Round the World with Ridgway

Books by John Ridgway

A Fighting Chance (with Chay Blyth)

Journey to Ardmore

Amazon Journey

Cockleshell Journey

Gino Watkins

Storm Passage

Round the World with Ridgway
(with Marie Christine Ridgway)

Round the World with Ridgway

John and Marie Christine Ridgway

HOLT, RINEHART AND WINSTON   NEW YORK

Copyright © 1978 by John and Marie Christine Ridgway
All rights reserved, including the right to reproduce
this book or portions thereof in any form.

Published by Holt, Rinehart and Winston,
383 Madison Avenue, New York, New York 10017.

Library of Congress Cataloging in Publication Data
Ridgway, John M
Round the world with Ridgway.
1. Whitbread Round the World Race.
I. Ridgway, Marie Christine, joint author.
II. Title.
GV832.R5   797.1'4   78-11848
ISBN 0-03-043751-2

First American Edition: 1979

Printed in the United States of America
1   3   5   7   9   10   8   6   4   2

Contents

To all those who stayed at home and made it possible
Lance and Ada Bell
Lady D'Albiac and Rebecca Ridgway

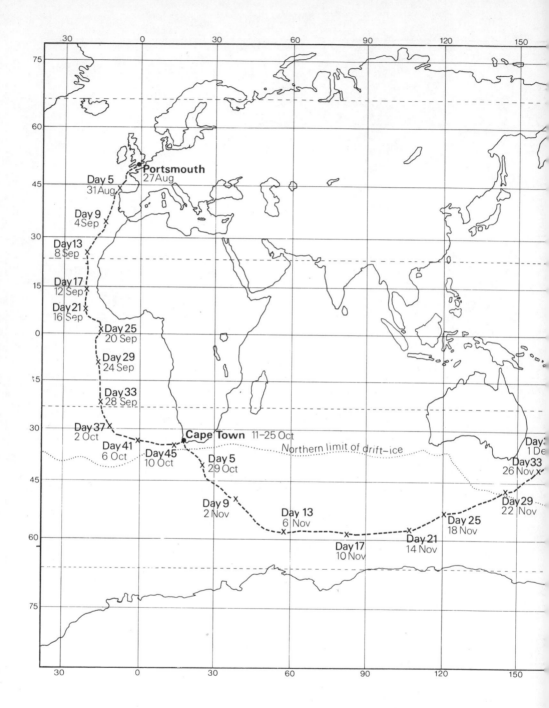

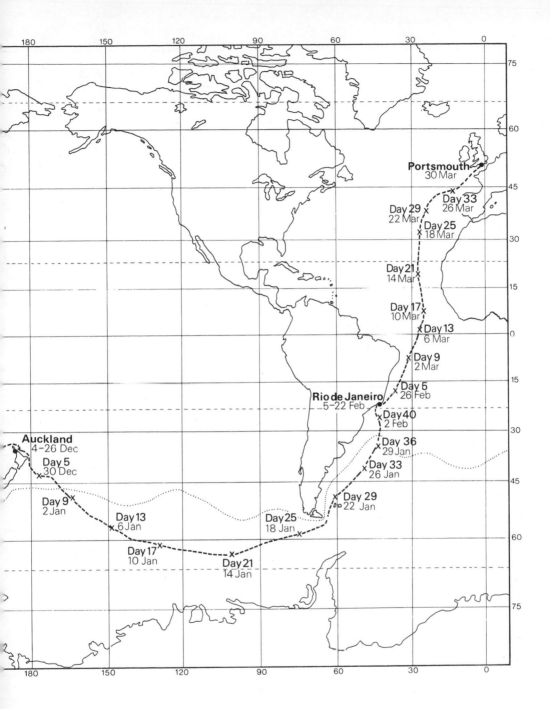

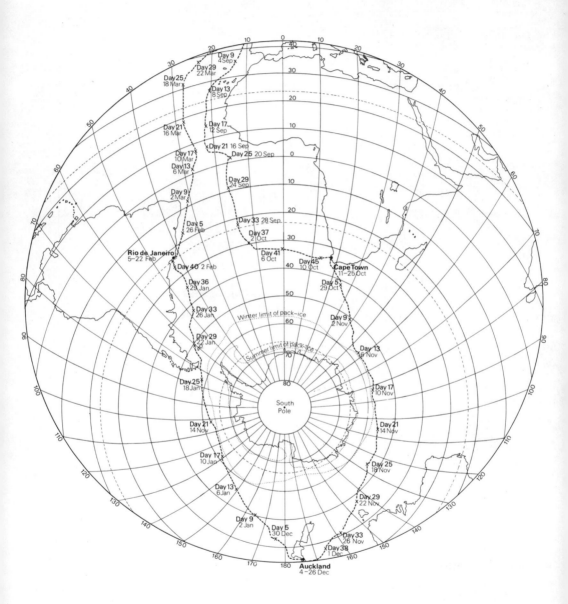

Day 9
4 Sep
Day 29
22 Mar
Day 25
18 Mar
Day 13
8 Sep
Day 21
16 Mar
Day 17
12 Sep
Day 17
10 Mar
Day 21 16 Sep
Day 25 20 Sep
Day 13
6 Mar
Day 29
24 Sep
Day 9
2 Mar
Day 5
26 Feb
Day 33 28 Sep
Day 37
2 Oct
Rio de Janeiro
5–22 Feb
Day 41
6 Oct
Day 45
10 Oct
Cape Town
11–25 Oct
Day 40 2 Feb
Day 5
29 Oct
Day 36
29 Jan
Day 33
26 Jan
Day 9
2 Nov
Winter limit of pack-ice
Day 29
22 Jan
Day 13
16 Nov
Summer limit of pack-ice
Day 25
18 Jan
Day 17
10 Nov
South
Pole
Day 21
14 Nov
Day 21
14 Nov
Day 17
10 Jan
Day 25
18 Nov
Day 13
6 Jan
Day 29
22 Nov
Day 9
2 Jan
Day 5
30 Dec
Day 33
26 Nov
Day 38
1 Dec
Auckland
4–26 Dec

Subject	feet	metres
L.O.A.	58·00	17·70
L.W.L.	47·50	14·48
Beam	14·50	4·42
Draft	8·30	2·54
Headroom	7·00	2·13
Sail area	1314·00sq	122·00sq.
Rating	41·30	

	lbs	kgs
Displacement about	42000	19051
Ballast (lead)	17151	7789

Number of berths —12

	gallons	litres
Water capacity	360	1636
Fuel capacity	150	682

Engine —Lister 15 h.p. SW2 MGR 2

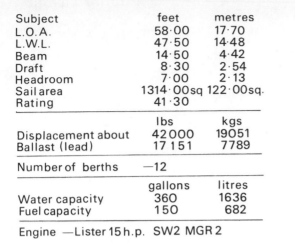

Yacht *Debenhams*
(Bowman 57)

Designed by Holman & Pye,
moulded by Seaglass Ltd.,
and built by Cape Wrath Boatyard,
Balnakeil, Durness, Sutherland
Scotland.

Interior Layout

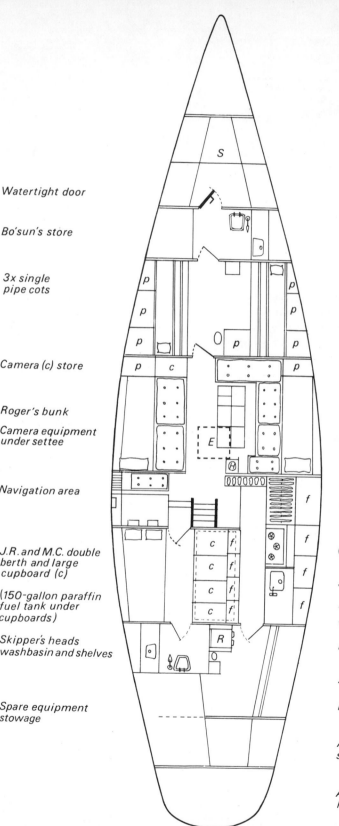

Chain locker
and stowage

Forepeak

Sail bags on
bunks and in bins

Watertight door

Bo'sun's store

Heads
Washbasin and
medical kit

3x single
pipe cots

3x single pipe cots
and storage

Personal (p) lockers
Main mast

Camera (c) store

Watertight door

Saloon table
and settee

Roger's bunk

Camera equipment
under settee

Noel's bunk

Engine (E)

Heater (H)

Boot rack

Navigation area

Oilskin rack

Food lockers (f)
(also under floors throughout)

Stove

J.R. and M.C. double
berth and large
cupboard (c)

(150-gallon paraffin
fuel tank under
cupboards)

Sink

Draining board

Watertight doors

Skipper's heads
washbasin and shelves

Radio (R)

2x pipe cots

Mizzen mast

Spare equipment
stowage

Aft cockpit
sheet locker

Aft sail
locker

Authors' Note

In addition to a standard sailing log and day report book, the authors kept written diaries for each day while at sea, J.R's being first dictated on to tape, M.C.R's written longhand in exercise books. Typewritten copies of the complete diaries were later revised, cut and put together and each day's entry headed by details from the *Debenhams* log. The purpose of this editorial process was to include the most interesting passages of both accounts with their independent viewpoints of the same events, and at the same time to revise the punctuation and phraseology or to add explanations of any obscure or private references. But there has been *no* attempt to add to the diaries any benefit of hindsight; they should therefore be read as essentially a record of events and states of mind as they occurred during our circumnavigation.

Preface

About the authors

JOHN RIDGWAY

There was something unusual about the circumstances of my birth at Billericay, Essex, in England on 8 July 1938, but for some reason I have never looked too deeply into it. Maybe the reality would not live up to my romantic notion of the sailor's love-child in the orphanage. As Freud is supposed to have once said, 'sometimes a cigar is only a cigar'. Anyway I was adopted and had a rather confused childhood. Parents gave me good homes and the opportunity of a good education which I wasted by concentrating on games at the expense of studies. Having little in common with my father, a successful civil engineer, I left school at seventeen and joined the Merchant Navy.

After one voyage to South Africa I found the deck space too confining for the restless athletic 'motor instinct' which has troubled me for so many years, so I left. In the early summer of 1956 my father announced that I had had my choice of career, now he would put me into Lloyds insurance in London. While he was in hospital with appendicitis I had my National Service call-up accelerated, and eventually found myself at R.M.A. Sandhurst as an 'Army Entrant', which was a polite way of describing those who had insufficient academic qualifications to make the orthodox entry.

I achieved advancement at Sandhurst through boxing. With more enthusiasm than ability I became Captain of Boxing and this helped me into the Parachute Regiment, which was just forming a permanent cadre of regular junior officers in place of the two-year-tour-from-other-regiments system which had obtained previously. As the first of these subalterns to join the 3rd Battalion, my five straight years' duty with the unit was therefore unique and I was

greatly influenced by the three commanding officers under whom I
served. These unusually able men were widely different in their style of
command but they were ambitious. The command of a regular Parachute battalion was a priceless opportunity to demonstrate their ability. I had stepped out of the frying pan and into the fire and they roasted
me. For five long years in the Middle East, Europe and Canada my feet
scarcely touched the ground in my efforts to find dark corners in which
to escape from their scorching gaze. I never achieved the standards they
required. All three became generals, one Chief of the General Staff
(that's head of the Army). The only nightmares I ever have concern
causing military displeasure during those years.

In 1964, aged twenty-five, I married Marie Christine D'Albiac and
left the Army. We went to live in the remotest part of Britain, where the
North West Highlands sweep down to the lonely Atlantic Ocean. There
we found Ardmore and became crofters, fifty miles from the railway
and three miles from the road. Access is by boat up a sea loch. There is
no electricity and no mains water at Ardmore and only one other family
lived there when we found it.

With Marie Christine at Ardmore I found the security I needed so
much. Together we returned to face the world. I rejoined the Parachute
Regiment and with Chay Blyth, an old friend, rowed across the North
Atlantic in ninety-two days from USA to Eire in 1966. Life changed
again. Two others attempting the row at the same time as Chay and I
were drowned. I felt we were lucky to be alive; in a sense the rest of my
life was a bonus.

After a short spell with the Special Air Service Regiment, I spent fifty
days sailing alone in the race to become the first man to sail non-stop
alone round the world. Unfortunately my voyage ended in Brazil, my
yacht having been damaged in a collision with a TV boat at the start. It
would be easy to say I would have won the race but for the damage (I
had started a week before my nearest competitor and over two months
before the last), but I don't think I would have made it anyway. During
the voyage I thought a lot about Ardmore, and on my return to Britain,
Marie Christine agreed I should leave the Army again. With my
gratuity and the small amount of capital earned from books and things,
we returned to Ardmore with our one-year-old daughter Rebecca and
built the John Ridgway School of Adventure during the winter of
1968–69. For the first couple of years we were lucky enough to have the
tremendous help of Rod and Jeannie Liddon.

The school is based on three principles: self-reliance, positive thinking, and the concept of leaving people and things better than you found
them. The seasons run from March to the end of September with
expeditions in alternate winters. In 1970–71 I led an expedition of four
complete strangers to make the first journey by foot, canoe, raft and

boat from the farthest source of the Apurimac Amazon high in the Peruvian Andes down to the mouth on the Atlantic seaboard of Brazil. In 1972–73 two instructors together with Marie Christine and me made the first crossing of the Gran Campo Nevado Icecap on the west coast of Chilean Patagonia. The winter of 1974–75 was spent sailing down to the Spanish Sahara, Cape Verde Islands, and back through the Azores to Ardmore with three instructors, Marie Christine, our daughter Rebecca and me.

After that we entered the era of the Big Boat. I felt the usual economic strains of a weakly struggling forty-year-old independent 'little man', and the somewhat oppressive realization that the old body was beginning to creak a bit.

MARIE CHRISTINE RIDGWAY

Up to the time I met John, when I was just eighteen, I'd led a fairly conventional and also extremely happy and secure life.

I was born in Dublin at the tail end of the war. My Irish mother had returned from long spells abroad with my father, an air marshal in the Royal Air Force, to see my brother and two sisters, who had spent the war with my grandmother in County Wicklow. Communications at that time were difficult and the first news of my birth was misleading; 'to Sybil D'Albiac, a son' was announced in *The Times*, and it was a few days before the correct news reached my father that he had a third daughter, not a second son. My father was nearly fifty when I was born, quite a bit older than my mother. Because she had had the hard choice of being with him or her children during most of the war years and had chosen the former, my parents had missed much of the pleasure of seeing the rest of the family growing up. Perhaps this is the reason why I received so much love and attention; I was brought up in an atmosphere of great love, happiness and fun for which I am forever grateful.

After the war my father became the first Commandant of London Airport – a job he held for ten years, bringing it from Nissen huts to the mighty complex it now is. As a young girl I used to roller skate through the empty No. 1 Building while it was under construction. My brother meanwhile was learning to drive the family car – a maroon Humber Hawk – on the network of empty roads in the Central Area. We lived a few miles from the Airport in the then quiet village of Longford on the old Bath Road, in a large Tudor house, perfect in summer but like a refrigerator in winter. At that time John lived in Datchet only ten miles away; he is six years older than me so I don't suppose we would have had much to say to each other even if we had met. I went to a preparatory school in Windsor daily on a greenline bus with my sister, Susan. From there I went on to a boarding school near Gosport, again following in my sister's steps, not distinguishing myself at all in any field. From time to time I was compared rather unfavourably with my sister, who showed far more leadership, sense and style than I was able to muster. I left at sixteen and was sent to Belri, a finishing school in the fairytale town of Arosa, six thousand feet up in the Swiss Alps. Here we worked hard, being allowed to speak only one hour of English each week. I learnt French, German, typing and shorthand and a few more typical finishing-school subjects such as deportment, foreign customs and history of art. However, my main efforts went into the skiing every afternoon; whatever the weather we were out on the slopes or touring in the mountains. I was there for six months and look back on it as tremendous fun. From Switzerland we were driven to Italy to see Florence, Venice and Rome and we caused a stir in every city: two mistresses, one in front and one at the rear of this party of thirty seventeen-to-eighteen-year-old girls – too much for the Italian males, who mobbed us wherever we went. For the final three months of our studies we ended up at Roquebrune, sandwiched between Monte Carlo and Menton on the French Riviera. I remember tennis and swimming each afternoon and sneaking out at night, with the threat of instant expulsion if we were discovered adding spice to the sorties.

Once back at home my main aim was to become independent; all I wanted in life was a flat of my own in London. Looking back I rather regret now not having finished my studies, but I remember how stubborn I was in my aim to be independent. Then followed twelve months in London with a job at the Arts Council during the day and parties and dates every night of the week.

I met John at a mutual friend's roulette party where the odds had been worked out very much in favour of the players. I had an unbelievably big pile of chips in front of me and looking across the table I noticed a good-looking fair-haired man with an equally large heap. Our eyes met between turns of the wheel. He came round. 'Shouldn't we join forces?' he suggested. From then on I saw a lot of John. He was an entirely different person to any in my normal circle of friends; there was a restless and troubled quality in him that drew me to him. It wasn't long before I fell desperately in love with him. I knew I would follow this man to the ends of the earth, if that was what he wanted. We became engaged, he sold his flash white sports car to buy my ring, and we married on the first day of spring when I was just twenty. We moved to the north of Scotland to start the struggle of trying to earn a living. John had just left the Parachute Regiment and apart from leadership skills he was not qualified in any other field. We must have looked a pathetic sight, love's young dream, as we knocked on doors from Ullapool to Cape Wrath trying to find a job and a home. On a short trip to Ireland to a cousin's wedding I showed a dear great-aunt a photo of the house we were planning to live in; I thought she would fall off her chair as she rocked back and forth in helpless mirth. Our love nest was a ruin; no roof, just the outside walls still standing, a highland pony scratching its back in the empty doorway. An attractive but desolate photo, not what one would expect to see in an estate agent's window. However, in the end we didn't move into the ruin but found Ardmore instead, three miles from the road and twenty miles down the west coast from Cape Wrath.

My life had certainly taken a different turn. I didn't admit it to John but I was far from happy in this lunar god-forsaken land which seemed so inhospitable to any form of life. 'If I keep quiet about it, he'll get sick of it of his own accord and then we'll move back south,' I used to think and sure enough we did move south. We had both managed to get jobs at the Kinlochbervie fish pier, I as secretary to the fish salesman and John mending fish boxes and working on a salmon coble. However, John felt he couldn't go on forever doing this so we turned our backs on the wild mountainous coastline of Sutherland and headed back, tails between our legs, with friends and family chanting 'I told you so'.

John went through a very miserable phase in his life. He had failed to make a go of it on his own in Scotland; he knew he wasn't cut out for the Army; but what else could he do? So swallowing his pride he asked to be taken back into the Regiment. It was shortly after this that we heard on the radio a David Johnson talking about a trip he proposed to make that following summer, rowing from America to Britain. I laughed out loud but John listened attentively: David Johnson was looking for a partner. On our return south John contacted him but it was obvious from the start that they would never get on. 'Well, I'll just have to do it myself.' I was torn two ways. I felt such a trip was close to suicide, I loved him, I didn't want him to die and yet having failed in Scotland I knew he was desperate to achieve something unusual for his own self-respect. So in spite of entreaties from family and friends to me to stop him, I felt that I should help him all I could in what he had set his mind to do. On 2 June 1966 Chay Blyth, whose first sea trip this was, and John set out in a twenty-foot open rowing boat from Cape Cod USA for Britain. Ninety-two days later after two hurricanes and countless privations they landed on one of the Aran Islands in Galway Bay. Their plan was to make a reverse charge call to my uncle in Dublin and borrow money for their fare home. To their absolute astonishment they found most of the world's press waiting there to turn them into national heroes. Our overdraft was paid off and we were on the crest of a wave, all the worry and heartache was gone and I had John with me again. To the great amusement of the press, nine months later, Maureen Blyth and I gave birth to daughters. Life had turned sweet again for us, although I couldn't forget that the other two, Johnson and Hoare, who had set off at the same time, were never seen again; their upturned boat was found by a Canadian frigate a few months later. The knowledge that he and Chay lived and the other two died has never been far from John's thoughts in the years since. Conventional ambition was now a thing of the past. We would live at Ardmore and build a School of Adventure.

Before moving north for good, John had a shot at two more of his ambitions. He passed the stiff selection course and became a Special Air Service Officer and a few months later, on unpaid leave from the Army again, he attempted to circumnavigate the world without stopping. As a number of others were planning a similar voyage, the *Sunday Times* jumped in and declared it a race for the Golden Globe Trophy (eventually won by Robin Knox-Johnson). John was hit at the start in the Aran Islands, where he and Chay had landed two years previously, by a pushy television trawler; damage sustained started to give trouble south of the Equator, forcing John to abandon his attempt in Recife, Brazil.

In the winter of 1968 we again moved north to Ardmore with our good friends Rod and Jean Liddon and their little boy Jamie. We worked harder than we'd ever worked in our lives before, building the ninety-foot timber building by the water's edge on Loch a' Chadh-fi. I was mainly involved with the office work, and would type two-page letters in answer to the briefest enquiry. It was necessary to make this huge effort in order to let the world know we had a good idea in offering holidays in canoeing, rock climbing, sailing and hill walking in this beautiful and remote area. Perhaps I was more mature by now for I had come to love this lonely part of the world. True, there were no shops, parties, or crowds of people, all things I had looked to in the past, but I now had an eighteen-month-old daughter and a husband whom I had nearly lost. Our first season we were full and luckily for us it has continued full ever since. John's theory is that if you run an Adventure School you've got to be adventurous, so we evolved a pattern of going on an adventure every other winter in our closed season, October–February. In 1970–71 John led an expedition from the Amazon's farthest source to its mouth. I was left behind to keep the mail answered and with extreme bad grace waved goodbye to John at London Airport. The three other members of the expedition were an army medic, a photographer, and a Spanish-speaking, Olympic lady skier. I was quite cross and unreasonably jealous. John had been gone about a month when I received a telegram: 'Come and join me in Iquitos – John.' I hastily looked up its whereabouts on the map; Mummy kindly offered to look after our daughter Rebecca and before I had time to think twice, I was on the plane and bound for the Amazon jungle. Contrary to John's fears, I didn't make a fuss about the heat, insects or any of the other problems to be encountered. We enjoyed each other's company and the experience set the style for future trips, such as one across an ice-cap in Patagonia reached by rubber dinghies through the Magellan Straits. Another year on a family trip with Rebecca when she was seven, we sailed with three instructors in our Nicholson 32 to the Spanish Sahara and Cape Verde Islands via Madeira and the Canaries and returned in December, stopping at the Azores. John's book on this voyage was to be called *Journey to the Sun* until the last two weeks, when we nearly sank off Ireland in the grips of a winter gale. It then changed to *Storm Passage*.

I'm still surprised to find myself cast as a tough adventurous type of woman by others when they hear of John's and my type of 'holidays'. I love my comforts, good food, pretty clothes and don't consider myself tough in the slightest. It's just that I don't like getting left behind.

I

Prelude

'Why are you going?'

'Because I can.'

A great many people would like to embark on a great adventure with a clearly defined objective such as a sailing voyage round the world. The reason that few have ever achieved their dream is depressingly simple: they can't. 'I wish I were going,' they say, 'but I must be on the 8.32 train to London tomorrow morning.' The mortgage, the bills, licences, hire purchase commitments, rates, children's education. These are the things of which dreams are made – and broken.

At Ardmore, near the northern end of the west coast of Scotland, we live in a typical stone croft-house whitened with lime, without electricity, central heating, or double-glazing, some three miles from the road; and the easiest access is by boat up a sheltered sea-loch. As a reward we are able to do without some of the ties of a more conventional life-style. We stumble along through the mist all the same, as harassed as most people; but every now and then there's a break in the cloud and the way ahead seems clear.

Such a time it was when we decided to build a big boat.

Early in 1975, Donald Hugh, our postman, walked out to Ardmore through the rain bearing a most important letter, from the tiny village of Durness, fifteen miles away up on the north coast. The small, precise handwriting explained that one Arun Bose was starting the Cape Wrath Boatyard, and there was one particular sentence which struck a chord with me. 'I do hope you will support my new venture.' 'Sounds just like us ten years ago,' I said to my wife, Marie Christine, passing the small blue sheet of writing paper across the kitchen table. A minute or two passed while we both continued sorting through the rest of the day's post. The only sound was the hissing of the old brass Tilley lamp on the wall behind my rocking chair by the window overlooking the loch. Outside it was already dark on a still February afternoon, and Donald Hugh would be limping back along the rough, hilly footpath towards the Achlyness sub-post office four miles away. Dear old Mrs Fraser would be waiting for the outgoing mail, impervious to the fumes from her ancient paraffin stove, well wrapped up in her black overcoat. She wouldn't miss a single one of the two or three cars passing along the single track coast-road up on the hillside above the lean-to post office at the end of her croft. At least the present mild spell meant that Michael was on time with the mail on his fifty-mile drive in the battered old red bus from the railway at Lairg each day: unlike the snow and ice of the previous month when the diesel had frozen in the pipes beneath the cab and it had needed a blow-lamp to thaw them and get the bus going again on the high ground between Overscaig and Merkland.

'Why don't you and Lance go up and see what his work's like?' Marie Christine said, referring to Arun Bose's letter. 'Maybe he could build the new dinghy you're wanting.'

A couple of days later, Lance Bell and I drove into the ex-RAF camp which now served as a home and workshop for several families who have come to the far north-west of Sutherland to make their living practising handcrafts. Lance's twenty years in a Teesside iron foundry had left him with scant regard for candle-making and tie-and-dye, and I was prepared for no real increase in the enthusiasm now. Lance and his wife, Ada, both in their late fifties, had been with us for eight years. They called a spade a spade, and I valued their realism.

The fifteen-mile drive in the old grey van through the steady rain had not been particularly cheering, as Lance had gone to some lengths to outline his conviction that 'them 'irsute buggers should get back to where they came from and get on with some proper bloody productive work'. If Mr Bose managed to convince Lance of his workmanship then we'd really be on to something. I could see straight away that he wasn't very impressed by the tiny eight-foot pram-dinghy which lay on its side half-finished among a jumble of tools in the narrow concrete bunk-house. It looked as if this was all Mr Bose had ever made. Lance spared the man hardly a glance, but he was much more interested in an ancient black band-saw; its massive cast-iron construction soon had the pawky Teessider talking nineteen to the dozen about his favourite topic: iron foundries. This was very lucky in a way because Mr Bose was painfully shy, small and neatly built with long, straggly black hair and bright, dark eyes behind spectacles. His beard reminded me of the Sikhs I had known at Sandhurst. It looked as if it had grown wild, never known the touch of a razor. I put him about twenty-three and half Indian by his complexion. The small black-rimmed spectacles gave him a curiously studious look for a boat-builder. My own stabs at conversation were hopeless. I couldn't hear his replies.

'Shall we go through to my mother's workshop?' he whispered at last, and we followed him along a low corridor in the cold, dark building and into an open area at the far end which was set up with a couple of intricate wooden looms at which Noelle Bose, a lively Nottingham widow, of striking appearance and firm opinion, was weaving the tweeds she made for a living.

'Arun made these, you know,' she said proudly, as soon as we'd been introduced. Lance looked at the precision work of the looms, and then back at Mr Bose, as if seeing him afresh. This fellow must be pretty good, I thought. Better see if we can get him down to Ardmore for a while.

A couple of days later, I was walking on the top of Ardmore with Marie Christine and our seven-year-old daughter, Rebecca. It was one of those precious highland winter days: flat calm with an endless blue sky. There was a dusting of snow down to sea level. Under foot the turf was gripped firm by the frost, the silence broken only by the occasional cry of a gull, and the timeless suck and hiss of the tide on the rocks two hundred feet below. We could see forever. The Hebrides, a good forty miles across the Minch, were as clear as I'd ever seen them, and just behind, the still white peaks of Foinaven, Arkle and Ben Stack etched the sky. Rebecca burned off her Sunday lunch by running on ahead and sliding across the ice-covered puddles among the peat-cuttings. Marie Christine and I were wrapped up in warm, short coats. Our conversation turned to my current worry; whether or not to get the big boat for the Adventure School.

We'd been lucky to avoid the worst effects of the present economic crisis; our savings were in the building society instead of the stock market. But now inflation at twenty per cent a year was rapidly reducing the money we'd put away for a rainy day and our old age. The best idea we'd had was to buy something on a housing estate in Inverness and lease it to a tenant; but this seemed rather tame and I thought it didn't deserve to be a success.

'Put it all into a boat, then, and to hell with it. Anything to stop you worrying about it,' Marie Christine said rather crossly, bored with the dreary subject. Any further discussion was halted by a wail from Rebecca. She'd gone through the ice, fallen and skidded to a halt on her backside in three inches of freezing water. By the time we reached her she was up on her feet. With fists clenched and scarlet face, she shook with screaming fury.

'Just like her mother,' I laughed, but that didn't go down too well.

Early in March we began the month's course we run each year for the instructors prior to the start of each new season. Rebecca was home from school. It was half-term at Ada Bell's Academy for Young Ladies, whose headquarters was the blue house, half a mile from our house on the other side of the wood at Ardmore. It may have been small with only one teacher and one pupil, but oh my, it was strict.

On Mothering Sunday morning Rebecca and I cleaned the house and rearranged some of our books on the new shelving Arun Bose had put up for us under the eaves on the landing between the two bedrooms. Arun had also painted several of the smaller school boats, and generally been most helpful in getting the place on its feet again in time for the first course due to start at the beginning of April. I'd already asked him to build the new fourteen-foot loch-boat we needed.

He stayed at our house for a week, and one evening we discussed the idea of a bigger boat; just how big I couldn't be sure – but Arun was keen to build it.

Charley Elrick, the Kinlochbervie postman, had taken a couple of days off to install our new peat-fired Rayburn in the kitchen, and things were looking up with the first signs of spring.

All through March I wrestled with the figures to see how we could possibly afford to build the kind of boat I had in mind. While tramping across the hard snow up on the three-thousand-foot Foinaven Ridge with the instructors' course I was trying to decide what size of boat would be right. I had already agreed to enter Jamie Young, one of our instructors, in the *Observer* Single-Handed Transatlantic Race 1976, so most evenings were spent planning for this in *English Rose IV*, the thirty-foot sloop I'd sailed alone across the Atlantic in 1968; but deep in the school septic tank, shovelling the residue into black plastic buckets, I could think only of the big boat. It was the same thing when scrubbing the bottom or anti-fouling our thirty-two-foot sloop, *English Rose V*; my thoughts always came back to the big boat.

The idea had a bit of a setback at the end of the month, however, when I decided a trip to Stornoway in *English Rose V* would make a good end to the instructors' course. I spent the whole night being seasick into one of those black plastic buckets with Murdoch McEwan. I thought the smell was familiar.

However, once back on dry land with the buildings Cuprinolled, sailing dinghies launched, canoes on their rack, and the spring sun shining on the still waters of Loch a' Chadh-fi, the idea of the big boat came flooding back. In fact, so much of an obsession did it become that we went scuba-diving in the snow to re-lay moorings for the big boat when it arrived.

Not everyone was keen on the idea, but I suppose that only made me more stubborn. Heckie and Hughie, crofters from next door, came in for supper one night, and Lance and Ada came down from the blue house. Over copious draughts of Marie Christine's home-made beer, and Ada's famous Yorkshire puddings, Lance announced his view:

'Bloody daft. You've no slip, no moorings and no pier. The whole place has changed from the first year we were here. You're getting carried away with yourself.'

Heckie and Hughie looked at their plates. Ada looked uncomfortable, and wished Lance hadn't had so much beer before he'd come down. Rebecca saved the day by suggesting we play dominoes. I had a most uncomfortable feeling that the old blighter was right.

Time marched on. Jim Archer Burton's boys from Westerleigh School near Hastings loved sailing down to the Handa Island bird reserve in the two yachts, but I thought how much better it would be in one big one – maybe a Bowman forty-six-foot ketch. But I had to be realistic. Where would the money come from?

Arun was at the school quite often, working on the boats, and one day we came up with the idea of a sea-angling boat which would double up as a work boat for the school. It would be expensive, but it would help establish Arun as a boat-builder.

On the first of May, Mike Williamson of the Highlands and Islands Development Board drove the hundred miles from Inverness to discuss the idea of a twenty-eight-foot sea-angling boat as an aid to local tourism. Marie Christine, Mike, Arun and I sat round the kitchen table before lunch. Mike put forward some very convincing reasons for the sea-angler: a grant and a loan from the Board towards the capital cost was a distinct possibility, but he couldn't say more. It was up to the Board to decide.

'You know, what we really need is a proper sail training yacht – a Nicholson 55 sloop – like the *Adventure* which won three of the four legs of the Round World Yacht Race last year. The Joint Services Sailing Centre has eight of them. They must be well proven. How would the Board like to help me with one of those, Mike?' I asked, and he looked up from the sea-angling brochures in surprise. Arun looked startled too.

'Well, I don't know. I doubt you'd get a grant, but a loan might be possible, of course. It's up to the Board entirely. Not me. I can only make recommendations,' he replied softly.

'But would you recommend it?' I asked again.

'Well, I'd have to know a lot more about it first.'

'Okay. Let's talk about it. Here's a line drawing of the boat.' I spread out the blueprint across the table, and I could see Arun squinting at it most carefully. Half an hour later, with nothing left to discuss, I said, 'Well, what do you think, Mike?'

'I know what I think,' came Arun's reedy voice. 'I'd much rather do the sea-angler first.'

My eyes rolled up to the ceiling, and I lashed out with my right foot trying to kick him.

'Well, I'd be prepared to submit a case to the Board,' Mike smiled. 'But as I said earlier, I think it would only be a loan.'

After lunch, Marie Christine and I took the two men back across the Loch to their cars, and after saying goodbye we took a Land-Rover out to a remote deserted bothy called Lone, which Sinclair MacIntosh, the factor of the Westminster Estate, kindly allows us to use for the businessmen's courses. We got there well before the instructors arrived with their small groups of various levels of fitness from Ben Stack and Arkle. Next day I would take the fastest group along the Foinaven Ridge, but first Marie Christine and I would spend the night at Lone with the course.

While we lit the fire and got the meal ready we talked about the latest turn of events.

'What do you think it will cost to build *Adventure*?' asked Marie Christine.

'A lot more than we've got,' I said, pessimistic but realistic.

'And if we get a loan from the Board, and Arun fitted it out up here?'

'Well, we might just manage it. One bad season and we'd be bust.'

'Do it. We won't have a bad season.'

'How can you say that? The oil crisis. A recession; inflation; VAT . . .' The words sounded like boulders on my back.

'I think it will be all right,' she smiled.

I grinned. Thank goodness for Marie Christine! I'd never make it alone. The idea of a Bowman forty-six ketch had nagged my mind for several years, so I rang Alan Hallett at the Emsworth Boatyard. A spry, white-haired, retired Captain, Royal Navy, with a distinguished war record, Alan had been particularly helpful when I'd visited the small, compact yard the previous autumn. To me it looked as if he ran a pretty tight ship there.

'Thinking of the Whitbread Round the World Race in '77, are you?' the clipped naval tones came up the wire from the south coast. I wasn't, but maybe there was something more to it.

'Maybe.'

'Well, the forty-six is too short on the waterline to qualify. What about a fifty-seven-foot ketch?'

'Ha, ha, ha, ha. No mun, no fun!'

'Well, we have an owner – a Mr Palmer – who might be interested in you skippering a fifty-seven for him. Are you interested?'

'I might be. Could you send up all the details on the fifty-seven, Alan? I'll think about it.'

I put the phone down and worked out the cost of the seven-hundred-mile call at peak rates. One of the old Camper & Nicholsons' slogans is supposed to have been: If you need to know the price, sir, the boat is not for you . . . What was I letting myself in for?

We had the ladies' course on now – twenty of them, aged thirty to sixty-five. There wasn't a lot of time for dreaming about the big boat.

With the coming of June, the weather turned fair and the croft assumed a green mantle, giving it the look of a billiard table as we came in with the boats of an evening.

I went to see George Davidson, the Kinlochbervie harbour master, about the chances of fitting out a Nicholson fifty-five on the old disused pier of the little fishing village a few miles to the north of Ardmore. George, a kindly East Coast fisherman, now retired to Kinlochbervie, quickly gave his assent. The fishing boats all used the new pier now. All I had to do was buy the hull and deck and transport it seven hundred miles on a giant truck, diverting round all the low bridges and narrow roads on the way.

We were wondering how to celebrate the tenth year of the John Ridgway School of Adventure in 1978. A sail round the world seemed suitable, but for blunt economic reasons it would have to fit in between the end of the 1977 season and the start of the '78 season. The Whitbread Race took too long because of the stops at Cape Town, Auckland and Rio de Janeiro – roughly nine weeks wasted in all. I had read somewhere that the clipper *Lightning* had made it from Liverpool *via* Australia and back to Liverpool in 158 days, or roughly five months, including the time spent in Sydney, in 1854–55. We might go for an attempt to beat that record by sailing non-stop round the world with a crew. On my fingers I worked out how long it would take from 1 October to 1 March – exactly right for the period between the two seasons. The boat's working life at the John Ridgway School of Adventure wouldn't be interrupted and if the voyage was from Scotland to Scotland the Highlands and Islands Development Board might find it good publicity if we broke the record.

After a visit to the Board in Inverness there seemed to be a fair chance they would loan me ten thousand pounds towards the cost of a new sail training yacht. I was absurdly flattered by this confidence shown in the school by an outside body; so much so that I asked my friendly bank manager over for tea on the following Sunday. Fraser Wilson drove the fifty miles from the Bank of Scotland in Lairg with his family, Ellen, Brian and Siona. They were much more interested in our stubborn grey Connemara pony, Boy Blue, than in my excited plans for the boat. But as they were leaving, Fraser said he could see no reason why the bank shouldn't advance me ten thousand pounds on the boat if the Board loan fell through.

June ran on into July and daylight was now no longer twenty-four hours. The weeks for twenty businessmen were replaced by fortnights for sixty young people.

Camper & Nicholsons knocked £2,000 off the price of their Nicholson

55 hull and deck, but they wanted £800 for the special plans of *Adventure*. Sloppy grey days sailing in the Minch sometimes made me want to forget the whole thing. I'd read all the books. I knew all about escalating building costs, and the late deliveries in such a venture. How on earth could it ever prove worth while? At the back of my mind a little voice kept saying, 'Aha! Come on! It's the only way to be alive again. You witter on about a fourth dimension in living, but the spark's gone right out of you!'

Alan Hallett of Bowman rang up on the day when I had decided to write and confirm my order for the Nicholson 55 hull and deck which Arun was going to fit out in a field near Chichester.

'Don't sign anything until you've heard from us,' Alan said dramatically. Next day he dropped his price £6,200 and agreed to let Arun work on the boat in the Bowman yard at Emsworth.

As far as the school was concerned, the Bowman fifty-seven-foot ketch was infinitely preferable to the Nicholson 55 sloop: there was double the accommodation. The Highlands and Islands Development Board confirmed an £11,400 loan. All that remained for me was to plunge the family into debt. I flew south for two days and signed the contract for a Bowman 57 ketch, hull and deck to be delivered to Emsworth from Seaglass in Alresford on 16 October 1975. The avalanche had begun. I felt a sense of relief at being committed.

As soon as I got home I began scuba-diving in earnest to lay the moorings for the big boat which I planned to sail up in a basic condition in January 1976. Meanwhile, the climbing, canoeing, dinghy, and off-shore sailing, hill-walking and swimming, and survival, went on apace as we neared the end of the 1975 season.

Friday, 31 October 1975 dawned wet and misty on the Brighton sea-front, where we were staying with Marie Christine's mother. There was no time for that awful morning run across the pebbles on the beach. It was 5.30 and the windscreen wipers weren't working properly on the Land-Rover as Marie Christine and I set out for Alresford. The road glistened darkly on a gloomy autumn morning. The great adventure seemed a fool's errand. Flasks of hot coffee and sandwiches cheered us up. It was a pretty big day for us.

Arun had been waiting since five at the small Seaglass factory on the untidy Alresford industrial estate. Jervis Head supervised the loading of the big white whale on to the low loader with a crane.

The fat lorry driver had a very young assistant and as the crane lifted the hull (less its keel, for clearance of bridges) from its cradle, the rudder skeg crunched on the concrete, knocking a big chip out of it. I told myself to look nonchalant.

'We'll patch that up at Emsworth. No bother,' said Jervis.

Where will you be when we go round the Horn? I thought to myself.

A bevy of police motorbikes arrived, and the cavalcade got under way through the leafy Sussex lanes, with the Seaglass sign swinging crazily on the stern. We drove on ahead after a while; the worry about possible accidents, pylons, low bridges, was all too much for me.

Eventually, the convoy entered the narrow confines of King Street, Emsworth. With motorcycle headlights blazing and motors gunning, the giant hull seemed higher than the houses. Did we really own it? The tide was out so the truck drove straight along the foreshore close to the old brick wall, and up to a crane waiting alongside a timber jetty in front of huge boat-shed doors. Soon the elegant hull – a bit odd without its keel – stood comfortably in a steel cradle on the slipway. From the beach I looked up at Arun, high above me on the deck, and thought, 'It's a big jump from that eight-foot pram dinghy at Balnakeil.'

In the Land-Rover Marie Christine was drawing colour schemes for Ratsey spinnakers. The spending spree was well under way.

One thing didn't go to plan. Jamie Young had fallen in love with Mary Fleming, one of the girls who had helped with the cooking at Ardmore during the summer. Not only was he now unsure about entering the Single-Handed Race next year in *English Rose IV*, but he needed some persuasion to join Arun in the petrol Land-Rover for the winter, even though it was now fitted with curtains. However, in the end the two-man Cape Wrath boatyard got under way. Their target: to transform this ugly white duckling into a majestic swan, fit to sail the seven hundred miles to Ardmore. The time available was two and a half months, 1 November 1975 to 18 January 1976.

Her first journey (photo J. Archer-Burton)

As Marie Christine and I drove hopefully north, the cause of my headache wasn't only the noisy diesel Land-Rover. My costings were worked out to a ridiculously fine edge.

At home we found Lance and Ada moving their furniture from their home in Teesside – sold after eight years absence – up to the Blue House. Lance was now the crofter at number 80 Ardmore, a strange number really since there are only five houses on the remote peninsula. Next door, Granny Ross, well over eighty, was coming home after an eighteen-month absence on the far side of Loch Laxford where she had been pining away for Ardmore. Heckie and Robert carried her up the steep croft from the shore on a chair. Ardmore hadn't been quite the same without her in her rocker by the sitting-room stove.

We were now set on the idea of breaking the record for a sailing ship around the world, and we planned to sail non-stop Ardmore/Cape of Good Hope /south of New Zealand/Cape Horn and back to Ardmore in the winter of 1977–78. Marie Christine's first positive action was to have her appendix out at the Royal Northern Infirmary, Inverness. Once this was accomplished we felt we really had to make the trip. Convalescence was accelerated by a splendid white Christmas at Ardmore, followed by the usual hectic Highland New Year, involving bottle-laden tours of the district by day and by night, and long starlit tramps through deep snow back to Ardmore. It is the unplanned which makes the memories: recovering a well-known local figure from a snow-covered wall on which he had collapsed in a compromising drape behind a friend's house at two in the morning; still later pushing a wrecked brand new car off the remains of a mail-box after the driver had mistaken his turning by three miles; then picking up the driver's wife in the snow where she had been dropped some time before the nocturnal accident; dancing to piano and accordion with friends' relatives, who had travelled seven hundred miles from London by train and bus to be home for Hogmanay; in bed with 'flu when the strength ran out after too many nights on the footpath home.

Our first project for 1976 was to sail the fifty-seven-foot ketch up the west coast of Britain from Emsworth, near Chichester, on the south coast of England, to Ardmore on the north-west coast of Scotland.

Marie Christine stayed at home and I travelled on 8 January.

Richard Morris-Adams, a shrewd and always optimistic ex-marine, had agreed to undertake the task of raising sponsorship for the Round World record attempt. Richard was a veteran of two businessmen's courses at Ardmore, so I had every confidence that if anyone could find the backing it would be he. With his firm, Counter Products Marketing Limited, working on the project, I soon got to recognize the cheerful telephone voice of his secretary, Yvonne.

As the irrepressible Richard drove me down to Emsworth on Tuesday, 13 January, in the cosy seats of his smart BMW, I felt reassured and the sun shone. The heater and the taped music took the chill out of life.

Emsworth was cold and wet but Arun and Jamie had performed miracles. The keel was on, the masts and rigging up, winches and deck fittings installed; the small motor was fitted, and anti-fouling and decks were painted. Below decks the accommodation for ten was basic; without windows the effect was like living in a cold, dark tunnel lit by a solitary paraffin lamp. When my eyes got used to the dark I found the galley, navigation area and forward heads had all been fitted in a temporary sense. On the floor of what was to become the saloon was a huge pile of teak-faced plywood boards: just about all the timber to be used in fitting out the yacht over the next eighteen months. Arun and Jamie had achieved the single most critical phase of the entire project on time – living on the job in the frosted tube.

All week preparations went full ahead to get the boat ready for sea. Sixteen sails and all the running rigging had to be tried for size. Water, fuels, provisions, navigation books, charts and instruments were all stowed away. It looked a little peculiar happening to a boat in mid-winter, high and dry in a cradle above the tide; and it was this last which concerned us most – for the high spring tide was officially Saturday, 17 January, but it certainly didn't look as if she would float, much as Ego Dridge, the yard foreman, tried to assure us.

The crew of ten instructors and ex-instructors appeared in dribs and drabs as the deadline drew near. Some of them could not afford more than a set time away from hospitals and universities.

Came the Saturday and quite a crowd of well-wishers assembled up at the end of the muddy creek. Ego had four launches standing by. Her flags were hoisted, sails made ready, and the crew pottered busily up and down the freshly painted blue decks. Excitement rose with the tide. It was such an important moment for us. The muddy brown water crept up the keel towards the bright red boot topping. On board, a yard engineer ran up the Lister engine for the first time. I turned the wheel this way and that, master of my destiny; then the water stopped rising, hovered, and began to fall.

'The glass is too high,' muttered Ego, drily. 'The tide's not getting into the basin. Be all right tomorrow though.'

I felt rather foolish. It didn't bode well. The supporters drifted away in embarrassment. Chris Ratsey, who'd come over specially for sail trials in the Solent, was stranded as we'd agreed to drop him off at Cowes. The crew retreated to a pub, and then watched a rugby inter-national on television at Lawrence and Sheila Mountford's house which overlooked the yacht. Their hospitality did a lot to help dispel the gloom.

'If we don't make it tomorrow, it'll be 17 May,' I said glumly, thumbing through the tide tables for the third time and peering through the window at the stranded yacht.

'We could take you all out to the downs for a walk if the tide fails,' said Sheila consolingly.

'I'd have to think of getting back to work,' said one of the crew.

Next morning there were fewer observers, it being Sunday. Ego's father, Jack, was there, dressed in a smart navy blue reefer with black buttons. Jack had made most of our running rigging, and as the tide rose around the cradle once more, he talked of his pre-war days as an oyster fisherman in winter, and paid hand on the old J-class boats in summer. The look on his honest square face betrayed his doubts about the tide. But at noon the cradle was pulled away. Up the slip it went, drawn by two oily hawsers, snaking down from a winch somewhere inside the cavernous sliding doors. Now the yacht leaned heavily on her port side against the old pier, firmly stuck in the mud. The situation was critical, but Ego had it figured.

'Hitch that warp on to one of your main halyards, John,' he drawled in his Hampshire voice, showing absolutely no emotion at all.

Jamie deftly bent on the warp which was led to the stern of a launch out on our starboard side. Props churned the water to foam, the top of the main mast arc'd across the grey sky, and suddenly she was afloat, laid over on her starboard side. Another launch tugged at our stern, and the curious trio inched astern and into the main channel.

Down below Arun had the Lister diesel going full tick astern on its first ever run on load, and smoke curled up from the damp asbestos lagging on the exhaust pipe.

'What an ungraceful start to your life,' I muttered. 'At least, it's Marie Christine's birthday, though.'

There wasn't much time for thought. We hit a flimsy marker post in the channel, although the towing launch seemed quite unconcerned. Then our engine failed, and Arun wriggled below the floorboards to make some minor adjustments.

'The nine hundred miles to Ardmore will be quite a good sea trial,' Jamie grinned in his shy way. We'd made similar trips together in both previous winters; rather harrowing they were, too.

A quick swing of the compass in the Solent soon after the launch turned back at the Chichester bar, and we were headed for Bembridge Ledge and the open Channel. The wind began to rise steadily as we made south-west, close-hauled against the southern side of the Isle of Wight. It was a dreadful night of discomfort and vomit.

'What the hell's that?' I shouted, as the boat was suddenly filled with a terrible clattering sound. I thought we must be scraping the side of a ship. 'Is this the way it's going to end?' I muttered, theatrical to the last.

'It's the engine. She's going so fast it's started itself on the propeller in gear,' cried Neil Scobie in relief, his red head dipping below the floorboards to follow the beams from anxious torches. We jammed baulks of timber against the shaft; they smoked in protest even with the motor in neutral; but in the end we got it all lashed up and silent.

Dawn found us storm-tossed near the Casquet Rocks, just north-west of the Channel Islands. By noon we were in Lyme Bay, off the south coast of England again – the wind was now south-west force 9. Another night of black despair, in the very pit of seasickness. Some of the crew were changing their minds about sailing round the world. In the event, only Arun of the ten people on board did come on the main voyage.

Next morning we found Brixham, as the weather forecast spoke of north-west force 11, but the smart coastguard launch told us not to stay at our anchor outside the harbour for more than twenty-four hours as the weather was going to get worse; so we moved on to Falmouth next day, and just in time too, for a trawler was sunk alongside the wall inside Brixham harbour that very night, along with a lot of pleasure craft. Falmouth is a nice, quiet little spot to spend a few days in winter, even in the snow. Sadly, several of the crew had to return to work, but John Irwin flew over from Belfast to join us for the next stage. Short, dark, and powerfully built, John was a great asset in the Irish Sea, where the weather kept up a steady force 8 to 9. But when the forecast gave 10 he suggested we head for Bangor, his home just outside Belfast.

We picked up a mooring in Ballyholme Bay in sight of the yacht club and John's family home. Everyone went ashore except Mary Fleming and me. I didn't dare leave. After a while the wind rose sharply and the mooring began to drag. Mary and I had some excitement dropping the main anchor, but we failed to get the engine to start. The rest of the crew, who'd seen the drama through the steamy yacht club windows, just got back in the Avon dinghy as the southerly storm set in bad for the night. The anchor watch lined up yellow street lamps and waited for trouble.

'We're dragging,' came the cry at five in the morning.

The grinding rumble made the alarm unnecessary. Everyone was lying tensed up on the floor, life-jackets already fitted.

'Arun. Get the motor going, full ahead. Jamie. Stand by to get some sail up,' I shouted, and people dashed hither and thither, lumpy and clumsy in their warm gear, oilskins and life-jackets. Fear blanked their faces like white labels. On deck, the vicious crescent of rocks at the end of the bay was right across our stern and much, much nearer. I had that dreadful resigned feeling: anxiety, my old friend.

'She's moved a couple of hundred yards, but I reckon the engine has helped the anchor get a hold again,' cried Scobie against the wind at the wheel.

We kept the little fifteen-horsepower motor running full ahead, and she held. At first light, a coastguard Land-Rover came down and parked in the rain on the shore road, barely a hundred yards on our starboard side. Jamie held up one of the floorboards for them to see the message '2182' he'd written chalked on the wood, while I got the long red Callbuoy radio going on that distress frequency.

'This is Desmond Irwin speaking,' came the broad Ulster burr, quite unhindered by the crackle of the radio. 'I can get a fishing boat to tow you if you like,' continued the welcome voice. John Irwin waved acknowledgement to his father from the cockpit. Perhaps we could have managed without, but it was grand to feel that heavy rope pulling our bows out to the open bay and away from the road and rocks to starboard and close on our stern.

The seventy-five-foot Norwegian-built green trawler handled us with ease. She was just leaving nearby Bangor harbour for Belfast, in company with all the other fishing boats; the southerly storm was too much for such an exposed place. Desmond waved from the bridge as we cast off to make our way up to Belfast docks under storm sails. It had been a close thing. Funny my hair doesn't turn grey.

The following day we sailed on the last leg of the delivery trip to Ardmore. John Irwin had commitments in Belfast, but he fixed up for Dicky Gomes and Brian Low to come on with us in his place. They were familiar with the south-western coast of Scotland, and so we made for the scenic route north inside the islands. Our route read like a travel brochure and was twice as beautiful: Mull of Kintyre, Sound of Luing, Gulf of Corrievrechan, Ardnamurchan, Mull, Skye.

2

Preparations

At last the two-masted white Bowman with her trim blue decks lay proudly at the new mooring sheltered from the wind below the most northerly wood on the west coast of Britain. From the garden gate I would look down on her and think: 'You're going to sail right round the world, south of the three great capes, and back to this spot.'

But there wasn't too much time for thought. February quickly drew into March 1976, and the instructors' course began. There was all the painting and peat-cutting to be done once more. Arun worked on *English Rose IV*, the thirty-foot sloop which had been blown over on its side up on the beach during the storms we had met on our way up with the Bowman.

Jamie Young looked on anxiously. I had sailed the boat alone from Eire to Brazil, and his chance was coming in just six weeks. He'd leave Ardmore bound for Plymouth and then a place on the *Observer* Single-Handed Transatlantic Race. On arrival at Newport in Rhode Island he planned to turn right round and sail directly back for Ardmore. A tall, shy, well-built young man of exceptional strength, Jamie had been with us for seven years since leaving Dunrobin School over on the east coast. After meeting Mary his thoughts had been shared between her and his single-handed race. It was the time of his life.

Bob Burns stepped into our lives one fine March day during the instructors' course. He was to become one of the watch leaders on the circumnavigation. He comes from the seaside town of Brighton on the south coast of England and has always been troubled by the possession of too much energy and a love of the sea and ships. At the earliest possible age he joined the Royal Navy as a boy sailor and discovered the unlikely natural talent while in training of being able to sit happily on the button of a seventy-foot high mast. Combined with this is a great love of runs ashore in the evening. After twelve years in the Royal Navy, during which he rose to the rank of leading seaman, the rigours of countless runs ashore in various ports had laid waste some of his closest friends and he found himself almost alone in not having taken the pledge. On leaving the Navy he used his talent for heights and worked for the government in the erection and maintenance of television masts sometimes as high as 1,200 feet. These TV masts are usually situated atop bleak moorland hills and the maintenance circuit became tedious after some years. Bob's eye was caught by the possibilities of working at heights aboard rigs in the fast developing North Sea oilfield. A man who is keen to run a small gang of hard-working, hard-playing fellows soon found himself at home with the rough Texan oilmen whose sole objective was results. Here 'Barby' became a trusted and reliable achiever in the difficult world of oil exploration out on the cold and treacherous waters off the north coast of Scotland. The snag with this kind of life is that the pay is good in return for the hard work and stress exacted by the job, and the method of operation is to spend two weeks on the rig and then two weeks ashore, accompanied only by the pay, which is very difficult to hold on to. And there was always the mortgage to pay on his flat in Brighton. A solitary and unmarried man of thirty-seven, Bob was already only too well aware of the path down which he could easily go on a two-week-on, two-week-off basis and so he took to touring the countryside in his Volkswagen minibus, which was known to all and sundry as 'Nellie'. On one of these trips round Scotland he saw the sign pointing to the John Ridgway School of Adventure as it stood beside the narrow single-track coastal road on the west coast of Sutherland. A few months later he wrote to me suggesting that he would like to help at the school during his periods away from the rig. At first this seemed to be an ideal situation but I soon realized that he was much older than the usual team of instructors, who are in their early twenties; this caused trouble, particularly with Tony Dallimore, who at twenty-two had never come into contact with the like of Bob Burns but who was equally able to call a spade a spade.

The businessmen's courses were much improved with the advent of the Bowman. While the walkers did the two-day mountain expedition, we were now able to take those who were keen on sailing out to the Hebrides, and the lonely islands made just the right holiday contrast with their normal busy lives.

When the boat was not at sea Arun would be down, hard at work on the fitting out, often accompanied by his brother, Neil, a student of naval architecture at Glasgow University. Neil is practically Arun's double, and as they tend to wear matching clothing they're usually mistaken for one another by strangers.

'We were wondering if you wouldn't be better entering the Whitbread Round the World Race in August '77 to April '78. It'd be so much more interesting stopping at Cape Town, Auckland and Rio than going non-stop,' Arun murmured quietly one May morning as he fiddled with the teak off the hatch cover he had just brought down from his Durness workshop. Behind him Neil nodded in agreement.

'Don't think we haven't thought of it, old top,' I replied. 'There are two problems, though. One: we can't afford to leave the school for so long; and two: I doubt we'd keep up with a fleet of racing boats.'

'Well, you could start and end earlier next year, and start and end later in 1978,' Neil chipped in, cute as ever.

'I wouldn't worry about the boat speed. You'll not win the race, but you could do well enough if you've got a good handicap,' Arun added.

That evening I put the idea again to Marie Christine.

'Oh, I'd love the three stops. It'd make up for all the misery in between,' she cried, full of enthusiasm.

'Well, I don't think we could afford the time.'

'Oh, you always say that. What's the point of living? There's no point in spending all your time denying yourself.'

I'd heard all this guff before. Lance would call me a Puritan again if he could hear the conversation. I felt like replying with that henpecked-husband line: 'Yes, dear, I'll take the dog for a walk.'

'Let's just think about it for a bit,' I compromised.

Early in June, Richard Morris-Adams rang to say he'd interested ATV in making a film of our voyage and that Charles Denton, Head of Documentaries, would like to come to Ardmore to discuss the idea. Although I could see the value of the film in terms of attracting a sponsor, I was apprehensive about carrying an unknown two-man film crew right round the world. After ten years' experience of TV film crews, I was painfully aware how temperamental they can be.

Charles Denton's visit coincided with an unusually hot July weekend. A charming, astute-looking fellow of about forty, Charles wasted no time in getting to the point as he and I sat in the sun alone on the back of the boat. Not only did he feel a ninety-minute film of the voyage should be made, but that a further thirty-minute film of a businessmen's course could make a useful introduction to be shown at the start of the trip.

When I suggested that we might enter the race with its three stops, he agreed this would help his logistics as far as the removal of film and equipment was concerned. We both agreed the choice of film crew was of paramount importance. By the time Charles left for London, Marie Christine and I felt we could rely on him to produce an interesting documentary; but we continued to worry about the film crew.

On 15 July we were delighted to hear Jamie's voice on the phone from Newport, Rhode Island. He'd crossed the Atlantic and was setting off back to Ardmore within a few days. I only felt sorry that he would not be coming with us round the world; but affairs of the heart have a way of overcoming all obstacles, and the circumnavigation was clearly seen as an obstacle.

I was concerned to pick a large crew of instructors for the race, so that it would truly celebrate the tenth anniversary of our starting the John Ridgway School of Adventure. The best way to select the team was to have a trial voyage in the autumn.

We chose to sail in early October from Ardmore to Madeira, then on to the Azores and so back to Ardmore. This voyage we had made two years previously as part of a longer trip described in my book *Storm Passage*, and I knew it would be a real trial in winter.

Fitting out continued apace. We went forty miles across the Minch to Stornoway to repaint the bottom with red anti-fouling, and came back vowing to build our own pier at Ardmore to lay the boat against on spring tides. The good ship *Loch Inchard*, a local seine netter of some sixty foot, came twice to help us lay our new moorings behind Paddy's Isle. Tony Dallimore had come to Ardmore as an instructor following his medical student brother, Nick. Short and taciturn, with a powerful neck and stubby fingers, Tony is a blunt, effectual character, who sees people in simple terms and is therefore able to make quick decisions. He is good at organizing and has a natural, forceful style of leadership. Coming from a small village in Somerset, with both parents working in education, he went to a grammar school and this was followed by three years in Glamorgan College of Education from which he emerged with a Bachelor of Education degree, but he has had no practical experience of life beyond his education. Competent and well qualified in sailing and canoeing and easily able to absorb the necessary skills of rock climbing and hill-walking, he was to become in 1977 the most efficient chief instructor I have had.

It was soon clear that Tony had plenty to offer and so I made him a watch leader for the trial voyage to the Azores.

Charles Denton had become Programme Controller of ATV during the summer and Richard Creasey, son of the prolific author John Creasey, took over as producer of the film from Charles. Richard and I got on very well together. We had much in common: confused family background, poor academic record at school, fierce enthusiasm. In London he kept fit by cycling to work, and at Ardmore he soon took to the daily cross-country run. It was agreed that ATV should pay us £3,500 to make the film of our voyage, and this included our feeding the two-man film crew for a total of nine months. Not a lot of money in a project which was costing around a hundred thousand pounds. Still, it was a start, and maybe it would encourage that mythical creature, a sponsor – although there was no sign of it up to now.

The 1976 season closed on 2 October, when the last businessmen's course finished; and on the very next day we sailed for Madeira and the Azores with a crew of sixteen, which included two ATV film crew, Marie Christine and Rebecca. It was rough right from the start, and several people were sick before we'd gone far from the mouth of Loch Laxford.

The film crew were Roger Deakins and Peter Berry; both in their late twenties, they were surprisingly inexperienced, having only recently left the film school. Slim, pale, and total novices as far as sailing was concerned, they were very different from the much younger, open personalities of the instructors; and although Peter Berry's ear-rings and the sophisticated veneer of the TV men appealed to the more impressionable, most of the crew looked on with amused anticipation. For freelance newcomers to the TV business, Roger and Peter had a great opportunity. But while a good ninety-minute documentary could establish them, the reverse also applied – an expensive flop would do them no good at all. It was rumoured that Charles Denton called after them as they left his office:

'Remember: fellows who make mistakes don't work for me too often.'

They clearly felt they were in for a real mind-blowing experience, and they certainly got it. The east wind which had blown across the now snow-covered peaks for the past three weeks changed abruptly soon after the start to forty knots from south-south-west right on the nose. All hope of a pleasant run down the Minch through the islands was gone. Instead we were tacking into a gale to get past the Shiant Islands. The boat was nothing like fitted out inside – after all, there was still another year to the deadline – and many slept on the bare boards in the saloon, sharing the same black bucket to be sick in.

The internal lighting was just a Tilley lamp and torches, and Peter the sound recordist developed an alarming death-rattle style of vomiting, which was all the more dramatic in the dark.

The second evening found us close under the red lights of the Tiree Beacon. Darkness brought the wind, and by midnight fierce squalls had smashed a forward stanchion and snapped a genoa sheet like so much string. An ominous swell was rolling in from the Atlantic, and the glass tumbled. The forepeak was flooded through the leaking anchor hatch, and the watertight ice protection door prevented this water from coming aft in the bilge. The boat took on a nose-down attitude and shipped still more water until the forepeak holding most of the sails was full to the brim. Bob went down through the fore hatch and emptied it with buckets. It took a long, long time. He blocked up the anchor chain hawse pipe with rags, and this almost stopped any more water getting in.

By the afternoon of the third day, 5 October, we were still tacking to the south-west in that big bit of sea between Barra Head at the southern end of the Hebrides and the north-west corner of Ireland. Conditions were pretty squalid, and for a lot of the day we had to run the main engine to charge batteries.

Filming was sporadic. As the day drew on the wind increased to sixty knots from the south-west, and the crew weakened. Only Bob and Tony remained untouched by seasickness. In the bare after-cabin the water floated the floorboards, knocking them in an irritating way against the side of the hull under my scaffolding pipecot as the boat heaved.

Marie Christine and Rebecca in the port side had not left their bunks since we had left Ardmore. On the morning of the fourth day when Rebecca opened her eyes, the corners of her mouth slowly drooped as she realized where she was, and the tears welled and silently trickled slowly down her cheeks. Mother and child played all sorts of games to take their minds off their plight. Bob cut bread into soldiers for Becca's boiled egg and told her his granny was an orange lollypop; but no matter how often Marie Christine and Rebecca sang 'My Favourite Things' there was no getting away from the situation.

When the wind reached seventy knots and more, the seas washed away the spray hood over the main hatch and flooded the chart table. It was time to lie ahull. One man sat on watch in the cockpit. Fourteen of the sixteen bodies were incapacitated by seasickness. I knew full well what the conditions would be like on the trip home from the Azores in December, when we would be without both Arun and Bob who had to return to their work. There was too great a risk of major damage with such a weak crew, the results of which could be catastrophic for the circumnavigation next year.

Bob was heartbroken when I gave the order to turn for home, but he was realistic: it was for the best in the long run. We had a memorable seventy-two mile run in eight hours under the spinnaker back up the Minch as the wind eased. Dick McCann narrowly escaped decapitation when the boom vang broke in an accidental gybe.

At twenty, Dick was to be the youngest member of the crew for the circumnavigation. His father was a squadron leader in the RAF and separated from his mother who was an occupational therapist. He had a sister of sixteen still at school and his education had followed the same unsuccessful path as my own. Leaving Kings School, Bruton in Somerset with four passes at O-level at the age of eighteen in July 1975, he carried with him the advice of his physical education teacher who was an ex-Parachute Regiment sergeant. 'McCann, there are two types of people in this world. There are the intellectuals, who are as weak as wee wee, and then there are the others who must use their bodies. You are not one of the intellectuals.' On leaving school Dick spent a year helping to teach games at a prep school in Devonshire and often worked on a local farm as well. The stubborn side of his nature, which had so tormented his teachers, showed itself again one day in a narrow Devonshire lane up which Dick was slowly making his way with the tractor and muck spreader. A local big noise behind the wheel of his shiny new Jaguar so aggravated Dick by blaring his hooter to overtake, that Dick pressed the switch which activated the muck spreader and altered the appearance of the Jaguar to such an extent, that Richard McCann found himself before the local magistrate, appealing for the understanding of the bench that muck spreaders often run amok.

Short and well built, Dick was very conscious of not being an intellectual as the physical education master had told him. I hoped the sunny side of his nature would prevail over the stubborn side; fifty-seven feet was a small space for an athlete who had difficulty in expressing himself in words.

We were back at the mooring under the Ardmore wood by eleven o'clock in the morning, and Lance and Ada were so surprised that they mistook the yacht for some other casual visitor. For all its brevity, the trial had been a success. Of the sixteen crew only Marie Christine, Bob, Tony, Dick and I were really on, with maybe a couple of possibilities. Even Arun joined the ranks of those who'd seen quite enough to know they didn't want another thirty thousand miles. The film crew, Roger and Peter, were still keen though pale. Roger felt, and looked, as if he would overcome the seasickness, but I couldn't forget Peter's agonized appeal one bad afternoon: 'Look man, I just don't seem to be able to kick this seasickness bit.' At least they now had some experience – there was insufficient time and too much to do, for me to begin again with another TV crew.

A great party was held that night in the wooden house down by the shore with steaks rushed fifty miles from Lairg on the mail bus. Much home-made beer was drunk, and several faces looked older. At one point, thirty-seven-year-old Bob announced his philosophy of leadership.

'You'll never get men to work for you unless they hate you. Make them hate you and they'll work wonders,' he cried, beer mug in hand, and I saw several heads come up from their fruit salad. I didn't agree either; this didn't fit in with the views of instructors in their early twenties, and that line was to stick in my mind.

A hasty conference held next evening by the light of the Tilley lamp up in the croft kitchen included most of the probable crew for the trip. It was agreed that we lacked an experienced ocean racer and that plans be put in hand immediately to find a person or persons who could help us work up the boat during the next summer, 1977, in readiness for the start of the race on 27 August.

Everyone went their various ways for the winter. Arun proposed to start on the boat again early in the new year. In the meanwhile he had a backlog of other work urgently needing his attention up at Durness. I could see the chance of the boat being properly prepared slipping away.

The yacht lay alone and secure on her massive new mooring under Paddy's Isle, half a mile south of the croft. Lance kindly agreed to build and fit the framework of the saloon as weather permitted during the winter. He was stepping into the breach once again just when the need was greatest – even though he disliked the whole idea of the circumnavigation.

After a brief holiday in Eire we returned to Ardmore. Following Marie Christine's example of the previous year, I entered the Royal Northern Infirmary in Inverness and duly had my appendix out as a precaution for the voyage.

All the while I pondered the problems of the crew. Clearly the greatest mistake I could make would be to choose the wrong crew. I was constrained by wanting the team to have Ardmore as a common strand of interest and this meant choosing from a very small selection of inexperienced people. At the same time I realized that we needed that stiffening which an older, more experienced ocean-racing hand could offer. Seven hundred miles from London, selection of that man was a bit of a conundrum. I placed an advert in *The Times*, and another in our local pub. In the end, neither was productive. *The Times* people were unsuitable, and the locals, although keen, just could not afford the time away from fishing – combined with the almost certain lack of a place on a fishing boat on their return to Kinlochbervie in 1978.

Early in 1977 a circular arrived from the Royal Navy Sailing Association, who were organizing the event for the sponsors, Whitbread. Attached was a list of those who had applied for crew places. I chose the most likely people for our purpose and offered them each a place on a week's selection course to be run at Ardmore in the last week of February. Those selected would be required to help work up the boat during the summer and help run the John Ridgway School of Adventure on our return after the voyage, from April to October '78, all food and accommodation to be provided free from summer '77 to October '78 – but there was no pay. On *Great Britain II* the crew were paying £4,000 per head for a place on the boat.

The selection course was geared to run at the end of the instructors' course for the 1977 season. And so it was that an accountant, an art dealer, a teacher and a Tasmanian world traveller, all in their early thirties and unknown to one another, joined the Royal Highlander in Euston station on the night of Friday, 18 February, plus Roger and Peter from ATV who urgently needed more sailing practice. When they boarded the northern train for Lairg at Inverness on the Saturday morning, they began to pick one another out from the other passengers. Once on the mail bus they could hardly avoid each other.

'This is my scene,' announced one big fellow, producing an expensive yachting book – which another candidate took to mean he'd written the book himself.

Others described voyages they had made as the old red bus rumbled through the snowy mountains on its one and a half hour journey to the west. They were met at the mail-box by Tony Dallimore, the new chief instructor, who drove them along the track to the school in the Land-Rover, and then brought them by boat the last mile across the sea-loch to Ardmore.

There were flurries of snow and floes of thin ice on the water. Ardmore is a quiet and remote place in summer, and that cold week in February it could have been on the moon.

The days started early and finished late. A morning at sea, a three-mile cross-country run through ice and snow around the sea-loch before lunch, and then to sea again in the afternoon was the pattern of the week. In the evening we had one fellow up at a time to supper in the croft, and this was followed by films or talks down in the wooden house with the others.

By the end of the week, Peter Brand, tall and wiry, was the one we thought most suitable for our own particular style of carrying on. Peter, aged thirty, comes from Tasmania, where his father is a motel pro-prietor and his mother helps run the motel. He has a brother of twenty-eight who is an industrial chemist and a brother aged twenty-four who is the assistant manager of the motel. He went to school in Hobart and followed that with three years teacher training in Hobart before doing two years of teaching at a primary school in Hobart to complete his non-graduate diploma in teaching. Tasmania was not big enough for Peter Brand so he started to travel, working his way around the world. Jobs have included tin-mining, apple-picking, dish-washing, steelworks, engineer's mate, electric supply in Alice Springs, freezer-hand in Darwin, truck driver, linesman, headmaster of an aboriginal school of thirty children, and cowboy. While he was in Darwin he met a Canadian nurse named Penny who became his fiancée and together they travelled the world, taking a sailing ketch to Timor and then on through South East Asia by road, rail and sea to Nepal and the Himalayas, then through India by train and by sea to Mombasa from where they camped their way through Africa, down to Cape Town where in 1973–74 Peter was the mate aboard a fifty-foot cutter named *Active* of the Off-Shore Sailing School. From there they travelled up through Namibia, through Rhodesia to Kenya and on through Ethiopia, up the Red Sea, through the Sudan and on to Egypt before flying to England. In London Peter became a hod carrier for seven months which strengthened his willowy frame and his pocket to such a degree that he and Penny were able to tour Europe before returning once more to London. His ambition is to settle in British Columbia and start his own sailing school which would include bushcraft and ski touring. His interests are skiing, music – he plays the guitar – trout fishing and woodworking. Indeed he is so keen on the woodworking that one of his ambitions in life is to build his own log house in Canada. Good with his hands, he is one of those people who are very fussy about the end result.

Tall, thin, bespectacled, intensely sincere and sensitive, Peter saw the voyage as the fulfilment of a life's ambition and a big step in the starting of his own Adventure School in Canada.

Many people came and went that spring, and we were glad to see familiar faces on three of the other boats when at last we came to the start of the race.

Roger Deakins and Peter Berry did their sailing, gripped the cold wet ropes, tottered round the run, and were determined to come on the voyage with us.

The season was soon going at full tick. The boat was alive with the sound of hammer and power tools whenever she was at the mooring. Jubilee Pier was gradually taking shape under Lance's hand. A twist of fate had us starting a small salmon farm in the sea-loch, in this the busiest of all years at Ardmore. Moorings for cages had to be laid; old telephone poles rose from the croft like an Alexander Bell nightmare to form the framework of the drying green for the net cages. Thousands of tiny salmon smolts came by truck from Uist. Many died because the distance was too great, but most lived to get the project off the ground. I had plenty on my mind.

One night as I finished serving supper to the businessmen in the wooden house, one of the instructors called to me from the stairs that there was someone outside to see me. It was Steve Lenartowicz, an able instructor from 1972.

Short, athletic and now aged twenty-six, Steve is highly articulate, intelligent and competitive. Some of this drive may have come from his background. His father is a retired Polish upholsterer living in Hounslow near London with Steve's English mother, who is a part-time teacher. His father left Poland just before the Second World War, leaving behind the Iron Curtain a son whom Steve had never met but about whom he sometimes wondered. Growing up in the harsh world of a London suburb with his unusual name, Steve soon learned how to make his own way and at the age of fifteen he became the Hounslow Junior Champion Orator by dint of having learned a *Time* magazine essay word perfect before the finals, which he then spouted as the original thought of a fifteen-year-old schoolboy in such a convincing manner that the panel never doubted him. An average grammar school education led him to Manchester University where he achieved a first class honours degree in physics. He surprised his teachers by declining the opportunity to become a professor in physics and instead opted for a career in teaching. After a further year he attained a teaching certificate at Bangor University, and then moved on to teach physics and outdoor activities at a secondary modern school in a rough part of Manchester where most of his pupils were West Indian. After three years at this school he was ready for a move and the idea of the voyage paralleled his personal ambition which was simply: achievement.

The harsh memory of the five-day October trial faded with the spring sun of a new year, and I was delighted when Arun agreed to re-join the crew, but just a little surprised when he whispered that he'd like to be a watch leader. Shy and quiet, almost to the point of total silence, Arun would seem to be the most unlikely character of the entire crew to make a watch leader, but as the man who built the boat I owed it to him to at least give him the opportunity. His watch soon became known as the 'cruising watch' but in reality I doubt very much if the boat moved any slower while he, Peter and Dick were in charge. Arun was an unusual person. His Indian father came from Bengal and had died some years previously leaving Arun as head of the family. During his four year apprenticeship he won the Boatbuilding Apprentice of the year 1970–71 prize awarded by the British Shipbuilding Industry Training Board. I felt it was only the difficult family situation which had prevented his going to university like his younger brothers. The family moved to Durness in 1974 and Arun started his own Cape Wrath Boatyard some twenty miles from Ardmore. The family lived and worked in the Balnakeil craft village where his English mother opened a shop to sell the products which she weaved on the looms that Arun had built for her.

In spite of the almost inaudible voice Arun used to communicate with others on the boat, his presence was very much felt as he had fitted the boat out from scratch, helped at different times only by Lance, Colin, Jamie Young and his own brother Neil. There was never any doubt at all but that Arun knew the answer to every technical question about the boat's construction. He could almost say how many turns each individual screw was embedded in the hull!

This particular decision highlighted a difficult situation which was to affect the entire project – everyone thirsted for responsibility: Tony, Bob, Arun and Peter Brand all needed responsibility to maintain their motivation.

Bob and I went through a very bad patch over personal matters which concerned the differing ways of life at the John Ridgway School of Adventure and the oil rig. In the end we both agreed he should give the voyage a try; but at thirty-seven he would clearly never work under Tony, whom he thought a rather supercilious twenty-two-year-old.

The yacht on duty at Ardmore 1977. On a young people's course, Rodrigo from Spain imagines what the trip will be like

The best thing seemed to be to make them both watch leaders on a level footing, with Arun leading the third watch. This left Peter Brand, who at thirty at first seemed to be the most experienced sailor. He wouldn't be happy under any of the three watch leaders, so I made him mate; that is, second in command under me but part of Arun's watch. This hierarchy was to prove a mistake.

As usual with boats there are problems with the delivery of parts, and the phone bill grew to frightening proportions as I tried frantically to get things sent from seven hundred miles away. The crew now was: Peter, Bob, Tony, Arun, Dick, Steve, plus the ATV men, Roger Deakins and Peter Berry. Marie Christine and I had decided Rebecca was right in choosing a boarding school near her grandmother in Brighton rather than coming with us on the boat. I felt there were two more places available, but I couldn't fill them suitably, although there was a constant flow of prospective crew members to and from Ardmore.

Then one day Arun told me his assistant, Colin Ladd, was keen to come. Colin was nearly as quiet as Arun, and although he'd been working on the boat for five months, Marie Christine and I hardly knew him. He had quite a lot to offer.

Aged twenty-five, with a freckled face and rather soulful look, Colin comes from Rickmansworth in Hertfordshire. His father is a chartered mechanical engineer with B.P. in London and his mother is manageress of a ladies' outfitters shop in Northwood. He had followed his fiancée to the craft village at Balnakeil, where she was planning to make a living from selling the tapestries she intended to make there. Study at the Royal College of Art in London does not necessarily lead to a successful business career, and Colin was not entirely convinced of the financial viability of life in the north-west of Scotland. He met up with Arun Bose and set to work as his assistant, thus making a one-man boatyard into a two-man boatyard. The main project in hand at the time was the fitting out of my boat for the voyage around the world. Arun and Colin became firm friends but it was only after some six months that Arun suggested to me that Colin might be a member of the crew.

The voyage was to be a giant step for Colin who had a degree in mechanical engineering, and whose experience of two years as a structural design engineer working on missiles for the British Aircraft Corporation at Stevenage had left him with strong feelings of discontent. He had been offered a place at aviation school by British Airways to become an airline pilot, but he had turned this down on the grounds of insufficient interest. He already held a yachtmaster's certificate for offshore sailing and had spent several years in dinghy racing. Other interests included nature and classical music, and he could play the piano. His fiancée agreed to postpone their wedding, planned for 17 December 1977, so that Colin could make the voyage. Colin looked to be the most easy going and pleasant personality of anyone in the crew. He seemed to be in the happy position of having no responsibility but plenty of ability.

David Burnett of William Heinemann Limited, a powerfully built figure with a permanently worried expression under tousled black hair, came up to Ardmore to discuss a book of the trip. Sadly, he lost the nails off both big toes after trying the run round the loch as part of his research. By coincidence, David knew Richard Creasey, the TV producer, but only by sight, as he also cycled part of the same route to work each morning in London.

I'd like to think the Ardmore run inspired them to international class, but there was a setback. On the week before the publisher's visit to the far north-west, the TV producer, deep in thought, ran into a steel rubbish skip standing innocently at the kerb. His bike was wrecked, and a shoulder dislocated.

However, they eventually met up in a smart West End restaurant (the publisher recognizing the TV producer by his casual attire and the sporty shoulder sling he carried). A few days later I received a note in David's thick, italic writing: 'I had lunch with the hunter. Such a nice boy (*only* 33, he told me). He was really helpful. Put the might of ATV behind us. Helped me up from the table, anxiously enquiring after my toes ...'

Shortly after this Richard Morris-Adams arrived from London with Monica Dixon and Simon Weaver from Barwell Sports Management, a public relations firm representing Debenhams, the department store giant. The four of us met on the yacht at the mooring under the wood. The sun shone hotly. The boat was in chaos. Arun had spots of white paint on his specs and his hair looked none too tidy. Monica, a glamorous Anglo-Swede, was dressed interestingly in leather. Richard had warned me she was a sailing expert; but Monica said that although she'd been a fund-raiser for the British Olympic Sailing Team she confined her sporting activities to the shore owing to seasickness. Simon, however, had the lean and hungry look. He was to push me hard on the run. I took them on a quick tour of the boat; then while examining the Blake's marine toilet installation adjoining my cabin, Simon made a suggestion.

'What would you think about naming the yacht *Debenhams*, John?'

I looked down at the toilet, and tried to imagine how twenty-five thousand used one-pound notes would look piled up in it.

'It has a certain romantic ring to it,' I grinned, and the deal was struck.

The bank manager thought it was a good idea too.

Where would the other seventy-five thousand come from? That was the problem. There was the three thousand, five hundred from ATV; the advance on the book would bring a bit – just how much depended on the publishers' success in sub-leasing overseas editions. Then there was the eleven-thousand-pound loan from the Highlands and Islands Development Board, but it still left a big gap. I scraped the barrel, cut down on inessentials on the boat, held long discussions with Arun, and worried about it. Would the ceiling be one hundred thousand pounds; was there enough in the building society; what about Rebecca's education, our old age ...?

And there were just one or two more problems. Peter Berry, the ATV sound recordist, phoned Richard Creasey from Indonesia to say that a doctor had advised him not to take up sailing because of seasickness. Creasy looked around him for a replacement. Not every wife wanted her husband to sail away round the world. There was only a month to go, but he managed to find Noel Smart, an energetic thirty-three-year-old Geordie, complete with a Mexican moustache.

Noel had covered a lot of ground in his life. His father, who had died in 1970, had been an electrical engineer in Newcastle upon Tyne, where his widowed mother still lived. Noel was an only child and had been to state school until the age of eleven before going on to a private fee-paying school in Newcastle, where he stayed until the age of fifteen before leaving to join a firm of accountants which his father had wanted him to do. This lasted for only six weeks. Noel had plenty of energy and immediately tried to join Tyne Tees Television which was just starting at that time. They took him on at the age of fifteen on condition that he went to the Newcastle upon Tyne College of Art and Industrial Design where he spent three years to gain a diploma in photography and then immediately became an assistant cameraman with Tyne Tees Television at eighteen.

Moving to ATV, he was a full cameraman at the unusually early age of twenty-two. He kept this job for the next eight years before growing tired of the routine, also he could not see his way clear to becoming a director. His discontent with his work coincided with the breakdown of his marriage and Noel left his wife and two children to take up the life of a charter yacht skipper around the Greek islands with a girlfriend. This pleasant life lasted for three years before he grew tired of it also and returned to England and freelance work, again in the television world.

Noel was clearly a different type of person from me. While I had chosen the rest of the crew very carefully, of course he would not have been on the voyage if it had not been for the fact that he was a last-chance half of the ATV film crew. He never seemed to ask a question of others and could change his views twice daily to suit the conversation. I could find no principles or ideals which either held his interest or troubled his conscience. I felt sure he wished to skate along on that hard, varnished surface which covers the realities of life and I could never reach him as a person. When we came to the point in our meeting where we discussed his leaving his wife and two children I said, 'Does this mean that you are another cold, heartless, selfish swine?' There was a long pause while he looked at me across the room. Then he replied quietly, 'No, it does not,' and we left the subject. That was the only time I felt I ever really spoke to the real Noel Smart.

No sooner had we laid the yacht against Jubilee Pier for the first time than we discovered the new Gori propellor had sheared one of the teeth in its folding mechanism. Fortunately, Canpa agreed to replace it immediately. We had less luck with the anti-fouling. It had been applied badly in Stornoway the previous summer and now the bottom looked like a travelling seafood bar. We decided to change paints to International Hard-Racing White. The firm very generously agreed to give us the paint to see how it would stand up to a thirty-thousand-mile trip. The snag came when we tried to get the old paint off. In fact, this anti-fouling scheme became the biggest single problem left. We used special paint remover from International with scrapers and scrubbing brushes between the tides. Once off, the next stage couldn't be done until we'd lifted the boat out of the water for several days eight hundred miles away on the south coast at the Rank Marina on the Hamble River in Hampshire.

Our excellent dehydrated food came from Batchelors Catering Supplies, so we had no worry there, and Caters of Debenhams kindly helped too. There was still one more place on the crew for a cook. I didn't want Marie Christine to have to do any more cooking, because the boat was practically paid for by the cooking she had done at Ardmore in the past ten years.

John Covington, aged thirty, appeared on the scene; a Falstaffian figure who had dabbled in many things. He was described by Duff Hart-Davis in the *Sunday Telegraph* as 'a splendidly built cook' but perhaps a more realistic zoological description would be 'a man gone to seed'. Short, round and troubled with blood pressure, J.C. (as he came to be known) joined the crew with the sole responsibility of being the cook. Whatever the weather, when it was time for porridge he could produce the porridge. It was a difficult job, and difficult he found it. In order to lift his prestige a little I added the title of 'sail trimmer' as he had had quite a bit of experience of weekend racing in smaller yachts in the North Sea. His father was a director of a large corporation and his mother is a J.P. His younger brother flies Harrier Jump jets for the Royal Navy and J.C. sometimes feels he hasn't really lived up to family expectations.

While his father was in the Army J.C. attended eleven schools around the world, ultimately achieving seven passes at O-level (one more than me) while at Maidenhead Grammar School. After a brief stab at the insurance business he joined the Parachute Regiment but left after the recruit training stage. He then wanted to be a pilot in the Army but this was not possible for him and he failed the Royal Navy medical for the Fleet Air Arm. Instead he became captain of a Thames river boat for a year before moving on through the chocolate bar, computer and agricultural seeds areas of commerce. During this time he was married at twenty-one, and divorced at twenty-five, without children. He felt he shouldn't have married, doesn't know what happened to his wife and he feels he shouldn't think about it any more.

Before joining our crew, J.C. had spent a year driving trucks in Saudi Arabia. His job was to transport goods from the stinking hot port of Jhedda to towns inland at a basic pay of £300 per week, in a six-wheeler Mercedes complete with frigidaire and 225-gallon diesel fuel tank. The job was hot and arduous for Europeans. His prime cargo was cement, for Saudi Arabia is the world's biggest building site and Saudis are very bad drivers. 'When they crossed the desert in the old days the camel did the thinking. Now, with the motor car, there is no one left to think.' J.C.'s ambition is to do and see things and his interests include yachting, cooking and a sufficient consumption of beer to keep the frame filled out.

3

Ardmore to Portsmouth

The 2nd of August came all too soon. The boat was in chaos, the decks piled high with stuff we couldn't find a place for below. But everything had to be squeezed in somehow. Half a day passed while the squeezing went on. Up in the croft, Marie Christine played Racing Demon with Rebecca to while away the time. We were on such a tight budget that we had to take everything we needed to effect repairs on the way. We even took the builder, Arun. There could be no turning the boat over to expensive yards along the way.

In the early evening, with the boat looking more like a laden barge than an ocean racer, we hoisted the sails, and heeling gently to the lightest of breezes, we slipped our mooring and headed silently up the loch bathed in shadow. As we passed the headland below the croft, the eldest group of the last course gave us three rousing cheers which rolled back from the surrounding hills. On the other side of the water, way up on the top of the hills, still golden with the evening sun, the two younger groups appeared like rebel tribesmen, and they gave three huge cheers.

'Three cheers for the course,' shouted Bob from the foredeck, and we answered like mad.

At the wheel I could hardly see for the tears. I was thinking all sorts of things.

Soon we were out in Loch Laxford and heading for the open sea. The blue dinghy astern turned for home. We waved goodbye to Rebecca and her granny, Lance and Ada, and Molly Ross from next door. The sound of their outboard was soon lost behind Paddy's Isle. We were alone. As we passed along the north shores of Loch Laxford I looked at the rocks, the rough grass and heather. A few of Heckie's sheep were nibbling at the yellow seaweed. Nothing has changed, I thought; fourteen years and nothing's really changed. What a fine place to grow old in!

A thirty-knot south-wester soon cleared the cobwebs. The challenge I had set myself was on. We had to get right round the world and back

Tony Dallimore

Peter Brand

John Ridgway

Marie Christine Ridgway

Steve Lenartowicz

Colin Ladd

Bob Burns

Dick McCann

Roger Deakins

John Covington

Noel Smart

Arun Bose

here by mid-April next year. Could I pull it off? The eight-hundred-mile passage down the west coast, round Land's End and up the English Channel to the Hamble River near Southampton took six days. We had much to practise. Skies were blue and calms frequent. It was ideal for the shake-down cruise I had in mind. In spite of all our well-laid plans we had never sailed together as a team until now. The initial watch system was: J.R. and M.C.R. and J.C. (cook), out of watches; Watch 1 was Tony Dallimore, Colin Ladd, Steve Lenartowicz; Watch 2, Bob Burns, Dick McCann, Noel Smart; and Watch 3, Arun Bose, Peter Brand and Roger Deakins. Each watch did a tour of four hours on deck, then eight hours off. Thus the boat was sailed easily twenty-four hours a day.

Whenever a complicated sail change was called for, like spinnaker drill, John Covington and I were called on deck. I would take the wheel while J.C. manned the winches in the main cockpit; and the duty watch of three worked the foredeck. The system worked well and was adopted. I wished later that we had tried some alternatives, but there was so much to practise, I felt a steady rhythm was best at the time.

Richard Creasey, the TV producer, travelled with us, and although he suffered agonies of seasickness, it did give him an idea of how the voyage would go. The main alteration was to place Roger and Noel in the same watch as they felt they couldn't make a film unless they were together. Bob, at thirty-seven, seemed best suited to handle the situation, but it created one watch significantly older than the others, and I was to regret this. I had high hopes that Bob would be an ally and an example as our ages were so close, but this was not to be, and even on this short passage we had warning shows of temper – but I left them unheeded.

Peter Brand was easily accepted as the man with most experience of big boat work, and with race fever gripping the younger fellows he had no difficulty in getting jobs done in his position as mate. Everybody worked full out.

Marie Christine recorded in the diary which she was to keep throughout our days at sea her thoughts on leaving home for the next nine months:

> Spent day of departure feeling in a dream, having taken a seasick pill in the morning, with ensuing drowsiness. But I was determined not to be laid out once on the boat. We had all gone very easy on food and drink for the last forty-eight hours – no beer, no second helpings – and it seems to have worked for me up to now. Mummy and Becca helped to give an air of normality to what was to John and me a day of trying to remember everything and more; carrying heavy bags down the hill to the boat which was to be our home for the next nine

months. Feeling the doubts and fears of the future and the sadness of leaving Rebecca for such a chunk of her precious childhood; the worry we were causing Mummy and Lance and Ada. The day was overcast, windy and wet. The boat seemed in chaos. Stowage was still going on, everything was damp and dirty. How could I choose to leave my warm secure home and friends and family for this new hostile environment where I was likely to get ill for three-quarters of the time, terrified out of my wits and physically cramped and uncomfortable? The trip had been something we'd been planning for two years, the dream of a lifetime for many, but for me not an overriding ambition, but an opportunity that I felt I couldn't turn down. John had said he wouldn't go without me, not that that was hanging over my head, but we didn't want to be apart.

Up at the croft Mum and Bec were playing a ferocious game of Racing Demon. Bec had had a cold and was being kept in and Mummy in her normal way was helping us all to keep going with

Becca and kittens at Ardmore

cups of tea or coffee and meals for anyone who appeared and, at the same time, sorting out the cupboards – in her words, 'battening down for winter'. Winter at Ardmore sets in with the first autumn gale. Overnight the leaves are burnt or fall off the trees and with the frost the wood mice come into the warmth and shelter of the thick-stoned croft, making cosy nests between the three-foot-thick rough stone walls and the matchboard lining. Always on our return from winter travels, the first rush round the house was to see what damage the mice had done: John's despair at finding the cork handles on his fishing rods eaten away, his best shoes gnawed, books and blankets; opening up drawers and finding silk and wool chewed – they never seem to go for manmade fibres. So questions like 'Where is the rat poison? Couldn't we leave the cats here for the winter?' and my thinking, 'Soon I'll be gone off on my trip round the world. Have I got the oregano? Must remember the tin opener. Hope the right type of loo paper arrives today – our last chance – off the mail bus.'

We eventually took everything we had to down to the boat – stowed it all in poly-bags in the many cupboards Lance Bell had put in for us in our tiny cabin. Arun Bose was still busy bringing on and fixing items such as the table, tools etc., and Bob and Peter were also involved with last-minute additions, so we waited out of the way up the hill. Our last supper was eaten. John fell asleep at the table, a quick catnap before the worries of the night. Then down the hill we went, clutching various items such as straw hat and blue bucket, a few books I felt I had room for, and my shopping basket with my tapestry. I waited in the dinghy with a swarm of midges having their last go and then out to the boat and on for the beginning of the thirty-thousand-mile trip.

Quick hugs and kisses for Bec and Mum, Lance and Ada and away. The sixty-six boys and girls from the Ardmore course were on either side of the sea-loch out of which we were to sail. The dinghy we had come out in was following us as we hoisted the mainsail and genoa ... Rebecca waving frantically with a wide grin on her face – very pleased not to be going with us. The trial in the autumn had put her off for a long time. She had remained quite firm in spite of her father's entreaties. But here was I, waving goodbye to her just eight months later.

It was soon time for them to turn back as I waved farewell to them and the tiny figures on the hillside. We had to look forward not back. I rushed below and quickly stowed some items that would move around in a rough sea, sobbing privately in our cabin. The rest of the crew settled straight away into the routine of four hourly watches, three on at a time. John Covington, our cook, made up the flasks for the night and on hearing a heaving sound from on deck I got into my bunk at top speed, not bothering to take off my clothes. If you suffer from seasickness the best place to be (apart from sitting under a tree) is lying horizontal in your pit.

After a short time John came in. He had been sick and was feeling in need of comfort, so he climbed in and we found to our relief that there was just enough room for two people in our small bunk, although half-way through the night I thought my hips would be crushed on the port tack with John's weight pushing me on to the leeboard.

We soon got the hang of flying our brand-new big-boy sail, which blossomed out red, white and blue beside the radial head spinnaker of the same colours as we ran downwind. The daily ration of two bottles of Fonseca Bin 27 port was less easy to handle, however. We decided to have a happy hour each day to take the tension out of the air, and this took place before supper. It certainly affected those of us unused to much alcohol.

One evening, beneath the thousand-foot basalt cliffs of Dunvegan, off the Isle of Skye, I could have sworn the water was running up a waterfall. Later J.C. (who suffered no such effects) berated us all for not keeping a steady course as we rounded the Lizard running under full sail and met the fleet of some two hundred and fifty yachts coming the other way on the Fastnet Race. We had had the port at lunch on that day. Someone noticed the name *Debenhams* and shouted: 'I want to change my shoes.'

'Sorry. Closed all day on Sunday,' replied J.C.

As we finished each bottle of port, Fonseca had asked us to put in a special message offering three free bottles for every message returned to Fonseca and throw it over the side. The racers were far too keen to pick up the bottles we threw over on that day; and we saw several of our competitors in the Round the World Race go by as they were using the Fastnet as a work-up.

'*Nazdrowie!*' cried the extrovert half-Polish Steve as one of the last boats went by just before dark. The crew looked startled and then waved wildly. The Polish entry hadn't met many fellow countrymen out in the Channel.

At seven o'clock one August morning as the mist rolled silently across the smooth waters of the Hamble River we nudged gently alongside the Rank Marina fuel jetty; the start of our race round the world was barely three weeks away and there was much to be done.

We had come south especially early to be at the centre of the British yachting industry and to take advice from the various manufacturers whose equipment was in our boat. Within the hour, *Debenhams* was lifted out of the water by the travel-lift and work begun on the long business of clearing off the rest of the anti-fouling and starting on a new process with International Paint. I found an office and a phone, and so the same day we were visited by the International experts who gave us precise instructions on how to use the perfect sunny weather we had to achieve the best possible anti-fouling. It involved five days' work and the crew really put their backs into it.

Visits followed from Proctor Masts, Barlow winches, Canpa steering, Shipmate stoves, and many others. Parts were taken away for servicing, strengthening or replacement. We were getting first-class treatment.

Arun and Colin continued to work on the fitting of new winches and the electrical system to support the huge Pentland Bravo radio which was installed by Greenham Marine, while Bob painted the decks anti-slip blue. Everyone else was on the anti-fouling. Rob Humphries came down to advise us on how to get the best possible rating for our handicap and actually helped Commander Banfield, the official measurer, with all the plumblines and measurement. But it was to no avail in the end. The Bowman 57 never was built to race; fast cruising, yes, but special lines to circumvent the rating rule, emphatically *no*; and we were to find out what that meant soon enough.

One afternoon just after we'd been put back into the water, now proudly sporting pristine white anti-fouling, smart red boot-topping and topsides agleam with polish, we got our first idea of the sort of

River Hamble – new anti-fouling and she is all set

Rebecca at Portsmouth before the start

competition we were up against. We were alongside one of the outer pontoons at one end of the marina, among the still empty berths specially reserved for entries in the Round the World Race.

It had been an unusually slow Fastnet Race with little or no wind, but at last the leaders were back. An immaculate sixty-five-foot dark blue Dutch aluminium ketch with cream decks and masts took her place in the berth next to us. This was *Flyer* – the favourite. I just stared at her, absorbing the impression of power. From somewhere below decks came the hum of a generator – 'a hyper-super dreadnought spinning across the bay'. An old line from something I'd learned at school surfaced in my mind.

'Oh, what a ship!' I muttered.

'They say he spent half a million on her. Specially built for this race, you know,' said an all-too-cheerful member of the marina staff at my side.

'Well, I guess there'll be plenty of rumours between now and the start,' I smiled, feeling anything but confident.

'It's no rumour. She's just won the Atlantic Race – by a couple of days too. She went over to the States to collect her new sails from Hood's, then raced back.'

'Who's the owner?'

'That tall blond fella. They say he's sold one of his businesses for ten million.'

Half a million to have a go at his life's ambition still leaves him nine and a half million.

'Ah, well. Thanks for telling me,' I said, suddenly anxious to hear no more.

'Look. Here comes *Condor*. See that yellow mast? It's ninety-three-foot high – biggest to be put in any yacht since the war, and four people can lift it. Made of carbon fibre, see . . .' The man went on and on. And wasn't I the one who'd given his mother-in-law fifty quid to buy a carbon-fibre golf club? What would a ninety-three-foot mast, thick as a tree, cost?

'Well, I'll have to get on with studying the charts now. Thanks for lending us the trolley.' I jumped leaden-footed aboard *Debenhams*. 'You've bitten off rather a lot. What are you like at chewing?' I asked myself, mindlessly stuffing charts in cupboards.

A week before the start we sailed the half a dozen or so miles to Vernon Creek in Portsmouth harbour. H.M.S. *Vernon* is a Royal Navy anti-submarine warfare establishment, and the little creek was just large enough to hold all fifteen yachts entered in the race. There were heavy timber pontoons to keep the smart hulls off the high, oily concrete sides of the rectangular inlet. A crane and artificial pool were available for those keen to wash their sails; naval liaison staff to help with workshop facilities; and scores of other things like press offices, information caravans, and even a special bank for those in the race.

As we came in Bob had us all dressed in our red North Cape polar jackets, and he heralded our arrival on his bo's'n's pipe. We were quite overcome when the other boats actually broke into applause.

'Pass your pudding!' came a hearty Naval voice from the pontoon.

Marie Christine blushed. Was he being rude?

'I think he means a fender,' said one of the crew, hastily throwing one ashore, not really seeing why it couldn't just dangle from the rail. Yes, we were very much the country mouse come to town. Inverness, the port of registry, was stencilled on our stern – you'd think it was the moon.

And so a week of activity began which was new to many of the crew. Suddenly, we were film stars. Crowds gazed down at us all day long from the high sides of the creek. Friends, relatives, journalists, manufacturers, officials, radio and TV men, all queued to come aboard and see round and talk about what we were about to attempt. Every night there was an official function for us to wear our fine Debenhams blazers, parchment coloured flannels and special Hardy Amies silk ties. We mingled with the other crews from other nations, who were equally smartly dressed.

The Press Office listed the odds as published by Ladbroke's, the bookmakers. Half a dozen boats were named, but *Debenhams* came in

John and Marie Christine Ridgway

Debenhams resting at Anchor at Ardmore

Preparations: the pier at Ardmore where we fitted her out

Anti-fouling: a long, chilly chore of scrape, scrape, paint, paint

The Red Coats: Front row (l. to r.) Steve, Bob; 2nd row JC, Dick, Tony, Arun, Roger, Colin; Back row Peter, Noel, Marie Christine, John

Debenhams off the Isle of Wight with 30,000 miles to go

the 'bar' section. The experts had assessed us as strictly cruising. They didn't like the steps on our mast, or the fluffy baggy wrinkle in our shrouds; and the massive steering oars Arun had built and lashed on either side of the aft cockpit just made them laugh. Each one of these was a three-man lift, but they'd get us home if the rudder fell off in the Southern Ocean.

Clare Francis's elegant Swan 65 lay inside us. A splendid flag flew from her forestay. It depicted a naked lady astride a swan on a blue background, completely overwhelming the white lettering of 'Debenhams' on a pale blue background which we were flying. It came from the roof of the Southsea store. We persuaded the store manager to lend us a nude female dress model, and ran that up the forestay until it was level with Clare's flag. She took the joke very well, and Jacques, her French husband, offered to throw anyone who was bothering us into the sea as they crossed *ADC Accutrac* on their way to us. In any case the laugh was on us in the end because the model stuck up the forestay, and it was some time before we could get it down; while catcalls rang out from all over the creek.

The scrutineering of the boats by race officials took most of the week. We were well prepared and, if anything, erred on the side of safety, so there were no problems. Some of the other boats looked as if they would never be ready in time: welding and hammering went on all hours of

Noel supporting our answer to Clare Francis

day and night. Great piles of exotic foodstuffs littered the pontoons, particularly beside the Italian entry, *B & B Italia*.

Everyone seemed to have last-minute problems. Even Cornelius van Rietschoten found at the last moment that his new sails for *Flyer* didn't fit. Before coming to *Vernon* he'd had some trouble with his crew. Cornelius was out to win.

'There'll be no reading books on my boat. Hell, no!' he cried at a party one night when Marie Christine told him she planned to read hundreds of books and learn to play the guitar. He ran a dry ship, too: no drink on board at all. One of the crew objected to the tough regimen, and Cornelius told him to buckle down or leave. He left. A spokesman for the rest of the crew told Cornelius that the rest wanted to leave in sympathy.

'I'm going to buy you a beer now. When I come back I want to know all those who want to leave, and I want them off the boat by this evening. I'm sailing with you or without you.' They all stayed.

Condor, the mighty British hope, was most plagued by unreadiness. No expense had been spared to rush this maxi-racer through the builder since she started building in October the previous year. But she was far from ready to race round the world. At three in the morning of the night before the start, Robin Knox-Johnson was up the mast changing the spreaders. Inside the boat teams of builders seemed to be working round the clock. Robin and his co-skipper, Les Williams, came in for a lot of good-natured chaffing for their obvious unreadiness, but they took it all and dished out some stick in return. The cost of their boat seemed much greater than any of the others, and apparently it was all borne by one man.

It started to rain heavily in mid-week, so I needed a hat of some sort. All I could find was a thick camel-leather cowboy hat I'd got in the Spanish Sahara for a sun-hat. It kept the rain off all right, but once sodden it became rather pliable. I noticed people looking at me in this funny hat, so I decided to keep on wearing it and to hell with them.

Marina cowboy just about sums up our chances, I thought. It brought forth some wry comments in the press.

Debenhams gave a press reception organized by Monica Dixon. After Mark Barker, the managing director of Barwell Sports Management, had outlined Debenhams' involvement in the project I was called out to answer questions.

'Are you a serious competitor in this race or is it just another adventure for you?' asked a rather sallow-looking photo-journalist.

'Well, I'm rather competitive by nature. We don't have a very fast boat, but I hope we'll do well in the second and third legs in the Southern Ocean – probably not so well in the first and fourth legs.' I replied with the first thing that came into my mind, but that was really the sum of my hopes at the time. 'As far as the adventure goes, there are two things I hope to see: the icebergs and really big seas in the Southern Ocean.'

All the time the question of finance kept nagging us. We were into a very expensive game. In the wings, soon to be forgotten, were several other boats which just didn't make it to the start for lack of funds.

The ugliness was brought home one morning as I came out of the BUPA medical which all the British crews were given free. Dick McCann was waiting outside. He was close to tears.

'I can't find the engine spares anywhere. There's a fellow on the quay demanding payment and it comes to hundreds of pounds. Put me off the crew. I'll get a job and pay you back if you have to pay for them.'

'Don't worry, Dicker. We'll sort this out okay.' I felt rather cross. At the quay among the crowd I met what can best be described as a 'heavy' debt-collector. He wouldn't come on to the boat: the parts must be brought to him. If he didn't have them by two o'clock, he would have a writ nailed to our mast. I can't say I liked his style and I felt inclined to let him do his worst. We never wanted the parts and we couldn't be sure we'd ever received them; or if they'd come they might well have been taken away again by the engineer who brought them. They were only one of a thousand and one things that had been going on during that week. When we next looked up to the quay we saw the 'heavy' had gone.

I rang Listers, and next morning they sent down Alistair Thompson, who sorted it all out. The 'heavy' was in fact from a firm of distributors of engine parts and not from their factory. Dick found the unwanted parts and handed them back. All was settled, but for a while we had seen another side to things.

On the night before the start Marie Christine banged her hand on the iron ladder up the side of the quay. One of the three diamonds on her engagement ring fell out and sank into the murky water. People said it was lucky. I thought it was lousy.

At last the morning of the start came: Saturday, 27 August. At 6.30 in the morning it was raining lightly as I made my last circuit of the HMS *Vernon* grass running track. When would we run again? By ten o'clock the crowds on the quay were so dense it looked as if people were in danger of being squeezed over the edge and into the water.

'I'm going out now,' called Clare Francis, inside us and up against the pontoon.

'Me too,' I replied. The little Lister coughed into life and slowly we reversed out of the creek. Old friends waved from the crowd. With my cowboy hat moulded to my head in the heavy rain and the throttle a crude line up from the engine across the deck to my position at the wheel, I had the feeling I was driving a chariot to the start of a great race. In a way I was.

4

Leg One – Portsmouth to Cape Town

John: At twelve o'clock on a rainy Saturday, 27 August 1977, the cannon fired from Southsea Castle to signal the start of the Race around the World. English Rose Kitchens appeared to have failed in their attempt to fly a giant hot-air balloon to celebrate their kitchens and our entry in the Race – even though our boat was no longer called *English Rose VI* but *Debenhams*. Close by the Castle a hardy band of followers stood dripping under their banner, which read: 'There is only one Boss – Ridgway'.

The cannon also signalled the end of my personal race to get to the start, two and a half years of exciting hopes and fears. We were off.

Out on the water, under a lowering grey sky, we found ourselves at the centre of an awesome occasion. Thousands of boats thronged the area of the start, making the various marks impossible to distinguish. It was the first 'ocean race' any of us on *Debenhams* had ever entered. 'Sailing will never be the same,' someone said quietly to himself as we picked up speed through the choppy Solent water. For me the wrung-out, wet-rag feeling of exhaustion at the end of preparation changed dramatically to one of exhilaration.

We came to the start line rather hesitantly, but all the same we managed to get very close to the line by the time the final cannon fired, though we could perhaps have been moving faster. From the outset we found ourselves in a duel with *Adventure*, the sloop entered by the Combined Services, and *Treaty of Rome*, a German ex-Admiral's Cup racing boat entered by the Common Market countries. We were cut off by a passenger boat on the leeward side of these two yachts; and so when I tried to overtake them I had to swing across their sterns and try and get up on the windward side. I found this rather difficult as the wind kept changing in both direction and strength. Around us I was very conscious of crowded boats shouting things like 'Merry Christmas' and 'Hope it goes well for you, John'. With five and sometimes six sails up we had our hands full. The grey sea itself was very confused, as big boats, the frigate HMS *Stubbington*, and large pleasure cruisers motored about in all directions. Only a few yards out on our starboard side, I could see a man in a black cap with chin strap riding *Treaty of Rome* as if he were a jockey. Young Dick was still unsure of himself after the encounter with the engine parts debt collector and he had a spinnaker sheet jam in a self-tailer, and then when we came to turn west down the English Channel at Bembridge Ledge buoy – only three miles from the start – we found that we couldn't really handle the rapid change needed from the starcut to the radial-head spinnaker. We spent rather a long time achieving this manoeuvre, and some of the other boats began to pull away from us.

Once we'd sorted it out, the *Willventure* and the *Sonar* – two launches which were bulging with friends and relations – turned for home; and very sadly we saw Rebecca waving frantically from the open window in *Sonar*'s cabin. Marie Christine and I probably wouldn't see her again until we returned to Portsmouth seven months later after riding our chariot right round the world.

Quite soon we were alone in the Channel with the other boats in the race scattered around us. *B & B Italia* was behind us and *Adventure* out on our starboard side. I noticed that *Treaty of Rome* seemed to be cutting south across the Channel towards the French coast, perhaps to try to gain some advantage from the Alderney race that night.

A big frigate passed us close by and the scene was dominated by the fifteen yachts in the race, each with its gorgeous bulging radial-head spinnaker and accompanying bright big-boy sail laid out to leeward. Light aircraft, helicopters, launches, and finally the Trinity House flagship, *Patricia*, left us alone. Now it was each boat for itself and six and a half thousand miles down to Cape Town.

As the excitement eased, the crew soon dozed away after the tension of the start.

Soon it was evening and the NE wind got up to about twenty or thirty knots on our stern as we roared down the Channel into our first night of the race. The big spinnaker had the sea bubbling over our stern. Hands got sore and arms ached holding the wheel against a quartering sea.

At ten o'clock on a black moonless night Bob called me to help change the radial-head for the smaller and stronger storm spinnaker. After midnight, when the wind eased, the duty watch failed to change up again to the radial-head, and some of the other yachts pulled away from us. But at least we didn't start off by blowing out two £1,500-spinnakers on the first night like one of the other boats.

Marie Christine: Nobody on board *Debenhams* had a completely peaceful night. I think all of us kept remembering things still to be done or last-minute items to be taken. Up at 6.30 – a grey drizzly day. John went for his run with Captain O'Kelly and I decided to make the most of my last hot bath for probably the next seven weeks.

Back at the boat the breakfast discussion was taking place – tactics for the start, and where each person should be positioned. I was told to sit on the stern and keep out of the way, which suited me fine. Richard Creasey, the ATV producer and our seasick companion from the trip down from Ardmore, offered to wash up the porridge bowls while the rest of us tidied up the boat for our departure from *Vernon* at 10.30. There was an air of excitement as we stowed away the gear. Bec and Mummy arrived at the pontoon and John and I hugged and kissed them goodbye. Mummy was close to tears but Bec just looked a bit bewildered. My heart felt like breaking in two, but we were committed and the only way was to look forward. Back on the boat all was looking shipshape. We were ready.

'Where's the – owner of this boat!' Bob shouted, pointing to a small spectator yacht moored three out from us. *ADC Accutrac*, Clare Francis's boat, was also all set to leave the Vernon Creek and they were inside us – and now we were stopped by this outside boat whose skipper had gone missing. Tempers were ready to fly and when the missing man did arrive, Bob gave him a scalding. Soon we were making our way out into busy Portsmouth Harbour, waving goodbye to the many friends who had come to wish us well. A stunt flyer was high above us, turning over and over in his small plane. Spectator craft were increasing in number and we were all most conscious of the possibility of a collision. Steve Lenartowicz was posted as lookout on the pulpit, his loud voice carrying better than any of the others. Soon he sighted the *Willventure*, a launch hired by ATV for friends and family of those on our boat. They were to stay with us till we were well off the Isle of Wight. We had an hour to sail around in order to position ourselves well for the moment the final cannon was fired by Ramon Carlin, winner of the previous race. Then we would shoot over the start, which was a line between the ancient Southsea Castle and one of the forts out in the Solent. The fourteen other yachts were manoeuvring with a lot more confidence than us. We crept slowly towards the line as the last seconds to midday ticked away – and BOOM – the final cannon fired. A great cheer went up from all of us on *Debenhams* and we were off. *Condor* had gambled well, her mighty yellow spinnaker pulling her at great speed well ahead of the fleet – around us multi-coloured spinnakers brightened the grey day and lashing rain. *Flyer*, *ADC Accutrac*, *Neptune*, *King's Legend* and *Great Britain II* had gained speed on us as they had approached the start line and they were now ahead of the rest of the field. We were abreast of *Adventure* and *Treaty of Rome* and all the way out to Bembridge Ledge Buoy we tussled for the lead. The launch Mummy and Bec were in circled us a few times and finally waved goodbye – we were now on our own except for a few low-flying aircraft still taking photos of the brave boats as they set out on their 27,500-mile journey that would take seven months or more. Circling the globe to face storms, icebergs, intense heat, doldrums – and what else? Each person must be wondering what lay in store for them. Would they be able to face up to the test they had taken on?

Suddenly the 'happy hour' was upon us and with great merriment we drank two bottles of our Fonseca port and chucked them over the side with the printed messages stuffed in the bottles and the corks stuck firmly back in place. I watched the bottles bobbing away behind us as we sped on through the gold-tipped water. The sun fell gently from the sky and the silhouettes of *Tielsa* and *Gauloises II* stayed out on our starboard horizon till darkness turned them to twinkling white and red lights.

After a good first supper of avocado, then mince, peas, tatties and a rather plastic strawberry mousse, we settled into our routine of watches and washing-up. John and I turned in quite happy with our tiny cabin; we were well used to it, having lived in it for the past month.

The night was windy and John went up to help change the spinnaker. Bob and Noel together had had to hold the wheel to keep the boat on course, but by morning we had slowed down to almost no progress at all.

Day 2: *Sunday, 28 August   Noon position 49° 00' N, 4°40' W*
Day's run 110 miles   Course SSW   Wind Variable, 1–2
Barometer 1025

Marie Christine: I led the seasick stakes by being sick twice over the side. Arun and Steve didn't look overbright, though – the sea was lumpy and the lack of wind didn't help morale. We tried all manner of sail changes. By mid morning disaster had struck. There was not enough wind for the radial-head spinnaker and it soon wound itself tightly round the forestay in two sections like a giant hourglass. Bob went up the sixty-foot mast in his bosun's chair and swung forward on to the forestay. Try as he might, he couldn't unravel the tight binding which the multi-coloured sail was now twisted into. John was called and he went up the forestay too. No luck. This was a race and we couldn't afford to waste precious time like this. Eventually after two hours of furious struggling the beautiful sail unfurled. We were once more on our way but each of us was thinking to himself of how much distance we had lost from our competitors.

At about breakfast time there had been a flapping of wings. A yell went up from those on watch. 'It's a hawk' – 'It's a swallow!' The dark fluttering creature eventually found itself a resting place hidden in a coil of rope on the mast. Our visitor was a tiny bat; perhaps it came from the Île de Batz on the near-by French coast.

Just before supper time, Peter turned on the radio and we all heard loud and clear our call: 'Hello, *Debenhams*. This is *Adventure*. Do you read me?' Peter wasn't quite ready to transmit and in any case we were a bit nervous about the procedure and so we thought we'd rather put in our two weekly calls towards the end of the week when our position was better – or so we hoped. So we let it pass and *Great Britain II* came on with her position and sightings of other boats. It seemed we were thirty miles *behind* all the others. Why? and what could we do about it? 'Chuck the beer overboard, we're carrying too much weight,' someone suggested. 'But it's valuable liquid. We'll need that when we get into the tropics.' 'We must speed up the sail changes. That's where we are losing time.'

In fact we were worrying somewhat unnecessarily. It turned out, later that evening, that we weren't as far behind as we'd thought. The big red sun sank into the sea and a full moon rose in its place and still we weren't moving much. The T-shirts Richard Morris-Adams had given us yesterday had 'Round the World with Ridgway, It's Quicker than Rowing' emblazoned across our chests. John suggested we add: 'Only Just'.

Day 3: *Monday, 29 August   Noon position 47° 51' N, 5° 48' W*
Day's run 113 miles   Course SSW   Wind WSW Force 3
Barometer 1023

Marie Christine: At dawn we saw the lonely finger of Ushant light-house abeam on the port side and we headed across the dreaded Bay of Biscay under full sail. The bat has gone. 'I ate it in the night, crunching the legs was delicious!' claimed Dick.

Steve's birthday. A cheery breakfast party with cards and presents for Steve, who had recovered from his seasickness of yesterday. All of a sudden he turned to me and said in a calm voice, 'Marie Christine, will you take the wheel? I'm going to be sick.' With that, he went to the lee rail and got on with it.

We are all dogged with doubts about our position. The wind is still too light for us. Does it all boil down to finance? We are loaded up with huge steering oars, coils of spare rope and wire, as well as lots of Arun's tools in case of emergency repairs, whereas the other boats will have only the minimum on board; if replacements are needed, no doubt they will pay for them when they reach port. In a sense we are set for an eight-month voyage. We are a competitive crew but perhaps not to the degree required in what has turned out to be a very professional bunch of boats.

John Covington (J.C.) is handling the cooking really well – I am so grateful that his being with us lets me out. The queasiness persists and I would have found cooking an awful struggle. Hot curry and rice for lunch and then a blowout of a birthday supper: two bottles of port (between twelve), asparagus soup, and lovely ripe avocados (given us by our old friend Louis Fulford) with a delicious dressing of tinned tuna and mayonnaise, followed by steak and kidney. Finally there was Steve's birthday cake, given him by his friend Hilary and iced by J.C. under my guidance. It was carried on deck with fourteen yellow candles (all we had) burning brightly. Steve cut it into twelve and we made pigs of ourselves as we munched through great mouthfuls of rich, sticky fruit cake. Hilary, somewhere in Manchester, is certainly a great baker.

All attention then turned to the radio; the race chat show had commenced. Again we were keeping quiet, hoping for a better position later in the week. Nothing very startling was revealed; they all seemed in good spirits and it was comforting to hear the voices come up around us. John and I wanted to phone Mum and Bec but Portishead Radio had a long list of calls to get through. Peter tried every so often to no avail while I waited patiently in J.C.'s top bunk in the tiny aft cabin which is also the radio shack. We listened to a series of rather depressing calls – seamen calling their wives, who all sounded fed up. One in particular seemed to have saved up all the bad news. Their son had smashed his car up by going round the corner and hitting a concrete lamppost and then she told him that someone had tried to get his motorbike going and had wrecked that too; the poor fellow at the end of the phone sounded more and more disheartened. Peter tried to make contact again with Portishead but had no luck so we agreed to try again tomorrow.

Day 4: *Tuesday, 30 August   Noon position 45° 41' N, 5° 39' W
Day's run 158 miles   Course SSW   Wind S Force 3
Barometer 1016*

Marie Christine: We got through quickly at about 10 a.m. I heard Mummy's worried voice, 'Where are you? Are you all right?' I think she thought we'd been shipwrecked and were ringing from Spain. We spoke to Bec who sounded none too cheery either. John and I both felt perhaps we would have been better not phoning.

A growing feeling of 'What am I doing here?' kept with me all day. I missed Bec and Gran enormously and began to feel very homesick. I am a prisoner on the boat with an eight-month sentence ahead of me. I long for the soft sounds, smells and colours of Ardmore: the green hazel and birch wood tangled with honeysuckle and briars which cover the hill to the water's edge. Ardmore, 'big hill' in Gaelic, is on one side of the sheltered sea loch a' Chadh-fi. To reach home involves a two-mile walk along a rough, hilly track through heather, bog and mire and finally through a rickety gate and up a steep waterfall. This is a trickle in summer but in winter or after rain it really lives up to its name ... and woe betide any person who comes out without their wellies on!

At the top of the waterfall is Upper Ardmore. There are two houses, one stone built and the other blue-painted corrugated iron with stone gables. In this second house live Lance and Ada Bell, both in their fifties, who moved north from Teesside nine years ago and have become the lynch pin of our existence at Ardmore. Ada has been like a second mother to Becca; she was taken on by the local Sutherland education authority to teach her from the age of five to seven, it being too far for

Lance and Ada held the fort at Ardmore – the worst Highland winter for 30 years

Rebecca to go daily to the local school at Kinlochbervie, while she was too young to weekly board. People were puzzled at Rebecca's slight Teesside accent whenever they met her — Scottish, perhaps, but why Teesside? Until I explained her unusual education at the blue house. One-teacher, one-child — a new experience for both Ada and Rebecca and one which they both enjoyed. Lance, a perfectionist at all he does, now has three fine gardens dug out of ground once cultivated, but long since reclaimed by rushes and bog when crude draining systems were neglected. The exterior of his house would withstand any winter gale, and inside Ada keeps it warm and perfect. The cosy Rayburn stove in the centre of the end wall in the kitchen heats the water, cooks the food, ferments the buckets of beer which stand behind it and keep them warm. Like us in Lower Ardmore they have no electricity. The ranges burn peat which we cut early each summer and lighting is by paraffin Tilleys — old brass lamps passed on to us with the houses and polished to a brightness which shows up faces distorted by their convex shape.

To reach Lower Ardmore you continue along the winding rocky path through the light- and shadow-dappled wood which would take it over completely if Lance didn't hack at it from time to time. The wood has a life of its own, depending on the seasons; spring usually comes late in the north-west of Scotland, but after a day or two of warm sunshine in April the leaves burst out and the wood is throbbing with life. Blackbirds, thrushes and chaffinches fly about in a frenzy of nesting, while primroses and violets push their way up through last autumn's leaves and moss.

Through to Lower Ardmore — past the ruin where Old Simon lived. Heckie Ross tells a story of how Old Simon and his sister moved to one end of this house when the roof started to fall in. And how he and Ninnie sat there one evening with Simon's dead sister lying on her bed in the same room, and just how frightened they had been when the door suddenly opened and then slammed shut on that perfectly calm night, all for no apparent reason.

Then to our house: two and a quarter bedrooms upstairs, the quarter being Becca's tiny one under the eaves; and downstairs our sitting-room. It can look quite like a sitting-room — one wall lined with books and John's roll-top desk — but most times it takes on the appearance of a very busy office: two filing cabinets, two typewriters; John and I churning out letters, plans, or just paying the bills. The peat fire hungrily consuming lump upon lump of peat brought up from the shore on our backs in sacks each day. The walls are lined with matchboard and (apart from far too many books) there is a fine ceramic sea trout, so realistic you would think it might blink. It was taken from a plaster cast of the fish caught by a proud fellow up at near-by Loch Dionard. To his dismay, when the clay model was baked, it naturally shrank an inch or two. He wasn't happy with this so had a model made from the cast in plaster. He had an exact replica of his fish, and we found the unwanted beautiful ceramic model lying in the potter's shop at Durness.

Above the fireplace is a large picture of Winslow Homer's 'The Fog Warning', given to John by a charming American journalist in memory of his row across the Atlantic. It is of a hard-looking halibut fisherman turning his head to the sound of the fog horn from his small dory; the warning is sounded by the mother schooner away out on the horizon and if the fisherman does not get back to his ship before the fog comes down, then he may not survive. Below this on the mantelpiece and scattered around on every flat surface is the miscellany of three expeditions to South America and Africa – a broken pre-Inca flint axe-head from near Machu Picchu, gourds, giant fishscales, models of horsemen made from crude latex by Amazon Indians (the gringos' mouths definitely do turn down at the edges, an indication of how the Indian views the white man); rounded boho stones and giant mussel shells from Chile, goats' skulls – all fine souvenirs but a duster's nightmare. Through to the kitchen, with a sleeping cat permanently curled in a soft ball on the ragged carpet in front of the Rayburn. The rocking chair at one end of an extending kitchen table – we never know who will arrive along the track in need of food and shelter. The winter is full of surprises. It may be just three of us for supper or thirteen. So the cupboards around the walls are well stocked to sustain invasion or siege.

In the house beyond us at the end of the path lives old Granny Ross, now in her eighties, her son Hector and a daughter. They have a life dictated by the crofters' calendar, bringing in the tups, wintering, lambing, cutting the peat, planting the tatties, clipping, cutting the hay, dipping and taking the lambs to the sale, all this interspersed with a bit of lobster fishing, a lot of church going and always time for a kindly chat and a laugh from Granny Ross, who beams and splits with mirth at the antics of the queer folk who have come to live next door where she was born. Human nature is such that even faced with perfection, one must turn away from it to appreciate what it is. But to the present: there is so much to be gained from our situation if only it wasn't all marred by feeling permanently ill.

On our last long voyage it had taken me six weeks before I felt well enough to get going on anything that required any effort. Perhaps that is the most crushing part of seasickness. It leaves you feeling limp and apathetic, which in turn demoralizes you, making any effort seem too great. I noticed this with Arun who on shore never stops to draw a breath, he is so busy, but lying in his bunk in the aft cabin, his pale face surrounded by a mop of black tangle, his hands lying limply at his side, he could hardly muster strength to eat and certainly not join in the banter of the more robust in the main saloon.

I made a great effort and sewed two patches on the seat of Peter's jeans, herringbone all the way round. They look pretty fancy, but I doubt if they'll stand up to too much wear. When the sewing machine is out I will need to strengthen the stitching a bit.

John has been moaning for the last two days that all he does turns to marshmallow. The main area of dissatisfaction with him is the navigation. He has always managed it well enough in the past, but at the moment he and Steve are working together on it. Not the ideal pair. Steve, a good mathematician, approaches it from a different angle to John. John has the formula written on a fablonized board so that the calculations can be entered with a chinagraph pencil and then rubbed off with a handkerchief ready for next time. This board has been with him on his row across the Atlantic with Chay, his attempted circumnavigation when he had to put into Recife in Brazil, and our trip to the Cape Verde Islands, so it's a well-tried formula. But somehow the combination of the quick mathematical brain of Lenartowicz and the painstakingly careful method of Ridgway did not work and after hours of sun sights, moon sights, careful time-keeping and endless calculations, a wail would go up 'Where are we?' or 'We can't be *there*'. Particularly demoralizing since the gap between us and the others seems to be widening.

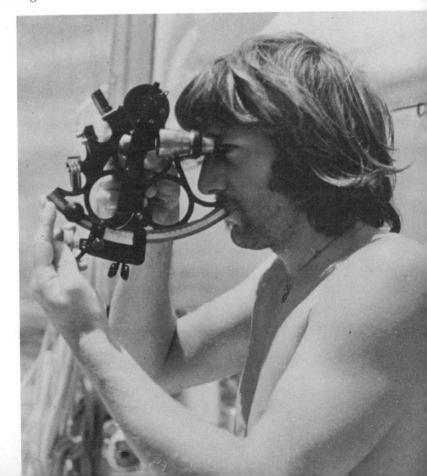

Steve taking a sight

Day 5: *Wednesday, 31 August   Noon position 44° 00' N, 8° 20' W*
Day's run 115 miles   Course SW   Wind W Force 3
Barometer 1017

John: At breakfast time we seemed to be aimlessly milling about in the Bay of Biscay with very light and variable winds, there was no sign at all of the storms for which the Bay is notorious. Somewhere ahead is the western end of the north coast of Spain – but where? 'I'm sure that's land over on the port bow,' called Roger, the shy and lanky TV cameraman. Already he is named 'Hawkeye Deakins', and if he saw land then at least half the crew would be ready to believe it's there – and they were soon lending plenty of vocal support to that notion.

Up to now Steve and I have been pretty much on our own as navigators, and the rest have been just a little sceptical of celestial navigation. 'Okay, alter course to 200 magnetic,' I called. 'We'll close the coast and confirm the celestial nav.' 'Oh yeah!' smirked Tony, annoyingly cynical as usual; to my way of thinking a watch leader should strive to unify not divide the crew. Maybe I should change him.

By mid-afternoon we were pretty close in under the mountainous coast around Coruna. A big white ketch appeared to be coming out across our bows; but as she was not using her mizzen – that's the sail on her second, shorter mast – we all reckoned her to be an old charter boat coming out to see who we were, for a bit of a chat perhaps. Anyway, Steve and I were greatly taken up at the time with the alarming calculation of our afternoon sight, which put us all of thirty-three miles inshore of the arrogant Tony's radio direction-finder fix. 'Pre-1935', sniffed Peter, our tall, wiry Tasmanian mate, from the main hatch, as he peered through his specs. 'It's the old rounded white bow – that's the giveaway.' Nobody argued; it really wasn't that interesting. Again, we're distracted by the second sun sight, which gives us almost the same position as the first. At the chart table, Steve and I were wondering how we could maintain some scrap of credibility for the celestial navigation department if both these positions right in front of the land were proven wrong.

'It's Clare! It's Clare!' came the shout from up on deck. 'On the sails, K 1888. It's Clare Francis.' Steve and I scrambled up the short ladder through the hatch and into the main cockpit. Everyone was jumping about with glee. We weren't last after all, and *ADC* at sixty-five foot is eight foot longer than *Debenhams*, so she would have to give us a couple of days on handicap to Cape Town.

ADC Accutrac is a series-produced yacht of the Swan-65 type which has proved ideally suited to long-distance racing. *Sayula I* – the winner of the first Whitbread race – was a Swan-65. ADC (a BSR company) bought the yacht – worth around £250,000 and originally known as

Pulsa – early in 1977, and re-fitted her for the race. Clare has a crew of twelve including her husband Jacques Redon, and Eve Bonham, who finished third with her in the Round-Britain Race in 1974. *Accutrac*'s two-masted ketch rig, like *Debenhams'*, makes for easier sail handling in rough weather – each sail is smaller than a sloop's – and is highly efficient in the stern winds which we hope will prevail over a large part of the course.

Clare Francis, born at Thames Ditton in 1947, has been sailing since the age of five and is probably best known for her exploits in the 1976 *Observer* Single-handed Transatlantic Race, in which she finished thirteenth out of a hundred and twenty-five starters, and set a new world record crossing time for women of twenty-nine days. The effect on our morale of catching the much bigger *ADC* after five days is electric, and this is reinforced by confirmation that our sun sights are correct. Tony's radio fix was at fault. There are going to be very few radio fixes on this trip round the world, but a hell of a lot of celestial navigation. Steve is delighted, looking just like George Best after he'd scored a goal.

ADC continued on across our bow, and then in the evening she tacked out to sea while we found a lucky off-shore breeze close under the land which carried us more to the south-west.

Later in the evening five of us crammed into the tiny aft cabin/radio shack heard Clare Francis in a somewhat resigned voice state her position – and ours. Our secret was out, not that anybody had shown much curiosity about *Debenhams'* whereabouts, except for *Adventure* on the first night. So we turned in feeling a lot better about the boat, our position, and life.

Marie Christine: I feel as though I'm in a fog and spend useless time either sleeping or reading. The large bottle of surgical spirit I bought before we left perhaps will be put to some use after all – to treat my bed sores!

J.C. made chilli con carne for lunch. It was delicious. I had forgotten about the alarming noise the pressure cooker makes when the pressure is up and the flame low. Normally, it just murmurs but this cooker takes no chop from a lurching sea and angrily hisses back. Surprisingly, hot spicy food seems the best at sea for all stomachs.

We are close to the north coast of Spain now. It looks really lovely. Little villages lying by the sea beneath the hills. You can even smell the freshness of the land.

Day 6: *Thursday, 1 September   Noon position 42° 59' N, 9° 40' W*
Day's run 119 miles   Course SSW   Wind WSW Force 3
Barometer 1021

John: We have been tacking down the west coast of Spain towards the

Portuguese border. The wind was very light indeed and there were patches of fog about. *ADC Accutrac* was quite a long way astern, her mast showing just over the horizon.

Another big white ketch appeared on our starboard bow and we seemed to be catching her too. Maybe this was *Japy Hermès*, which started life as the *Flying Angel of Upnor*. She was designed and built to sail in the 1976 *Observer* Single-handed Transatlantic Race. The renamed *Japy Hermès* is crewed by twelve students from the Marseilles College of Engineering. For them the race is not only a competitive challenge, but apparently an opportunity for the practical application of their researches into life-saving techniques, which has been part of their curriculum. Without something nasty happening it's difficult to see how they're going to practise.

Japy Hermès has been extensively re-fitted for the race with a completely changed interior layout, and some modifications to the superstructure carried out to specifications set by the Architects Association of Marseilles. The sponsor, Japy Hermès, is part of the Swiss-based Hermès-Precisor international group, which manufactures typewriters. The yacht is sailing under a French flag, but members of the Swiss company will greet the yacht at each port of call, because the route covers key points in the sponsor's international chain of companies; this will prove a valuable back-up for the crew, not only materially but also for morale. The skipper of the boat is Jimmy Viant. He is twenty-five years old and he raced with his father, André Viant, in *Grand Louis*, which finished third over-all in the 1973–74 race. Jimmy skippered *Grand Louis* in the Atlantic Triangle race while his father took on a new boat, *Katsou*. André Viant finished second over-all and Jimmy third. All of us on board are very pleased to be catching up with *Japy* because at sixty-two foot and a bit she will be giving us time on handicap to Cape Town as well.

With all this light weather in place of the usual Portuguese northerlies the result has been that the boats have bunched up together and are waiting for those strong following winds which will allow the bigger boats to stride away.

The crew is delighted with the sightings of other bigger boats. Some of them have been homesick and lovesick as well as seasick. Peter, Colin, Tony, Noel and Roger have all been rather withdrawn and this has really bucked them up – I don't suppose I'll ever be able to persuade them all that the Race was not the main purpose of the voyage.

Marie Christine: It dropped calm in the night and the rigging made a clanging sound just like an empty wardrobe with wire coat hangers rattling in it. J.C. gave me my regulation quarter-mug of cold water for teeth and half-mug of hot water for washing at 7.30 the next morning. We go through this curious procedure each morning. I pass my two mugs (one for teeth-cleaning water) through my little window across to a hairy arm extended from the galley window. Both windows open into the centre cockpit. It was surprising what a good wash I could have with just one mug and a flannel. But, oh, how I would love to wash my hair, it's one of the worst deprivations of being at sea. At present I am wearing it up and covered by a scarf so it doesn't look too bad, but it's beginning to itch.

Peter has stuck up two mirrors in our cabin and heads and I've three more photos to put up. It's quite like home. And a real luxury to be able to shut the door on the rest of the boat. At the front of our bed we have a lovely colour photo of Bec, given to us by our friend Richard Morris-Adams. She is balancing on a log at the obstacle course in the wood at Ardmore. She has an expression of great concentration as she nears the end of her task.

Unless you are blessed with a vast private income or fortune, it is close to impossible to take part in a race of this nature without the aid of some sort of sponsorship. We were only too happy to accept the £25,000 Debenham's had agreed to pay us in return for us calling the boat *Debenhams*. Monica Dixon and Simon Weaver from Barwell Sports Management acted as intermediaries, efficiently arranging all sorts of details, from press releases to compiling a list of inside leg measurements for the smart blazers and trousers we were supplied with. All correspondence for this was filed away in the 'major sponsorship' file. We also had a 'minor sponsorship' file which contained all my requests to various manufacturers for items such as clothing, food and a limited amount of equipment. I had been delighted at the response and probably out of about forty letters, thirty-five replied with promises of help. Also kept in this file was our correspondence with Mentzendorff, Palace Street, London SW1. On one of the April businessmen's courses was a certain Martin Dawson, a charming fellow from Halifax, who seemed to defy all the rules which I'd had drummed into me about what would lead to a healthy life. He drank and smoked and yet had plenty of wind for the early morning runs – most mornings he beat me. As Ada and I cooked the supper in the tiny kitchen in the wooden house, he would come in with large glasses of whisky for us and insist on helping, much against our wishes. Then two months later, when there was a phone call late one night, I knew straight away who it was when John answered with 'Hello, Martin'. He had been in touch with an old friend of his in Oporto who made port and had suggested we take some with us for the trip. 'Well, why not?' said I. In spite of John's protestations that we should be running a dry ship, we ended up taking enough port for us to have two bottles every

We loved our port — MC, Tony, JR

night for the whole trip. Would we be the first circumnavigators to come back with gout? We were now only about one hundred miles from Oporto and Bruce Guimaraens who made the port, and there had been an idea that if we got in touch he would come out and wave or pelt us with peaches and tomatoes or whatever. However, in spite of our very patient radio operator at Portishead, it transpired that Mr Guimaraens was away for the next four days and could not be contacted. So that was the end of that idea.

While we were through to Portishead, they asked if we could take down a sixty-word telegram for *Condor* and then try and get one of the other boats with a VHF radio to transmit it to them. Apparently their radio was not working, which meant having to put in to the Canaries to pick up a spare set. It would be quite a blow to them, particularly as the radio has nothing to do with the sailing of the boat, but the race organizers have made it compulsory for each boat to radio their position twice weekly. This is for safety purposes – if a boat fails to report then other competitors and shipping in the area can be on the lookout. Failure to report results in a penalty.

Day 7: *Friday, 2 September   Noon position 41° 42' N, 10° 24' W*
Day's run 104 miles   Course S by W   Wind W Force 1–2
Barometer 1020

John: We're pretty well becalmed all the time up until about lunch-time; and I felt that getting nowhere was getting on people's nerves. So Peter, Bob and I made out a list of jobs for completion, each before noon – idleness is going to lead to a dead ship. This 'doing nothing is doing wrong' approach won't go down very well with the younger, less experienced members of the crew, I'm afraid – but we'll have to force it through.

The heat and calm ahead will surely aggravate the long-standing feud between cold brusque young Tony and the quick-tempered old Navy hand, Bob. Well, it's my job to cool it.

During the lunchtime discussion, Bob was left alone at the wheel. Unfortunately I was concentrating so fiercely on composing the purple passage of my speech to the crew that I didn't realize that Roger, the cameraman, and Noel, the sound man, were filming down in the cabin when they should have been up on watch.

'Clare is just streaking away,' cursed a frustrated Bob from the main hatch. 'Will someone pass me the glasses so I can see how she's doing it?' In that lunch hour Clare took *ADC* from back on our port quarter, along the horizon and up to a fine point on the port bow. Half an hour later she was gone over the horizon – and we still lay wallowing in the calm, with me feeling all sorts of nasty things about the watch on duty.

'I won't say anything,' said Dick tight-lipped after one of my harangues. Still, the wind came up for us too and soon we were on our way again. As the day wore on the sail area changed up through starcut spinnaker to radial-head and a mizzen staysail; and 8 knots became our average. The evening radio chat with the other boats put us pretty well up for our rating, with two bigger boats, *Tielsa* and *Japy Hermès*, notably behind us.

As the boats came under my scrutiny, so I found myself studying the boats, skippers and crews portrayed in the official programme compiled by the *Illustrated London News*. It seems rather like Field Marshal Montgomery hanging Rommel's photograph in his caravan before Alamein. I tried to imagine the strengths and weaknesses of each race entry, based on the problems I'd had myself in simply getting to the start line.

Sheer finance is a factor. Unfortunately, it's a major factor in the winning or losing of each leg. For example, if *Condor* can afford to have helicopters flying radio sets around, it looks none too well for us once the spinnakers start to burst.

Marie Christine: Another calm night with little progress. The sea is smooth like gently undulating grey silk.

It's Colin's birthday and he is twenty-five. We gave him a card with 'When you're too tired for wine, women and song – hire someone to do the singing'. J.C.'s face lit up. Apparently his brother sent him this very same card five years ago and they're still sending it back and forth. Still J.C. should have a good long rest from the first two on this trip. Come to think of it, there's not been much singing lately either. We all need wind. Racing brings tension and excitement to this trip.

Suddenly a shriek went up from outside, 'Whale!' A *huge* whale surfaced, blowing about twenty yards away from the boat. A real beauty. He came up again, even closer, but I think he was camera shy as there was, by the time he came up a second time, a barrage of photographers lining the deck: Steve, Colin, me, Dick and Roger and Noel with their hi-fi stuff. He didn't reappear until later and then far off with a mate.

We were asked to move very gently about on deck; any heavy movement can make the boat lurch and in these calm conditions spill the wind out of the sails. I lay down by one of the teak window frames and continued my rather protracted job of scraping off the varnish. I had done four with another two big and small to go. We watched *ADC Accutrac* pick up the zephyr of a breeze and move ahead of us on the port bow. There were a few rather unworthy comments about 'Could they be charging their batteries? With a 108 h.p. engine?' But the sea is like that and we just happened to be in a calm patch.

By evening the wind was increasing and we sped over a glassy smooth sea with the gay starcut spinnaker a riot of red, white and blue, drawing on us.

Day 8: *Saturday, 3 September   Noon position 38° 40' N, 12° 02' W*
Day's run 214 miles   Course SSW   Wind N Force 5–7
Barometer 1020

John: At ten o'clock in the evening I was safely wrapped up in bed. There were a few loud bangs going on as the radial-head spinnaker filled again after the odd gybe or broach. It was a pretty dark night with a scrap of moon and we were surfing along at up to 14 knots. Tony, Colin and Steve were the watch on duty, and just about everybody else was in bed. CRACK!

'Halyard's gone,' Tony's cry rang out from above.

I rolled out of my bunk, struggled into my life harness and told Marie Christine to go back to sleep – all in one go.

'Be sure and clip on,' she called after me as I closed the cabin door. Once up on deck I made my way aft to the wheel.

'It's not the halyard,' someone called, 'it's the spinnaker. It's blown out.'

Not one of us had ever seen this before. At £1,200–£1,500 a time it isn't really encouraged. I noticed I was muttering to myself in frustration at the back of the boat . . . 'There are no more cars in the garage, daddy.' There wasn't any way I could buy another one of these spinnakers. Colin, Tony and Steve were full of remorse and very good about it, and after we'd got the storm spinnaker up in its place and salvaged the wreckage I went back to bed with a bit of a headache. It's going to be some time before I forget the sight of that ruined radial-head framed in pale moonlight. How lucky we were to recover the main body of the sail! Once torn out of the frame, it got caught around the forestay instead of blowing away free over the side into the night.

Day 9: *Sunday, 4 September   Noon position 35° 30' N, 13° 23' W*
Day's run 195 miles   Course S by E   Wind N by W Force 5–6
Barometer 1021

John: As soon as possible in the morning Bob got on with the remaking of the big radial-head spinnaker, sticking it together with two-sided sticky tape given him by Simon Richardson back in the Hamble, and then zigzag stitching twice over it with the machine. Bob reckons it may take anything up to five days to repair it to a reasonable shape. 'I feel like a warden at the Tate Gallery after a robbery. I've got the frame, but I haven't got the painting,' Bob cracked. But he's very reluctant to let anyone else help him with the work, and this will not be practical as other repairs pile up later on. We pushed on at 8 or 9 knots with a tri-radial, but it's not nearly as big as the radial-head; and in the evening we heard that Charley on board *Adventure* was sewing like mad as well. They blew their radial-head about the same time as us.

I'm standing in for Bob on watch at night – but they don't do that in the services: the skipper doesn't stand a watch, so Charlie is mending the sail and standing his watch, so his repairs will take longer. Without a mizzen mast, of course, to set extra sails on, they're falling behind us at last. Everyone is a bit quiet after the events of yesterday. I've laid a course for the Canaries, and by evening we're the most easterly boat in the fleet, but we're pretty well up for our rating. I want to be east, but I also want to avoid being becalmed among the islands as I have in the past at Madeira, the Cape Verdes and the Canaries. Once you get in among those islands you nearly always get becalmed.

I'm worried about Tony (23) and Bob (37). They are both inclined to retreat into enraged silence under the pressures of leading their watches. Tony finds Colin (25) and Steve (26) older, mentally quicker, and more worldly wise. Bob drives Roger (28) and Noel (33), cursing them in turns both good- and bad-naturedly, which they respect; and these three are gradually edging apart from the rest of the crew by reason of their age and experience. Bob's life as a junior rank in the Navy has conditioned him to obey orders; he cannot cope with discussions particularly if they include the younger, brighter minds of the university graduates. There is a gulf there which he intends never to bridge – it bodes ill for the voyage. While Bob is adamant the helmsman stands feet apart with both hands on the wheel and his watch trimming the sails, Tony will steer with one foot on a wheel spoke in light airs and read a book if nothing is happening. It's rather a contrast.

Day 10: *Monday, 5 September   Noon position 32° 49' N, 14° 27' W*
Day's run 180 miles   Course SSW   Wind NNW Force 3–4
Barometer 1022

John: After a pleasant night watch – I was standing in for Bob again from midnight until four o'clock in the morning, with Roger and Noel – I went to bed and was up again at eight o'clock for breakfast, and a very busy day.

We had trouble hoisting the starcut in place of the storm spinnaker. With just about everybody on deck and in position, Dick began taking in the halyard on the spinnaker winch while Bob pulled the sail up by hand. One turn on the drum was not enough. It sprang off and Dick felt the halyard bite into the back of his neck. Fearing the chance of a hanging, he braked the halyard with his bare hands; and the weight of the half-hoisted starcut spinnaker burned the rope into his palms and the back of his neck. Right at the back of the boat on the wheel the first thing I heard was Dick's sudden yelp of pain – then I saw him thrown to the deck. There was quite a bit of milling about, and I could see that the huge multi-coloured cloud of sail was collapsing into the sea. 'Come up to windward,' came Tony's urgent shout from the bow, for we were already running over the right-hand edge of the sail. I brought her up all right and with everyone's help the sail was safely brought back aboard. Then Steve, eager to treat his first patient, led Dick below and began to dress his wounds, which were very painful – rope burns are just like any other kind of burns, and the sun and sweat didn't help to ease the pain.

That sail change ended up in taking an hour and ten minutes. In stark racing terms when compared with the other boats, it was no surprise that we found we'd fallen behind by the time the positions were declared over the radio at seven in the evening. Too many of us look for excuses when we should be focusing on unavoidable facts. We are slipping back.

Based on previous experience in this area, and the winds the other boats are having, I'm planning now to go to the west of the Canaries to avoid getting becalmed anywhere near the islands; it's clear from the progress *Tielsa*'s been making that the Trades are well off-shore. The weather's warming up now and the crew of *King's Legend* ahead are suffering from a lack of suntan oil. Our crew are all pulling well, and the repair of the radial-head is coming along very nicely with Bob and various helpers, whom he grudgingly accepts from time to time, working away all day long in the cockpit.

During the night we made 8 to 9 knots on a broad reach south-west towards Palma, the north-western island of the Canary group. There is a faint danger of hitting the unlit and uninhabited Selvagen Islands, which are only 400 feet high. I reckon we are passing well to the north of them, but on a dark night no one's too sure of anything.

Day 11: *Tuesday. 6 September   Noon position 30° 41' N, 16° 46' W*
         Day's run 166 miles   Course SSW   Wind N Force 3
         Barometer 1025

Marie Christine: Bob set up work again in the centre cockpit with the sewing machine, sitting cross-legged and muttering oaths if the machine became temperamental over the zigzags as he wound furiously away with the handle. The weather is warmer each day now we are past

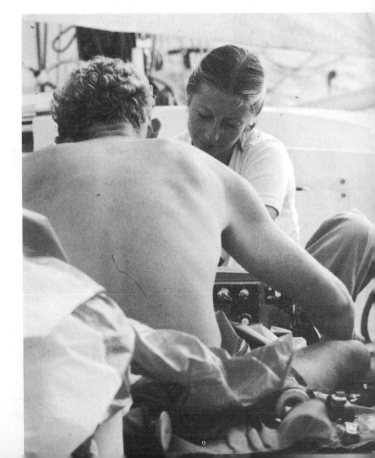

*Bob and MC repair
torn radial-head near
Madeira*

Madeira. We are still one day behind the rest of the fleet, but we are all settling in well to life with each other.

As we had slowed down Tony had dangled his fishing line off the stern, and there was a great yell of surprise when after about two hours of nothing he felt a fish on the hook. All those on deck, except Bob who was scornfully not going to be put off by such frivolities, rushed in different directions, me to get my camera, Steve to get a bucket. But it's all in vain. The fish got free. However, within five minutes there was another bite and this time Tony hauled it on board. It was a fine Skip Jack Tuna (as Peter called it), a fish about twelve inches long and weighing about one and a half pounds. It was all bright and shimmering as it lay flickering in the black bucket, and Colin deftly finished it off by breaking its back. We were all thinking how delicious a fried tuna each would be for supper. But it was not to be, for this was the only one caught. However, J. C. cooked it up with onions and lemon juice and served it with rice for an hors d'oeuvre. We may not be the fastest boat but we certainly are living well.

Day 12: *Wednesday, 7 September   Noon position 29° 00' N, 18° 51' W*
Day's run 149 miles   Course SSW   Wind NW Force 2
Barometer 1023

John: A calm around midnight has done little to help things. The morning passed slowly with only a force 2 northerly wind in place of the expected force 4 to 6 north-east trades. It was a cloudy day and we didn't see anything of the island of Palma, which we left some thirty miles to westward in mid-afternoon. Where is the wind? We appear to be slower than all the other boats at the moment. No doubt there are

Medic Steve inspects Dick's hand after rope burn

plenty of reasons for this, a heavy boat, slow sail changing, the loss of the radial-head spinnaker for three days. Possibly we just don't carry the range of sails the other boats do; and those we have we don't use to the best possible advantage. No one likes to be last, though. Morale was a little improved by the appearance at lunchtime of splendid mince and mash pies, and cheese and onion pies made freshly by Marie Christine.

We are probably carrying the greatest weight of any boat, because we intend to do our own repairs if at all possible, and so have a lot of tools and materials. We also have 170 gallons of paraffin, weighing about three-quarters of a ton. Much of the food that we have is to last us right round the world ... And anyway we're doing this for fun, aren't we? There's little point in making excuses. We're doing the best we can with what we have. We must enjoy it or it's all a waste of time. The most dangerous times for morale are the calms.

Marie Christine: Washed my hair with two cups of warm water – not a lot of rinsing but it feels better. Have offered to do the cooking for J. C. It's calmer and I don't feel sick. Bob's spinnaker is at last finished. We stopped it up with rubber bands and hoisted her up gingerly. She opened out and flies beautifully. It's hard to imagine she'd been in shreds only three days ago. Bob has a big grin on his face. I don't think he really thought he'd manage it. I decided to try out the oven on the paraffin stove. J.C. lit it for me and I got to work making pastry for cheese and onion pies and one of mince that had been left over from the night before supper. The baking trays wouldn't fit in so I took the wheel for a moment while Arun, who was on watch, bent back the un-necessary metal at either end of the dishes. They went in fine and were cooked just in time for lunch at twelve. In the afternoon I made some brown bread and a chocolate cake. I kept on hearing groans from Dick ('Marie Christine, are you trying to torture me?'). The enticing smells were wafting through the aft cabin hatch directly in front of the wheel. We had curry and rice with peanuts fried and salted and an unlikely but delicious combination of finely sliced onions and fresh oranges tossed in oil and vinegar. We're running out of fresh fruit now but we still have plenty of tinned. And then we finished off with the sticky chocolate cake. I felt better for having been able to contribute something towards ship life and went to bed cheery for a change.

Day 13: *Thursday, 8 September   Noon position 26° 33' N, 20° 22' W*
Day's run 189 miles   Course S by W   Wind NE Force 3
Barometer ?

John: Rolling along down the trade winds (which are mild to my way of thinking), somewhere off the west coast of the Sahara Desert. The increased heat is making for a general air of lassitude. Few of the crew have ever known heat beyond the English summer. Sun, glare, and the lack of salt are all going to have an effect. My job is to watch and see they don't lose efficiency. It's my plan at this time to let each individual share in decision-making, using the lunchtime discussions to keep open the channels of communication. I've found with young instructors that the main thing they seek after school and college is the chance to feel responsibility, whether it's navigation, sail plans, radio, engine, or medical – all these things offer opportunities to escape the boredom of just being a small cog. Also I'm letting everyone take their turn at the helm, rather than using only a few selected helmsmen. Personalities emerge when things are not going well – people just can't help themselves – and I feel it would be foolish not to allow them to vent their feelings and ease the sting of their frustration in trying to solve the problems for themselves. I've always operated in this manner. I remember at the age of twenty-one in the Parachute Regiment I was even then accused of running my first platoon 'like a Soviet'. I've always believed in letting everyone use his brains, but at the same time it's vital for the leader to be ready and rested, to be able to take firm control in case of emergency. Unfortunately Bob is stubbornly opposed to this easy style of leadership.

Marie Christine: It gets hotter all the time. We should be in the tropics by tomorrow. Progress is erratic. *Condor* and *33 Export* have both had to stop for repairs but not for long. There's a lumpy sea and I am not feeling too brilliant again. We sent a telegram this morning to wish Becca good luck with her new school. I do hope she is happy there. John and I spent an hour on the pulpit watching the water as we sped through it, wondering if it was all worth the effort. We saw some flying fish, curious creatures that take off from a wave and glide just above the surface for up to fifty yards or more.

Day 14: *Friday, 9 September   Noon position 23° 08' N, 20° 40' W*
Day's run 194 miles   Course S   Wind E by N Force 4–5
Barometer 1021

John: One of the three thermos flasks, used by watches for hot drinks at night, broke at two in the morning. We're going to have to build a rack for them in the Southern Ocean – we will get replacement liners for them in Cape Town because they'll certainly be a godsend among the icebergs.

The paraffin navigation lights are not working too well. We go so fast that the draught under the cracks of the sliding backs blows them out. Maybe we could build a packing at the bottom to seal the crack. They save so much electricity.

In the early morning we made a phone call to Richard Creasey at ATV and he quotes Proctors – the mast makers – at £300 for the spinnaker pole ends to be delivered to Cape Town. This is about what I expected, and I fear we'll have to get them, otherwise we're going to end up without being able to use spinnakers at all. Rolling along at 8 knots we're running due south now on our eighth consecutive day under the spinnakers; and the heat's growing steadily worse. We're about 240 miles to the west of the Sahara Desert. Slowly we do seem to be catching the opposition – but it's very slowly. *33 Export* is behind us after calling in at Madeira, and *Condor* also was delayed in picking up her new radio. *Adventure* is only twenty-eight miles ahead now, and *Gauloises II* is 300 miles ahead and *Condor* is already going back up through the fleet, seemingly still without a radio which works.

Marie Christine: Two weeks at sea. J.C. made a celebration supper and some delicious white bread. We had an 'abandon ship' drill on deck just before lunch in the heat. To add a menacing touch, there was an evil-looking black shark circling the boat. Roger's not feeling too well – probably slight sunstroke. J.C. is running a sweepstake on when we expect to get to Cape Town. I have said forty-two days (six weeks from Pompey) and the guesses range on up to fifty-four days. My guess is not calculated at all, only wishful thinking. I have read five books since the start of the race. John and I had a little party in our cabin last night, just the two of us. We split a can of beer which I hadn't drunk at supper and finished off my peanuts from two days ago. I shall have to find a new hiding place for my private non-perishable leftovers. There is a small ventilation hole where, squirrel-like, I was hoarding them. But now John automatically feels to see if there's anything there. Colin has now screwed down the two loose floorboards in our cabin, in case of capsize. It's a good thing because we have an assortment of jams, oil, pickles and whisky kept down there, and I dread to think what it would do to the cabin if they all broke.

Day 15: *Saturday, 10 September   Noon position 20° 09' N, 20° 35' W*
Day's run 164 miles   Course S   Wind ENE Force 4
Barometer 1020

John: Dick got hit in the face by a flying fish at two in the morning. At first he thought it was Peter Brand throwing bits of rope at him. Next thing was that two more landed on the deck, and I think they're going to be cooked by John Covington.

We had a bit of a problem this morning with Peter Brand unhappy about the helmsmanship of some people – notably Steve, who in fact has never done any helming at all before he set off on this trip. It boils down to Tony's watch and the mistake I may have made in putting all three young people together. They feel, I think, that they're being picked on by the other older people on the boat such as John Covington, the sail-trimmer, or Bob, who's obviously a lot older and more experienced in life but not as experienced in sailing, except for the fatal flaw that he thinks he knows it all. Communication with Tony is very much a one-way business. In spite of his bull-like manner he is of course as sensitive as the next man; easily stung by any reference to his thinning hair or the rate he is putting on weight, he feels he is second youngest on the boat yet this in no way diminishes his desire to lead. Bob's watch started by referring to Tony, Colin and Steve as 'the cadets', but after Bob had repaired the spinnaker they blew out he called them 'Dallimore's doomwatch'. All of this does nothing to heal the old wounds between Bob and Tony, and on top of this Tony despises Arun for being too timid and un-racing in outlook. I notice Tony seldom talks to or encourages any of the others. His attitude is one of dull sullenness. How I hate these clashes of temperament, but how inseparable from leadership they are. They're really trials of strength, I think, and they will go on and on until, I suppose in years ahead, I'll become too weak to keep things going along the lines I want. Maybe that's evolution! Peter and I had a chat with Tony up in the bows, watched of course by the rest of the crew on the stern, and I feel sure the problem is really one of shyness on Tony's part. He's a very valuable man, if only he'd give a bit. This is no place for a cold fish.

It's difficult to have a private conversation with Peter, the mate. If we go up into the bows then the duty watch back in the cockpit wonder what we are discussing. Down in the saloon there are always at least four others who will leap into action if anything controversial is mentioned. While he welcomed the job as second-in-command in the first place, I feel Peter, a sensitive soul, is unwilling to enforce unpleasant duties on the others so the job will probably devolve on me.

In the evening at 1800 hours GMT, when the boats all speak to one another, I sent a message to the skipper and owner of *Flyer*, which has only broadcast once in the race so far. 'Cornelius. This is John Ridgway. I'm sure you're listening. When you get to Cape Town I know you will take on a complete new set of sails. I would like to buy some of your old ones.' This brought an immediate response from *Flyer* which Pierre Fehlmann, skipper of *Disque d'Or*, relayed to me. 'My position is 15 degrees 15 minutes north, 25 degrees 20 minutes west.' This put him almost through the Cape Verde Islands but in an unlikely position unless he had risked the calms and gone between some of the islands. It was almost as enigmatic as *Neptune* saying they were 315 kilometres from the Canary Islands. Anyway, we are now only twelve miles behind *Adventure*, and those ahead are running into calm weather.

After supper, Noel, Roger, Marie Christine and I played Scrabble in the cabin, lit by the paraffin storm light as the boat pushed smoothly along in the night at around 6 to 7 knots.

Marie Christine: Well into the tropics now and it's boiling hot at night; I had to move to the bottom of the bed. We are not far off the Cape Verdes; I hope nothing forces us to stop at these desolate islands – I remember it all so well from our last trip.

The boat is going well now, with our daily discussions at lunchtime. John has got a good team spirit. Everyone seems at last to be pulling in the right direction.

Day 16: *Sunday, 11 September   Noon position 17° 34' N, 21° 15' W*
Day's run 156 miles   Course S   Wind ENE Force 2–3
Barometer 1018

John: As it was Sunday I kept off the noon discussions, and allowed the day to drift along like a holiday. No work in the morning and the same light winds as usual. People sat around reading, and not reading – just sitting with their feet in buckets of cold sea water! I gave a short talk on navigation in the morning to five or six people who were interested in learning how to do the noon-sight to get the latitude.

There was a bit of a row in the evening between Tony and Bob over the big-boy sail. This sail dips in the water in certain light conditions,

Dickie keeping cool

and then there is the threat of tearing the sail as well as the slowing effect of its dragging in the water. Bob has no time for this fancy sail, but Tony and Colin consider it vital in light weather.

By giving J.C. the sail-trimmer's job, we've got one more link in the chain of command to slow down decisions. Peter Brand is a fairly tense sort of fellow and every so often he blows up. How pleasant to have somebody other than myself to do it, but I doubt he'll last. He and J.C. had a good go at each other, about the speed of decision-making – but it clears the air.

We're pretty well level with and ninety miles east of the Cape Verde Islands by three o'clock in the morning. Bob signalled with the Aldis to a passing ship, but we couldn't read the speed of her reply, and she disappeared across our stern in disgust.

Marie Christine: The Great Heat is upon us with the usual thirst and lethargy. J.C. is wisely keeping a strict watch on our water consumption. He's keeping it to not more than six gallons per day. In other words, four pints per person for drinking, washing and reconstituting the dehydrated food; not much, but I think we are better off than some of the other boats. *Treaty of Rome* said they were getting thirsty over the radio last night. John's prickly heat is troubling him, intense itching on parts of his legs and arms and tiny blisters which he is trying very hard not to scratch. I cut his hair up on the bow. It's the coolest place to be, with the air spilling from the spinnaker flying above.

J.C. is still managing well with the cooking with great good humour, which I consider a miracle. He doesn't appear to notice the heat at all in spite of his great bulk. As the sail-trimmer he is called out to give advice from time to time, having more experience than any of us of ocean racing; but some people don't value it too highly. For me, the best thing of the day is the delicious draught of Rise and Shine which J.C. has been giving us from time to time. We had a glass this evening just before bed – which belies its name!

Day 17: *Monday, 12 September   Noon position 14° 43' N, 21° 13' W*
        Day's run 123 miles   Course S   Wind NNW Force 3
        Barometer 1016

John: There was a change of wind soon after midnight and we handled the changing of the spinnaker without loss of boat speed on a dark night.

The morning brought a large school of big, black, scarred dolphins who were quite happy to lollop along with us at 6 knots for several hours.

'FIRE!' called Colin, his ginger head coming up over the saloon table

Colin's electrical fire

from his usual place down in the forward starboard corner of the saloon, where he always seemed to be fiddling with the electrics. Within the space of half a minute the saloon was filled with acrid, grey smoke, which billowed up from the four 150-ampere batteries stored under the corner seat. People started to cough, and all the electrical switches were thrown. Arun came on to the scene, and I began to think of Drake's plan to douse fires using hogsheads of human urine, which sadly we haven't got. Still, Chubb's extinguishers have much the same effect and the fire was quickly put out – but we are left with powder everywhere and many feet of burned out wiring. Arun and Colin spent the rest of the day cleaning up the mess, which isn't much fun at the best of times, but in the tropical heat as the wind died away to nothing at all, it was very lucky that they were both so immersed in the design and building of an improved electrical system, which would effectively isolate the positive and negative terminals, that they ignored the heat.

This was by far the hottest day so far, and the effect was especially noticeable between noon and five in the afternoon. The heat seems to fuzz the brain a bit, and some of the sail changes were not really as sensible as they might have been.

As well as the dolphins, we passed two yellowish-brown turtles, one of which Steve described as about the size of a dead calf. We saw a ten-foot shark, whose length we judged from the distance between its sinister black triangular dorsal fin and the tip of its tail which occasionally broke the surface.

At dusk a small black swallow-like bird with a long V-shaped tail and a red face landed on the guard-rail after much nervous circling of the boat. It appeared to be very tired, and as its confidence grew so it looked for more stable places to land. Next thing we knew it was in the saloon, hotly pursued by Peter Brand, our nature-lover. After a while, Peter emerged from the saloon with a cardboard box which had 'Made in USSR' stamped on its side. 'He'll be all right,' drawled the nasal Tasmanian, 'I've put him in here for the night.' And so it was. But me, I reckon I'd be pretty frightened, shut up in a dark Russian box for the night. These swallows, it seems, are fairly frequently visiting the other boats in the race and some of them have had as many as four aboard at one time.

Day 18: *Tuesday, 13 September   Noon position 13° 50' N, 21° 30' W Day's run 66 miles   Course S   Wind SE Force 0–1 Barometer 1016*

John: We made only some twenty miles between eight at night and eight in the morning, and the spinnaker would hold up no longer. So then it was the light genoa, main and mizzen, slatting about in the swell. After breakfast I listened to a French plane speaking with the French boats. They hadn't moved far in the night either. A telegram from Portishead radio yesterday had warned us of the plane, but in fact it didn't seem very interested in the British boats.

The heat bore down as we crawled along at 2 knots. Oh, for a good heavy rain shower like the one *Disque d'Or* reported last night on the radio. They apparently collected 200 litres of drinking water. More breeze after lunch helped cool the fevered brows, and we were making 6 knots closehauled on a south-easterly breeze for a while, but it didn't hold.

Fish jumped all around; smallish fish marauding the flying fish, and directly on our bows were four really plump tuna-like fish. They would take none of Roger's lures: not the Torbay Tweaker or the Eddystone Redgill, nor nothing. As they dived at the bow they presented a bright purple iridescence from the angle of their bodies – head down, tail up.

Magnificent sunsets and vast seascapes make the pattern of our days. It's foolish to let our poor position in the race lessen the grandeur of the experience. Still, as General Patton once said: 'Victory is the best morale-builder.'

With the night came a short light drizzle, but no real rain – and all the time it's stifling hot.

Day 19: *Wednesday, 14 September   Noon position 12° 03' N, 21° 24' W*
Day's run 74 miles   Course S   Wind E Force 2
Barometer 1018

John: In mid-morning great plum-coloured clouds loomed up. It *had* to rain. Bob hung the grey inflatable collision mat below the mizzen boom while Tony and I rigged the green canvas collision mat, that Hillary Ashford had made back at Ardmore, below the main boom. Nearer and nearer came the grey curtain of blessed, delicious rain. Everybody was on deck with their shampoo and soap – and lo, an archway appeared in the curtain, and we sailed right through. It was rather worse than no rain at all: there was just enough drizzle to get the hair covered with shampoo – but not enough to get it off. It hadn't rained a single drop in eighteen days. Still, just being near the area where it had rained helped to freshen the air a bit.

After a splendid rice pilau lunch of rice, pineapple, chicken and onion, I found Peter Brand lying up in the bow with a home-made spear-gun made up from a broom handle, two nails and a length of shockcord.

'Straight from Hawaii and Hobart,' he cracked, sporting a blistered right hand. 'I'm going to get me one of those fish.' And he pointed down at the iridescent purple fish speeding along in the shade of the bow.

After a few near misses we called up Steve and employed his First Class Honours degree in Physics to eliminate the refractive error. Meanwhile I grappled with the problem from a different angle. I'd seen a fish take a biscuit packet from the surface once when Chay Blyth and I were rowing across the North Atlantic. All these tuna – or were they dorado? – seemed to come up to the surface occasionally as if they were looking for insects. I threw some small light balls of silver peanut packet ahead of the fish as they came up. BANG! One took it, and I'd found the solution. It wasn't Roger's Torbay Tweaker but the Debenham Dibbler they wanted. Using Roger's light fibreglass rod and a fifteen-pound nylon monofilament line, I made up a floating lure using a size 6 hook with a Wrigleys Spearmint silver paper body for weight, and a quarter-inch square of white polystyrene for buoyancy; a flick of the wrist and it shot out a few feet ahead of the bow. There were a few interested rises, and then BANG! He was hooked. The line burned my fingers as it came off the drum of the reel. For a short while I managed to keep his head above water, but as soon as he dived he had the remorseless pressure of the boat speed with him – and the line broke at the hook. The rest of the crew were greatly impressed, but the fish didn't come back for the rest of the day, even though I waited for several hours – with a thirty-six pound line instead of the fifteen on the reel. The answer was to have sufficient power to lift the fish cleanly out of the sea and on to the deck in one smooth action, never letting it use the boat speed on its body.

Day 20: *Thursday, 15 September   Noon position 10° 37' N, 21° 48' W*
Day's run 116 miles   Course S   Wind ESE Force 2–3
Barometer 1018

John: M.C. and I sat up in the bows in the cool of the evening, with a fair breeze, and then that golden moment as the huge sun forms a dew-drop with the horizon, then just away leaving pink-edged clouds right across our heads and beyond, into the fast darkening east.

The evening radio brought sad news. *Condor*, perhaps the most exciting boat in the race, has broken her ninety-foot yellow carbon-fibre mast at the lower spreaders. She's retired from the first leg, and will motor to Monrovia and then on to Cape Town. This is a very sad blow for the dashing Les Williams, hard in the wake of his troubles with *Burton Cutter* in the last race. Maybe this is not a race for exciting boats after all; perhaps they should all be very well tried before setting out.

Marie Christine: Another awful night, breakfast was an ordeal with cheery chat amongst the fellows. I felt exhausted, an outsider and unable to join in. What was I doing here – I wasn't the slightest bit interested in sailing, navigation, suffering, or being part of the team. I helped with the washing up and crept back to my room with my cup of cold water to wash in, misery flooding over me in the ovenlike room. John came in and I told him I'd had enough. I was a failure as far as his sailing was concerned. Why should *I* go on suffering? John's face looked horrified when I told him I wanted to get off at Cape Town and not go on. I wasn't contributing anything to the running of the boat. I don't like crowds, and being cooped up with eleven other men I was finding oppressive. The failure was entirely with me. I couldn't make the effort while feeling unwell all the time. I was pathetic and I knew it. John comforted my sobs and pleaded with me to go on with him – so I suppose I will. There seems no way out without letting him down. If I come back from this trip there will be *no* more sailing for me. The awful thing is it's going to get worse; legs 2 and 3 will be terrifying as well as uncomfortable. John, practical as ever, thought my main problem was that I wasn't getting enough salt. He could be right. I sat around for the rest of the day on deck doing my windows and felt a bit better after my despair of the morning.

We have a lot of birds on the boat now. The heat is intense and they flutter below into the main saloon and sit about in unlikely places. We have rigged up an awning over the aft cockpit to afford some shelter for the helmsman. A good way of keeping the feet cool is to put them in a bucket of sea water, changing when it heats up too much. There is a big swell from the south now which is meeting the northerly one that's been

Swallow and Arun

with us all the way down. The sea out here behaves in a most strange manner. There are great areas of smooth calm and then we pass through turbulent patches of confused water stretching from east to west which would appear to be currents. In spite of the great heat and proximity of the doldrums we made good headway today.

Day 21: *Friday, 16 September   Noon position 8° 46' N, 21° 40' W*
      Day's run 90 miles   Course S   Wind Variable Force 1
      Barometer 1018

Marie Christine: Am trying to make a big effort to be positive about this trip. I wasn't helped by being sick over the side after breakfast. The wind has altered direction and is now coming from the SW so we are close-hauled and hitting the oncoming swell. A rain shower for us after lunch. We all managed a good wash this time as well as hair and clothes. Washing was festooned from every available line and, as the ebullient J.C. said, 'We look more like Sketchleys than Debenhams.' It cheered us all up no end and also the fact that we were moving so well. We also collected two gallons more rain water. But with only ninety miles covered in twenty-four hours we'll be stuck here for ever.

Day 22: *Saturday, 17 September   Noon position 7° 11′ N, 21° 30′ W*
Day's run 146 miles   Course SE   Wind WSW Force 4
Barometer 1016

Marie Christine: Been at sea for three weeks. J.C. made very good brown bread and chocolate cake which came out of the paraffin oven at a rakish slant. However, once covered in icing, it looked not unlike Handa Island at home – wedge-shaped – and it tasted delicious.

Making good progress still – could we be out of the doldrums?

The swallows are all dying – they won't eat or drink anything. The poor things seem resigned to their fate.

Day 23: *Sunday, 18 September   Noon position 5° 29′ N, 19° 30′ W*
Day's run 160 miles   Course SE   Wind S by W Force 4
Barometer 1015

John: We spent the day bashing into a lumpy southerly sea. Little happened, but we just hung on and tried to get used to the new uncomfortable motion, very much leaning over to one side and bumping up and down. This affects people differently; Arun, Marie Christine, Steve and I feel pretty sick – and I think Roger does a little bit, too. Bob, on the other hand, has gone quiet and is rather snappy, and he doesn't seem to want to talk about anything. After twenty-two days this is a bad sign, I fear, as there must be at least another twenty days to come before we reach Cape Town.

The heat in the 'swamp' – which is what they call the forward compartment where six of the crew sleep – is very bad, with the hatches necessarily closed now to stop the spray coming in. So tempers are getting more than a little frayed.

On the evening radio we learn that *Condor* is now fitting a new mast in Monrovia – the capital of Liberia – and we find ourselves at 5 degrees North moving slowly, with *Great Britain II* 5 degrees South – that's 10 degrees of difference, which is 600 miles between us. Close behind them are *Flyer* and *King's Legend*. *Adventure* and *Treaty of Rome* – two boats that we raced from the start with – are still pretty close to us after all these miles.

The Aldermanic John Covington is still doing great stuff with the food, and I think everything will be all right once we get out of this awful heat.

Marie Christine: Bad night. Very bumpy sea now as we bash into the SE trade winds. Too sick for anything more than glass of water for breakfast. Sat up on deck and spent the whole morning discussing Dick's future. I think we'll have to find him a rich widow. Peter is going to emigrate to British Columbia where he'll live with his Canadian fiancée Penny. They plan to buy some land and run holidays for Americans. John and I offered advice and pointed out pitfalls. We both feel like a couple of old-timers, having been running our school for ten years now. There are many similarities between Ardmore and Peter's scheme. He has various books and maps on British Columbia with him and has been studying them intently. One drawback is that he has just discovered an annual rainfall of 100 inches in the area where he was planning to settle.

Have just finished my eighth book of the trip. It's a great temptation to read all day long. Later this evening after I'd got into bed, there was a terrific shower of rain. Both John and I put on our bathers and went out into the cockpit for a good wash. Not the most pleasant shower of my life – it was pitch black and the boat was well heeled over and lurching through the night, but with our life harnesses on we managed a pretty good scrub. If I hadn't been so hot and sticky before I would not have bothered.

Day 24: *Monday, 19 September   Noon position 3° 25' N, 17° 40' W
Day's run 173 miles   Course SSE   Wind WSW Force 4–5
Barometer 1017*

Marie Christine: Went up on deck in my nightie to see a nosy sperm whale. It was jumping vertically out of the water to get a good look at us

Lunch for the helmsman

with its plate-sized eye focused on us. You could even see its huge mouth hanging half open.

A grey lumpy sea today. None of the seasick brigade, Arun, Steve, John and me, are looking that bright. I could only manage a glass of lemon juice for breakfast. At least I'll be getting quite thin at this rate. Spent a mopey day alternating between lying on my bunk feeling I was mouldering away and up in the stern getting wet and blown. The secret is to keep your mind occupied – talk about anything under the sun. With most people it's reminiscing.

Peter radioed our position through to *Spinnaker* in the afternoon and was told of a call for us from Southampton Boat Show. Clare Francis was to have spoken but they couldn't hear her. 'Would John say a few words instead?' Playing second fiddle is not quite John's idea of how it should be. However, he went ahead.

Heard on radio tonight that *ADC*'s engine has broken down so they will not be joining in with the chat show from now on. Bit of a blow for them. They'll have to eat up all the contents of their deep freeze pretty smartly.

Day 25: *Tuesday, 20 September   Noon position 1° 23' N, 15° 30' W*
Day's run 181 miles   Course SSW   Wind SE Force 5
Barometer 1018

Marie Christine: Another lousy night, squashed against the leeboard with the boat at this angle. Will I ever get used to it? Within the next twenty-four hours we'll be crossing the Equator. It's more like the North Sea, grey and lumpy.

Made an effort at breakfast to help and washed up afterwards with a bucket of salt water in the cockpit and rather grubby tea towels. Thank goodness we're not all so thirsty any more. Getting on much better with everyone now. I'm afraid it's just my moods that make me feel apart. Took a Maxalon seasick pill after breakfast which had bad results on me. Just after John had scored a 72 on the Scrabble I felt very queasy and had to go and lie down. He naturally thought it was his score that got me down! Our cabin is at least cooler now we are going into the wind. With the sea breaking over the boat all forward hatches remain shut and the swamp and main saloon are very hot and airless. They're feeling it particularly at night – we'll have to get Arun to fit ventilators in Cape Town.

Day 26: *Wednesday, 21 September   Noon position 00° 48' S, 17° 03' W*
Day's run 192 miles   Course S   Wind SE Force 5
Barometer 1019

John: We crossed the Equator during the night and so King Neptune duly came aboard – that's myself complete with crown and trident – at 1100 hours in the morning. Mr Robert Burns – a many times crosser of the Equator in the service of Her Majesty aboard everything from cruiser to hospital ship in the Navy – elaborately performed the duty of Big N's agent. Marie Christine was dressed in white; having crossed the Equator by dug-out canoe from south to north on the Amazon, she acted in the capacity of Aphrodite. Messrs Dallimore, Ladd, Lenartowicz and McCann were inducted as vassals of the realm with soapy water shaves. The proceedings were closed with oodles of Mercier champagne – courtesy of Dr Dixon of BUPA – and certificates were issued for the unfortunates. The whole thing was 'proper 'ansome', as Bob put it.

All day long we bashed along at 8 to 9 knots under No. 1 yankee, No. 1 working staysail and a full main.

The tracks of the other boats are spread out on the big chart of the south Atlantic in the main saloon bulkhead, and at mealtimes we all chew over the pros and cons of going north or south of the South Atlantic High, which is still a great many miles to the south of us. If we go round the southern side, which is probably faster, it means we've got to go about four thousand miles from our present position. If we go

Crossing the line: MC. JR. Bob in cockpit; Tony behind

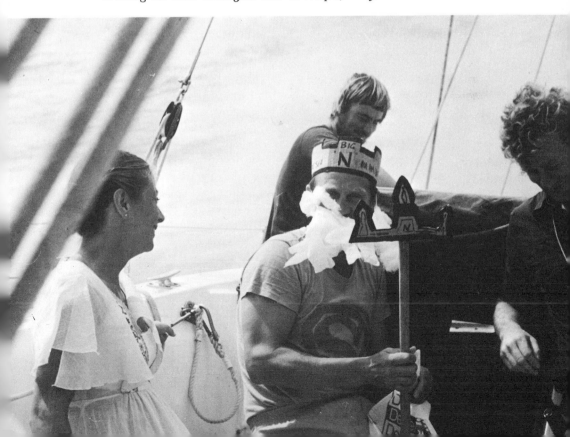

along the northern side then we could save as much as a thousand miles. Luckily, in the position we are at the moment, we can watch the tracks of some of the boats ahead of us and see what luck they're having with the High – and perhaps follow them.

Day 27: *Thursday, 22 September   Noon position 3° 46′ S, 17° 41′ W*
Day's run 196 miles   Course S   Wind SE Force 5
Barometer 1019

Marie Christine: Still not resorted to sleeping on the floor – but almost – the heel is quite severe. We end up crushed against the lee in spite of being head to toe. I bruised my forehead with a crack from the sextant case which is screwed in just above my head. My hips and back are quite bruised as well. I'll arrive at Cape Town black and blue at this rate.

Grapenuts for breakfast. We had the usual discussion over which course we should follow – it depends largely on the position of the high pressure area. We've been listening to a forecast each morning from a French ship broadcasting to the French yachts in very fast, indistinct French. It gives the isobars and millibars and goes on for almost ten minutes. I now have a notebook half filled with columns of figures

King Neptune's equatorial champagne: Roger, JR, Bob

which Tony tries to make sense of and puts up on our wall chart in the saloon in chinagraph pencil. Also marked on the chart are the other yachts' positions which we try to get each evening on the chat show. Up to now, everyone has been fairly generous with information on their positions and weather but for two nights now we've had no word from *King's Legend*, who had been coming up regularly, or from *Flyer*. They are both past about 16 degrees South but perhaps are not letting on whether they are going to the west or east of the expected calm areas of the High which we will all be trying to avoid. All the boats are making good progress now with a fairly general south-south-east wind of about 25 knots. We also heard that *Condor* will be setting off from Monrovia on Sunday with her new mast. They haven't hung about.

The day started grey and lumpy but by lunchtime we moved through the cloud out into brilliant blue sky and sea – the equatorial sun burning down on us. A perfect day - enough to chase away any suspicion of queasiness. A glorious day to be alive, passing flying fish, dolphins, violet Portuguese Men o' War, and stormy petrels as we speed south. We have covered 196 miles this 24 hours. Judith of *Treaty of Rome* was most indignant when one of the other yachts mentioned that an American radio programme had suggested that the crew of the European entry was having trouble getting on with each other. 'Not at all – we are getting along fine,' her well-bred English voice shrilled back. What a daft question anyway! *Japy Hermès* are taking their sick crew member to Recife; apparently he has kidney stones, poor bloke. He must feel terrible, letting his boat down as well as the pain from lack of proper medical attention.

Our situation in Chile, when we were two months away from any medical help, is not unlike this. Steve can patch up minor accidents and relieve symptoms and pain but anything major would involve taking the injured man to shore – not so easy in the Southern Ocean. We must all take care.

I fished out my handbag from the heads where it was wedged behind a pipe. (John bought it for me from a fancy boutique in Buenos Aires.) It took me half an hour to remove all the mould which had grown on it in just under four weeks at sea. I felt the same had happened to me when I removed my black T shirt for a wash in the heads, made almost impossible by the lurching sea. Even my lovely brown back had a creeping mould of peeling! John wittered on about sunburn and how it was inevitable with me as he unwillingly rubbed in my Alliage body lotion. But how could any suntan last when it was rubbed all night long against a terylene lee cloth?

I spent the afternoon out on deck marvelling at the dazzling sea and the brilliant sky. The wind freshened by late afternoon and we changed down from the genoa to the No. 1 yankee with the wind blowing at over

25 knots. I took seventy-two photographs, more for myself than any publication up to now, since this was the very best day of the trip and how I would like to remember it. A perfect orange sun dropped into the heaving sea and tropical darkness was upon us. This would be the shortest day until we cross back into the Northern Hemisphere next March.

Our resolutions regarding food faded as the spicy aroma of another giant curry wafted up heralding supper. Only Tony was firm and he had nothing all day, except what was left of his peanuts and a can of beer.

Day 28: *Friday, 23 September   Noon position 6° 52' S, 17° 47' W*
Day's run 200 miles   Course SE   Wind E Force 5
Barometer 1019

John: The storm petrel which came on board last night was taken care of by Nature-boy Peter, who stuffed this one in a cardboard box and pencilled 'A Pigeon' on the outside. In the morning it looked a little more tousled than when it first came aboard but when Peter put it over the side it swam about in the wake all right – until it was left astern with a rather shocked look on its face.

Sailing 200.7 miles 40 degrees off the easterly wind stands testimony to the bumping; but the bumps are a small price to pay for the speed. We certainly are going well now.

A tropical bird with a long white streaming tail came to see us in the morning; the sun shining through its snowy plumage made it seem a lonely dove of peace from far away. Maybe it came from Ascension Island, which is only a couple of hundred miles to the east of us now.

Later on in the afternoon, a grubby grey gannet paddled its wings above our masts, but it soon lost interest and pushed off disgruntled. In the sea, the flying fish are larger, and bright sun shows their wings in palest blue as they skate off the waves away from us. Now we're seeing Portuguese Man o' War jellyfish again – bigger ones this time. These translucent purple sails, which are so easily capsized as we go by, just as easily come upright again after we've gone.

The twelve persons aboard *Debenhams*, with this brilliant sunshine, are in good heart and at ease with one another. This is a most important factor for the future.

Marie Christine: First day of Southern Hemisphere spring! Had a vivid dream of J.C. heading a mutiny and throwing John and me overboard. I dream more and more vividly out here than ever at home.

After the usual breakfast discussion it seems likely that we will go east of the High, a shorter route but a bit of a gamble with the wind. It is hard to say where we are placed in relation to the other boats as we are heading south-west and south-east as well as south. But on a southerly basis we are now ahead of *Adventure* and *Treaty of Rome* and on a level with *33 Export*. We might not be last after all!

The squalor of the saloon table goaded me into giving it a good scrub after breakfast. It had got to the state where there were hairs stuck all over the white paint, and stale butter, crumbs, sugar, trickles of tea and old eggshell lodged between the middle section of the table. One hour later it looked clean after an attack with salt water, detergent and a stiff brush. Half-way through this simple task, as I battled with my stomach and the sliding bucket, I couldn't help but think, 'What am I doing here?' None of the heroics for me. Am I not really just a housewife at heart? How happy I would be to be back at home now with order and cleanliness around me. Instead, I'm in a boat lurching and heeling at 35 degrees, eleven men as my companions, who for seventy-five per cent of the time talk about sailing, which I am not particularly interested in. And squalor is everywhere. I felt rotten all morning till John called me up to see the white-tailed tropic bird.

Making good progress. The mutual suffering brings us seasickers closer together.

Day 29: *Saturday, 24. September   Noon position 9° 43' S, 17° 04' W*
Day's run 194 miles   Course SSE   Wind E Force 6
Barometer 1021

John: The good progress continued with about thirteen hundred miles in the past week. With this cutter rig 40 degrees off the wind the boat moves very sweetly indeed.

'Killer whales! Whoopee!' squeaked fearless Dick McCann – the lavatory man (he is in charge of the heads) – at 16.30 in the afternoon. Peter had seen them first of all, eight spiky dorsal fins knifing across our course a quarter of a mile ahead. They seemed to sense us coming and a pair of them altered course right for us.

'There they are – forty yards off,' Peter said calmly, as we all clambered out into the cockpit from the saloon. 'First time I seen 'em since False Bay by Cape Town,' he said.

'Watertight doors?' I replied.

But they stopped some twenty yards off the side of the boat and wallowed around, looking at us. The give-away white patches near their heads made them look surprisingly friendly. Rather like fishy giant pandas. All the same, I could only think of *Guia* – an Italian entry in the last race – which is now resting at the bottom – not so very far from here – in some three thousand fathoms of sea, her side stove in by playful killer whales as she returned to Europe from the Cape Town to Rio race.

Day 30: *Sunday, 25 September   Noon position 12° 44′ S, 16° 33′ W*
Day's run 197 miles   Course SSE   Wind ESE Force 6
Barometer 1022

Marie Christine: After all the port the previous evening, we left our bed as before instead of altering it and had another dreadful night! Felt awful all morning but made a big effort and went on deck in the afternoon. My mind was occupied talking to Arun and then Peter about India. Hope to go there some day. I felt very cheery by the evening. Wish I could get on to a more level emotional plane. I seem to alternate between utmost despair and reasonable cheerfulness.

The saloon is now pretty damp with drips from the ceiling and a long leak that has worked its way on to the wall chart, which is now looking soggy. I think we are all getting on well with each other.

This evening with the boat being so heeled over I stuffed a thick blanket beneath our mattress, hoping to correct the slant. This had the effect of raising John up so high that he was almost above the leecloth. I'm determined to sort the bed out once and for all, so I sent John into the saloon and got to work taking the mattress right out, making a deep well which I padded with spare charts, two karrimats, the sleeping-bag and finally our sheet. At last success — we had a super night!

Day 31: *Monday, 26 September   Noon position 16° 10′ S, 16° 15′ W*
Day's run 206 miles   Course S by E   Wind SE Force 5
Barometer 1022

Marie Christine: I couldn't find anywhere to keep the mattress, so regretfully threw it over the side! No point taking it all round the world ... but it seemed drastic all the same. I could have put it to very good use at Ardmore.

Spent the morning playing Scrabble with Tony, Steve and John. Much to their surprise, I suspect, I won hands down. John hates to be beaten and this was the start of a bad day for him. He went up on deck in a huff and got absolutely soaked to the skin by a sneaky wave which washed over the ship. Worse was to come; after working out the morning and afternoon sight we discovered we were two hundred miles farther west on our longitude position. This had come about partly because of three poor sights in the last two days and Bob not working it out correctly. Poor John was very depressed. On our giving out our position that evening over the radio, *Adventure*, who hadn't spoken to us for weeks, came back to us immediately: 'According to your position at 1800 hours, it would appear that in the last twenty-four hours you have done 300 miles. Is this correct?' Our maximum up to now on this trip is 206 miles, so no wonder they were worried! John explained the difficulties he was experiencing with twelve navigators on board and how our last two positions had been incorrect. This error could have lost us a day. On the other hand we may well find better winds and it could work out to our advantage. It puts us farther out to the west of the fleet. We expect it to be quite a race to the finish between *Gauloises*, *Treaty of Rome*, *Adventure* and us. *Great Britain II*, *Flyer* and *King's Legend* are closing in on Cape Town. They are nearly on the same latitude but have quite a way to go to the east. They say they have big seas down there (more seasickness to come). Before turning in, Peter pointed out the Southern Cross to me.

Nearly out of the tropics now and getting cooler, thank goodness. Finished another book.

Day 32: *Tuesday, 27 September   Noon position 19° 10' S, 15° 47' W*
Day's run 199 miles   Course SSE   Wind ESE Force 6
Barometer 1024

John: Still going well all day in the south-easterly trades. I lost again at Scrabble (while feeling seasick!); but the sights were good in the clear sunlit skies and I'm happy now about our position. It really needs me to work out the sight each day to be quite sure in my own mind that we are in the right place.

A black skua-like bird appeared at 12.30 while Peter was discussing with Tony's watch what they would like to happen if one of them was lost overboard. 'Go on with the race,' they all say. And if someone dies on board, they expect to be put over the side in the big-boy sail bag, weighted down by their own scaffolding bunk pole.

Marie Christine: Bumpy sea — we're all feeling sick. Sat out all afternoon in brilliant sunshine, watching the big flying fish down here. We had a big supper tonight, finishing with a huge chocolate cake on to which we poured port. It was delicious.

Peter got through to Portishead after supper and we placed a call to Brighton as it is Mum's birthday today. Got through quickly. She was delighted to hear from us. She said Bec was loving the new school, but hadn't wanted to go back after her weekend out with her. I didn't think this was anything to worry about, it was often the case when Bec weekly boarded at Kinlochbervie. I said we'd ring again when we were in Cape Town in ten days. Am I being over-optimistic? Arun then rang his mother in Durness, who seemed most startled to receive a transfer charge call from the middle of the South Atlantic. And finally Steve rang home, a conversation peppered with 'Over' at the end of each question and sentence. It's so exciting getting through that you tend to forget everything you'd planned to say   next time I'm going to write it all down in advance.

We went to bed feeling very cheery that all was well at home.

Day 33: *Wednesday, 28 September   Noon position 22° 09' S, 15° 28' W*
Day's run 194 miles   Course SSE   Wind ESE Force 5
Barometer 1024

Marie Christine: It is getting cooler all the time; I put on trousers this morning instead of shorts, which I've been wearing for the past five weeks.

The last of the eggs were eaten this morning, thank goodness – I'd gone off eating them weeks back and I found it really turned my stomach sitting next to a keen hard-boiled-egg-eater at breakfast when he cracked the shell and gobbled the smelly contents. In my unreasonable and queasy state it's almost more than I can bear. I find that with this lumpy sea and sickness there's a lot that makes me feel pretty bad. My sense of smell has become quite acute and to be downwind of greasy hair, stale breath and sweaty clothes ... it's all I can do to stop being sick. Not that I'm blaming anyone for uncleanliness; in fact, they are all making a great effort, but with only one mug a day of water to wash in and at any mealtime ten of us cooped up in the saloon, the air is quite stale, especially as when going into the waves it is not possible to open any of the forward hatches.

Lost at Scrabble to John. I felt sick – must be some connection – and couldn't face going on deck, so went and mouldered in my bunk. I thought of Bec and the things she hated on the Cape Verde trip: the taste of salt on the cups after the washing-up, my Sabatier knife which had gone a bit rusty and left black marks on bread, cheese and fruit. One of the requirements I reckon for a good sailor is a 'strong' stomach (not in the seasickness sense but somebody who isn't put off when things get squalid). Mild inebriation from the port seems to help enormously; perhaps it just dulls the senses slightly.

Day 34: *Thursday, 29 September   Noon position 25° 09' S, 15° 22' W*
Day's run 190 miles   Course SSE   Wind ESE Force 6
Barometer 1026

John: Squalls of up to 50 knots kept the sails pretty small all day; and the boat was bumping up and down as if on a concrete road. We are heeled so far that the drinking water is leaking from the port leeward tank and out of the galley tap, which is below that tank's water level. This is a bit of a nuisance because drinking water is at a premium now. Plenty of sea water is also coming in through the after-hatch and down into the after-cabin. Everybody is bearing up well to the stress, and I must try and keep them all at ease with one another. Tony and Bob cause me the most worry.

Marie Christine: Heard of amazing developments on the chat show last night. *Great Britain II* had been becalmed all day but she said a westerly breeze was springing up. *Flyer* and *King's Legend* were within sight of each other; it could be a very exciting finish.

Our first albatross appeared in the sky today, its great wingspan hardly moving as it glided around the boat, mildly curious. Later we saw it feathering the water with its spread wing tips.

John and I collapsed into our bunk feeling sorry for ourselves and I found a hidden packet of surprisingly crisp gingersnaps, which we ate far too fast. Finished reading Arun's copy of Farley Mowat's *A Whale for the Killing*, the sad story of how man has nearly exterminated the whale population and the description of people slaughtering captive whales purely from blood lust. It mentions South Africa as a base for whaling, although it is most likely run by Norwegians. I hope I don't come across anyone involved. It would be hard to hide my feelings.

Day 35: *Friday, 30 September   Noon position 28° 00' S, 14° 36' W*
Day's run 180 miles   Course SSE   Wind ESE Force 5
Barometer 1027

Marie Christine: Another squally day with the boat heeled over and I feel quite sick. Will it ever pass?

Colin and Steve spent all morning working out our proposed route to Cape Town taking into account the northerly current that sweeps up the coast. We don't want to get becalmed just north of Cape Town, as the current will carry us northwards. We expect it to take fourteen days! Cape Town seems to be getting farther away, not closer. John is not too optimistic about our situation. The westerly boats are now making great strides. Have we decided on the best route? We are now heading south-south-east.

J.C. produced a delicious cheesecake for pudding tonight.

Day 36: *Saturday, 1 October   Noon position 28° 29' S, 12° 34' W*
Day's run 123 miles   Course SSE   Wind S Force 2
Barometer 1025

Marie Christine: It fell calm during the night. Great gloom over breakfast: it would seem we're right into the High! It's strange to dread the High like poison out here when at home we almost pray for one. Here a calm sunny day is depressing beyond words! It's hard luck on Steve and Colin, that following their suggested course we should have gone into this calm. John is really down-hearted. What a way to spend the winter – worrying constantly about our position with other boats. We both think our only chance on the next leg is to follow an unusual route and either come in first or really last.

How to avoid South Atlantic high?

Everybody is throwing off their clothes to get a bit more sun. We all look a very mouldy bunch now after ten days of jumpers and coats on – pale and peeling.

Interesting developments on tonight's chat show. We are now three degrees farther to the east and the wind is picking up a bit where *B & B Italia*, who is just south of us and where we were yesterday for longitude, is now quite becalmed. If only we could get a better weather forecast! *Great Britain II* is still not moving, *Flyer* and *King's Legend* have managed to keep going to the east. They should be in Cape Town soon. The chart on the wall in the saloon on which all our tracks are marked is gazed at like a crystal ball. We mark the weather in chinagraph on the perspex cover. We sat after supper for a long time with the torch on the chart trying to decide on everyone else's chances and on our tactics. It gets dark around about 7.30 and for some reason we have never fitted a light in the saloon.

Day 37: *Sunday, 2 October   Noon position 29° 20' S, 12° 00' W Day's run 95 miles   Course S by E   Wind SW Force 2 Barometer 1024*

Marie Christine: After breakfast and the usual discussion about lack of progress, the conversation turned to jobs to be done in Cape Town.

Both John and Arun had made lists and, comparing notes, it looked like a month's work. How long would we have in Cape Town, anyway?

Feeling well, I offered to help with any job planned for today. We decided it would be a good day to try to fix the leaks in the main saloon. All day like dervishes, Tony, Steve and I unscrewed the teak lining from the interior of the saloon and removed the ceiling till we had exposed the bolts and nuts which held in place battens outside, to which could be fastened the storm boards. Arun reckoned this was where the leaks were coming from. We worked hard at stripping these and rebedding them with a thick white gluey substance. Much to our surprise we got all twelve stainless steel battens off and rebedded by six that evening, also all the lining back in place. I even learnt that the screw heads should either line up with the grain of the wood or else face from fore to aft. The sun shone down and the boat was moving slowly. Arun worked away at the hatch cover he was building and Colin drilled a hole the size of a lemon through the deck, through which the chimney from our paraffin stove would go — we'll need it in the Southern Ocean.

After John and Arun had decided there was enough work for a month to be done in Cape Town, John, who still hadn't cheered up much said, 'Sod it, let's have a party tonight.' In our cabin John and I had twenty-four bottles of whisky which hadn't been touched. It was decided that we would celebrate with whisky and Steve would make some Atholl Brose. The party started with J.C. bringing on doorsteps of

Hot work for Arun and Colin in Doldrums as they make new hatch cover for Southern Ocean

ham and pineapple, asparagus, creamy potato into which had been added finely chopped raw onion and a tasty rice salad. We gorged ourselves. Then followed the potent Brose; added to toasted oats were two pounds of thin amber honey, half a bottle of Long John whisky and two tins of our precious cream. It tasted like nectar. Finally cheese and port. The whisky bottle circled the table and the conversation and singing got louder. We left the debris in the saloon and moved out into the chill starlit night. With guitar, accordion and mouth organ we sang all the songs any of us could think up. Punctuated with John's 'Another bottle of port?' we had, in Bob's words, 'a mighty 'andsome party'. Arun's seasickness overcame him and he lay in the skuppers retching over the side, but undeterred. His voice could be heard singing along with the chorus.

We finally turned in after midnight. The entry under 'fuel consumption' in the log book was six bottles of port and two bottles of whisky.

Day 38: *Monday, 3 October   Noon position 31° 30' S, 10° 46' W*
Day's run 195 miles   Course ESE   Wind SSW Force 5
Barometer 1018

Marie Christine: The wind got up in the night and we scudded along. I woke with a pain in my belly which persisted all morning and finally shifted by mid-afternoon after three paracetamols. John was most attentive and kind. There was nothing he could do but it was a great comfort having his sympathy.

I put on my waterproofs and went on deck. It's really quite cold and windy now. We have in our wake quite a collection of birds; stormy petrels; a slightly larger bird, which I think is a Cape Pigeon, but Dick christened the Zebra because of its distinctive black and white striped wings; a larger black bird; and the even bigger, mighty albatross.

Some of the boats ahead had been hit by sudden stormy weather. *Gauloises* had suffered a broken spinnaker pole. *Tielsa* had a spinnaker blown out. *Great Britain II* had been broached and had lain on her side for three minutes with the mast's spreaders in the water! Luckily none of the three boats had suffered anything worse, but we took it as a good warning that at all times life harnesses must be worn on deck. I can't help but wonder what would have happened if this had hit us last night during our party on deck. The weather is a mixture down here in the South Atlantic of cold fronts, highs, and depressions. *Treaty of Rome* and *Adventure*, who are north-east of us, are becalmed. We are shooting along and the boats ahead of us even have too much wind! *King's Legend* and *Flyer* are within sight of each other and they have no wind. They haven't far to go now. How frustrating for them!

Day 39: *Tuesday, 4 October   Noon position 31° 55' S, 7° 12' W*
Day's run 165 miles   Course E by S   Wind S by W Force 3
Barometer 1020

John: The glass rose during the day as the depression moved ahead of
us. The sky cleared and I was able to get a fix at noon which confirmed
my dead reckoning that we were going well to the east, straight towards
Cape Town. But in the afternoon the wind died and soon we were
putting up the rickety radial-head in force 2 to 3 from the south-west.

Positions in the evening radio show were pretty comprehensive, and,
all things considered, we're well-placed and should get some time in
Cape Town to effect repairs and prepare adequately before the next leg.

I was called by Arun at 10.30 on a black moonless evening to help
with a change of the radial-head down to the storm spinnaker, as he
could see a squall coming up from astern. I wasn't really wide awake
when I took the wheel over from Dick and he passed it to me very
quickly – just as the boat began to broach on a big quartering swell.

'Helm to port, John. Helm to port,' I heard Bob bellowing from the
forward cockpit as the precious radial-head spinnaker thrashed in the
broach.

'The mast's coming down. The mast's coming down,' Marie Christine thought she heard Dick cry from her bunk down in our cabin, as she
made her way rapidly towards her life-jacket.

With more than a little difficulty we got the sail down as the squall hit
us; and it took both Arun's and Bob's watches, plus John Covington
and me on deck. And there was a hole big enough to walk through in the
sail as it came down. We still made 7½ knots with only the main up, and
it was back to 10 to 12 knots again as soon as the Ratsey storm
spinnaker was set.

The clocks were put forward at 11.30 in the evening and we all felt a
bit apprehensive about the weather. Bob took the helm, and I urged a
discussion on the next steps to be taken if the wind increased further.
The next squall was not far astern.

Marie Christine: Still scudding along with a good wind and in the
right direction. Steve and Colin's route, taking currents into account, is
certainly paying off now we are on a route heading slightly to the south
of Cape Town and the boat is going well.

John and I both feel sick. It is just something we have to be resigned
to. We lie in our bunk thinking a lot about home. Johnny keeps
describing a vision of a winter breakfast in the kitchen: snow flakes
whirling outside the window, Pussy sitting on the sill miaowing silently
to get in for her share of the warm stove, a full sack of peat standing close
by; the copper pipes cracking with the heat of the water, and me putting
on the clean tablecloth, plates of crisped black pudding and soft fried

eggs; hot mugs of tea and home-made bread and marmalade. And then a sleepy Becca shuffling down the stairs in her slippers and dressing gown, lifting up the sleeping cat and sitting silently at the table with thumb in mouth and cat in arms. Planning the day ahead: a walk to Loch Dughail for driftwood, or, if the snow settles, tobogganing down the steep hill to the shore just outside our gate ...

But it's Tuesday, 4 October 1977 and John and I are somewhere in the South Atlantic, seven thousand miles from home. Becca has flown from the nest and away to boarding school. It's the present, not past nor future that matters. Will John and I ever be rid of the restlessness that drives us away from home to travel, endure, struggle and survive? No sooner are we away and committed than we want above all else to be home again. I've said it before (and I hope I won't have cause to in the future): 'Never again'.

Day 40: *Wednesday, 5 October　Noon position 32° 38' S, 3° 48' W*
Day's run 189 miles　Course ESE　Wind W by S Force 6
Barometer 1022

John: The decision was made for us about what to do if the wind increased, because somewhere up in the darkness on the foredeck there was a great crack and the storm spinnaker broke loose.

'Guy-stop's gone,' shouted Bob, and everyone started squirming about the heaving decks. I hung between the mizzen mast backstays, just behind Bob, at the wheel, trying to make out exactly what the situation was.

'The pole is still attached to the spinnaker,' I said to Bob. 'It must have been the wire guy itself that parted.'

'Better hope the forestay doesn't go too with all that banging,' he warned gruffly, handing the wheel over to me.

Torches flashed, and the job of getting the storm spinnaker down was soon done. Arun's watch set about stopping up the sail again into its bag ready for re-hoisting while Bob's team reefed the main.

At around two that morning the storm spinnaker was flown again, breaking two of the guard-rail stanchions with the new rope guy in the process. The speed was on again, and we should have dropped the main at that point, I think.

Everyone was in a state of some shock that the wire had broken. We'd never had any trouble with it before. Suddenly, people were only too much aware of the power the sail exerted in the cold, dark night. I handed the wheel back to Bob, and J.C. started making coffee for the other watch. I went down below, and I'd just got my oilskins off in the saloon when there was another great BANG.

'Guy's gone again,' J.C. said quietly from the cooker, and we quickly donned our oilskins once more.

This time the cry was that the strop at the end of the spinnaker pole had gone. 'I think we should abandon spinnaker practice until daylight,' smiled J.C., and I nodded wearily as I made my way up the steps and through the main hatch out into the darkness. We got the spinnaker down again, and everyone but Bob's watch made their various ways to bed. It was after three o'clock by this time. Tony's watch let Arun's team have a lie-in at breakfast, but I decided that we should stick to watch timings in future to preserve a routine in the long periods of bad weather to come on the next leg. Tony accepted this without good grace.

The day rolled past under double-reefed main, No. 2 yankee and No. 2 staysail. Everyone was pleased with the progress we were making towards Cape Town.

But on the evening radio chat show I started off with, 'Hullo, *Treaty of Rome, Treaty of Rome, Treaty of Rome* – this is *Debenhams, Debenhams*. Do you read me? Over.' There was no reply. Nothing. We no longer had communications. Maybe it was because the aerial on the backstay was broken by the strain exerted on the forestay in the spinnaker shenanigans of the previous night. Having no radio gave me a very lonely feeling.

Day 41: *Thursday, 6 October   Noon position 33° 12' S, 00° 04' W*
Day's run 185 miles   Course ESE   Wind S by W Force 4
Barometer 1031

Marie Christine: Stormy night. Wind lessened and so did our progress during the day. Made great efforts to join in and forget the seasickness. It worked up to a point. Mended Dick's split jeans – he thinks he's no longer a 30-inch waist. I would agree, having now mended both his trousers and shorts. Peter made efforts to fix the radio but nothing worked, so I wonder what the other boats will put our silence down to.

Creeping towards Cape Town, we have today crossed the Greenwich Meridian – only a few more days to go and then, no seasickness, baths, clean clothes, fruit, letters from home! That's my order of preference. The fellas still rave on about pints of lager and bitter which I wouldn't even consider.

I went outside for a blink of sunshine, and saw many various and beautiful birds all around us. It is very cold now and I came in chilled. John has quite a cold – although where can he have got it from? He was quite amazed when I suggested it wasn't possible in this sterile, salt laden air. Maybe it's the feathers from the sleeping-bag we're now using. John is allergic to birds. He's never come across it before, but then we're using them in such a confined space.

I got some jam out from under the floorboards in our cabin and was disgusted to see everything down there awash in oily paraffin water. Fortunately we've only stowed bottles and jars there so they won't come to any harm. But I'm collecting the paper gollies off the back of the jars for a brooch for Becca. The last two will be rejected by Robertson's for health reasons. They look evil. There is much water still in the heads, which swirls around when we're heeled over and splashes right up to under the wash hand basin. I have always to put my boots on to go in there now. The only other shoes I have are pretty sodden gym shoes which caught a generous dollop of sea water through our open window the other night!

Day 42: *Friday, 7 October   Noon position 34° 03' S, 3° 12' E*
Day's run 165 miles   Course ESE   Wind WSW Force 4
Barometer 1029

Marie Christine: After a fairly flat night I felt rather well for a change, so I gave the table a good scrub and sorted out our room. What a difference it makes, feeling well!

Played Scrabble with the usual team of John, Colin and Tony. John won. Then a second match with just me, Colin and Steve, which I won. John and I are quite childish in the delight we take in winning. Perhaps that's the missing element in this trip – might be altogether different if we were in the lead!

Still radio silence. I expect *Great Britain II* will be in by now. We're eating up the miles. Peter excelled himself making pancakes for us all after supper until very late. Arun and Dick did well up on watch – pancakes kept on coming up through the after-hatch.

Day 43: *Saturday, 8 October   Noon position 34° 58' S, 6° 47' E*
Day's run 174 miles   Course E by S   Wind NW Force 5
Barometer 1020

John: A stormy night. The squalls beat us. First the storm spinnaker strop goes and we got it up again only after much struggle. In the early morning Tony broached the boat and we had to let the sheet go, and then they couldn't get it in again in the squall – so the spinnaker had to be dropped. We got it in okay under bare poles, and this was one of our bogies laid, for we had feared that it might not be possible to do it without the mainsail to blanket it.

I was unhappy about the 'mental plonk' attitude aboard the boat.

Everybody talks of Cape Town but still we're many hundreds of miles away. The squalls will not beat us.

Peter had a row with Tony up on the foredeck about the cleanliness of his watch compared with that of the other watches. Tony can't be bothered to wash down the cockpits and decks when his watch is on before breakfast. Peter told him he would give him a hard time at Ardmore next summer when their roles were reversed and Tony was running the show again.

We had the Ratsey storm spinnaker up in the morning, and the tape which secures the head-ring to the swivel parted right up at the mast head. This was another bogey of ours because the spinnaker then lay like a great red, white and blue carpet on the water dead ahead of the boat — and the danger is that you run over it. Anyway, I was at the helm at the time and managed to steer to windward a bit, and we pulled it in from the stern, so there was no damage done. I organized a hot toddy for all, after a brief plan of action given outside in a bright sunlight. Cleanliness is the key word to try to improve the stagnant mental attitude that we have.

Will she broach? Pete watches the speedo

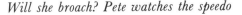

In the evening we passed many strips of bright luminescence on the surface of the sea. I think that perhaps these are squid which sometimes are left stranded on the deck by big waves.

I was up twice in the night for spinnaker gybes and guy trouble. Come the dawn we had a 30–40 knot wind and we were under the No. 2 yankee and No. 2 staysail with the main double-reefed, but everybody was cheerful.

Marie Christine: Quite rough in the night – heeled right over at one stage, enough for water to come through our window and that wasn't from a splash over the coach roof! It tipped Noel right out of his bunk and Bob fell on to his gear, bursting his 'frou-frou' as he calls it, leaving a cloud of talcum powder descending over the swamp and occupants.

Up on deck the sun was shining and quite a big sea running. Saw a sperm whale (I think). It surfaced very close to the boat but we were able to see it following us as it swam through the following waves. A magnificent sight.

Everybody is in good spirits, although there were some sharp words exchanged up in the bow between Peter and Tony. It can't have been very serious as it had blown over by lunchtime.

Six weeks out from Portsmouth; I have lost my bet of forty-two days to Cape Town. We expect to be in by Wednesday. Just starting my fifteenth book, *Lord of the Rings* – wish I had Becca to read it to. Celebratory cheesecake for pudding was delicious. Weather now very squally.

Day 44: *Sunday, 9 October   Noon position 34° 55' S, 10° 06' E*
          Day's run 185 miles   Course E by S   Wind SSW Force 6
          Barometer 1015

John: The wind got up and up during the day and by six in the evening we had 45-knot gusts from the south, and a building sea. This was just the time for some practical experience with the trysail which goes up on its own track in place of the mainsail in extreme conditions. J.C. at the wheel had the speedometer needle jammed up against 15 knots on the end of the dial. Down in the saloon this motion felt as if we were riding a toboggan down the Cresta Run. Spray obscured our windows in a good imitation of snow. I took over the helm while they were rigging up the trysail with a No. 3 yankee and No. 2 staysail. Out of the corner of my eye over my left shoulder I suddenly noticed that the sun had gone out. A large wave was poised to break right over our stern. Some excitement ...

During the night there was much bumping, and I was worried about unnecessary damage, but just as I got up to discuss the need to run off the wind a bit, the wind began to ease.

With the dawn we were back up to full mainsail and No. 1 yankee. The crew are in fine form, and I'm well pleased with the sailing efforts of the TV crew, Noel and Roger. They go well with Bob to make up F troop; and their maturity is an asset which nicely balances the youth of the instructors.

Day 45: *Monday, 10 October   Noon position 34° 38' S, 13° 22' E*
Day's run 185 miles   Course E by S   Wind SW Force 6
Barometer 1020

Marie Christine: The gale lessened in the night, so we put up more sail. Cape Town is all we can think of now. At noon sight there were 260 miles to go. Bob says 'F' troop is suffering from Channel Fever – an old Navy term for the excitement of nearing home as ships come up the English Channel. John produced the outrageous idea that he wouldn't mind missing Cape Town and going straight on to Auckland. It was met with much booing and hissing.

Blue rain-washed sky and spring sun helped us further on our way. Quizzes and Scrabble (with Tony winning today) took up the afternoon.

The wind lessened all day; we really don't want a calm now. But there is still quite a sea running. One large wave sneaked into the aft cockpit and just caught Arun, who was coming out of the aft hatch. He was soaked. A fair dollop of water went into the aft cabin, wetting J.C.'s sleeping-bag amongst other things. Water is again swirling around under the floor in our heads. Arun found what was wrong with the pump and fixed it – most of the bilge water has been pumped out at last. Went to bed feeling excited.

Day 46: *Tuesday, 11 October   Noon position 34° 22' S, 17° 18' E*
Day's run ?   Course E   Wind W Force 4–6
Barometer 1025

John: In the early hours we set the storm spinnaker and then the noon sight put us exactly in position for the classic southerly approach to Cape Town; so we gybed to the starcut spinnaker and raced for the blue line of the African continent.

After forty-five days at sea it is unforgettable. The grey days faded and I'm left with a magical moment of finding the right spot.

We crossed the line just after ten in the evening, and I was really touched by the sincerity of the welcome from the crews of the other boats who were already here – each with some fairly hair-raising tales to tell. There are four more boats still to come, and we're all looking forward to the Southern Ocean, and the magic moments that will certainly come in between here and Auckland.

Marie Christine: A spanking wind keeps us going. I feel great today, could do anything. There is a festive air about the ship. J.C.'s secret cache of beer was brought out to have with the celebration lunch of fried hamburgers, tinned tomatoes, mash and peas. 'You could imagine eating this in a café in Manchester,' interjected John just as we were raving about the delicious food in front of us. Fortunately J.C. the creator didn't hear. It is funny how something different tastes *so* good. The Batchelors food has been excellent. The beer came up from the bilges in the galley and was coated in a filthy paraffin-water mixture.

The high spirits seemed to fail somewhat in the afternoon. Colin and Steven began to regret the ending of the routine which had become our life of the last six weeks, unanxious for contact with the outside world again. In many ways a spell in port could be most upsetting to the harmony which we had succeeded in creating between the twelve of us. There was bound to be over-eating, over-drinking, bad heads, bad stomachs. Some able to spend more than others, groups going out of an evening inadvertently leaving somebody out. For myself, I could only feel excited.

John sighted land at 1.25 p.m. and won the Galaxy chocolate bar offered as a prize. At 10.04 in the evening we crossed the finishing line marked by two amber blinking lights. Sirens hooted, a green flare was shot into the inky sky by some watchers ashore. We had come 7,367 miles from Portsmouth in forty-six days. The first leg was over. A yacht club launch came smartly out to lead us safely to our moorings. As we approached our berth we warmed to the sound of cheering, motor car horns, klaxons, anything that made a big enough sound. John started singing, 'All are safely gathered in', thinking we were the last boat of the fleet to make South Africa and that this was the reason for the big reception. But no – we learned from Admiral Steiner who leapt aboard to welcome us that there were still four more to come after us. Bottles of champagne were thrust up at us from a sea of faces on the catwalk. The party had started! A blissful shower, clean clothes that hang loose on me now. Letters from home – all these dreamed of treats piling on top of us – for these alone I'm glad we did it.

5

Cape Town Interlude

John: It was close to midnight when we were finally secured to one side of a pontoon which stuck out from the frontage of the Royal Cape Yacht Club; the vacant other side awaited the next boat in. We were all pleasantly surprised at the warmth of the welcome, particularly as it was so late. Admiral Otto Steiner, Chairman of the Race Committee, and John Fox of Whitbread, brought champagne and beer. Bernard Deguy, skipper of the French yacht *Neptune*, brought a bottle of wine, to return one I had sent to his table in a Portsmouth restaurant on the eve of the race. The extrovert members of our crew, Bob, J.C. and Steve, quickly led the others into an all-night fandango.

Next thing I know I am sitting in our darkened saloon (we have no light fitted yet) and *Treaty of Rome* comes in to take the berth on the other side of our pontoon. The whole of our crew is well oiled by this stage and, led by Steve with the gas foghorn, mouth trumpet and Tannoy loud-hailer, they set to in earnest to give the smallest boat in the fleet, the Common Market entry, the biggest possible welcome. I always feel foolishly embarrassed at this sort of carry-on and tend to hold back on the booze in case of a crisis. The saloon, indeed the whole boat, quickly filled up with wildly cheerful, drunken people bent on having the time of their lives. Cigarette ends and matches were everywhere, the gas blowlamp was aimed erratically at the Tilley lamp, bottles and glasses spilled, people gabbled nonsense in some languages I understood and others I couldn't comprehend. Another skipper, nearly paralytic, sobbed his heart out to me, trying to justify his poor performance on the first leg which had almost ruled out his boat's chance of winning the race over-all. My own spirits declined with the reaction to forty-six long, long days, and the knowledge that we had only completed an easy quarter of the course, with the serious stuff coming up next.

Next morning, picking my way through the debris of the night before, I felt depressed. We were eleventh out of fifteen; the three boats still out couldn't beat us. It could have been worse; if we'd been independent I wouldn't have cared – after all we were just trying to sail round the world in time for the start of the next season at Ardmore. But we weren't independent; I had taken money from Debenhams, ATV and Heinemann, and reassure me though they might I knew they would have preferred me to do better. I knew the boat was no racer, that no one in the fleet had thought we would do better. But still I wished we *had* done better and I allowed it to depress me. There had been no let-up for a long time and not much respite in sight either. My depression affected the crew; they were young and inexperienced and had each without exception in his own way tried his hardest. It was unforgivable that I should depress them – but I did, there is no escaping the blame.

The crew's reaction to the long forty-six days at sea was mixed and the results unexpected. Bob and J.C., faithfully followed by Dick, set off on a drinking rampage which depleted their funds and left them unfit for urgent work on the boat for several days. J.C. didn't achieve anything very effective on board during the whole fortnight in Cape Town and this was not well received by the hard-working younger members.

Peter, the mate, was met by his fiancée Penny, who had flown out to meet him in Cape Town – a perfectly reasonable and pleasant plan, as everyone would have agreed at sea; but it had the unfortunate effect of isolating him from the crew when he moved off the boat to stay in an apartment. As mate, and being Tasmanian, he was already a little apart from the rest, and also only J.C. had been less well known to everyone at the start.

'Y'know, I thought I was taken on as an ordinary foredeck hand,' he told me earnestly, over a cup of coffee in a quiet corner of the yacht club one afternoon. 'I just want to enjoy the trip and be one of the crew, I don't want all the hassle of being unpopular – getting Tony and Dick and so on to do things they don't want to do – I don't enjoy it at all.' I sympathized with him. Why should he? We didn't really need a mate and if he didn't want to be one that was just fine. I could handle the job myself. Making unpopular decisions was not new to me. We agreed quietly to drop the role of mate on the next leg.

Arun, subdued as ever, waded into the long list of jobs he had left for Cape Town just as soon as he landed. At sea he was chaffed by the other watch-leaders, Tony and Bob, for being too timid and un-racing with his sail changes. He stoically endured continual seasickness, but was some distance apart from the rest of the crew in a philosophical sense, as he felt the thoughtless destruction of a craftsman's work at sails, rigging, etc. in a race to be a crime. Also he abhorred living in a noisy crowd. Although five years younger, he had won Peter's respect. At first the Tasmanian told me he doubted if he would be able to serve under him without occasional outbursts, but Arun's range and depth of thinking was always quietly portrayed in his neat effective command of the boat. He never showed a flicker of concern for his position as a coloured man ashore, although the ill-concealed contempt of some of our hosts towards him enraged the rest of the crew.

Roger and Noel clung together like limpets. Roger was always silently concerned about the present and future of his film. Unwilling to communicate with me, he was grappling alone with the problems of making a film about leadership without any experience of the subject. Noel, older and much more experienced, was a great support for him; he kept all conversation at a very shallow level, giving nothing away about himself. I felt they made an error of judgment in siding strongly with their watch-leader, Bob, who at thirty-seven was a well-formed 'character' for the film. In so doing they isolated themselves from the other younger watches. The total age in Bob's watch was ninety-eight, in Arun's seventy-five and Tony's seventy-three. Those extra twenty-three years of experience I felt could have been put to a wiser use than the 'F troop rules OK' T-shirts they had made in Cape Town. At a stroke it made Roger's view of the film subjective rather than objective. The ATV film crew were able to arrange hotel accommodation and hire a car. This glamorous expense-account living was powerful medicine to the younger, more impressionable – and skint – members of the crew. It was ATV, not the skipper, which took the crew out to dinner.

Bob's descent into silence when below decks towards the end of the first leg boded ill for the future. His open dislike of the precocious Tony, contempt for Arun's timid watch-leading, and a smouldering resentment towards me, carried over from our dispute in the spring, set F troop apart in the boat.

The individual watches were well formed; the crew were surprised to discover that even after forty-six days on fifty-seven feet they still preferred each other's company ashore. Only J.C. really wandered off on his own in an alcoholic haze, and most people were able to recognize his worth at sea. Individuals sympathized with his problems and felt grateful they were not in his moccasins, particularly when at his most maudlin he would recount the turmoil of his past.

The facility of STD dialling on the phone to loved ones at home in the UK proved a snare. It was impossible to speak without a mental picture of twenty-pence pieces falling into a black pit like a shower of Smarties. Tony and Colin, even Noel, suffered severe blows to their morale, when the hitherto secure relationships with girlfriends showed signs of strain under the 'How are you?', 'What did you say?', 'Well, this is a very expensive call' routine.

Colin had been quiet on the voyage. Like his close friend Arun, he had missed the final briefing from me and Richard Creasey, the ATV producer, at the croft on the night before we left Ardmore. I had not had time to go through it all again with them. The boat allowed nowhere for a private conversation, and I felt Colin was unsure of what it was all about. I really didn't know him very well and I wasn't much the wiser by Cape Town. Able and thoughtful, he was not sufficiently stretched as an ordinary crew member and I expected him to underline his presence on the next leg. In his case the phone problems were serious as he had planned to marry his fiancée, a recent graduate of the Royal College of Art, on 17 December 1977, but had postponed the wedding to come on the circumnavigation.

Tony had a difficult position for a twenty-three-year-old who had scarcely left Britain before. He was the second youngest on the boat and had grown into his position as chief instructor at Ardmore. Experienced and well qualified in the various activities, he had met thirty-seven-year-old Bob's eccentricities with a stone wall, and there had been a collision of wills, causing wounds which had never healed. He was possessed of great energy and was a driver of his watch, preferring the bald-headed offensive to diplomacy in his dealings with people. Tony broke things . . . a lot of things. The cost of his education had been met by the State; material things were expendable – to be replaced by 'others' as required. Unfortunately I filled the category of 'others' in our present relationship and Tony was by far the most expensive instructor I'd ever had. Now he had moved into an arena where damage was financially crippling, and this placed a severe strain on our relationship – not for nothing was his watch nicknamed 'Dallimore's Disasters' and 'Doomwatch' by the sailmender, Bob. Steve and Colin were an important couple of years older than their watch-leader and in most things they were a shade too experienced for him. He found they could trip him up, whether it was spelling at Scrabble, sailing theory, navigation or whatever; so Tony retreated into a ferocious silence, seldom entering discussions and avoiding the televised meetings like the plague. Overt rebellion was only expressed in a refusal to carry out maintenance tasks required by Peter as mate, and marked reluctance to have the decks washed down when his watch was on duty just before breakfast. A watch-leader's position was priceless experience for Tony, but for me it was going to be just an added burden. While he never shirked hard work and drove his watch hard I wondered how long it would be before he matured sufficiently to realize that as watch-leader a good part of his energy could usefully be deployed in leadership aimed at achieving the over-all success of the circumnavigation. Loyalty and morale, strategy rather than tactics – only Arun seemed to grasp those principles. Bob was a disappointment, but then it was I who had given him a second chance. Perhaps I should have spent longer looking for more experienced watch-leaders.

Steve had made his presence felt. In spite of seasickness he never shirked work on the foredeck. A naturally cheerful fellow with an engaging manner, he absorbed each new experience like a sponge; navigation took only a text book and a couple of days to master and he let no one doubt his ability as the medic. Some of us felt his loud voice was talking to us as if he were still the teacher and we the pupils, but nevertheless he was always willing to discuss any subject with wit and sympathy. Perhaps the most positive sign of his stability was that he appeared perfectly content with his role on the boat; he was not one of those who felt they must prove they worked harder or were smarter than the watch-leader or could do much better than the skipper.

The cook's job is not a happy one on an extended voyage with limited ingredients and facilities. Some boats had deep freezes and exotic foods; our basic ration was the range of Batchelor's Catering Supplies. J.C. wanted to come on the trip so badly that he offered to be the cook, knowing that was the only way he could get on the boat. His behaviour on our arrival at Hamble from Ardmore had been a demonstration of his wish to get off the boat after only a few days cooking. I kept him on, against the advice of others who were surprised at my decision, not for his own good but because I didn't think last-minute changes a good thing. J.C. had cooked for forty-six days without a break on the way to Cape Town, and none of us could complain about his efforts – from my angle he could behave as he liked in port so long as he cooked every day to Auckland. That was our arrangement. He suffered by not being in a watch because he lacked the comfort of being a part of one of the three-man teams. The younger fellows mocked his shortcomings and 'F' troop sometimes put him down cruelly, so it was natural that on our arrival in port he should look for friends on the other boats. He was not long in finding them, either. Quite soon, to my alarm, J.C. became one of the most popular characters in the fleet, and I found myself scurrying for cover if I saw his great bulk weaving towards me along the quay, in often not the smartest of gear.

The youngest was Dick. Easy-going and friendly, he was still unsure of himself after the unpleasant incidents with the engine-parts debt-collector back in Portsmouth and nearly getting hanged by the spin-naker halyard. In two seasons at Ardmore he had shown himself to be happier with people than the irksome business of 'work' on the main-tenance side of things, so I did not expect to find him one of those who look for jobs to be done; he was good at being told what to do, like the winches and engine, which were his specific duties, and being left alone to keep them in good order. I was sorry to see that Dick shied away from any discussion with the university graduates, preferring the company of Bob whom he jokingly referred to as his uncle, but who had not had the benefit of Dick's expensive education. I rather feared his father might feel that I had led the boy astray.

For me the most alarming aspect of our two weeks in Cape Town was the terrific expense most of the yachts went to in repairing and renewing their gear for the next leg. It seemed crazy to fly riggers out from Europe just to check the tension of wires supporting a mast. The number of new spinnakers appearing to replace those destroyed on the voyage from Portsmouth made me wonder how we would ever get right round the world without buying more sails.

As for the entertainment in Cape Town ... well, I'll leave Marie Christine to describe that side of things.

Marie Christine: Our first night of the two weeks in Cape Town set the style with a party on our boat that continued most of the night, leaving me with a two-day hangover. Bob and J.C. had eyes like road maps at breakfast; it had been a long spell of abstinence for them and they were both going to make up for it.

Our fantasies of steak and cool lagers soon became reality. One famous night at Walter's Grill, Steve ordered the largest steak they had. When it arrived – a giant of well over three pounds – he couldn't believe his eyes. He ate as much as he could, wrapped up what was left and four of them ate it for breakfast the following morning.

Our main problem was which of the several invitations each evening to accept. Each boat had been adopted by one of the Rotary Clubs. Ours was the Fishoek Branch. Bill and Grace Edgecombe took us all out to the Cape of Good Hope Nature Reserve – perhaps the highlight of our stay. This peninsula full of wild life – like baboons, springbok, and ostriches – was a fine contrast with the grey ocean which had been our world for so long. Gerald Wright, the enthusiastic chief game warden who showed us round, took us all back to his home for a *braai*, a South African barbecue. While fires were being lit and meat cooked he showed us round his own unusual menagerie: a graceful lynx who made a deep, guttural purr as she circled and rubbed against me; a pair of guinea fowl, Hopalong and Cassidy (the former had only one leg, thought he was human and spent most of his life sitting on the centre of a revolving clothes line); and a beautiful bat-eared fox which slept at the foot of the Wrights' bed each night. I watched the mainly insect-eating fox raise one paw as if pointing and turn its huge ears to the ground, catching the minute sounds of insect life, then stab with its sharp muzzle at the grass for a tasty morsel. The weaver birds were busy building their swinging nests in the high trees behind the house, for this was spring in southern Africa.

We had much to do on the boat, so days were spent, especially by Arun and Colin, adapting, adding, and reinforcing. It was hot; the south-easterly wind would get up mid-morning and blow with great strength till late evening, carrying with it blankets of grit and soot from the picturesque steam engines which serviced the docks.

For the first week a dark cloud hung over the fleet of twelve boats now in. Radio contact had been made with *Japy Hermès*, which had been delayed by putting a sick man off at Recife, also with *Condor* which had been to Monrovia for her new mast. Reports were coming in daily about the dysentery which had hit them and how they were down to only two able men. But nothing had been heard from *33 Export* for at least three weeks. Officials were trying hard not to look worried but word reached us when the first of the two Shackletons flew out to look for the sleek, yellow-hulled boat from which during the last race her skipper, Dominique Guillet, had been washed overboard and lost. Was this an unlucky boat? So much superstition still surrounds the sea and boats. We didn't dare speak of it but I think we all thought the same. The following day she was officially posted 'missing'. *33 Export*'s back-up team had been waiting at the yacht club for a few days; even the fiancée of Alain Gabbay the skipper was waiting. Then on Sunday, 16 October at a party given for us we were telephoned with the good news that she had slipped in quietly. *Condor* and *Japy* also arrived that night. We were all in.

The crews from the three last boats were in good shape. From what we'd heard I'd expected to see a fleet of ambulances and stretchers taking off *Condor*'s crew but their problems had been sorted out by their ship's doctor. We all had a lot to tell each other. It was good to see the faces behind the voices which we had got to know well on the chat show, to see where they broadcast from and the general layout of the other boats. Barriers of suspicion were down and we were all friends, eager to help each other, feeling so much in common.

The relief from seasickness was constantly on my mind. I felt so well again on land that when I met a man who thought he could help to cure us I wanted to know more.

Dr Roy MacCallum had been one of the best Springbok scrum-halfs of recent times. He had interrupted his playing by going to America to study chiropractic, a philosophy and science which comprises a system of manipulating the segments of the spinal column for correcting the cause of disease. John and I agreed to have four sessions with him and the next day we made our way to his surgery out in the suburbs.

I nervously didn't know what to expect; John, having been to an osteopath, thought the treatment would be similar. We waited our turn in the small room adjoining his surgery, until the door opened and Roy ushered us in.

John first. He leant his chest on an upright, sectioned, cushioned board which Roy lowered till John was horizontal, arms hanging down limply either side. After asking him to relax absolutely, Roy set to work manipulating his vertebrae. As he worked down his back he pushed a foot pedal which brought up a section of the board and raised a particular part of John's back. It sounded awful when twice Roy pressed a certain spot and a cracking sound came from John's ribs. John lay there limp. I felt sure there would be some indication from him if it was hurting.

After working up and down for a few minutes he finished by twisting John's head sharply to left and right, again with an alarming cracking sound. John just lay, not moving ... and for one terrible moment I wondered if this tough scrum-half had killed my husband in front of my very eyes. But John got up slowly from the bed and it was my turn. I felt as though I were going to the guillotine but Roy's gentle but firm hands helped me relax and I made great efforts to quell the panic when he exerted pressure and caused the cracking sounds that had so alarmed me when I watched John. I must be mad or desperate to subject myself to this. Is the seasickness really so bad? Then we were out in the waiting-room making a further appointment with Roy's energetic Scots father, who must have told the waiting patients who we were, for as we left they wished us good luck.

We walked shakily to the near-by station to catch a train for Cape Town. Roy had warned us that for an unfit person the effects of a first treatment could be similar to being hit by a bus. John and I felt terribly unfit. At Ardmore we try to run three miles each morning usually before breakfast, and had missed this therapy at sea. We felt overweight after a week of gluttony in Cape Town and out of sorts. Later on in the day John's back began to hurt really badly. Should we go on with the treatment? We decided we would and in all had four sessions which Roy very kindly did for free. Each time we felt easier and more relaxed until John's aches and pains disappeared completely. But would it cure the seasickness?

The days in Cape Town were passing quickly; life for us twelve had fallen into a pattern.

Peter had his love, Penny, who had flown out from England to resume a theatre nursing job she had held a few years ago. It all worked out well and the second evening in she invited us all out to dinner, a gargantuan feast cooked by herself and her friend Sandie. Penny was always ready to help with any problems any of us had and before we left presented us with armfuls of cakes and biscuits.

Bob and J.C. were quite keen to make up for lost time on the drinking and struck up firm friendships with the people in the bar at the yacht club. Bob had plenty to get on with in the way of sail mending and attending to the rigging and would be back after the midday session but

J.C. more often than not was nowhere to be seen. He made a great number of friends, including a charming English lady who took him completely under her wing for the last three days. During that time whenever we saw him he had a beatific smile on his big face.

Colin, Arun, the loquacious Steve and Tony made a number of girl-friends. The worry was who and how many were going to turn up for the final farewell. Two admirers of Steve and Colin's did appear on the morning of the start, weighted down with a cool bag full of bottles of champagne and ice. The swains were amazed by the gesture, particularly as they admitted to having only treated the girls to a cup of tea. Such is the glamour of a round-the-world sailor!

Roger and Noel became quite urbane again. They hired a bus, drank, ate and smoked as though each were going out of style, swooned over the good-looking Cape Town girls and wondered what film-making had to do with going to sea.

Dickie had a rich aunt whom we had all joked about before arriving in Cape Town, till Dick got quite cross. However, she turned out to be a 'good sport', according to Dick, and took him out from time to time. The rest of his time was spent eating steaks and in the bar with his old pal, Bob. He became a hero amongst the rest of the racers for punching the nose of a journalist who had gone too far, from Dick's point of view, with gossipy remarks about John.

We all benefited from the spell on dry land except John, who got a cold and felt depressed. What was cheering was that the crew preferred to spend their evenings with each other. The six weeks from Portsmouth to Cape Town had not been too great a test of our friendship. We still liked each other.

6

Leg Two – Cape Town to Auckland

Marie Christine: The starting gun fired for the third and final time and three seconds later we shot over the line. A gambled racing start and we were first over the line on our voyage to Auckland *via* the Southern Ocean, the icebergs and storms lying in wait for us. Racing tactics came into full play as a knot of boats sped towards us. 'Hold your course, John,' yelled Tony as the giant *King's Legend* tore straight at us. It was our right-of-way ... but surely they won't slice us in two? With seconds to spare they altered course and squeezed through the closing gap between ourselves and *ADC*. 'Mad Dog' from Georgia up on the bow as lookout shouted with his well-known loud voice: 'We're Americans,' whilst the cool, blond Hans Savimaki at the wheel made a rude but friendly sign as they passed within feet of us. We were on our way again, our boat once more alive and we ourselves a close-knit team with a common aim.

In a mood of elation we kept our lead down the spectacular coast. We wondered at what looked like a calm patch close in and thought of tacking farther out. 'We'll keep on course – it's an oil slick from one of the wrecked tankers up on the shore,' shouted John. Two tankers had gone aground close to each other one stormy night during the winter. They were being towed to Japan for scrap by a Japanese tug, by a very thin rope for the job which broke in a heavy swell. They had become quite a tourist attraction and we'd also been out to view these two craft laid up on the rocks like stranded whales.

J.C. was busy trimming sails at this crucial time, so hearing murmurs about food I went below to see what I could find. I felt this was my first test. If I survived the sickening effect of the galley within the first few hours of being at sea it could mean a 'cure'. Within a short while I'd passed up twelve bowls of coleslaw given us by Grace Edgecombe, slices of luncheon meat and chunks of good home-made bread spread with the last of our Cater's butter from Portsmouth. I came up with my own bowl, feeling fine – perhaps the excitement of the start had

JR riding the chariot out of Table Bay
while Tom Woodfield looks on

banished seasickness from mind, then back down again for our favourite pudding ashore which Sandie Lillington had again kindly made for us, generous wedges of banana and caramel in a biscuit crumb base, covered thickly with cream. I still felt fine. We sailed on, passing the Sangkop Light, upon which the rollers remorselessly broke, shooting plumes of spray high into the air. 'Steer to starboard, John, there's something coming up in the water,' shouted Steve from the bow. 'Don't worry, that's a basking seal,' yelled back Peter. 'It'll move.' Instead of one flipper and a fat sleek body showing on the surface suddenly two flippers waved and the seal splashed hurriedly out of our path. What a rude awakening!

By evening only *33 Export* and *Neptune*, the two French sloops, were close to us. We could see far out to sea the silhouettes of the rest of the fleet at the start of this most demanding of the four legs. Down below we badly missed our port and drank a glass of wine instead. The ten cases of Fonseca Bin 27 port had arrived on board a ship the previous evening but despite all our efforts and those of the yacht services chief at the yacht club, Archie Peacop, we had to leave without it. Although we did have on board 480 cans of beer and some whisky, we still hankered for the port.

The presence of our new navigator, Captain Tom Woodfield, was a great lift to morale. He was going to find us a far southerly route through the icebergs to Auckland. Going this far south meant less distance, 6,700 miles as opposed to the 7,500 handicap route that most of the boats would take, if they kept in the Roaring Forties' latitude. We were expecting to go into the Shrieking Sixties close to the Antarctic continent. This move really appealed to John's dramatic nature. I was not so sure, but at least we should see more wild life. 'Penguins, sealions and whales are all plentiful down in this region', Tom had told me. He should certainly be an expert on the Antarctic. Now in his early forties, a mild yet authoritative man, Tom had spent twenty years in this region with the British Antarctic Survey in command of the survey ship *John Biscoe*, and later the *Bransfield* each carrying a total of a hundred or so, made up of crew and scientists. He had been fortunate enough to take his new wife on his last tour down there before being offered a position with Trinity House as one of their ten Elder Brethren. John and I had met him and his wife briefly at a party given by the officers of HMS *Dolphin* on the night before the start at Portsmouth. Amidst potted palms and to the strains of a naval band playing in the background, he mentioned to John the advantages of a southerly route. One, more daylight; two, westerly winds but not the vicious gales and high seas of the Forties; and three, a shorter route.

As much as anything else because it seemed the bolder course, John was quite sold on the idea. Tom said that he would send charts and more details to us in Cape Town. On our arrival there we found a letter from Tom mentioning how much he would like to join us for this second leg if we wanted him and if he could manage to get leave from Trinity House.

After our position as eleventh in the first leg John was determined on a greater attack. By a rather circuitous route he got a message through to Tom! 'Can you join us Cape Town – Auckland?' Tom arrived on Sunday and the race started again on Tuesday. I showed him round the already crowded, and at that stage disorderly, boat and I wondered what thoughts were going through his head as I pointed out to him his bunk, a seat in the main saloon, and the small space in a food locker for his gear. Some change from his luxurious quarters as master of *Bransfield*! But he never showed any dismay or shock; perhaps this was what he had expected. That night John, Tom and I had managed to escape with some South African friends to one of the best restaurants in South Africa where between courses we discussed our tactics for the next leg. The contrast of sitting with a fine view of the glittering lights of Table Bay at a table spread with damask and adorned with Mason's stoneware, sparkling crystal in the light of the candelabra, compared to our first supper afloat, hot spicy curry eaten out of plastic bowls with a spoon, shoulder to shoulder in the cramped saloon, I felt would show up the compatibility of our thirteenth crew member. He seemed at home with both situations straight away, helping hand out the bowls and assisting with the washing up. He was one of us.

Day 2: *Wednesday, 26 October   Noon position 35° 32' S, 18° 12' E*
Day's run 128 miles   Course ESE   Wind SE Force 3
Barometer 1018

John: As the light increased we could see no sign of land. South Africa was gone. Our next landfall was North Cape on the North Island of New Zealand, more than seven thousand miles away. Around us we counted eight of our competitors.

'We must head south — that's where the wind is bound to be,' said Tom Woodfield, speaking from twenty years' experience in command of a British Survey ship in the Antarctic. Short and broad with thinning dark hair, Tom was yearning to return south once more after an absence of seven years working in London as an Elder Brother of Trinity House, the people who maintain our lights and buoys around the British Isles.

Our tacks at one hour east and half an hour south paid off, for by two in the afternoon the wind veered south and freed us to sail 143 degrees true, our Great Circle composite course for Auckland, New Zealand. On this heading we were to windward of all the other twelve boats spread out to leeward, and we planned to go farther south than all our competitors, save a good mileage by cutting the corner and steal a bit of a march on the rest. Unluckily, this happy situation did not last. As the wind fell away in the late afternoon, so the boats passed us one by one. It takes a good man to be last.

We caught a small tuna for supper, and *Gauloises II* ghosted by a hundred yards to starboard during the radio show. A glorious moon shone down on the wreckage of our lead by the time I turned in.

Marie Christine: John, Arun and Steve are all looking queasy; Steve has been sick and Arun and John have bad headaches. John can't believe that I'm all right; neither can I, really. Everyone seems pleased to be back in the old routine again. Much laughter and reminiscences of the Cape Town stay. There is a distinct advantage of staying on board in port. I didn't get used to a bathroom with hot water close by, a soft mattress or large bed, so life is just the same except for the angle.

By afternoon, in spite of our position to windward of the other boats, they overtook us one by one. By evening we had dropped behind and so had the wind. John's morale plummeted. Still, we had been in the lead for a while.

The antibiotics John had been taking for his sore throat had had the usual effect of depressing him but I felt this would soon change. He and Tom seemed to be getting on well.

Day 3: *Thursday, 27 October   Noon position 36° 48' S, 19° 33' E*
Day's run 124 miles   Course SE   Wind SW Force 3
Barometer 1017

John: I had trouble coping with the slowness of our progress in the light airs which prevailed all day. Something in my nature cannot stand the idea of the other boats drawing ahead of us; yet, of course, there is nothing we can do.

The wind piped up in the afternoon, and at last we seemed to be in the Roaring Forties. Boat speed now made fishing a thing of the past.

Marie Christine: Not much wind till afternoon. In the calm it's surprisingly warm. Colin sat out wearing only shorts. I fell asleep up on deck and woke up with a bruise on the bridge of my nose where my sunglasses had dug in. Another fish was caught – small consolation for going so slowly; but the calm seems fairly general and none of the other boats are moving fast.

However, the wind picked up and by afternoon we were singing along in a gale. Sitting in the aft cockpit I watched the seas mount as one squall succeeded another, the breaking crests of grey waves beheaded and flung aside by the infamous Roaring Forties wind. We sped along once again, our boat proving her seaworthiness. From time to time waves would break on to us in the cockpit, sneaking over the side and hitting me where I sat, square on the back with surprising force and warmth. We were just in the Indian Ocean and the few inches of tepid sea water swirling around in the cockpit-well warmed our chilled feet.

Today is Arun's birthday. After supper, with a bit of stage management, J.C. and I appeared simultaneously from either side of the main saloon bearing brightly candled cakes: J.C. from his galley with a rich fruit cake Arun's mother Noël had made for him, and iced by J.C., and I from our cabin, which runs parallel with the galley, with a real fairytale chocolate cake topped by a cherry, baked for the occasion by Peter's Penny in Cape Town. Amidst great singing Arun blew out all the candles on both cakes in one breath and proceeded with the difficult task of dividing both into thirteen.

Day 4: *Friday, 28 October   Noon position 38° 56' S, 21° 12' E*
Day's run 207 miles   Course SE   Wind WSW Force 4
Barometer 1014

Marie Christine: The stormy weather continues and we are able to make good progress on our southerly route. We are well south of all the other boats except *King's Legend*, who are pulling out all stops it seems to win this leg from *Flyer* or anyone else!

I'll have to watch my step below. Each time I disagree with Bob he thinks I'm trying to pick a quarrel. Nothing like this ever occurred on the first leg because, feeling so sick, I never felt like talking, let alone disagreeing with anyone, but in my present cured state it is a different matter. We're good friends really but the situation lends itself to disagreement. Anyway it helps to pass the time.

It is all hypothetical now, but if we had managed a further seven miles each day on the previous leg we would have come fourth and with only two miles more each day we would have beaten *Tielsa* and *ADC* – a fact to remind ourselves when we're not feeling so keen. Steve can calculate anything.

Dramatic news over the radio tonight: *Gauloises II*, skippered by our friend Eric Loizeau, was seen running under bare poles this afternoon by *Adventure*. A few minutes later Eric's voice came over the air: 'My rudder is broken and I am making for Port Elizabeth under jury steering. I will get a new rudder there and hope to see you all in Auckland.' This was very sad news indeed as *Adventure*, *Gauloises II* and we were in the same whisky team and we had struck up a great friendship with Eric and would miss his cheery voice each evening in halting English with: 'How are you John, my dear?' At least the fact of it happening here meant he could get back to South Africa. We were soon reaching the point of no return: no shipping farther south to rescue us, airplanes to spot us or land to call in to if things went wrong.

Day 5: *Saturday, 29 October   Noon position 41° 34' S, 25° 04' E*
Day's run 211 miles   Course SE   Wind WSW Force 6
Barometer 1015

John: Peter is still very quiet. Missing Penny I suppose. We agreed to play down his role as mate on this leg, but being so miserable isn't cheering anyone. Bob is already bad-tempered – with thirty-five days to go!

A cold front came through during the day with squalls up to 60 knots. The storm spinnaker halyard parted, and this sail was laid out across the sea to leeward. This time it was only a matter of routine to haul it in. At least half a dozen boats damaged sails during the day, and *Great Britain II* ran over and lost a spinnaker. *Adventure* hit a small whale head-on during the night, and *King's Legend* was knocked on her side. There were no injuries, however, but just cuts and bruises, and one man bruised his back rather badly

Marie Christine: Bumpy sea and much wind as a cold front came through. Arun was sick at breakfast and John and Steve looked rather pale. I stuck a strip of plaster behind their ears, a remedy sent by a South African lady who had heard John and me talking on Cape Town radio about our visit to the chiropractor. Sadly it had no effect. I feel they are not open to suggestion enough; if only they could *believe* it would work. I am sure that's half the reason for my cure. But then it works two ways: I am as gullible as anybody and frequently duped.

It is getting much colder now. We lit the small paraffin stove in the saloon. It warms up the place and is particularly nice if you're sitting right next to it.

John thinks that the seamanship is forgotten in favour of the racing and encourages our crew to watch for chafe and keep clipped on at all times. The main thing is to get safely to Auckland.

The increasing cold is causing quite a bit of condensation in our heads (toilet), also on the outside wall by our bunk. I covered this with a rather nasty quilted plastic in Cape Town. Much to the amusement of the others I coated half the wall with thick engine grease, thinking it was glue which was in exactly the same coloured tin. It took about an hour to remove all traces of it before I could start again with the glue. Not a star on the 'do-it-yourself'! Still, the end product helps a bit, although there are a few drops of water on it.

Day 6: *Sunday, 30 October   Noon position 44° 05' S, 28° 02' E
Day's run 185 miles   Course SE   Wind SW Force 3
Barometer 1017*

John: The wind eased a lot and we crept along with a starcut spinnaker. As it was Sunday, the meals were rather special; and Marie Christine made some bread and also a shepherd's pie with peas for supper.

We are by far the most southerly boat of the fleet, and Tom has warned us all to keep a sharp lookout for icebergs.

Marie Christine: Calmer day – everyone in good spirits. I had a go in the galley, started by making soda bread which was not a great success but I felt so good I offered to do the supper for J.C. Mid-afternoon I made some rock buns which we ate by the stove with real piping hot coffee and life seemed quite pleasant for a while. My efforts in the galley for supper went down well, except for the washers-up. I seemed to have used every utensil in the galley! It's too cold and stormy outside now for this so we heat up some sea water and wash up in the sink in the galley; still in a black bucket, as water in the sink does not drain away. John and I are very cosy in our bunk, all the problems of the last leg sorted out.

Day 7: *Monday, 31 October   Noon position 46° 25' S, 31° 06' E*
Day's run 182 miles   Course SE   Wind SSW Force 3
Barometer 1013

John: Albatrosses, black skuas, cape pigeons and silver-grey petrels wheel about the boat at whatever speed we're travelling.

More food is being eaten by everyone and we all regret having had to leave the ten cases of Fonseca Bin 27 port in Cape Town.

Because of the possibility of icebergs, we have arranged our daily clock so that it gets lighter at four o'clock in the morning, but dark by eight in the evening. This ensures that the watch at four to eight in the morning has daylight, for it is in those early hours that we reckon that vigilance will be at its lowest ebb. On this clock arrangement, it's easier for us to make the inter-boat radio contact at nine in the morning. Also, I have another chat in the early afternoon with Dave Leslie, the skipper of Her Majesty's Sail Training Yacht, *Adventure*. Dave kindly gives me the weather forecast and sends our position to Race Control in Portsmouth, England, twice a week, using a morse frequency which *Adventure*'s radio operator works directly to an army unit in Blandford, England. As *Adventure* is likely to be the boat going next farthest south besides us, it is most comforting to think we have this close communication in these cold, empty, grey seas.

At our Hallowe'en Party in the evening Tom Woodfield told us tales about his twenty years with the British Antarctic Survey; like the time when he found his ship steering through a mass of grey fragments floating on the surface of the sea, which he took to be disgorged by whales. As he was close to the South Sandwich Islands at the time, he checked the echo-sounder and was a little surprised to find the depth registered at 15 fathoms, instead of the 1,000 fathoms shown on the chart. The grey stuff floating on the water was lava, and his ship was directly over the summit of a new volcano which was rising smartly up to the surface. Tom's greatest problem was to decide in which direction to steam to avoid having the ship lifted out of the sea from under him.

Marie Christine: Each day it is getting colder and soon we will see icebergs – no problem in the day but in this area you can get wind and fog together which is a frightening prospect in the night if there are icebergs around. I must pack an emergency bag of clothing in case we have to abandon the ship. (I wonder how long I'd survive.) Up on the deck today I had to come down after only two hours – my feet and fingers were numb and that was with plenty of warm jerseys, socks and full waterproofs on. The crew are managing well – no complaints from any of them. It can't be a lot of fun at night sitting for four hours in the cockpit.

In the middle of last night John went out to check on progress. He sat down in the dark at the chart table and got a mighty shock to feel something damp and solid on one-half of the seat. It was Peter, who woke with a start. Arun's watch had just worked out a system of one of the three spending half an hour down below to warm up before going out on the helm.

Nobody felt much in the mood for a riotous Hallowe'en party although Steve wore his witch's hat. He looked quite comical, earnestly discussing some matter or other with a pointed black hat on and long black woollen hair dangling from it. I think he'd forgotten he was wearing it.

We are well south of the rest of the fleet and everyone is conscious of the necessity to be alert at all times in this cold and lonely part of the world. This is no time for having one too many drinks.

Day 8: *Tuesday, 1 November   Noon position 48° 07′ S, 34° 11′ E*
Day's run 212 miles   Course ESE   Wind WNW Force 6
Barometer 1016

John: A glorious day of blue skies – ice-blue, you might say – and roaring wind. We made 212 miles and the sea and swell were bordering the alarming at 50 to 60 knots of wind.

The cold is not unbearable, although other boats are finding it bad, they say – to us it's much like home. The heater is now being used quite a lot and the scientists, Colin and Steve, are researching ways and means for toast-making on it.

With a yankee sail poled out on the windward side and the main on the other we get along pretty well; but during the night we had to take the pole down and fly the yankee loose on the same side as the main, and this made for a night of crashes and bangs.

Tom is suffering from severe headache and sickness. He is confined to bed but this is awkward as he sleeps in the leeward seat in the saloon, which is used by the rest of the crew for relaxation during the day. A partial solution is to have him sleep in Marie Christine's and my cabin by day, and back into the saloon by night.

The shock of the hasty preparations in UK, the flight out, and the comparatively primitive conditions on board the boat combine to make a way of life rather different from that Tom fondly remembers as master of his own ship for twenty years around Antarctica. Add to this the softening effects of seven years of 'carpet slippers and commuting on the 8.32' and a job more nervously demanding than physical and it is no surprise that spending several hours a day out on deck in severe conditions has brought on an attack of migraine-like headache, which he has suffered in the past. At forty-four Tom is surprised at the youth of the instructors aboard; they are mostly in their early twenties and Tom is very aware of being twice their age. Marie Christine quickly noticed this and she has gone out of her way to make him feel welcome by spending much of each day chatting with him in the saloon. This new situation suits her very well as she was particularly conscious of having no one to talk to on the first leg when she felt so low with seasickness. Since being cured by the chiropractor in Cape Town a new and friendly face on board is especially welcome.

The three watches are now well separated in outlook. Arun, Peter and Dick are rather deprecatingly nicknamed the 'cruising watch' by the others, who regard themselves very much as racers. Tony, Colin and Steve who used to be the 'cadets' are now known as 'Dallimore's [Tony] Doomwatch' – this name was thought up by Bob, Noel and Roger (proudly wearing their own 'F troop rules OK' T shirts bought in Cape Town). Bob and Tony have always regarded each other with wariness bordering on frank dislike since some trouble back at Ardmore in the spring. The name 'Doomwatch' springs from the long hours Bob spent mending the radial-head spinnaker Tony's watch had blown out on the first leg. As the one who pays the bills I'm rather in sympathy with Bob on this because Tony's natural impatience and drive to get things done has made him by far the most expensive instructor I've ever had at Ardmore.

Marie Christine: Washed my hair in a pint of precious fresh water in a bucket – quite a balancing feat as the boat tends to lurch around.

Going along at a terrific rate – exhilarating on deck in the brilliant sunshine and blue sea. With the cold, crisp air it's almost like being in the Alps. Inside you hear a mighty rushing sound as the boat slips off the waves.

Colin gybed the mainsail this evening; it whanged over to the other side with an almighty force, breaking a snatch block – quite alarming. John feared for the mast.

Day 9: *Wednesday, 2 November   Noon position 50° 24' S, 38° 53' E*
Day's run 205 miles   Course ESE   Wind W Force 5
Barometer 1010

John: Still sliding along on the cold, grey sea which is now down to 2½ degrees Centigrade, and the air only a little better at 3½ degrees. Another 200 miles reeled off.

Everyone stayed surprisingly cheerful and coped with the unpleasant conditions with enthusiasm. Down below, life could hardly be improved. We're buoyed up by the knowledge that our course lies dramatically to the south of all the fleet, as illustrated on our race progress chart on the main saloon bulkhead. The other boats also show a distinct interest in our position. Goodness knows I kidded them enough in Cape Town that we had an ice-breaker coming out from London and how Tom had actually written the Antarctic pilot.

It was good to hear from Eric Loizeau that he was already at sea again and hot after us in *Gauloises*, after fitting a new rudder in Port Elizabeth. 'I hope we'll do something in "le whisky" prize after all,' he laughed, across the air waves from eight hundred miles astern.

Marie Christine: Worrying news this morning from *King's Legend*. One of their men has a suspected broken back. They were trying to get advice from *ADC*'s medic and also the doctor on *Condor*. It is hard for us to hear much now we are just into the Fifties. Judith from *Treaty of Rome* came over loud and clear and finished with a message that Philippe, their skipper, sent me a kiss – a nice touch of gallic charm.

Most people are now wearing their North Cape polar suits – entirely scarlet from head to toe with the complete gear on except where eyes and nose peep out. They are good and warm but make the wearers look rather like pantomime boiled lobsters.

John and Peter tuned in at eight this evening for two reasons: no word from *Tielsa* for the last three days and we thought she might still be trying to get through on this frequency at this time and we also wanted to test our Brookes and Gatehouse Homer Heron for receiving transmission from *Adventure*. They could hear us speaking on our main Pentland Bravo radio but we were unable to receive them clearly. We tuned in to hear two of the yachts discussing having seen what they thought was a distress flare. Steve, Tony and Colin had just come down talking about a brilliant shooting star they had seen. We wondered if they could be one and the same; discussing the direction we decided not.

Not a bit of luck with the Brookes and Gatehouse – we may soon be out of touch with the other boats. Very cold in our cabin now but once in bed with a hot water bottle I begin to thaw out.

Day 10: *Thursday, 3 November   Noon position 52° 28' S, 43° 27' E Day's run 206 miles   Course SE   Wind NW Force 6 Barometer 1000*

John: Fog. Tom gazed into the grey blanket all morning and most of the afternoon. We managed to hold the 8½-knot average which gives 200+ miles each day. Good for distance but disastrous for hitting bergs.

Rehearsals for sighting and hitting ice went satisfactorily. It is really very exciting. I sat below and read a novel about merchant banks, and as a result I resolved to pay off all my debts on return to Ardmore – it's a bolder, more maverick thing to do. I sincerely don't want to owe anyone money, even if it has to be unprofitable to be out of debt; and I sincerely don't want the burdens of wealth either.

We're worried about bergs going aground on the recently discovered Ob Bank, which is not very far from us now. Bergs could easily go aground in 135 fathoms – that's 810 feet – and Tom told of seeing the 100-fathom line – that's 600 feet – often marked by huge bergs with only 60 feet above the sea. That would mean about 600 feet of ice below the water.

The fog dominated the day and pressure told in different ways on different people. Colin, for example, normally a quiet and confidently tireless fellow, nodded off to sleep in the saloon after lunch with an open book of electrical circuits on his knees. A few hours later after a dog-watch spent peering into the fog he suddenly said with some anxiety: 'Going on as we are now is like trying to find the unlit entrance to Loch Laxford in the dark, only without a chart.' The aldermanic John Covington, for example, normally bluff and cheerful, now took the peril of the bergs and our failing inter-ship communications with a very straight face. My own comment that I found the situation rather exciting and that I wasn't worried raised no answering smile from faces around the saloon. At night there was vigorous and sensible protest from Bob Burns on deck if any chink of light showed to impair the night vision of those straining their eyes into the dark blanket through which we were running at 8½ knots.

I felt the strain myself. Unable to sleep, I couldn't stop my mind from wondering what 600 feet of berg below the surface would look like – thousands of years of consolidated rock-hard ice. Whichever way we turned, there could now be nothing but icebergs.

'I'm a bit surprised the water temperatures are so low,' Tom Woodfield cautiously said. He had spent longer than anyone else peering into the fog that day. Am I doing the right thing? I kept asking myself, tossing and turning in the bunk. Why am I taking the risk?

There was no answer. I just kept on wondering what the berg would look like – and we slipped on through the foggy night.

Marie Christine: 'The visibility's down, John, to two hundred yards.' Bob's voice interrupted my dream. It was now three in the morning and the wind was blowing a steady force 7. This curious combination of wind and fog with the menacing possibility of icebergs close by that we couldn't see was now upon us. Immediately after breakfast Tom, with his beige balaclava pulled on well and wearing his laced-up arctic boots for the first time, stationed himself just outside the hatch in the centre cockpit on the lookout for bergs. It was a daunting thought. They could be any size, two hundred feet high, two miles long . . . He had enough experience not to predict anything more than just their presence in this area. On a clear day it would be easy to avoid them but in this poor visibility we would have little time to change course and veer to windward.

During the day the glass dropped from 1011 to 998, which added a further sinister touch. *Adventure* came on in the morning and said they thought we were in for a big blow. In 'F' troop's words, 'We're doomed, we're all going to die!' We could still joke but in truth the situation was far from cheering. Tony took the water temperature by placing the thermometer in the forward heads – a cunning way of getting the information without having to go out. It registered 36.2 °F and the air was 38 °F, cold but we were now more acclimatized. The saloon was all we could wish for; those not on watch huddled around the table, the stove pumping forth the heat as we read books, talked, dozed. Dick and I had a sewing 'bee' going. With an enormous embroidery needle he was cobbling together a split in his red polar trousers with black thread while I was laboriously putting in a new zip on Noel's jeans.

The day wore on; no icebergs sighted, less wind and Tom insisting he stay on watch. He finally came in after four and instructed the new watch exactly what to look out for. It was no joking matter now and Doom Watch went out through the hatch intent on their purpose. Feeling unsettled and wanting to take my mind off our situation I offered to do the supper. 'I'll be out of a job; you'll not be wanting me next,' wailed J.C. Far from the truth! It is fine cooking when you feel like it but different altogether keeping it up meal after meal. I made a sharp lemon sponge with icing for pudding and a spicy curry with a salad of onion rings and oranges covered in French dressing.

Although busy in the galley I could still hear snatches of worried conversation. The fog wasn't lifting and it was getting dark. It was decided to alter the sails to an easier rig for going about if we had to. It took the two watches on deck quite a time to get it done. Bob leapt up in rage, 'They're worse than an Irish parliament – what about my poor sails!' and with that he charged up the hatch to find out what the hell was going on.

We turned in about nine, knowing there were five and a half hours of dark and fog ahead. 'Get your survival bag ready, Marie Christine, and we'll sleep in our clothes tonight,' John told me as he got into his sleeping-bag, fully dressed with boots already stuck in the legs of his waterproof trousers and jacket both lying on the floor close at hand. 'Turn that light off,' bellowed Bob. 'We can't seen a **** thing up here.' So by torchlight I continued my task of getting two more jumpers, a jar of face cream, camera and film, diary and photo of Bec to put into my bag. What use would any of those things be in water that was only just over freezing and hundreds of miles from help? I lay on my back trying to relax the knot of fear in my stomach. John was unusually silent, the responsibility heavy on his shoulders.

Day 11: *Friday, 4 November   Noon position 55° 13' S, 46° 19' E*
        Day's run 190 miles   Course ESE   Wind W by N Force 5
        Barometer 998

John: We kept the clock so that it would get light at two in the morning. The boat was at its most vulnerable between three and seven in the morning. Three o'clock in the morning courage is a rare quality – daylight is much safer than darkness.

We came out of the fog in the early hours and by mid morning the Ratsey storm spinnaker was doing its usual good job. As the wind fell, so Tony's 'Doomwatch' called for the big-boy or blooper sail to be hoisted alongside the storm spinnaker. Bob Burns' 'F' troop were on watch at the time. Bob likes to run the ship when he's on watch, and while he would sometimes ask for advice, he never liked to be given ideas from those below. Predictably, he was so irascible that J.C.'s attempts at setting the big-boy were doomed to fail, and he took it down again. From that moment Bob went into one of his black moods, and when, later in the day, with the big-boy set by Tony providing a much more suitable course than could be managed without it, the sail burst along the whole length of a seam near the foot, he became really impossible. No one said anything to him while he sat in the cabin and glowered into the middle distance, and then stomped off to lie in his bunk.

This sort of result from the pressures within everyone's head is an everyday part of living in a confined space.

Marie Christine: No icebergs and no fog. We survived the night, though those on watch during the darkness look pretty tired this bright sunny morning. Still very cold but the pale sun holds a touch of warmth. Breakfast of hot porridge and condensed milk started disastrously with at least four people spilling their sticky contents either on the floor or (worse) on their neighbours. How glad I am I don't feel sick any more! That would finish me. The boat is lurching in an unpredictable way as we speed before a following north-westerly.

Darkness fell around seven and it was decided to put the clocks forward an hour, which means dawn will come at three in the morning. We have nine hours to lose on our way across to New Zealand. Taking this southerly route at 60 degrees south the degrees of longitude are about thirty miles apart as opposed to sixty miles at the equator. Once we go east we should manage at least six degrees east a day. Positions of other boats show *Condor* and *King's Legend* also sweeping south, but not yet as far south as us. The great debate at present is how can we keep from the other boats our position and situation. If they hear us saying 'no icebergs sighted yet' they are likely to come farther south themselves. On the other hand we can't give misleading information. John and Peter tried the radio at nine this evening and were unable to make any contact with *Adventure*, so the problem was averted for a while and we'll probably see ice tomorrow anyway. Tom reckons it is about.

Day 12: *Saturday, 5 November   Noon position 56° 39′ S, 51° 47′ E Day's run 196 miles   Course ESE   Wind W Force 7 Barometer 1001*

John: At three in the morning Arun woke me up to say that a squall was coming and that he felt J.C. and I should be dressed and ready to help if it became necessary to take down the storm spinnaker. Although I was sleeping fully clothed in my North Cape polar suit I still needed a short time to don oilskins, woollen dachstein mitts, waterproof mitts, neck towel, hat and boots – too long in this case, as the boat broached and the spinnaker halyard broke. Luckily by the time I scampered out on to the deck past drifts of snow lying in the angles of the cockpit seats Peter was already desperately trying to stop the boat from running over the spinnaker, which now lay in the water all along the leeward side.

I took the wheel from him and the miserable job of hauling it in began. Driving horizontal snow in a 40-knot wind from the squall soon

Breakfast time on Debenhams – Tony comes off watch, Colin looks on as Dick mops up spilt porridge

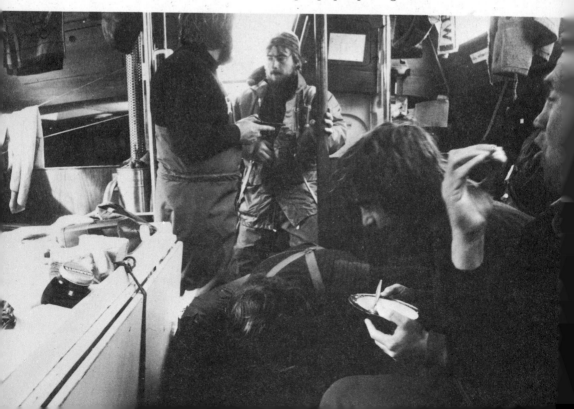

passed, and we were on our way again under reefed main and No. 1 yankee. I went back to bed, but my feet didn't really warm up again, despite the down sleeping-bag, until after I'd got up for breakfast.

All day the seas rolled up from astern – grey water, grey sky, grey cold. The pressure in the stuffy saloon stoked with paraffin and human fumes steadily mounts. We've never had a serious discussion on any subject outside sailing. In the happy hour, Noel and Roger came down from the first dog-watch with Bob – neither of them ate their supper, and Roger flared up and killed the conversation the rest of us were having about the society trends towards hire purchase, overdrafts and mortgages.

'I don't want to hear about your tax problems,' he said – and jumped into his bunk.

This crew was largely chosen for its compatibility, but that didn't include Roger and Noel – and unluckily their berths happen to be the only two in the saloon and they can't get away from the noise of conversation and taped music.

Marie Christine: At breakfast, discussing the temperature, J.C. said solemnly, 'It's minus one in my bunk.' A pause as we wondered what he was on about. 'Yes, I couldn't fit her in in Cape Town.' J.C. with his forty-eight-inch chest only just squeezed into his pipecot. He shared his bunk with a bird one night north of the equator but this poor little migrant swallow was found flattened and dead by morning.

Word came down from Tony on deck that there was ice on the foredeck. Snow flurries filled the grey sky and the sea was the colour of Welsh slate and humpy like Welsh hills. The day passed as usual with the watches of three going up every four hours. It meant waking up at least half an hour before to allow enough time for dressing. On would go three or four layers: T shirt, followed by long-sleeved shirt, jumper, then polar jacket for the top half. Bottom half would be red fleecy polar long johns, socks and then red polar socks. Next for the head a woollen hat without bobble, long scarf wound tightly around head, covering nose and mouth. Finally, red fleecy balaclava, only eyes peeping out. Henri-Lloyd Ocean Racer high trousers with braces, then jacket. Dachstein pre-shrunk mitts fitted inside the inner Velcro cuff; waterproof motor-cycle type mitts on top. Boots on, skiing goggles over the eyes, hood up and then out to do battle.

Down below those off watch mostly went to bed; the cold and effort on deck was taking its toll. The stove, draped with singeing, steaming mitts, hats and socks, was now the focal point of our living space. Lucky was the person who got to sit next to it, except that there were certain duties to fulfil: shift around the drying gear, prick the burner which had a nagging tendency to block, and at meal times 'make the toast'. It could only cope with three pieces of bread at a time and could take up to

Tom Woodfield in the Southern Ocean

five minutes to toast one piece, but there was plenty of time and not much to do.

We'd not managed to make contact with *Adventure* or any of the other yachts for two days. John decided to give it a go, fearing that *Adventure* would worry if we continued not to make contact with them. Because of the clock going forward it meant waiting until nine – everyone had gone to bed except those on deck and John, Tom and I. We sat in the dark saloon and swapped yarns about the past and people we knew. Peter came down from being on watch at five to nine and with his frozen fingers tuned in the Pentland Bravo radio set. John sat on an upturned drawer thrown away by *Treaty of Rome* in the icy radio shack in the hopes that we'd get through. Suddenly loud and clear on a different frequency came the dark brown voice of John Roberts from *King's Legend*. 'Any news of *Debenhams*? Any news of *Debenhams*? Over.' John picked up the receiver and spoke to them, giving our position. They were able to give us the position of all the other boats. We were well south of the fleet.

Adventure then came on. They sounded relieved and pleased to hear us. I think they had all been quite worried having not heard from us for two days.

'How is Marie Christine's seasickness?' Dave Leslie, the skipper, asked.

'She's fine but I'm not; I'm going to make an acupuncture appointment when I get to Auckland,' John answered disgustedly.

'We've got the latest ice report from Washington, John. I'm sure you'd like to hear it.' Dave's helpful Scots voice crackled over the airwaves. Tom leaned in from the galley where he had been helping me fill my hot water bottle, to look over Peter's shoulder and check that he had the correct figures written down. It was clear from Tom's face that we were pretty close to the pack ice before Dave had finished reading out the figures.

Dave finished up by saying 'I wouldn't advise you to go any farther than 57 degrees, John, or you'll be in it.'

Tom hurried back to the chart and after a minute's plotting said, 'We must alter course immediately.'

We were only sixty miles north of pack ice on the edge of the frozen area that is Antarctica. Tom was mildly surprised that it was still frozen at 57 degrees as he had hoped we could have made 60 degrees South. John and J.C. went on deck and they and Arun's watch altered the sails for an easterly course – now running parallel with the ice, *not* towards it. This manoeuvre took two and a half hours in the cold dark night. It was one of those providential situations which make you think someone is keeping an eye on you. We nearly hadn't bothered with the radio schedule that evening. It was pure chance that we happened to hear *King's Legend* on a different frequency and if we hadn't received the American satellite's ice report we would surely have been in it by morning.

I cuddled into my sleeping-bag, feeling like an ostrich. The more I pulled it over my head the less I could hear and I went to sleep feeling cocooned from reality. I was wakened by much noise; the wind was getting up and the watch on deck were changing sails. In the half light I could see John's mummified red shape with his ridiculous green knitted lady's golfing hat just poking out of the top of the sleeping-bag. It was right parky in our little cabin.

Day 13: *Sunday, 6 November   Noon position 57° 10' S, 57° 57' E*
Day's run 216 miles   Course E   Wind N Force 10
Barometer 986

John: The wind rose sharply a couple of hours after midnight on 6 November. During the day the barometer fell 21 points from 998 to 977.

The northerly wind rose to 60 knots for long periods and the 216 miles we made was the best this boat has ever achieved. The sea was rough and we were passing parallel to the pack ice some twenty miles to leeward. With two small headsails up the crosswind and sea were driving us down on the ice. The spray blinded the watch on duty, and even with goggles it was hard to see properly; the seas breaking over the boat seeped through the zips of their oilskins until they were soaked through.

Marie Christine: It was perishing cold on deck as we sped along with the storm under two tiny scraps of sail, 'running parallel with one of the most inhospitable shores in the world', in Peter's words. Constant vigilance for icebergs kept one man at all times on lookout as well as the helmsman. Worried about leeway in this northerly gale and steep sea, the helmsman steered a course north of east, causing the waves to break over the boat, filling the cockpits and drenching those on watch. Every so often we could hear a shout from the helmsman as a really big wave came towards us; inside the sound was deafening as tons of water poured on to the deck. The after-cabin was taking water at a great speed from a rope locker beside the aft cockpit and it was being pumped out every fifteen minutes. Otherwise the boat was relatively dry.

Roaring along under trysail

As each frozen watch came down I gave them steaming mugs of Bovril after they'd stripped off their wet gear. Gloves, scarves and socks were draped over the tiny stove but there was nowhere to put jumpers and trousers. It was a depressing situation for the crew. I think we all felt grateful we were in a sound boat; it can't have been far from any of our thoughts, 'What if we lose the steering?' The northerly gale would have us into the pack ice in no time at all. Another ever-present fear were the icebergs. The poor visibility caused by snow and spray did not help allay this. The day wore on, the glass dropping hourly and the worry mounting. The whisky was served out by very shaky hands when it came to 'Happy Hour'. We were now adding hot water and making a toddy of our drams – it was a good warmer.

I felt thankful I hadn't Becca here. The situation reminded me so much of our Cape Verde trip four years ago. Two days before Christmas on our homeward passage a hundred miles off the west coast of Ireland our Nicholson 32 had been swamped; a giant wave had sent a wall of water through an opening in our main hatch half filling the boat with icy Atlantic water. The panic to pump her out before another came and sank us ... And how Rebecca had wailed at my soothing words, 'Mummy, it isn't all right – there's a hole in the boat.' Just about all our clothing was soaked, including sleeping-bags, the paper decorations hung in limp festoons and Becca's little voice piped: 'This is the most horridest Christmas I've ever had.' Now I would do everything I could to survive, but this time I didn't have the extra burden of responsibility and worry for my child. That helped.

Tom, Peter and I sat in darkness round the stove waiting for the radio schedule at nine. John was having a quick two hours' sleep, trying to glean crumbs of comfort from Tom's answers to our endless questions. He had ended up by saying: 'You should get a bigger boat with a good, strong engine, then do what we used to do if the weather turned ugly: motor straight into the pack ice to a point far enough in where not a ripple disturbs the surface; have two gin and tonics and go to sleep for the night with the wind screaming around the still ship.'

At ten to nine I woke John up for the schedule. Peter, Tom and John went down to the radio and tuned it in, but there was nothing. Peter tried different wavelengths and frequencies but could only get the normal Portishead ship's telephone service. John radioed our position, weather and barometric pressure to anyone who was listening and switched off the set.

'Somebody was certainly looking after us last night – one night in four and that was the night we needed the ice report.'

We turned in, John and I getting into our sleeping-bags fully clothed. My feet were still icy when I awoke three hours later.

Dawn showed us ice in the rigging

Day 14: *Monday, 7 November   Noon position 57° 05' S, 63° 43' E*
Day's run 190   Course E   Wind NNW Force 5
Barometer 976

John: The wind eased in the early hours of the morning, and although the glass stayed at 976 we were putting up a tri-radial spinnaker in the sunshine by six o'clock. One hazard was the shards of ice three-quarters of an inch thick which fell from the masts as the sun warmed the air. A six-foot length of ice falling fifty feet from the mast could have caused some mischief, but Dick was the only one affected; some splinters cut the back of his hand.

   Glorious sun rewarded us for yesterday and the mizzen shrouds were hung with drying oilskins inside out, and gloves and pullovers, scarves, hoods and socks. We seem to be part of a huge slow-moving low-pressure complex which is moving at much the same speed as us.

The gaudy tri-radial spinnaker is an ill-assorted sail to set all day long – so close to the ice shelf. With a magnetic variation of 57 degrees west, it's not surprising that we will pass within three hundred miles of the Magnetic South Pole.

Everyone is so cheerful that it's a pleasure to be on board. Three years of work and worry – and now it's all unfolding as I had hoped. But a note in our official log reads: 'Great Circle course to 59 °S abandoned having regard to sea temperature and ice report indicating ice on 57½° parallel. Parallel sailing approx. along 57° commenced.'

Day 15: *Tuesday, 8 November   Noon position 57° 00' S, 70° 37' E*
Day's run 210 miles   Course E   Wind NW Force 7
Barometer 975

Marie Christine: Good progress in the night. Morale is high. Peter and John were able to join in the chat show between the other boats at 11.00, hearing *Treaty of Rome* very clearly. Philippe Hanin, their excellent skipper, sounded pretty low in spite of their very good progress. It's extremely cold with them; their heater has packed up and the temperature inside the aluminium hull is only 3 °C. We got the other boats' positions. *Condor, Great Britain II* and *King's Legend* have been doing very long runs each day. It looks as though they're only about two weeks' distance from Auckland. On handicap they would need to be. We think we are about three weeks away. Both *Treaty* and *Adventure* are making good progress. It was a blow for us about the ice being farther north, 57 degrees as opposed to 60 degrees south, as we have had to alter our course slightly, missing out on the maximum advantage of our Great Circle route.

I went up after lunch for some fresh air. I felt very cosy as I'd kept my boy's pyjama bottoms on under my trousers and I was wearing three jumpers under my oilskins. I took up the daily ration of Mars bars for those on watch and we sat hanging on as the boat coasted along the breaking waves. With the sun shining out of a clear blue sky, it was magnificent. The albatrosses don't like it this far south but there are great flocks of ice birds all around the boat (silver-grey petrels). But I miss the albatrosses really – it's hard to believe they can live for eighty years and that a twelve-foot wingspan is not uncommon.

I came forward, trailing my clipped-on safety line, and bent down to speak to John when suddenly *whoosh*, a giant wave came at me from over the coach roof. After it had gone I blinked the salt from my eyes. Sadly I'd not had my hood up. I could feel the icy water running down my front and back – my hair and woolly hat were soaked, as were my gloves. Screams of laughter came from the aft cockpit; at least it had amused them. I went back and joined Arun, who was on the wheel and who I felt was the culprit, Dick and Peter. It had happened many times to all of them and I had to laugh. I stayed out until I could feel my fingers no more and then went below and washed my hair in a pint of hot water, changed my wet jumpers and slowly warmed up.

I'd offered to do the supper for J.C. so I got on with making dumplings and peeling onions for the repast of mince and dumplings with mixed herbs, boiled onions and mashed potato, finishing up with steaming mugs of real coffee and oatmeal biscuits. The cooker is very temperamental in these cold conditions; it flares up if you try to turn up the flame, and you need about five minutes to light it now (instead of two), holding the blow-torch on the pipes to vaporize the paraffin. The fuel must be too cold for it to work well. I was close to screaming at times, what with the boat lurching, the cooker flaring up and the very cold water taking so long to heat. J.C. has great patience. I've never heard him exasperated. Matters improved when Tom passed a hot, stiff whisky in to me. How easy it would be to take to the bottle in this situation! A panacea for cold, fear, frustration, it sheds a rosy light over squalor. Just as well I'm not on the boat on my own.

Much later, as I lay in my cosy sleeping-bag thinking over the day's happenings, there was suddenly a loud tap on our window. 'Come up and see the Aurora Australis,' Peter called. It was hard to drag myself out into the cold but I felt I couldn't miss seeing them. I clambered out of the bunk over John and up the steps to the hatch in my pyjamas to have a quick peep. There in the dark, star-studded sky hung great curtains of pale light. It was a bitterly cold night so I didn't stay long to gaze at their shifting forms. I was glad I'd made the effort, even though I was shivering when I got back into my down bag. On crisp winter nights at Ardmore we see the Aurora Borealis, like sweeping searchlights their beams scanning the night sky. Now to have seen both Northern and Southern Lights I felt was a great privilege.

Day 16: *Wednesday, 9 November   Noon position 56° 55' S, 75° 46' E*
Day's run 207 miles   Course E   Wind WNW Force 5
Barometer 986

John: In the early morning we put up the storm spinnaker, but the halyard broke and so we're left with no spinnaker halyards at all. That's a fine state of affairs in this situation.

Marie Christine: The wind increased during the night. John was called up to help with a sail change. Unless it's an emergency he tends to lie there for about two minutes before jumping out and getting dressed. I always wake up and try to keep awake to make sure he doesn't drop off – sometimes it's an enormous effort. Most times I fall asleep while he's getting dressed and then wake again as he's undressing. For that brief moment of consciousness I can never work out why he's taking his gear off when he's meant to be going out!

Went out for a short while in the afternoon. There is heavy snow in the air; Tony, Steve and Col. were changing sails with bare hands. I felt very cold after ten minutes or so. I don't think I'd last long in a life raft out here with my poor circulation. The contrast between outside and in is enormous when the weather is wild. After supper we all sat in the dark telling stories. Tom has an endless store of Antarctic tales and Arun told a funny one about his pet python in India.

*Colin's frozen
rope trick*

Day 17: *Thursday, 10 November   Noon position 57° 35' S, 82° 19' E*
Day's run 194 miles   Course E   Wind NW Force 5
Barometer 985

John: Bob climbed the mast in quite a swell; and after a big of aggravation he managed to replace both spinnaker halyards.

We have snow showers each day, usually at the same time that 'dog-leg' Woodfield wants to take his sights. On this afternoon the snow fell continuously, piling up on the cockpit seats and sticking to the masts and spars. Narrow bands of blue sky marking frontal weather systems passed from one horizon to another in half an hour or so, but the wind seldom seemed to reach forty knots. During the evening it fell away until notes in the log reappeared bemoaning the lack of a spinnaker.

Marie Christine: Life goes on much the same day after day. My world is very much below decks. I made an effort with trying to keep the table clean and clear – gave it a good scrub after breakfast and cleared everything away, threatening dire results if things are left around.

We now have a torn blooper and yankee. It's hardly the weather to get mending them.

Played Scrabble in afternoon with Tom, John and Col. I find I'm getting quite irritable with certain members on the boat and really snapped at J.C. I'll have to make an effort not to upset the harmony. I have very little to do anyway; at least I can try and cheer up others. It's not easy, though.

Day 18: *Friday, 11 November   Noon position 58° 31' S, 84° 25' E*
Day's run 203 miles   Course E by S   Wind NNE Force 7
Barometer 990

John: 'If you wanna see an iceberg there's one on the port bow – quite close,' Dick mumbled as he poked his head into our cabin at one in the morning.

'It's only a bergy bit,' said Tom from the top of the main companionway.

'How big's that then?' asked Marie Christine in her pyjamas.

'Oh, about the size of a block of flats', he replied grandly.

For me it was unforgettable and one of the main reasons why I had come all this way from Ardmore at 58 degrees north to this berg at 58 degrees south; a jagged, luminous white island in the half-light of dawn, it lay motionless – the only solid thing we had seen since leaving Cape Town eighteen days ago. 'Yes, I'm here,' it seemed to say. 'My friends and I surround you – hit one of us and you die.' Two more came past before breakfast, both massive tabular bergs. Then at ten o'clock Tony saw another one directly on our course, and I decided to close on it for a good look-see. We passed a couple of hundred yards upwind of a magnificent sight – whites and blues, crashing waves, and with hundreds of birds feeding on the krill trapped at the foot of the ice cliff. *Debenhams* rocked violently on the backwash of the waves from the ice fortress. All day long we passed bergs of different shapes and sizes, their numbers steadily increasing. There was a heated argument at supper between cruisers and racers as to whether or not we should carry a spinnaker at night. Bob and Tony were for it – Peter against. Peter often has to put Arun's point in a dispute because Arun is inclined to adopt an inscrutable oriental pose, scorning the shouting match. I decided we should make all speed if the visibility was good enough. We were cutting quite a distance by coming this far south, and now we must

A white-out for the saloon

press home the advantage by trying to maintain hull speed without exceeding the controls laid down in the wind-speed/sail-size chart.

Tom volunteered to stand ice watch from eight o'clock in the evening until first light at about one in the morning. I find it difficult to sleep knowing that we are at the edge of the Antarctic continent in pitch darkness heading straight for icebergs and making 10 knots under the spinnaker; and all this with two of the three watch-keepers so short-sighted that I'd never seen them without their spectacles!

At ten o'clock the leaky window into our cabin opened.

'Can you come and give us a hand, J.R.?' came Peter's Tasmanian twang.

It was the beginning of a long, unforgettable night. I took the wheel while Arun, Peter, Dick and J.C. tried to get the spinnaker pole back off the forestay after an emergency reach to windward which had just cleared a couple of bergs. The speed dropped to 8 knots – there was no moon – the only light came from the hypnotic luminous glare of the bergs themselves. We began to encounter bits of ice – round about house size, but with only the roof showing – these were called growlers.

'Port ten!' called Tom from the weather shrouds.

'Port ten!' I called back. And so we went on jinking through the bits while the rest of the watch sorted out the rigging on the deck.

After a while I gave the wheel to Dick and moved forward to see Tom. 'I reckon the spinnaker is too dangerous to carry when the visibility is no good at night,' he said, out of the tube-like hood of his anorak, between calling the course to Dick.

'Okay. We'll drop it if things get worse,' I replied. With that we ran straight into a lane of ice bits, several of which hit the hull with ominous thuds.

'Drop the spinnaker. Call J.C.' I turned and shouted back to Arun at the main hatch. We slid downwind between two bergs close together; and then the No. 1 yankee, staysail, and full mizzen were hoisted to complement the mainsail and raise the speed again to the same 8 knots that we'd achieved with the spinnaker. But this time the boat was much more manoeuvrable; we could come up into the wind or free away at will to clear the bergs. If the wind got up or we were in trouble, we could drop sails very quickly.

At half past midnight, with first light nearly on us, I decided to go below for a nap, thinking I would be called to rehoist the spinnaker again once it got light. But it was impossible to shut my eyes with the continual thudding of ice against the hull.

Peter was in the radio shack trying to contact Portishead to find out who was trying to call us from London, as *Adventure* had told us during the radio chat show about this traffic awaiting us. Suddenly he rushed up on deck to get the sheets eased, and lessen speed. The bumping of the ice was too much for him. I followed him and we saw that we were now embayed in a huge area of loose ice surrounded by bergs of all shapes and sizes. Ahead lay a great wall of blank white some 10–15 feet high and stretching to the north and south horizons. This was pack ice, there was no way through. We must head north-west until we cleared it. 'I hope Tom realizes this is no ice-breaker and we don't have reverse,' were my first thoughts as I took the wheel from Bob. It was an exhilarating wintry scene. The wind rose sharply to 40 knots on the dial before me in the aft cockpit. Bob, Noel and Roger reduced sail with admirable speed, and we tacked to and fro through the growlers in a north-westerly direction back towards Cape Town. In spite of the gale force wind there was now so much ice on the sea that the surface remained smooth except for a long swell. It was like sailing through porridge, very lumpy porridge. I found I could pass within inches of pieces of about the size of a dining-room table, and only a few feet more were needed to clear the house-size chunks.

I could see that Tom was shaken by this dramatic turn of events. 'I'm sorry about this,' he said a couple of times, and I could imagine what was going through his mind as I looked north up what appeared to be the coast of a huge area of ice. We might be tacking north for hours while other boats could be running south-east straight towards the ice, for we had no means of telling how far it stretched to the north and east of us.

'Don't give it a second thought,' I said, trying to reassure him. 'I'm

In loose ice at dawn with 40 knots of wind

having the time of my life – it's really exciting and I'm sure we'll be all right in this with so little sail and daylight already here.' At the wheel I felt absolutely in control.

The gale force headwind was very cold on my face and steering was a bit hampered by my efforts to drag my neck towel up from the neck of my orange oilskins to cover my mouth and nose. I regretted wearing my tight seaboots, a size too small, because my feet were quickly numb.

Steve of Tony's watch had been in his bunk since coming off watch at eight in the evening and he wasn't due on duty again until four in the morning. His bunk is the middle one on the port side of the swamp. He was tired like everyone else, the days and nights of cold and more particularly wet were taking their toll of nervous and physical energy – the eight hours sleep through the middle part of the night were most welcome.

'I heard Tom calling the course changes to the helmsman at about eleven o'clock,' he told me, 'but it meant little to me and I soon drifted off to sleep again. Then a little while later I realized I was lying rigid and wide awake – we all were in the swamp. There was a noise like someone eating crisps in your ear. Sometimes there was a loud bang and often you could hear the pieces of ice bumping all the way along the hull. I was glad to get up and do something when Roger called us to give a hand at one o'clock.'

To get through the lanes of close-packed brash, I brought the boat up into the wind to take the way off her parallel to the lane before paying off and nudging through at right-angles. This was no problem. I felt great confidence in the hull at all times, and I only feared for the prop-shaft and rudder as we fell off the swells on to the ice. As far as I could tell, the passage of the ice along the hull always cleared both these danger areas.

After a couple of hours we passed into open water and headed east-north-east in full daylight at three o'clock in the morning. Really huge bergs were scattered all around us. All in all, this was the best time I'd had in years. All the worry of building the boat and entering the race was worth it for this single twenty-four hours of indelible memory. I turned in at five in the morning, a tired but truly delighted man. My feet were completely numb.

Day 19: *Saturday, 12 November   Noon position 57° 56' S, 91° 54' E*
Day's run 200 miles   Course E by N   Wind NW Force 5
Barometer 992

John: We sailed through bergs all day in fairly light winds under grey skies. Towards nightfall, the barometer began a spectacular fall, dropping eighteen millibars in six hours. The wind rose to gale force and beyond – and the course Tom needed to lift us a little north and away

The start at Portsmouth

Off duty in the saloon we might be three commuters
on the Piccadilly Line

Growlers are hard to spot in this visibility

Dolphins

A flying fish; hang-glider of the ocean

Loading up at Cape Town with fruit for the Antarctic

from the ice-shelf meant steering east-north-east, with the gale-driven hail and sleet beating hard into the begoggled faces of the helmsman and duty watch. Tom stood ice watch during the critical four-hour period of darkness. He was clearly worried by the frequency of ice, both bergs and growlers. His Arctic anorak had a flexible wire built into the front of the hood, and this allowed him to protect his face with the fabric bent into a tube in front of him. How lucky we didn't have this weather last night! The mast, spars and rigging grew a thick coating of ice from the moist atmosphere. Both air and water temperatures are below freezing. The winches were coated with ice, and when the No. 1 yankee was replaced by the No. 3, it came down like a pane of glass – frozen solid.

Marie Christine: We're in the ice. It's 2.15 in the morning. After passing several large icebergs during darkness, now in the early dawn everywhere around us are lumps averaging about the size of a house, some bigger, and many smaller ones. I'm writing this sitting at the chart table in my waterproofs with my abandon-ship gear on my bed in case one of the many bumping bergs holes us. All are on deck except the three who have been on watch since before midnight, who are snatching a quick rest. 'I've had all I can take,' said Peter. We are tacking through the bigger, house-sized bergs; the smaller ones thud against the hull of the boat. To starboard it looks like dense pack ice, white humps of ice passing us by in the grey sea. Shouts from the deck to John at the helm.
'Big one to starboard.'
'Loosen the sheets, we're going too fast.'
'Go to port.'
Next morning we had almost become embayed in the pack ice but by keeping going slowly when possible in the strong wind and bumping our fragile way through the brash we had managed to creep through the broken pack ice into clearer water by 3.30 a.m. The boat seems not to have suffered – no leaks anyway, only one broken stanchion. For at least four hours we were constantly hitting lumps of ice. Two large bergs had been seen at nine last evening by Tom and Arun's watch. They passed through these two giants and then the trouble began with more and more ice surrounding the boat. It appeared as though we were making our way into a bay of pack ice with large two-hundred-foot high glacial icebergs hemming us in. 'I don't like the look of this', Tom said to Peter who came down and got John. And from then on they fought to keep the boat moving, nosing its way through what was like a minefield to us. It started to get light at 1.30. We could see the bright ice blink in the sky from the pack ice and the bergs; smaller ones moulded into fantasy shapes of fairy castles and swans; the larger ones of two to three miles long, flat-topped and dazzling white, with dark blue fissures tracing

Noel sail-trimming as we race along

from their tops to where the booming surf broke below. And the brash which was all around us, lumps of melting ice approximately five feet square. 'For this alone it has all been worth it,' John murmured, gazing with red-rimmed eyes, tired after four hours at the wheel, at the receding pack and bergs that had hemmed us in. 'You can keep your Cape Horn – this is what I came for.'

Down below we tried to warm up. My hands had been numb and the pain was intense as the blood flowed back into them. By 4.30, after hot drinks we were back in our sleeping-bags – life had returned to normal but it was a night I don't think any of us will ever forget. We were all up for breakfast, looking bleary-eyed after the hard night. The wind had increased and we were going reasonably well. Icebergs dotted our horizon. Two of our sails were torn, No. 1 yankee again and the blooper. John suggested to Bob that perhaps I could take a turn at mending them as he felt we needed these sails. Bob was most put out at this suggestion. I can only think he takes it as a criticism rather than as a helpful suggestion. Unfortunately at the time I took great exception to his refusal to let me get involved – I felt sure with a brief idea from him I could get both sails mended perfectly well. I had done stitching on the Nicholson's sails and there was no magic involved. My blood was up and my pride hurt – we had quite a slanging match! It ended up with Bob mending the yankee on his own in the morning, by which time we were speaking again and I helped him in a very minor way with the blooper in the afternoon. I never met a more independent fellow!

After lunch those that could went to bed. Tom borrowed Colin's bunk, who was out on watch, as he'd had virtually no sleep since the previous night. Bob and I had the saloon entirely to ourselves and with gentle piano music playing on the tape we got on peacefully with our task of mending the sails.

After supper Tom went out to watch for ice earlier than the previous night. It was a bitterly cold night with heavy sleet showers. The glass had been falling all day but by evening it plummeted alarmingly: in six hours it dropped eighteen points, down to 965. It was clear Tom was concerned at the worsening situation – the visibility was almost nil, the wind was getting up all the time, gusting up to 60 and over, and there was ice in the area. We had passed many large bergs during the day. As the night wore on the rigging, spars, sails and winches became covered in ice. Even the Brookes and Gatehouse wind instruments froze, causing J.C., at the helm, to gybe. 'Could you come up, John? I'm rather worried about the situation.' John and I had awoken with a start from an uneasy sleep at the racket from the gybe. John was already out of his sleeping-bag, quickly flinging on his oilskins. The boat was shaking and lurching; it seemed as though we'd lose the mast at least. I lay in my bed straining to hear what was being said on deck above the screaming wind. It was a relief when daylight came at about 1.30 a.m. and we could see what was about us. The polar nights last only about four hours at this time of year but four hours in that driving sleet, spray and unseen icebergs had taken their toll of nerves and strength.

Day 20: *Sunday, 13 November   Noon position 58° 00' S, 91° 54' E Day's run ?   Course E by N   Wind NW Force 7 Barometer 966*

John: In mid morning the glass began to climb again from 965, and the sky cleared as the centre of the depression passed. Blue skies and 40 knots of wind made the growlers hard to spot in the dazzling surf on a big sea. On the 0700 GMT (noon local, that is) radio show, we heard that *King's Legend* had sprung a leak; she could sail all right on the port tack but was taking water if she had to go on the starboard tack. I made plans to accompany her if it became necessary.

Tom suffered a severe headache today and was sick several times, so he was put to bed in our cabin. Speaking to Judith on *Treaty of Rome* in the evening, after she'd told me that *King's Legend* was okay, I was interested to hear her say that she felt okay on the boat – even without the heater. 'It's funny how you get used to any state of comfort,' were her words. This is exactly my own feeling during my expeditions of the past twelve years. It's really the anticipation of discomfort which lowers morale. The body itself copes with discomfort in its own way.

During the afternoon the seas began to build again and the boat to move until it was as Bob said – a longitudinal washing machine.

I changed the routine to present our maximum power during the four hours of darkness – so the clock was put back two hours so that the dark was split between the two dog-watches, all three members of which were to be on deck spotting for bergs and growlers. Marie Christine and I also did a half-an-hour on deck and half-an-hour off routine; so there were four pairs of eyes searching for ice as we rushed along at around 10 knots. At one point, two bergs were seen at once, very close together and right ahead.

Bob altered course 45 degrees to windward and life became even more uncomfortable – and worse: alarming for those below. There's nothing like tossing about in the dark below decks and hearing cries like, 'Iceberg!' – 'Which way? Which way?' – 'Come up to port – there's another one!' – these three shouts all at once crossing each other, and then more crashing and banging. Usually, this is followed by someone dashing for the main hatch and shouting, 'I'm going up.'

Marie Christine: The morning was bright and sunny, a fresh breeze blew, and lumpy sea, an aftermath of the previous night's gale. John and I went on deck to look at a particularly impressive iceberg which we would pass close by. John took the wheel and steered the boat, to my mind, far too close. Birds were wheeling around the three-hundred-foot ice cliffs, with blue strata lines denoting its glacial origin. 'Watch out,' yelled Bob. 'There's a lot of large brash all around.' We were getting used to this slalom of avoiding the lumps but it still scared me. Once away from the bergs and brash I told John a story I had squeezed out of Tom the night before, of how the *Bransfield* had been nearly sunk when pack ice to which they had been tied up had calved and thousands of tons of ice had fallen on the ship.

We stayed on deck for a while enjoying the clear alpine-like air and the sight of dazzling white bergs dotting the horizon. John decided to alter the clock by bringing it forward two hours. It meant the two dog-watches shared the four crucial hours of darkness. As usual with any new suggestion it was met with a lot of grumbling and moaning. I kept quiet although I felt it was unreasonable of people to be so unreceptive to a change that would help everyone without putting more load on any one watch. Tom spent the day in our bed, trying to shake off a migraine. I'd managed a quick sleep in Colin's empty bunk in the 'swamp' in the afternoon while he was on watch. We were going fast through the darkness at seven so John and I decided to take half-hour turns watching for ice on deck. It was an almost impossible task to see the smaller house-shaped growlers as we sped through the sea so fast with breaking surf all around.

When I was out on watch no one saw anything until Rog and I simultaneously distinguished a monster berg, its ghostly loom appearing on our horizon as the boat lifted with the waves. 'There's an iceberg

MC on ice watch

off the port bow,' we called to the helmsman. Then another appeared, this time on the starboard bow. Darkness was all around; the occasional bright patch of phosphorous sped past on the surf, imagination turning every white patch in the dark night into a potential killer, but we got through. The polar twilight was slowly changing to dawn but gradually we could see more and with cold fingers and toes Colin and I swapped yarns while peering into the distance. Eventually I came down, heated the same water I'd now had for two weeks in my hot water bottle and wearily went to sleep in broad daylight, only to wake half an hour later still cold.

Day 21: *Monday, 14 November   Noon position 56° 00' S, 106° 27' E Day's run 209 miles   Course ENE   Wind NW Force 10–11 Barometer 981*

John: The next crisis developed as we were finishing breakfast.

Arun had spent a long time getting soaked through in the early hours with a hacksaw, cutting away the remains of the massive stainless steel kicking-strap installation from the main boom. It had broken through a three-eighths inch stainless steel rod on the previous day, and the jagged remains endangered the mainsail if we should have to gybe on to the other tack.

Right now we had to do just that – with a vengeance. Tony, Steve and Colin suddenly found themselves in a great highway of debris leading to an ugly upturned berg up ahead. I looked out of the port window at the for'ard end of the saloon, and I said as calmly as I could to the others, still finishing their breakfast,

'They're in a lane of growlers. I don't see how they can avoid hitting something.'

'John, you can't afford to hit anything in this sea,' snapped Tom. (It was blowing 60 knots in a huge sea.) 'I'm going up,' he added, crawling out of his sleeping-bag.

I jumped for the main hatch and smiled reassuringly at Tony on the wheel.

'Come on up,' his blue lips mouthed against the gale storm.

'More eyes. More eyes,' shouted Steve, by the hatch. My oilskins went on rather quickly. I clipped on to the weather jack-stay and slid aft to take the wheel from Tony. Ahead I could see down a hill strewn with road-blocks of ice, and at the bottom left-hand side of the roundabout formed by the overturned berg the road was blocked by a traffic jam of pale blue surf.

'Which way d'you want to go, John?'

Many eyes were on me.

'We'll gybe and go to the right,' I shouted.

This growler could sink us – spectre of the night watch

'You'll have to hurry,' called Tony tensely from the mizzen shrouds.

'Okay. Off we go. Take your time. There can be no mistakes,' I called – and they were quick. J.C. released the main boom preventer while others stood by the yankee and staysail sheet winches. The manoeuvres went smoothly and we skirted the berg on what was technically the wrong side. The whole surface of the sea was coated with a layer of white foam, making the growlers much harder to spot in time. The waves were so large that sometimes in a trough I was uncertain if I could avoid the growler I knew would be just over the next hill.

We made it. It was a memory. The cost: one speedometer impeller smashed by ice under the hull, one damaged winch overstrained by the boom preventer, the last of the snatch-blocks washed away in the gybe. Memories come expensive in sailing boats.

The bergs were huge with great cliffs and mountains in central plateaux – 'Nice scenery, but not long on beaches,' I said to Colin, who claimed each one was more spectacular than the last.

On the radio we heard that *Condor* had a man overboard, but that he'd been picked up almost straight away. *Debenhams'* motor couldn't push her against this sea. No one had better fall off.

Both *Great Britain II* and *King's Legend* were aiming to pass close to Hobart; *Great Britain II* with a man squashed by a spinnaker guy, and *King's Legend* with a split in her rudder skeg. There is plenty to make a skipper worry a bit.

Marie Christine: Eventually morning came by our ship's clock and with it the usual rather squalid breakfast scene, now made worse by the festoons of garments hanging around the saloon and a steaming scorched heap on the stove. Tom, still bothered by a bad head, sat in a corner saying little.

'There's ice to port, make for starboard,' shouted Col, standing in the shrouds, to Tony at the wheel.

'More eyes, more eyes,' yelled Steve to us below.

'John, come up,' yelled Tony.

Suddenly all hell was let loose. John had a quick look out of the port window. 'There's bits of ice everywhere! I don't see how we can miss them.'

'Whatever else, we cannot afford to hit ANY ice in these sea conditions,' yelled Tom, jumping up from the corner. 'I'm going on deck.'

There was a scramble as Tom, John and J.C. got into their oilies and rushed up. The boat was lurching violently now as evasive action was being taken by Tony. We were well downwind of a large iceberg and we had just hit a patch of bergy bits, each one the size of a house, perhaps a tenth showing above water. They were everywhere. The wind was blowing gale force and the waves were anything between fifteen and thirty feet. All about was breaking surf, ice and shouting. Most people rushed on deck to help. I made a dash for my cabin, put on oilskin trousers, got ready my survival bag, life-jacket and oilskin jacket, leaving them on my bunk ready for 'abandon ship'. That ready, I went back into the saloon. It was hard to keep upright; the boat was lurching violently to left and right. Bob and I decided we'd get on with clearing the breakfast.

'Only the unspeakable French would leave the breakfast dishes unwashed before sinking,' laughed the xenophobic Bob Burns as we set to in the galley.

'It's no time for joking, you two — the situation's bloody serious up there!' J.C. shouted to us on his way through to his and Arun's cabin, which was now awash. We were taking in a lot of water through the aft locker which had no seals on.

Eventually the shouting died down: the boat was again on course and relieved faces came back down. We had survived another nasty situation ... How long would our luck hold?

Day 22: *Tuesday, 15 November   Noon position 55° 30' S, 111° 50' E*
Day's run 206 miles   Course E by N   Wind WNW Force 7
Barometer 986

John: The days of storm appeared to be over by five in the morning, and so Tony ordered the poling out of the No. 2 yankee.

At breakfast, Peter delivered an impassioned appeal for people to mark their own clothing, to stop taking his from the stove. Bob followed this with a blast about the cleanliness of the saloon table. I was delighted at not having to say anything. It was getting done by popular consent – the message was home: morale depends heavily on cleanliness and order.

In spite of minor backbiting the team was in good order. Inter-watch sniping has stopped. Men with salt-white lids over strained red eyes, thinking of others besides themselves, heat army lemonade drinks for their mates up on deck. On ice watch at night, four pairs of eyes peering into the dark find a sense of comradeship and common purpose so valuable and yet so seldom found in everyday life at home. Perhaps this memory is the most satisfying aspect of this kind of venture – the sheer length and size of the voyage steadily shape it into a unique experience. Something which, once the mould is cracked at the end, cannot be built again. The second time would not be the same. Each of us, old and young alike, will be slightly changed by this.

Our new latitude taken at 0725 meant that Tom had to hurry to get it down before breakfast. We were rather taken aback to find that 55 degrees 35 minutes south, 110 degrees east, put us far north of our Great Circle for Auckland. The storms may have pushed us, and the current set us to the north – but a likely culprit is the compass. About only a thousand miles from the Magnetic South Pole the magnetic main steering compass was dangerously sluggish to react when the boat was thrown off course. The helmsmen, compensating for fear of the gybe, tended to head too far to the north, rather than towards the south and the pack ice.

Marie Christine: Darkness came around 3.30 and at supper Bob asked in all seriousness, 'What time is dawn tonight?'

'About 10.30,' answered Tom, grinning mischievously; he had enjoyed playing Father Time with our ship's clock.

Later Peter serenaded us softly on the guitar. Down below the boat felt more like an air balloon, gently rocking on the deep – 'not unlike a night club atmosphere', remarked Tom. I think it was the dark and the empty beer cans rattling round the table that set the mood.

Sometimes they loomed up out of the mist

Day 23: *Wednesday, 16 November   Noon position 54° 32' S, 116° 00' E*
Day's run 211 miles   Course E   Wind SW Force 7
Barometer ?

John: 'Mmmm. Hello, John. Our navigator suggests you check the magnetic deviation of your sextant. Over,' joked Judith from *Treaty of Rome* over the radio. Maybe we've got some magnetic metal near it; or because we're near the Pole, the magnetism of metal already near the compass is more effective. Whatever it is, we have certainly made a surprising move north – from 58 degrees south to 54 degrees south in two days. That's 240 miles. We've been going too far north and not nearly enough east. Everyone is a bit edgy about it, but there we are. It cuts away a great chunk of our Great Circle advantage over the others. There's nothing we can do about it. We're suddenly level with *Treaty* and *Adventure* and they have us on handicap. All that risk was for no advantage in the end.

   The wind was down, but as soon as we put up a spinnaker, another berg appeared ahead. The distinct increase in air and water temperature made life more tolerable, but the romance and excitement of the icebergs is almost gone. Some of us may never again witness the haunting beauty of the luminous bergs in the early polar dawn.

Day 24: *Thursday, 17 November   Noon position 54° 03' S, 120° 38' E*
Day's run 150 miles   Course E by S   Wind N by W Force 9
Barometer 994

John: At breakfast the conversation revolved about the changing clock. As we move farther east, so the clock has to be put on. When the ice watch was adopted a few days back, this cycle was interrupted. For some minutes it looked as if Thursday, 17 November might be cancelled altogether, but in the end it was decided to let it run until four in the afternoon, and at that point it would become midnight on Friday, 18 November.

Marie Christine: Peter gave me my first guitar lesson of the trip; he's started me on a lovely song. We retired to my cabin and sat on the bed. I'm really keen to learn. I must keep it up.

Lunch, then Scrabble with Col and Tom in afternoon. It's quite a pleasant way of whiling away the hours if you win – which I did. I think the main qualities required for success with Scrabble are greed and ambition. I must have both in abundance! Col, sitting crouched over his letters, thinking hard and long, occasionally rubbed his wrist. 'It's rheumatism, I think,' he mumbled into his ginger beard. The damp had brought it on. Everything is still running with condensation but we have learnt to live with it. Wet bedding is one of the most unpleasant aspects. Both John's and my pillows are sodden.

At 4 p.m. our ship's clock went forward to midnight. We had supper, a good tot of hot whisky each, a few more of Tom's stories and then bed. John was called out almost straight away and was up most of the night changing sails. He came back in at 5.30, frozen and none too cheery. I'm glad I am along to help him. I feel he needs my support very much at times; he's got plenty to worry about!

Day 25: *Friday, 18 November   Noon position 53° 48' S, 126° 12' E*
Day's run 214 miles   Course ENE   Wind NNW Force 4
Barometer 986

Marie Christine: 'Jet lag suffered by some crew members' was written in the log first thing. Breakfast seemed to come very early – midnight by yesterday's clock. I felt as if I'd been to an all-night party and had far too much to drink. Johnny went to bed after breakfast, tired out and feeling depressed. He still can't shake off the seasickness and the last day or two have been bad for him, and he feels that the two days of heading too far north have thrown away the only chance we had in the race.

Still cold but nothing like what it has been. The chilblains on my toes are almost unbearable at times when my feet warm up; they really itch. Otherwise I've no problems. Noel is suffering from a skin irritation on his body which he's had ever since Portsmouth. He says the itching nearly drives him mad at night. I've given him my Brewers Yeast tablets to try. They just might help.

The boat is going like a bomb. 'She's really loving these heavy seas,' Peter told me, coming down to enter the log on the hour, muffled up in all his gear. 'There is a heavy swell but she rides it fine.' Once or twice during the day we lurched heavily on a really large wave. 'Let's get these knives away,' warned John, picking up my ugly sharp kitchen knife, which had slid to the other side of the table. We'd been guzzling quartered oranges. 'If the boat goes over you don't want this stuck in you.'

It was close to these waters that *Sayula*, Ramon Carlin's winner of the last race, was turned over.

More Scrabble with Tom after supper. I'll certainly miss him on the next leg. At times with the others I feel a bit like the headmaster's wife but Tom loves to talk and answer all my questions about the Antarctic.

Johnny and I felt really cold in bed. I'd not bothered to heat the water in my hot water bottle and our feet were like ice. We tried imaginary running races with John doing the commentary and always just beating me at the post, however hard I tried to move my feet in the confines of the sleeping-bag. It helped a bit.

Day 26: *Saturday, 19 November   Noon position 52° 32' S, ?*
Day's run 217 miles   Course ?   Wind?
Barometer ?

Marie Christine: Beautiful bright, sunny day; slightly warmer, still strong wind blowing and heavy seas. J.C., thumbing through the log for this leg, reckons we have had gale force winds for two-thirds of the time and a lot of that has been storm force. Lucky we've been going with it!

I did some cooking in the morning, making bread, a chocolate cake for supper, rock buns and choc. chip cookies, which should keep us going for a bit.

'F' troop have cheered up today. They had all been rather silent for the past few days; it's a long time at sea to keep up the momentum. I spent the afternoon out, the boat cutting along the white-capped blue waves, dove pigeons and silver-grey petrels fluttering in our wake; John at the wheel with me and Tom sitting beside him while the 'cadets', Tony, Steve and Col, horseplayed in the centre cockpit. They ended by trussing Colin up like a chicken with the blue and white sheets. It is one way of getting rid of surplus energy.

Southern Ocean seas. Bob sail-mending while running downwind,
Arun at helm with Dick — another 200-mile day

We heard on the radio that *B & B Italia* has broken a spreader. They have quite a problem and could easily lose the mast. There are no steps on their mast so they have to go up in a sling to fix it while the boat rolls 60 degrees. They are quite close to us. John has offered help if they need it. 'I don't suppose they are carrying the forest that we are,' Arun quietly added. We have almost enough wood on board to construct another boat!

Before supper while John was resting in bed, Colin and I were putting jam away in one of the cupboards when we managed to scorch and melt the vinyl off a corner of one of the orange saloon cushions by letting it touch the paraffin stove. They'd cost a lot to make and I knew John would be fed up. Fortunately the burnt area could be tucked out of sight and we waited until after J.C.'s delicious curry before confessing our accident. John took it reasonably well.

Day 27: *Sunday, 20 November   Noon position 51° 24' S, 136° 34' E*
Day's run 194 miles   Course ENE   Wind NNW Force 5
Barometer 993

Marie Christine: Looking round the breakfast table I was struck how people's appearances have changed since Portsmouth and Cape Town. J.C. has grown a big, bushy, dark brown beard. When he wears his red North Cape hat cossack style you'd have thought he'd just walked out of the Kremlin. Others have followed suit. Bob, Steve, Peter, Roger, Tony, Noel, Tom, Arun and Colin had beards before. But now the only chins visible are John's, mine and young Dickie's.

A calm day, not much wind and a bit of rain. Scrabble in the afternoon with Tom, John, Col and me. It deteriorated at the end when I accused John of cheating, at which he snatched the score paper out of Colin's hand and ate it!

We dropped to only two knots at five in the afternoon; hardly any wind at all, then all of a sudden it sprang up and we shot along and heeled over with pots and pans clattering to the floor in the galley.

We thought we'd have a bit of a party in the evening. I had a good wash and changed into clean jeans. (I find I've lost weight.) J.C. was first into the beer and became very talkative. The rest of us were a bit reluctant to let ourselves go: anything could still happen – icebergs, storms. We had a real blow-out of a supper: chilli con carne, cheesecake, Fonseca port cake, and finally Steve's Athol Brose. The guitar was fished out and J.C. strummed some bluesy-type songs. He then went up and fell into the aft cockpit, much to the amazement of Peter, Arun and Dick who were out on watch. We all finally turned in about midnight, having heard from *B & B* that they were making for Hobart to repair their damage.

Pumping out the loo tonight I noticed no phosphorescence at all. It's been very bright for some time now; pumping in the sea water one can see bright specks of it. Perhaps we've moved into warmer water where there is less.

Day 28: *Monday, 21 November   Noon position 50° 24' S, 140° 27' E*
Day's run 192 miles   Course ENE   Wind NNW Force 5
Barometer 1002

John: The weather is noticeably warmer now at 51 degrees south compared with 59 degrees south. It's just about possible to live without wearing long-johns. There is a distinct border for the birds, too. The silver-grey petrels have gone and in their place are new kinds of birds from Tasmania called 'mutton birds', although they taste like oily sheep according to Peter, who comes from Hobart. But then he is a little short-sighted so I'm not sure that they are the birds he thinks they are; and with all that fuss about the Ancient Mariner and the albatross, I don't think we're going to be eating any anyway.

Day 29: *Tuesday, 22 November   Noon position 48° 04' S, 145° 03' E*
Day's run 223 miles   Course ENE   Wind W Force 6
Barometer 1002

John: The wind was perfect for the storm spinnaker and new records were set for four-hour watches at 39.5 miles on the Brookes and Gatehouse. The result of this was extra movement in the steering quadrant, so that we could no longer risk flying spinnakers until a new key-way is fitted in the quadrant, and this can't be done until we reach Auckland.

At night I spent hours on the radio with Peter for *B & B Italia*, who have now decided to make for Auckland instead of Hobart. We heard that another boat ordered £10,000 worth of sails in Auckland.

During the night the wind increased to gale force and beyond. The main boom-end fitting to the main sheet broke, and the £800 No. 1 yankee blew out. I was crestfallen. I'll be ordering no new sails in Auckland.

Bob and I have been unable to communicate at all for many days now. I just write my requirements in the day report book by the chart table. Bob's blowing out the No. 1 yankee will not help things.

Day 30: *Wednesday, 23 November   Noon position 46° 14' S, 148° 49' E*
Day's run 215 miles   Course NE   Wind WSW Force 9
Barometer 1008

John: The spinnaker pole heel-track on the main mast was distorted – probably at the time of the oversailing of the No. 1 yankee this morning.

The wind continued and the seas built up all day. We had to gybe after lunch to clear Tasmania, and one of the ten-minutely rogue seas swamped me at the wheel – sea water up your nose tastes just the same in the Tasman Sea as it does on Brighton beach. All night the heavy seas continued, and there were two really bad broaches at three in the morning while Noel was at the helm. He said they really had his knees shaking. Down below in our cabin we wondered if the boat was falling apart.

Marie Christine: A rough night. The wind built up steadily, gusting well over 60 at times with the frequent squalls. The large swell and occasional cross waves pushed the boat well over time after time. Everyone looked tired at breakfast after the worrying and uncomfortable night; most of all John. For him the damage sustained had cost about £1,000. We're involved in a very expensive game, without the necessary funds to push our boat to the limit required to win. We must be satisfied with making the passage.

The wind kept up a steady gale force strength with mounting seas. Exhilarating for the helmsman steering the boat as she surged at 15 knots down wave after wave; every so often he would yell 'Look out' as a large cross wave came racing like an express train towards us. Down below we hung on, wondering if this would be the wave that would turn our world upside down.

The aft bilge pump packed up, causing our heads to flood alarmingly. A sound like Niagara Falls greeted me as I went into my cabin after supper. John and Peter were on the radio again, so Tom and I got to work with the stirrup pump on the rushing water as it swirled around our ankles and up the well. A curious way for our guest navigator to spend the evening.

Day 31: *Thursday, 24 November   Noon position 44° 11' S, 152° 30' E*
Day's run 199 miles   Course ENE   Wind SW Force 6
Barometer 1020

John: At lunch the subject of the Auckland three weeks came up for discussion. As usual, twelve people could not agree on one single plan, so there had to be a compromise which satisfied no one completely. One of the main problems is the initial binge, which occupies a small percentage of the crew for the first three days and prevents the rest from carrying out any set plan.

There was talk on the radio of *33 Export* having broken her boom twice. The evening position certainly set her back a long way. Many of the boats reported problems of one kind or another from masts and spars to steering. The result of this leg is still very much in doubt. If there were to be a big storm maybe our steering would give up altogether on us.

Day 32: *Friday, 25 November   Noon position 42° 15' S, 155° 46' E*
Day's run 169 miles   Course NE by E   Wind SW by W Force 5
Barometer 1026

John: All day the wind fell lighter and lighter, until with the radial-head spinnaker and all sails set we gradually came to a stop. Down below I clinched the Scrabble with the words 'adjudge' and 'pencil' in the treble, whilst sucking oranges through a hole jammed up with a sugar lump. Very tasty.

Marie Christine: A calmer night with the glass rising and the sea

growing flatter. There is a general air of well-being about the ship as
people are able to sort out their sodden gear and have a good wash. J.C.
has lifted restrictions on our water ration as we reckon we are about
seven days from Auckland, if all goes to plan. Johnny can't wait to get
there; he is feeling like a caged animal, and a seasick one at that! As for
the rest of us, we're all quite cheery except for Bob, who has sails to
mend all the time and is getting tired, I suspect. He won't let anyone
help him.

Day 33: *Saturday, 26 November   Noon position 41° 18' S, 158° 35' E*
Day's run 76 miles   Course ENE   Wind Variable Force 0–1
Barometer 1029

Marie Christine: A day of great calm: 'no progress', or not much, with
only seventy-six miles on the clock. The slatting of sails and a grey fin
whale awash on the starboard quarter. Blue skies, warm sun on our
backs and albatrosses and cape pigeons drifting lazily over the water.
The boat was soon festooned with damp, mouldy gear airing and
drying in the bright sunshine. Shorts and sunhats were the order of the
day; toenails being cut after thirty odd days of thick socks and boots.
  During the morning we saw a fine humpbacked whale a short dis-

'F' troop. Airing clothes in Southern Ocean,
l-r Noel, Bob, Roger

tance from the boat, blowing at frequent intervals in the flat blue Tasman Sea.

A party supper of pâté and bread I'd made during the afternoon; ham and chocolate cake, washed down with four litres of red wine donated by 'F' troop, two bottles of champagne by 'Doom Watch' which they'd been given by some girls in Cape Town; and, not to be left out, Peter produced a box of Black Magic for the Arun's watch contribution. Tom and I washed up while 'Doom Watch' played hide and seek up on deck. Not very easy to find anywhere to hide on a fifty-seven-foot ocean racer, so Peter got the guitar and with Colin on his ancient, woodwormy, faded black and red squeezebox, those on deck sang songs, hymns, and carols with gusto.

Excitement is mounting as we near Auckland. Maybe only five days to go if the wind blows. *Condor* is now in Auckland.

Day 34: *Sunday, 27 November   Noon position 40° 21' S, 161° 12' E Day's run 174 miles   Course ENE   Wind NNW Force 4 Barometer ?*

Marie Christine: There is slight tension at present between Tom and John. We all get on each other's nerves at times, I suppose. John is obviously not too cheerful at the moment and showing little interest in anything. I feel this is partly due to the ever-present seasickness, the acceptance of the fact that we are not going to do as well as we'd hoped at the start of this leg, and the minor irritations of living at close quarters with people for such a time. It would seem that Tom can't understand John's lack of interest and thinks that as skipper he should be chivying everyone on. I can see and understand both sides.

I spent the morning away from it all up on the pulpit hidden by the genoa. The sun shone between white clouds and turned the dull sea into sparkling patches of blue. It was perfect and I realized that I had grown to love the sea; to find peace, excitement, exhilarating fear and comfort from its ever-changing surface. This feeling had grown over the months we had been at sea. I tried to recall how I'd felt at the start of our voyage in August. The ocean had then appeared to me a menacing presence; the calm was mere respite before a storm which could take us at any moment. We had now survived storms and ice, suffered heat, cold and damp, and our dart-shaped boat was true. Would there be any other existence to match this purity of purpose?

Later John came up to join me. He was shocked to find that a bolt had nearly worked itself out of the foot of the forestay. It would have needed very little pressure for it to have come out entirely and that would have meant no forestay and probably no mast.

Arun was called and was able to fit in a new split pin and knock the bolt back into position.

The wind slackened and by afternoon we were barely moving. I lay out in the centre cockpit, soaking up the sun. It was like a benediction after the ice. I'd never experienced chilblains itching from the sun's heat before but they would soon be gone in this.

(Jet in sky flying to Wellington first sign of life.)

Tom was telling Bob and me stories of sailing over to Brittany when on leave from the Antarctic Survey when John came up and in seconds upset us all by bringing up the topic of corruption in Government. I could see Tom bristling with anger, our mood destroyed, and yet poor John was in a depressed state and he certainly didn't feel in the mood to talk of jaunts abroad and I think would have preferred a diversionary, controversial discussion.

Later that evening, with everyone else abed or out on watch, Tom spoke out and suggested John snap out of his gloom as it was getting everyone down. I felt divided in semi-agreement with Tom and yet hating to hear any criticism of John. I've always felt I was his greatest champion and yet the first to criticize him to his face – a contradiction perhaps. That night John didn't sleep at all, the harsh words from Tom had produced an electric effect on him. Tom had been worried about loyalty and the morale of the crew, particularly concerning a recorded interview he had overheard the previous night. John was naturally concerned what people were saying behind 'closed doors' and not to his face. So after talking to me for half the night he went out on deck to talk things over.

Day 35: *Monday, 28 November   Noon position 38° 43′ S, 164° 33′ E
Day's run 128 miles   Course NE by E   Wind NW Force 2
Barometer ?*

John: On the one hand I feel we have lost our one great chance in the race through heading north instead of holding the Great Circle course. On the other hand I am oppressed by Bob's lack of communication and Tony's stony silence. On top of this Marie Christine spent all her time talking with Tom whose only involvement in the project was a short trip from Cape Town to Auckland. For him the loss of our advantage after meeting the pack ice was just a temporary set-back. I saw it differently. His style of leadership would be quite different from mine. 'There's no such word as can't in my dictionary,' he'd say. But I didn't mention the critical days after the pack ice which his headache had prevented him from navigating. I've spent nearly three years getting the boat built, and coming half-way round the world. I find it hard to listen to others telling me what they would do if they were in my place.

We drift along at about 3 to 5 knots in beautiful warm weather. 'Late November?' people kept murmuring delightedly, before they fell asleep on the deck for the day. And then it was over.

Japy Hermès, Tielsa, Debenhams and *Neptune*, all together in a thirty-mile radius circle according to the radio in the evening.

Nothing much happened all day except this excessively pleasant weather.

Day 36: *Tuesday, 29 November   Noon position 37° 34' S, 166° 36' E*
Day's run 139 miles   Course NE by E   Wind Variable Force 1–2
Barometer 1025

John: By dawn in the same small breeze we had another boat overhauling us on our starboard quarter. It was *Japy Hermès*. By late afternoon she had slipped over the horizon ahead of us. We were now level with boats that are faster than us, and the advantage we'd made by going farther south was exhausted.

Marie Christine: Still virtually no wind. We are stuck in an unusual high pressure area extending round North Island and well on into the Tasman Sea holding us, *Neptune, Tielsa, Japy Hermès, Gauloises, Treaty* and *Adventure* from our goal. The rest of the fleet is in Auckland.

I cooked a supper of cheese and onion pies, fresh crusty bread and finished off with dried apricots cooked in the pressure cooker and Carnation milk. Just as I was handing out the last plate of pud, Bob stood up to make an announcement.

He said he'd realized he'd been moody over the past few weeks. He couldn't help it unless there were certain changes, one being that nobody should speak to him for an hour after he got up and if we wanted him to stay on for the rest of the trip we should let him know, otherwise he was getting off at Auckland. Also he was fed up with John's puritanical viewpoint!

It was an emotional moment for him and I think we were all very sorry that he felt this way. John was as surprised as any of us, but talking between ourselves later it was clear that much as we wanted Bob to stay there weren't going to be any changes. Everyone else got along fine with each other, the fault sadly lay within himself. He'd been snappy with just about everyone at some stage along the trip with the result that people were beginning to avoid him. I felt it had come to a head due to tiredness; in spite of repeated offers of help from others to mend the sails he obstinately refused, determined to do this huge job on his own during his off periods when he should have been resting. It all seemed so unnecessary. In John's words 'a result of breakdown in communications'. He'd really only spoken to Roger, Noel and J.C., 'F' troop, over the last few days. I had given up days back for fear of having my head bitten off. He'd been fairly curt to me on a number of occasions. I was fond of Bob. We'd weathered a few storms together over the last two years; it was sad it had come to this.

Day 37: *Wednesday, 30 November*

John: And with the fifth day of calm, the beer ran out, and we were all just going up and down on the swell and listening to the lucky crews who'd reached Auckland by getting there before this Tasman high pressure system set in. For some reason it was just too much for some people. Late yesterday afternoon Bob made the shock announcement: 'I am thinking of leaving the boat at Auckland. It's all too puritan for me. I'd like you all to think about it and let me know as soon as possible.'

I spent the night without going to bed at all and discussed the situation of Bob with each of the watches on deck. Tony's watch felt that they had failed in allowing Bob to achieve a breakdown of communication and so isolate himself from the rest of the crew. They were all agreed that they were quite willing to put up with his bad temper and moodiness if he was happy staying on the boat. If he was unhappy, then the decision should be up to him. He could leave or he could stay.

This drama acted as a catharsis in the calm of the past few days, and everyone except Noel and Roger – who are Bob's watch members – became unusually cheerful. This coincided with a lift in the wind, and the fair chance that we will still beat *Tielsa, Neptune, B & B, Japy Hermès* and *Gauloises* on handicap.

I joined Bob on the foredeck that morning where he was mending sails, and decided to get down to matters straight away. Roger had told me the previous night that Bob had agreed to have the meeting filmed. I said:

'Well, I'll discuss this on television if you want it that way, Bob. Personally, I think it's a bit degrading. What do you feel?'

He replied, 'It's the first I've heard of doing it on television, and I don't want no TV.'

'Okay, then,' I said. 'Well, I've thought about what you were saying last night about leaving. I didn't go to bed last night, and discussed it at length with everybody else on the other watches – and they feel that they've failed by isolating you. If you're happy to stay on the boat being silent, they'll put up with the bad temper because they know you, and because it's you. In short, if you want to stay and go on as you are, that's fine. But I should say there's not going to be any change in the way things are run.'

'Well, it's nothing to do with them, is it, John? It's between you and me, isn't it?'

'If that's how you feel then I think it would be just as bad on the next two legs; and each one of them will be forty days in length, stuck in the same close quarters without any relief from the claustrophobic effect of the people being together and there won't be any more to drink than there is at the present time. So if you're unhappy it's probably best if you leave now. It's up to you.'

He paused a bit, and then said quietly, 'Okay. I think it is best to leave now, and with no recriminations, eh?'

There wasn't much more we could say. I got up and made my way back along the deck down to my bunk, feeling really miserable – and I fell asleep.

Marie Christine: Still trapped in the High: warm sun, blue skies but little to no progress. Bob's statement of yesterday has split the camp somewhat and cast a gloom over us all. 'F' troop are very pro-Bob and it seems to me they hold John responsible, with the result that if any of them are down below at meal times tension mounts. I'm sure this isn't peculiar to us alone; it happened on the last race that people left their boats and even on the leg from Portsmouth to Cape Town there were changes amongst crews. Everyone is keen to get to Auckland and away from each other for a break. If only the wind would return. We are so close now. John took to his bed early, suffering from a chill, sneezing his head off.

Day 38: *Thursday, 1 December   Noon position 34° 36' S, 171° 23' E*
Day's run 200 miles   Course ENE   Wind SE Force 5
Barometer 1019

John: Somehow we all got involved in a long discussion in the saloon after breakfast, while Bob's watch was up on deck – I wanted to clear the air about a couple of points.

Firstly, the film needs to be got off the ground, I feel. We have missed the sperm whale jumping, the pack ice, and the near-collision with the upturned berg; so I tried to direct people's thought for the first time on to the film, to encourage everyone to help with the capture of those fleeting dramatic incidents that occur on the sea. Roger must be kept informed and helped into action.

Secondly, I set up ideas for the reorganization of watches after Bob's departure. We soon got on to the closed door interviewing which Noel and Roger have been practising. Tom warned me that he felt I should keep an eye on it. I was upset really to have this extra pressure exerted, which I felt was coming from an unsympathetic film crew. Particularly unwelcome was the idea that the interviews should be conducted without my knowing that they were going on. I'd be reasonably happy – well, quite happy, really, for it to happen – so long as I know that it's happening, but doing it behind my back, that I didn't feel I was prepared to accept. Frankly, I feel that unless Roger and I are able to work together with open discussion, then the results of the filming will be seriously impaired.

Today began Toytown Navigation. Few people can have navigated the Southern Ocean with the use of Chambers Dictionary – which is also useful for other oceanic problems like Scrabble.

Arun produced the cosine formula for spherical navigation from Mary Bluett's *Celestial Navigation for Yachtsmen*. He then asked Steve what a haversine was. He didn't know, but Colin found the definition of a haversine in the dictionary, and it said that haversine is half a versine.

Tony the mad barber of Debenhams attacks Arun's mop

So then he looked up versine and it said 'one minus cosine'. Apparently, this means that a haversine is one minus cosine over two. Of course, I'm not really sure about this myself but I have to believe them.

With this information, Professor Lenartowicz, B.Sc. (Hons) in Physics, was able to write out a programme for our cheap plastic calculator.

Captain Woodfield was rather sceptical of this new form of navigation, which by-passed all his books.

Marie Christine: Sighted land, Three Kings Islands, after thirty-seven days out: a beautiful sight.

We are not a particularly happy ship at present. One or two seem to have it in for John, which enrages me. Hurry up, Auckland, we are all ready for a break from each other!

An evil-looking black shark's fin circled the boat a few times. I'd almost gone in for a swim yesterday. We spotted another yacht on the horizon during the late afternoon. It passed us one mile to port. What a beautiful part of the world to sail in! Here the air is crystal clear and fresh and the sea is free from the filth that surrounds Britain. It has not been turned into a giant drain for industrial effluents and dumping ground for rubbish and oil.

Progress is slow, the wind is blowing but not from the right direction and we could really do with the No. 1 yankee, which isn't fully repaired yet.

Day 39: *Friday, 2 December   Noon position Four miles E of Cape Wiwiki*
Day's run 169 miles   Course SSE   Wind E by S Force 5
Barometer 1019

John: We spent the night beating to windward under the lights of North Cape, New Zealand. Of all the nights when we needed a clear sky, it had to rain. The light of Cape Reinga blinked at us like a malevolent Cyclops through the mist and rain. 'You could get N.Z. to improve their system of lights,' observed Tom wryly at breakfast. One short flash every twenty seconds is not sufficient for the mariner to take a positive bearing. I'd always been so relieved to see a light that I'd never thought of it like this, but really I suppose it would help if the character included a long flash or at least a series of short flashes for this purpose.

By seven o'clock in the morning we were round North Cape and heading hard on the wind still, down the west coast of North Island; and all day this continued – tacking to and from the spectacular rocky coastline.

Marie Christine: Bumpy sea and tacking to get us around North

Cape; not much progress with the wind coming from the wrong direction.

I heated a huge pan of fresh water, washed myself from top to toe, gave my hair an extra good scrub and had enough water to rinse it this time. The boat was well heeled over so as usual I lodged the bucket in our heads and stuck my head into it, supporting myself where I could – in all quite a tricky operation. I just managed to get a good position when a shout from above, 'Lee-ho', warned that we were going about, and I shot from one side of the tiny compartment to the other, shampoo and towel skidding over the floor. Finally, my wash completed, I went on deck to hang out the first washing I'd been able to do on the trip. I dared not think how long I'd worn my black bra but anyway it was now clean and fluttering on the rails along with about ten pairs of pants and a few hankies.

'F' troop have cut themselves off completely from the rest of us. Curiously enough, Bob appears to be quite cheerful, or maybe he was just putting on a brave face. It could even be that he felt relieved he'd finally made his mind up to go. I felt a growing resentment from some of the others against John, holding him responsible for Bob's departure. It was a miserable situation, aggravated further by our lack of progress. 'F' troop and the boozers amongst the crew were desperate to get in for Saturday night but we couldn't be sure when we'd arrive. A fairly inebriated Sam from *ADC Accutrac* came on to talk to us on the chat show. They had been in Auckland for a few days now and I think felt for us stuck out in the High. It was grand to hear his cheery voice but it certainly brought home to some of the others what they were missing and at that time wanted more than anything else in the world – a real good night out with enough beer to get smashed.

Day 40: *Saturday, 3 December   Noon position Six miles NE of Poor Knights Island*
Day's run 93 miles   Course S   Wind SE by S Force 5
Barometer 1012

John: Our main problem now is that we don't have the use of the No. 1 yankee. It's still torn from when Bob blew it out a week ago. His policy of not allowing anybody else to work on the sails is taking its toll, and we're losing valuable speed by having no sail between the heavy genoa and the No. 2 yankee; and the result of this is we hear each day from *B & B Italia* on the radio that she's catching us. The distance was fifty miles on the evening of Thursday, 1 December, twenty miles last night, and now we're becalmed in sight of each other by the Chicken Islands.

'F' troop under Bob are another handicap; as the oldest watch they could have set an example, but instead they're a divisive influence. Forty days is a long time at sea in such a small, cramped, confined space.

When darkness came, a breeze sprang up and the heat mist cleared – and the race to the finish between us and *B & B Italia* is on.

Tom is trying to keep communications open with Bob, Noel, Roger and J.C. There are mumblings that they will all get off at Auckland. I would be delighted if I never had to see any of them again.

Marie Christine: John and Tom took turns to be up during the night to plot our course with land close to starboard. Come the morning there was a sharp disagreement between them about the course John had set while Tom was asleep. Tom said it had put an extra fifteen miles on our route and John disagreed entirely.

A beautiful day with the sun shining on the green forested land we had come half-way round the world to see. We weren't making much progress but no one on the ship could fail to wonder at the scenery that surrounded us – craggy forested islands to port and the mainland to starboard. I felt almost claustrophobic for a while; I'd become so used to our empty horizon and now land was crowding in on us.

We drank the last of the beer at lunch; the whisky had been finished two days back and I was dishing out tiny tots of brandy in the evening but we'd almost finished that too. Morale was low – Dick seemed particularly uncheery at the thought of his mate Bob going. Another disagreement flared up after supper between John and Tom about anchoring. The wind had dropped away completely and there was doubt about whether we were going backwards.

It was time for us all to get off the boat and get away from each other, maybe then we would feel different.

Day 41: *Sunday, 4 December   Crossed Auckland Finish Line at 0842 local time.*

John: By first light among the extinct volcanoes surrounding Auckland harbour we were neck and neck with *B & B Italia* in very light airs. I could feel the rebels up in the bows willing the Italians to beat us as they lounged about, making no attempt to help the sails round in the almost calm weather. The TV crew had gone on strike and decided not to film at all. Dick was more bolshy than usual and accidentally jammed the genoa sheet in the winch one short tack before the finish, with the result that we were stuck in irons for crucial seconds. It could have happened to anyone but it cut Dick to the quick.

The Italians had a speed boat full of supporters from their furniture firm of sponsors, all screaming 'Bravo, Corado, bravo.' A couple of launches of officials were out too. *B & B* crossed the line 37 seconds ahead of us after 7,500 miles – a victory that had a lot to do with morale – but luckily we beat them on handicap.

At the dockside on Marsden Wharf many of the crews had gathered to cheer and throw thunderflashes as we came in. They thought we'd done well in the ice.

Noel and Roger jumped off the boat on to *ADC Accutrac* as soon as we were alongside, and hardly had their feet touched the deck than they started chain-smoking.

I can well understand how Sir Francis Drake came to execute his best friend on his voyage round the world!

7

The Auckland 'Mutiny'

NOTE: This chapter describes (and was largely written) at a particularly low point in the two-and-a-half year long project. On reading the proofs I find it raw and jerky. I feel I did badly during this period. I was inept — I should have taken a firmer line.

John: We spent some three weeks in Auckland in glorious weather and as soon as the crew had landed from the boat we split into various factions. Roger and Noel moved into an hotel, hired a car and could offer these facilities to whomever they chose. For the rest, unlike Cape Town, Auckland presented some problems. The yacht club was miles away from the wharf in the docks where the yachts lay. The facilities on the wharf were the usual dockworkers' lavatories and washbasins, and it was some time before we all located the showers. In other words we all lived in a muddle on the boat and communication with the outside world was very difficult because the callbox at the end of the wharf was frequently busy or broken and midday in Auckland was nearly midnight in London. I was helped by Admiral Otto Steiner and his colleagues of Race Control who were staying at an hotel near by. Marie Christine was able to have a bath there and once or twice I made phone calls in the middle of the night to coincide with office hours in London. In short, the difficult situation which had developed during the last few days of calm weather before our finish was exacerbated in Auckland. The tremendous hospitality of the New Zealanders only served to make the problems more difficult because we obviously could not express our feelings in public at the private homes and parties of our hosts.

Peter Brand flew home to Tasmania soon after we landed to be with his family, whom he hadn't seen for two years. Marie Christine and I were able to get away for a week's complete break, fishing on Lake Taupo, perhaps the most famous trout-fishing lake in the world. The fishing and the solitude were just what we needed and luckily I caught fish on every day, between three and a half and six and a quarter

*JR's first
fish, a 6¼ lb
brownie*

pounds in weight. This was almost certainly the fly-fishing holiday of
my lifetime and I am sure it could not have turned out that way if it had
not been for the great help given me by Ted Bland of Heinemann,
Auckland, in organizing it.

On the way back to Auckland in the bus I said to Marie Christine:
'Things will not be quite what we may expect when we get back to the
boat, so we must be ready for anything.'

It was late in the afternoon after a long journey through the rain
when we finally arrived back on board. There were ten days remaining
before the start of our 7,500-mile voyage from Auckland round to Cape
Horn to Rio. In the saloon Steve was entertaining some people who had
given him a lift on his way back from a short holiday hitch-hiking in the
South Island. In our cabin I worked rapidly through a small pile of
mail. The situation in the rain that afternoon did not look too bright.

With Bob gone, leaving only a forwarding address in the South Island, Noel and Roger also hoping to be gone and in any case living in the hotel, I found a letter from Dick in which he also seemed keen to leave the crew. I moved through into the saloon and sat down at the chartroom table, sifting quickly through piles of instructions for the next leg from the Race Committee, meteorological reports and sundry bills, with the odd Christmas card thrown in. A small note in Arun's precise handwriting informed me that Richard Creasey, the ATV film producer, was expected very shortly in Auckland. His three telegrams of changing travel details rather confused me but I noted with some alarm that Arun, Colin and Tony wished to see me before Creasey's expected arrival. The saloon was crowded with visitors and Arun came out from the galley with his notebook and began explaining various maintenance problems that he had encountered in my absence. Then in his quiet voice he added, 'and I think I must go home to Scotland'. So saying he put a blue airmail letter in front of me on the chart table.

'This explains the problems, I think,' he said. 'It is not because I am not enjoying the trip but that things have reached a point at home where I can't afford to be away from the boatyard any longer.'

I quickly read through the letter from his brother Neil and had to agree that the work situation certainly demanded Arun's return.

'Well, if you have got to go, you have got to go,' I muttered glumly; and glancing up through the main hatchway I suddenly saw Richard Creasey on the dockside. As we went up to meet him Marie Christine muttered: 'We can sail the bloody thing home on our own if we have to.' But I found it hard to smile.

Over a very long Chinese dinner Richard was at great pains to try and help us solve some of the problems but I could tell from the way he waved his hands about that he was far from happy about the situation and as uncertain as I of the next steps to be taken. Just after midnight Marie Christine and I walked disconsolately back through the puddle-strewn streets to the boat where she lay at the wharf. I was unable to sleep at all during the night and I was unreasonably annoyed that Marie Christine was able to sleep. Tossing and turning I occasionally woke her up just to tell her how pleased I was that she was asleep. There really seemed to be no solution. The crew was down to seven and while this would make for a pleasant voyage home I just could not understand how we would be able to run the school, the salmon farm and the new fishing boat with so few people. All of these things were based on extremely tenuous financial foundations and it seemed to me as if my pack of cards was about to tumble down and maybe it served me right. I began to think of the past and in the yellow glare of the street lamps through our cabin window the past appeared to be a series of signposts leading up to the present disastrous situation. I have always believed that one should never make decisions when you are happy, hungry, angry or tired and I was the last two, but I could not get to sleep. At around four o'clock Marie Christine said rather grumpily, 'Why don't you try a prayer?' It seemed a good idea but I still could not sleep. I got up at 5.15 and went for a run through the empty streets. It was just what I needed and had so missed for the past several months.

The boat was deserted in the bright sunlight of a new day as Marie Christine and I ate a small breakfast in the saloon. I walked along the wharf and looked at the other boats, knowing full well that they all had their share of problems. Suddenly I saw a familiar figure, my old friend Stafford Morse. His woolly head could not hide the wide smile of greeting. He had come from Australia to meet us here in Auckland and down in the saloon we soon discovered that he was keen to join the crew and that his sailing gear was in the rucksack on his back. How pleased we were to see a smiling face in the right place at the right time and soon we were joined by Steve who was also full of beans after his holiday away from the boat. Then Richard Creasey appeared and said that Bob was at the hotel with Noel and Roger and that he was sure that the differences between us were very small and if we met that all three would continue on the next leg of the race.

It didn't take a very long chat with Bob in a café to resolve our difficulties and after that Marie Christine, Richard Creasey, Noel and Roger and I met and talked out our problems. In the early evening

Alongside Condor *at Marsden Wharf, Auckland*

when Marie Christine and I got back to the boat we found Jim Marland, who had been an instructor with us for four years, waiting on the quay. After a few minutes he told me he also wanted to join the boat and by the time we went to bed the crew was fourteen instead of seven – which didn't seem too bad a credit for one small prayer.

Next morning, after my run, I set about speaking with each individual member of the crew. I started breakfast at 7.30 in a small café near by and by the time I had seen half a dozen of them breakfast had gone on until three o'clock in the afternoon. The problems are best expressed in the letter Dick had written me a couple of days previously, when Bob, Noel and Roger were still off the crew. With him I tried to explain the answers to some of his questions:

Dear John,

I feel now that perhaps things on the boat have finally gone too far. When we left Ardmore I felt it was the proudest moment of my life, sailing around the world and with a skipper whom I had complete faith in. Now I feel that I can no longer sail with you unless a lot of changes are made. The crew were at first a close-knit group of friends but have now become divided in attitude towards the venture and I for one find it hard to get on with anyone except a few at the present moment and this is no way to approach the next leg.

I have no wish to persecute you in any way but I feel that you must be held responsible for a lot of the trouble on board. Your continual depression during the last leg was very hard to tolerate after four hard hours on deck. It is very depressing when everyone is doing their best to get the boat moving and then find that nothing seems to satisfy you. The film trouble was I feel unnecessary. You yourself said it was to be a true account of what happened but now seem to be trying to stop people airing their feelings without your consent: why? You should have nothing to hide. Nobody had said anything up till then.

The only way I can possibly carry on is by you either leaving and letting us race the boat back under a new skipper, which I would love to do, or by you changing completely. You may feel that this is an insulting letter and would wish me to leave the boat as soon as I return. If you do, then I am sorry. I really am far more perceptive than you realise. I can see that perhaps now the film and book are far more important to you than the race itself. It may shock you to hear this but there is no way I am anyone's fool. People should realise I can be leant on so far and no farther. Perhaps Tony could tell you a thing or two about that.

That is all I have to say John, but before I finish I would like you to know that up till now I have always defended you with everything you do, even to the point of rounding on someone because he had a go at you behind your back. Lastly, please do not think Bob nor anyone else had anything to do with this letter. It is entirely my own feelings. I at present feel very down and hope something can soon be done to clear the air. Perhaps Tom could do just that job if he came back to navigate us back on a straight course.

I thought this letter might well be connected with Noel, Roger and Bob; it was written on notepaper of the Great Northern Establishment – the hotel where the other three were staying.

'Well, Dick, I got your letter. What do you expect me to do in reply except say that you can burn in hell before I take you any farther. As you very well know, you can't step off the boat on to the wharf without people asking if there is any chance of a place on the crew around the Horn.

'The trouble is that you are twenty years of age and the youngest person on the boat. You expected this to be a difficult voyage but you thought that meant being cold and wet only. The true difficulty lies in the mental struggle of being confined for four forty-day periods on the boat and the solution to this problem is rather simple. What you need is a great kick up the arse and either your mother or father should give you that.'

Dick was livid. 'Don't bring my family into this,' he snarled.

Other people in the dockside café looked towards us.

'Oh, come on Dick, you can't make a great thing about your broken home. I have had it, others on the boat have had it, and we have all just got to put up with it,' I replied. 'The thing to do now is for you to ask me any questions that are on your mind so that we can discuss them frankly off the boat.'

Dick clasped his hands behind his head and rocked back on his chair, near to tears. 'I don't know what is going on,' he said.

'What exactly do you want to know, Dick?'

'Well, what are the watches going to be?' he asked.

'It seems certain that Arun will have to go back to England to get the boatyard back on its feet again,' I replied; 'he really can't see his way to being absent so long from his business and therefore we will have to change the watches.'

'I know,' said Dick, 'I just can't stand Peter Brand.'

'What do you mean, "you can't stand Peter Brand"? We have come fourteen thousand miles and been nearly five months shut up in that boat and I promise you I had no idea that you did not like Peter.'

'You know full well that we had had a row on the foredeck before we reached Cape Town,' Dick replied angrily.

'Well, I am sorry to say I had quite forgotten it; we have come some eight or nine thousand miles in the last eight weeks and a lot has happened. I thought you were able to cope with Peter as well as anybody had been coping with anybody else on the boat but now that I know this it makes my job a little easier. We will have two watches instead of three and you will both be in different watches.'

'Well, you have been so depressed lately,' said Dick.

'Yes, that is right, Dick, I have been very depressed and the thing is for you to try and help me because I am just an ordinary human being and not the superman you might have once thought I was. Life is not simply black and white and my feet are made of clay just as much as anyone else's. I heard that you had nearly got into a fight in my defence in Cape Town. Well, I don't know what that man said about me – but it is quite likely it was right.

'I had several problems on the last leg. For a start I saw the Great Circle route down to the ice as our only chance on the entire race to sail a shorter distance than the rest of our competitors. As you know, we reached the pack ice and headed north, losing part of our advantage, and then towards the end we were becalmed in the Tasman Sea while the bigger boats were already tied up in Auckland. I could not see a way around that and on top of this Marie Christine seemed to be always siding with Tom and this only made things worse.

'You asked in your letter which is the more important, the film and book or the race. Unfortunately they are absolutely interwoven. Imagine that each of the fifteen boats is like a financial iceberg. What you see at the wharf is in all cases only the tip of a lot of problems and we are only a small one but I think our situation is unique, whereas the other boats tend to fall into distinct groups. *Condor* may have cost £500,000 and *Flyer* £300,000 with *King's Legend* perhaps slightly less, but all three are backed by men of large private means. *Adventure, Treaty of Rome, Tielsa* and *Great Britain II* are run by organizations. *Japy Hermès, 33 Export, Gauloises, Disque d'Or, B & B Italia, ADC Accutrac* and maybe *Neptune* are all directly sponsored, as you can tell by their names, and as you can see by the firms which back them up at the various ports.

'We, however, are in a situation of our own. Our sponsor paid £25,000 for us to name the boat *Debenhams* and there is no further involvement, whatever our financial plight may become. This has advantages and disadvantages. I have agreements with ATV and Heinemann and because of that I cannot avoid a deep feeling of responsibility to them. When things go badly I find it a considerable strain. Our small iceberg cost something like £100,000 and the raising of that money causes me continual anguish, as much of it is dependent on the future. As well as this, none of the crew of our boat would have been able to get a place on any other boat before the start of the race because of our inexperience, so this is an extra problem.

'As far as the film is concerned, I was happy with things going as they were until the last stages of the last leg when Tom told me that as an Elder Brother of Trinity House he had attended a course to learn about the handling of television interviews, as a result of which he was very doubtful about the way the interviewing was going on behind my back on the boat. It did seem to be undermining my authority and it made for an extra strain. There could be no question but that I should know when filming was being done and by whom. The film will of course be made by an editor after all the filming is finished and so the content of the interviews does not bother me as I have every trust in the fairness of ATV. I would like to see a clearer idea of the film and its requirements of the crew explained by the film crew before we start the next leg because (if you remember) at the original meeting at Ardmore before we left for Portsmouth Arun and Colin were not present, and in any case most people have forgotten what Richard Creasey said because of the panic of getting everything ready at that time.

'You will also be pleased to hear that Bob is back on the crew because of course he wants to finish what he set out to do. Looking back now, I feel it would have been better if I had said to him that we should get back to Auckland, all take a breather for a week or so and then discuss our problems again, instead of telling him that he might as well leave the crew before we had finished that leg of the race.'

At the end of this Dick and I shook hands and got ready for the next leg of the race. But I don't think he really understood what I was trying to say.

My talks with the others followed much the same pattern, if not as severe. Of course each individual had his own particular concerns, not least myself.

Steve felt that maybe some people would use the film to defend themselves against what might come out in the book, and this highlighted a problem which few had considered at the start of the voyage. He also raised the point that the other crews seemed to relax aboard each others' boats whereas we seldom seemed to have visitors and I explained that our crew was generally rather different in outlook to the older, near professional sailing enthusiasts on the other boats, for many of whom the style of living was one they had been following for several years and so a lot of them knew each other from before. Steve said how he enjoyed the opportunity to develop a nodding acquaintance with the glamorous skippers of other boats as it was interesting to see what they were really like after having read about them.

Tony, on the other hand, was glad that we didn't give parties, as he was not interested in that sort of thing. He explained that he often felt very strongly that he was the second youngest on the boat, even though he was the chief instructor of the John Ridgway School of Adventure, and this made him apprehensive about working with Bob, Peter and J.C. under him when we got back to Ardmore again. Another strain was the breakdown in communications between him and his girlfriend back in England and his doubts about their future.

I was convinced that it would be better for Arun personally to continue the voyage, but in fact it was better for me if he returned to Ardmore as he could then deal with some of the problems which needed to be sorted out before we arrived home with the boat to start the new season.

J.C. had no money at all and for him this was very painful as he needed cash to sustain a social style which he found most important. He investigated the possibility of getting a job in Auckland, leaving the boat and starting from square one again but he was very much aware of his family's watching him from a distance. I felt it was vital for him to finish what he had set out on. There was a vast difference between starting at square one in New Zealand having failed, and starting at square one back in Britain having succeeded in what he set out to do and where he could hold his head up before his family.

Staff Morse appeared to be concerned only with the spectre of seasickness which had so nearly forced him to leave *English Rose V* and fly back to Britain on our voyage to the Cape Verde Islands in the winter of 1973–74. He was unaware of all the problems which lay ahead.

When Peter returned from Tasmania we agreed that he should formally announce his resignation as mate on the boat as this was an unnecessary position and indeed one which he had not needed to perform on the voyage from Cape Town to Auckland. He was happy to become an ordinary crew member without responsibility, as had been his first intention when he applied for a place on the boat ten months previously.

I took on Chris Barker, a twenty-two-year-old New Zealander who had befriended Steve, Colin, Arun and Tony. Chris's plan was to sail with us back to Ardmore and then work as an instructor during the 1978 season along with the others. He also hoped to be joined in Scotland by his girlfriend Terry, a three-quarter Maori student of architecture. I had some reservations about this arrangement. Privately I wondered if Chris's friendship with Steve, Colin, Arun and Tony was motivated by a wish to get on the boat.

Noel and Roger were holed up in their hotel and from the chain smoking I could see they were most concerned about their film and they felt as if they were mediators between me and the more vulnerable members of the crew, Bob, J.C. and Dick. I fully understood their inner struggle about the film as I had always found on previous expeditions the same despair about my books, but happily for me I had reached the point (which had always come in the past) where I no longer fear the blank sheet of paper. Half-way around the world I knew there was a book in it and I only hoped they would soon feel their film was 'in the can'. However worrying the next leg was for me there would not again be the pressure of fearing that there was really nothing to write about.

My diary completes the story of our final days in Auckland:
Thursday, 22 December 1977

The sails are back from the sailmaker and the mainsail still needs plenty of minor stitching which the sailmaker was unable to do owing to the press of work from other boats in the Race and the nearness of Christmas. Bob Burns had promised to be down at the boat for work bright and early on Wednesday, but he didn't come and when he didn't show up this morning either, I decided I must go and find him myself. The rumour was that he had 'flu and was in bed in his hotel room, which was being paid for by ATV.

Before leaving for the Great Northern Establishment to find Bob I heard that Colin had just received a telegram from his fiancée, whom he should have married on 17 December. It read: 'Leaving you and Balnakeil.' To make matters worse it looked as if she had gone off with Arun's younger brother. Arun is Colin's closest friend on the boat and he is leaving to go home as well.

As I walked up Auckland's busy Queen Street in the bright warm sun of the Southern Christmas I thought how the voyage so far had affected the lives of Tony and Colin. It wasn't the sea but the separation which had severed bonds which at the outset appeared unbreakable. Whichever way I looked at it it seemed unfair that Colin should be sitting disconsolately in the wharf shed doing Bob's work on the mainsail; he had had hardly a day off since our arrival in Auckland, while Bob hadn't done a thing for the boat and was being fêted by ATV as a returning hero.

I was surprised to find Bob sitting on his bed reading, with no sign of any medicaments.

'I came up to see how you were. We were expecting you back yesterday morning,' I said, sitting down with my back to the single room's solitary window.

'Well, I'm on penicillin; but I might as well tell you now. I was going to come down to the boat in the morning to let you know I've changed my mind again: I'm not coming back to the boat. An offer I've got here is too good to refuse. This racing is all right for the young fellows; I'm too old. I've got to take my chance and think about settling down out here.' The words spilled out and his face looked pinched and bitter.

'Well, I never thought you would just quit for a cheap trip to New Zealand – I wonder how everyone would have felt if I'd sold the boat in Cape Town and said, "O.K. fellows, I've had a good offer for the boat, the trip's over. Make your own way home." I don't think you for one would have appreciated that.'

'Oh, it's different for you. You're well set up.'

'All right, Bob. Have it your own way . . . I'm sorry it had to end like this. There really isn't much else to say.' I got up and walked to the door. 'Best of luck, Bob.'

I found a deserted lounge on the first floor of the hotel and sat down, painfully aware that the three weeks in Auckland had been spent on a fruitless clash of wills. Thousands of miles away across the Southern Ocean lay Cape Horn, quite careless of personalities.

'I thought you might like to be one of two watch-leaders – Bob's not coming with us,' I said to Colin, as he sat on a pile of red sail bags working away with palm and needle on the mainsail in the gloomy wharf shed. 'If you're feeling really down the best solution is hard work; it'll help take your mind off it a bit.'

'Yes, I'd like to be a watch-leader.' He smiled sadly. I felt awkward, remembering a similar situation in my own life nearly twenty years before. There was nothing I could or should say.

Colin mending sails in Auckland

We took everyone on the boat out to dinner that night and Colin had a lot to drink. The Italian crew bought us chianti and the French some burgundy. We gave them a bottle of Glenfiddich malt whisky. We had all had problems, but it was dark and warm and late in the restaurant and the musician played Italian and French songs for us. It was fun being on the Race. Colin weaved about a bit and clung to Marie Christine for support, but we got him to bed all right in the end. Marie Christine smoked a couple of cigarettes, a thing almost unknown for her, in an effort to help Roger feel she was on his side and understood the difficulties of making a film about all this.

Friday, 23 December 1977

This evening Marie Christine and I took Cornelius van Rietschoten out to dinner after he and I had played together in the crew golf competition. We went to a pleasant French restaurant called Clichy, just outside the docks. Cornelius is tall, athletic and blond, and looks a lot less than his fifty-one years. In my view he deserves to win the Race, which he has led since the start, because his is by far the best prepared challenge of all the entrants. He has provided his own money and a sufficient amount of his time to build and test *Flyer*, which is a special Sparkman and Stephens design in aluminium for the Race. Determined and proud, Cornelius intends to drive *Flyer* to the very limit on the next leg.

'Sometimes the boat broaches so badly the crew are thrown out of their bunks. They don't like dat – I really love to see it, especially the big talkers!'

His Danish wife, who doesn't like sailing and never visits the ports of call, has suggested he write a book about the Race. 'You must get to know your crew,' she says to him.

'How can I do that? I don't want to speak to them – I just say three words a day – that's enough. They do as I say or they get off the *Flyer*, that's all there is to it. There is no swearing, no drinking and no reading – just racing and I love it.' His pale blue eyes seem a little distant as he laughs.

Cornelius is a driver, who spends most of his waking hours at the wheel. He wants badly to win. He sold out the family electrical firm, founded by his great-grandfather, and started his own merchant bank with the proceeds. He can't understand how I could possibly allow a film crew to interview my crew behind my back while we are at sea. There is no discussion on the *Flyer*; the boat is driven on his decisions alone – he doesn't want to know what the others think. I have to admit that after the turmoil of the past few weeks I wish I could afford the same approach. But at least I have my wife with me and that is

Treaty of Rome *alongside* Debenhams *in Auckland*

something his money can't buy; thirty years older than his crew, he feels pretty lonely in Auckland and can't wait to get back to sea to continue the struggle.

Saturday, 24 December 1977

We gave a party for the crew and friends on board the boat at eight in the evening. Everyone crowded in and the drink flowed freely. Paul McCartney's new 'Mull of Kintyre' rolled out from the cassette player and tears pricked my eyes. Jan and Stig from *Treaty of Rome* helped J.C., Steve and Colin with 'Southern Ocean Blues'.

I awoke to find the saloon dark and empty. It had been a long three weeks in Auckland. Monday is the day.

8

Leg Three – Auckland to Rio

Day 1: *Monday, 26 December 1977   Noon position Auckland*
Day's run 81 miles   Course ——   Wind SE Force 4
Barometer 1019

Marie Christine: Down below it had a deadeningly familiar effect on
me as I tried to sort out loose items that would fly around once we got
moving. This time I knew only too well what we were letting ourselves
in for. Now the sun was shining brightly in the warm air, but soon the
boat would take on a besieged air as we headed south into the cold again
with the miseries of dripping condensation, damp clothes and bedding
and fear of the ice and giant seas. There was no way out. I couldn't and
wouldn't leave the boat at this stage, but it was with a heavy heart that I
set about my task. Perhaps it was all too close to Christmas for me to feel
enthusiastic; the last few days I had felt quite down, missing Rebecca
and family and home terribly.

Day 2: *Tuesday, 27 December   Noon position NNE of White I. volcano*
Day's run 100 miles   Course E by S   Wind NNE Force 2
Barometer 1022

Marie Christine: A different watch system: two watches of five people.
Colin and Tony as watch-leaders during the day, six hours on and six
hours off and at night three periods of four hours. J.C. is now part of
Colin's watch and the plan is for everyone to try their hand at the
cooking under J.C.'s guidance. We should have some interesting
results. I have offered to do one day a week. I could easily fall into doing
it all in the end, but that wasn't what John and I had in mind when we
took J.C. on originally back at Ardmore. It should be a more efficient
system for racing the boat as the five on deck will be able to handle sail
changes without calling on people down below. Having twelve hours on
watch and twelve hours off will also mean that during the off period

*B & B crossed the line 37 seconds ahead of us at Auckland.
Leaving Auckland we were neck and neck again*

most of the time will be spent in their bunks, 'not so much time for socializing', as Tony succinctly put it. It may have its advantages in that people won't get on each other's nerves while sitting around down below. Anyway, we'll soon find out.

The wind dropped off in the night and we are surrounded by six boats this morning all drifting about in light easterly air, willing the wind to get up. It'll certainly take us a long time at this rate, with 7,400 miles to go. On the horizon we could see the magnificent outline of the smoking volcanic White Island.

Life is settling into its normal pattern once again. Staff is sleeping in Arun's bunk. He has been very sick and can't keep anything down. My heart goes out to him – lying on his back surrounded by boxes of potatoes, oranges and a large box of bread kindly donated by *Adventure* at the last minute, which I couldn't refuse, as well as J.C.'s entire boot locker.

Alan still very pale, but says he's fine. He is totally absorbed with getting together the charts and navigation books. He has a curious method of taking a sight. He holds the sextant up to his face and places his lips on a circular tube on the lower part of it. The first time we saw this, John and I were agog. Did he blow through the tube and cause air bubbles to rise or – as John facetiously suggested – was he going to play a tune? Apparently neither: he had one eye weaker than the other and being unable to shut it he had to move the sextant so it was in line with his good eye. I still haven't gathered what part the tube plays, but I've got seven weeks to find out. He reckons it will take us forty-nine days to get to Rio – thus missing the Carnival, which would be sad. Alan says that Carnival is like very rich fruit cake and after forty-nine days at sea we might find it rather too rich.

Chris, our quiet young Kiwi, seems to have a true talent for fitting in. As part of Colin's watch he appears to be totally at home on the boat and when on watch is continuously aware of the boat's performance and is trimming sails whenever required.

After breakfast we threw ten empty port bottles containing messages over the side. Chris had added a postscript to one asking the finder to ring his family. He had left behind an elderly father, two brothers and a very pretty girlfriend. These bottles were left over from an impromptu party we had had on Christmas Eve. J.C. and Steve had been in fine voice and with Peter on the guitar, had belted out our very own 'Southern Ocean Blues' for what must have been at least half an hour. This racket had attracted other crews from near-by boats and we were soon crowded out. Our saloon hung with Christmas cards and lit by a Tilley lamp gave out a festive air. On the table sat two beer mugs, one stuffed with bright scarlet geraniums dripping blooded petals when knocked in the merriment, and the other with a stalk of heavily scented lilies I had been unable to resist in a flower shop as they reminded me so much of home. The flowers and cards had only two more days left before they would have to come down, as we stripped the ship bare for sea.

Later that evening, Col, Steve and I had escaped from the carousing to go to Midnight Mass. Col and I found an Anglican church and a million miles from home sought comfort and succour from the Christmas message.

Day 3: *Wednesday, 28 December   Noon position 37° 53' S, 178° 42' E*
Day's run 149 miles   Course SE   Wind Variable 1–2
Barometer 1022

John: The next dawn found us off East Cape in company with nine other boats still in light airs, but by noon the sails were slatting impotently and tempers were a bit stretched as the other boats drew away from us. *Adventure* appeared to be having some difficulty in keeping to her course in the almost flat calm, maybe due to the brand-new crew for this leg not being familiar with the boat; anyway it certainly gave us the opportunity to catch her. I went on deck and sensed a feeling that we would catch up the half mile or so by luck, while sails remained untrimmed and the heavy genoa sheets hung from the limp light genoa. The problem was that Tony had sensed that no one was keen to make the lunch and so he'd gone below to prepare the bread, cheese, and cold sausage himself, leaving no one actually in charge on deck. This resulted in Noel asleep on the saloon top, Steve reading up Alan's navigation manual in the cockpit, and Roger at the wheel exchanging light banter with Dick, who was draped languidly over the weather rail. All in all it was no recipe for victory, and I knew it. I sensed that the crew knew it too but didn't want to be reminded of it. If we relaxed our approach to the Race and were content to slip down the order from 11 towards 16 rather than aim for single figures I felt a dangerous situation could develop.

The problem is how to achieve the lift in morale. Some of the fellows really need a lead, particularly Dick, who would follow Noel and Roger up or down the scale.

My efforts at a lunchtime meeting of the crew out in the cockpit fell on rather stony ground, I felt. There was a collision of opinion between the two watch-leaders; Tony was adamant that the cooking and cleaning should be done by the off-duty watch, while Colin and everyone else felt the on-duty watch should do these tasks because there was no need to have five on deck unless the sails were being changed, and in any case as it got colder six hours would be far too long for anyone to stay out and a rotation among the five would be necessary. Also the off-duty watch really ought to maximize their sleep because under the new two-watch system everyone was half on watch and half off, instead of the four hours on, eight off, which they had become used to half-way round the world. Rather than force Tony to back down in front of the others I said I'd think about the two ideas and come up with a solution later.

As soon as lunch was over, and as the watches changed at 1400, I called Tony and Colin up on to the foredeck for a chat and we squatted down among the sails. 'Well, we have an interesting situation here, with two big watches of five the future of the voyage lies squarely in the hands of the three of us. It's quite a challenge for you two, because the morale of each watch will go up or down depending on your leadership. We have a problem with the cooking business, Tony; let's sort it out now. I really think it must be done by the on-duty watch.' Colin and I looked at Tony.

'Yes, I think you're right, but it looks as if on my watch Dick, Noel and Roger won't want to cook and Steven won't be able to in bad weather when he is seasick – that means I'm going to be doing a lot of cooking,' Tony said, more softly than usual.

'Well, we need a firm rota with everyone on it – they'll cook all right if

J.C. tells them when and lays out the materials in advance. What do you think, Colin?' I looked at the other watch-leader.

'I think it's up to J.C. to prepare the list,' he said. 'I'm sure the cooking must be done by the on-duty watch.'

'Any other problems? How do you think everyone's getting on? – Tony?'

'Fine.' (Tony is predictable, it's always either fine or hopeless; there is never any middle ground.)

'Well, watch Noel and Roger. If they become disheartened Dick will follow them down into the dumps, and we'll all suffer. It's up to you.'

He nodded his quick sincere smile, much more heartening than the oft-used alternative of monosyllabic cynicism.

'What about you, Col?'

'Okay. I was a bit unsure about Alan Green at first, I wasn't sure if I was to navigate along the coast on the first night or if he expected me not to. In the end I did it!' He grinned shyly through thick ginger hair.

'And Staff, Chris and J.C.?' I asked.

'Staff seems to have recovered from his seasickness, and I didn't realize just how keen Chris would be on the sail trimming. He's a great help but we'll see if he can keep it up. J.C. seems to be enjoying himself all right.'

'Yes, I think they'll be okay. Alan was pretty shook up by the forty-eight-hour flight from London and then that big swell on the nose made him sick. He'll settle down; his job must mean he can get on with people all right. Well, that seems to be about everything. Can either of you think of anything else?'

They both shook their heads. We felt at ease with one other, and that shouldn't be underrated.

'Okay, then, just remember it's up to the three of us. We have a new and I believe more efficient way of sailing the boat. For many of the crew this is the time of their life. Ahead of them lie the mortgages and other family responsibilities; let the three of us try and make it good for them.'

Tom Woodfield had left us in Auckland in order to return to his work in London. And so in the afternoon I decided I really must try and find out something about our new navigator, Alan Green. I got out my decrepit book of Instructors' Notes, asked Alan into my tiny cabin and had him sit down at the opposite end of the bunk from me and then started the usual inquisition I made of any candidate for an instructor's job at the John Ridgway School of Adventure – except Alan was thirty-nine and not looking for a job with me. A tall, thin, angular, heavily bespectacled man of cautious speech and studied politeness, he carried the marks of one who had weathered many a clash with difficult yacht owners and skippers, committee members and officials. Given that extravagant mixture of vulgar money, snobbery, ambition, national pride and plain brassy selfishness which is the essence of ocean racing away out on the extreme limits of a materialistic society, shy Alan Green had developed a tough skin and an extensive collection of verbal portraits of the villains, heroes, stars and superstars of the racing world in which he had administrated for the past nine years. Since leaving the Navy after National Service his life had centred on sailing. A ten-year career with a discreet Government Department 'which had a bit to do with communications and a lot to do with making tea' finally succumbed to sailing after Alan had invented and successfully run the Middle Sea Race from Malta for two years during his spare time. In 1970 he accepted a full-time job as Assistant Secretary (Racing) with the Royal Ocean Racing Club (R.O.R.C.), but the normal club political in-fighting had prevented his becoming full Secretary until May 1978. He wouldn't be drawn on the point of whether or not this was his ultimate ambition, but he was good at cleaning the saloon table and he tried damned hard at everything he did from cooking, through cleaning the forward heads to navigating the boat. I reckoned he'd be all right.

Marie Christine: Like yesterday, little to no wind. Hot sun is beating down on us. Staff is still not right yet and had breakfast in his bunk. Steve is burping a great deal, which is all part of the seasickness, and Alan reckons he's okay now. He's taken over Bob's bunk in the swamp and attached to its head is a huge yellow motorcycle helmet which he explained he will wear at the wheel when the sea is breaking over us. Staff revived at lunchtime and ate Tony's tabascoed tomato and onion soup with relish and again joined Colin's watch.

'D'you realize we're outnumbered?' J.C. murmured to Colin, looking furtively at the three southern representatives – Peter from Tazzy, Chris and Staff from Australia. 'Of course, they all look the same to me,' retorted Col.

Later in the afternoon John and I retired to our cabin and, feeling sorry for ourselves at the thought of forty odd days' confinement, ate a whole box of 'After Dinner Mints' with me peeling and dropping these chocolate bombs into John's and my mouth.

Day 4: *Thursday, 29 December   Noon position 40° 04' S, 179° 14' E*
Day's run 189 miles   Course ESE   Wind E. Force 3–4
Barometer 1023

Day 5: *Friday, 30 December   Noon position 42° 44' S, 176° 25' W*
Day's run 149 miles   Course ESE   Wind E by N, Force 2–3
Barometer 1018

John: The easterly breeze stayed light for the next couple of days and we sailed on fairly hard on the wind. *Adventure* and *Gauloises* seemed always to be in sight astern, which was encouraging to both watches who strained to keep the boat tuned and sailing at her best. Down below I worried about the two-watch system and hoped on hope that it would work well and the crew would settle down. As skipper I naturally accepted the blame for Bob's leaving as an indication of my own poor management of the crew and I feel desperately keen to heal the wounds. How I feel the fifteen-to-twenty-year gap in age between me and the main body of the crew! Sometimes I dearly wish they were older.

As we closed Chatham Island, *Adventure* bore away downwind of us but I could see her spinnaker plainly enough all day from the mizzen mast cross trees. *Gauloises* closed on us on a more southerly course which enabled her also to carry a tri-radial spinnaker. We tried to hold her off for a while with the starcut, but she passed us all the same so we reverted to the heavy genoa and our original course to weather the island.

Just before supper I had a chat with Colin and we agreed to move Chris to the other watch in place of Steve. When Tony got up for the meal we called him in and he agreed the change was a good idea as it meant a sail-trimmer in each watch. The boat has never been sailed more keenly – we held *Adventure* and *Gauloises* for four days. Had we raced them from Ardmore to the Hamble last August we could never have managed such a good performance; *Adventure* won three of the four legs of the last Race and *Gauloises* was third on the first leg of this Race and won the prize for the most outstanding voyage on the second leg. In the end they had only got away by going farther off the wind and carrying a spinnaker for more boat speed.

Marie Christine: We overtook *Adventure* this morning. Those on watch were dismayed that none of her crew said anything as we ghosted past close by, but then neither did we – anyway, what would you say in such a situation? We could perhaps have thrown them a can or two of beer as they have only one can on board and that's to be delivered intact to Whitbreads in Rio.

I have been feeling, and still feel, mildly depressed. There is so little for me to do, really. I could take over the cooking entirely but I'm not keen as I'll have a lot to do when I get back to Ardmore.

The two watches are sailing the boat really well now and don't need any help there. I never felt more keenly my position as passenger. Nobody is holding it against me, but now the routine and personalities have become so familiar there doesn't seem to be sufficient challenge to jerk me into action and out of my gloom. I think of Rebecca a lot and feel selfish at having left her behind for so long. Does thinking of Rebecca make me feel sad or is it the reverse, when I'm feeling low my thoughts turn to her? I hope I snap out of it soon.

The two watches are sailing the boat better than ever before. We appear to be ahead of *Adventure, Tielsa, Gauloises* and *Treaty*.

An area of chafe had caused a split in the heavy genoa and Col made a temporary darn in it during the night. As it was not in use during the morning we hauled it into the main saloon and set to work. I concentrated on the tear while Col attended to another area that had torn on the foot. With the help of the book *Care and Maintenance of Sails* by Jeremy Howard-Williams I found the correct way to repair it, which was to open up the seam which ran along the middle of the tear, patch both sides and then three times stitch the seam. Full of confidence to Col, I said I could easily manage this on my own; but as I proceeded I began to think of Bob and whether he hadn't been right all along to spurn my offers of help. The heavy sail cloth was slippery and thick with tallow, the palm I was using was huge and kept slipping and I dreaded using the machine which I feared would not go through the weight of the material. However, I persevered and by the end of the morning had patched the tear and sewn together the seam with the aid of the Read's zigzag machine, which performed perfectly. Col and I were pleased with our efforts and joked about going into business when we got to Rio! It was good to see a flicker of a smile on Col's face. He has been far from happy these past ten days, since the breaking-off of his engagement. What must his feelings be? Regret and heartache. And what could we say to console him? There wasn't anything I could think of. I crept into the swamp yesterday to wake him up for his watch and I see he still has the large photo of his girl stuck up by his bunk. I just hope he isn't suffering too much.

A good lunch cooked by Noel: chicken supreme, fresh potatoes, and green beans. I had three helpings of beans. At this rate I shall be getting fatter than I already am.

The great day has arrived for Tony to remove the twelve stitches put in after an accident he had when opening a tin of corned beef.

Sitting on deck in bright hot sunshine Tony had given the ranks of spectators that we had grown used to lining the quay and peering down at us a real run for their money. Never cautious, Tony had impatiently set to on opening the tin. It slipped and sliced into the soft fleshy part of his palm, thick with veins, where the thumb branches out. Crimson blood spurted high then fell, staining the blue and white deck as the crowd leaned across in horror. It was a deep cut and beyond the scope of our medic, Steve, who rushed up in a dither with an Elastoplast. Tony was taken to the harbour First Aid and given penicillin and twelve stitches, later replaced owing to internal bleeding of the wound.

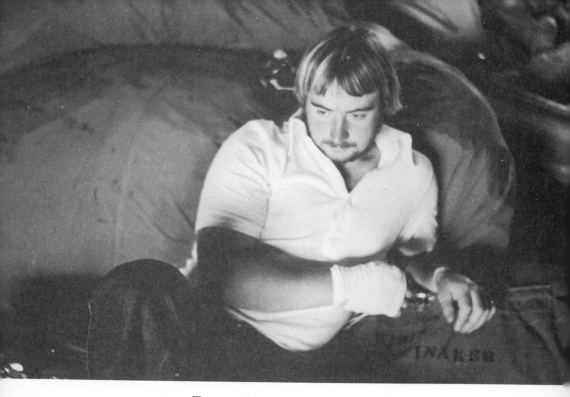

Tony nursing his twelve stitches in Auckland

Rog and Noel had the film whirring as Tony unwound the greyish crêpe bandage, exposing the ugly dark blood-encrusted wound. With razor-sharp scalpel and trembling hand, he cut the black stitches and pulled them out. He will need to nurse it carefully; the cut appears to have knitted together, but I don't suppose it would take much to open it up again.

I returned to my cabin feeling rather shaken by the spectacle. There was a quiet tap on the door and Rog poked his head in. 'M.C., would you mind if we asked you some questions on film?' I hated being cornered by the camera and felt I'd nothing positive to say, but seeing Roger's vulnerable eyes, how could I refuse? He and Noel had a difficult job to do; there was so much for them to capture on film which affected our daily lives, but most of it was impossible to film: Bob's growing discontent, Colin's telegram, friction between certain crew members. Unless there was a hidden eye recording everything all the time, much was bound to be missed.

Waiting for them to return to my tiny cabin I felt tears smarting my eyes; I knew what questions they would ask. Was I missing Rebecca at Christmas time? Was I glad I'd come? Was it the adventure I thought it would be? What did I hope to get out of it? What was it like being one woman with twelve men?

The first was easy and the most painful, but how could I adequately put in words the sadness I felt and selfishness that made me feel so guilty? I could hear in my mind six million viewers saying: 'So she should suffer — leaving her poor child for eight months. What does she expect?'

The other questions weren't so easy. My feelings seem to change from day to day; at times I think that what we have set out to do is one of the most exciting challenges left to man on this planet; other days and most of the time, it seems futile, an unbelievably boring, uncomfortable and unproductive use of eight months of my life. I never felt a great urge to prove myself or to impress others and sadly it was never, as it is for so many, my life's ambition to sail around the world ... Then what in heaven's name am I doing here? I suppose I came because John wanted me to and yet he isn't enjoying it much, either. Perhaps this isn't the time to make up our minds about what we are on — I must try and live each day as though it mattered and not wish for Rio or April when it will all be over. Who knows what I will have gained from the experience? I've learnt one thing and that is what a gift patience is. Would that I had more!

I cooked the supper in place of Staff, who I reckoned wouldn't last long in the galley. (Onion and orange salad, macaroni cheese, baked potatoes, followed by two apricot flans — quite nice.)

Day 6: *Saturday, 31 December   Noon position 42° 54' S, 174° 10' W*
Day's run 196 miles   Course ESE   Wind NE Force 6
Barometer 999

John: Now we are moving towards the International Dateline we have the chance of two or three New Year celebrations. The barometer has fallen 35 points to 985 from the start at Auckland and we logged 196 miles for the 24 hours to 0001 on Sunday 1 January 1978, our best yet. I wish I had spent more time in Auckland thinking out our course to Cape Horn, and less time worrying about three weak characters who saw New Zealand as a haven where they might start new lives far from the critical view of families at home. I would like to have gone farther south straight away, as I did from Cape Town.

We bowled along all day with an uncomfortably large swell coming in on our port and beam with a strong wind from the north-east. Staff and I were both sick, but the two watches each of five men are proving a much more efficient means of running the boat. I should have done this from the outset and let the prickly characters be damned ... when I think of the silly limits I went to to ease Bob's path and still he let me down. How clear it all is with hindsight!

The first New Year we started to celebrate at 2330 local time 31

December (1030 GMT 31 Dec.). Amid crazy messages passing between the boats on the radio, we consumed a couple of bottles of champagne, some New Zealand wine as well as port, beer and whisky. Also we ate half of the splendid fruit cake which we had had made and iced for the boat while up at Lake Taupo. Pale blue letters said HAPPY NEW YEAR AND GOOD LUCK TO YACHT DEBENHAMS.

From now on I plan to spend less time flattering the egos of the crew; they can sort out their bruises for themselves.

Marie Christine: More wind and we are speeding along well; the boat is heeled over considerably. It's a fact of boating life that one accepts the heel without comment but all the same it involves one in a great deal more effort in whatever one is doing. At meal times, food being passed from the galley to the saloon has to be held at the precise angle of the boat or else it spills. In spite of the square plate holes on the table, anything from a jug of milk to a box of sugar if unguarded will spill its contents on to the dismayed person on the downside. On the port tack it is quite restful sitting on the downside, except that your head is forced against the wall and to get up from that position requires a fair struggle. Perhaps one has slightly more control on the upside; with your legs stretched out and feet placed firmly on the lowered flap of the table you can brace yourself well. A slight problem arises when people wish to get through to the Swamp. You then have to lift up your legs quickly to let them through and slam them back before falling off. In our cabin to get something out of an uphill locker is a nightmare ... gingerly opening the door a crack, hoping to find and pull out the required item quickly before an avalanche of the cupboard's contents comes tumbling out.

Today I had to find the champagne for tonight's toasting in the New Year. We were on the wrong tack but I couldn't wait any longer. With care I opened the cupboard where I reckoned it would be, simultaneously the boat lurched to starboard and what seemed like the entire contents of three shelves came at me as if fired by a cannon: books, charts, odd shoes, whisky, brandy and the champagne. 'Well, at least the corks will fly off with a bang tonight,' I thought to myself as I watched the bubbles rising inside the green glass bottles. I feared the clatter would bring some curious person to see what was happening and I would appear the very image of a secret drinker sitting surrounded by whisky bottles. However, I managed to get them and the charts and the books and the odd shoes all away and shut in with no enquiries.

At 11.30 in the evening we turned on the radio. It seemed most of the other boats were on the air gaily singing songs and wishing each other Happy New Year. I spoke to Eric of *Gauloises* and Philippe of *Treaty* and wished them the season's greetings. Philippe sent a long smoochy kiss back over the air, much to the amusement of the others. *Condor* came on and Les in a soft voice said, 'The Major and I will sing a little song.' It was to Clare and Bumble on *ADC* and sounded an hilarious note of warning that the French were after them and they'd better get a move on! Just before midnight we opened the champagne and cut the cake. We sang 'Auld Lang Syne' and wished each other a Happy New Year.

Day 7: *Saturday, 31 December   Noon position 47° 13' S, 171° 15' W*
Day's run 165 miles   Course E by S   Wind SE by S Force 3
Barometer 985

John: Back in the world of albatrosses and jumping whales under huge rain-washed skies. We are already down to 47 degrees south and yet there has been no sign of the Roaring Forties ... So saying, with the barometer fallen from 1020 to 980 the snarl of storm was heard for the first time on this leg. A flurry in the afternoon from south-south-east died at dusk and then roared back at 50 knots from the same direction. A bumpy night followed.

Marie Christine: Again crossing Date Line today. A curious situation of having two more New Years today; at 1 p.m., our ship's time, it is midnight on 31 December back at home and at midnight tonight we are crossing the International Date Line for our third and final start to '78!

A day of steady wind and quite good progress – 180 miles – our best yet, but far from brilliant. While Alan and I were in the galley washing up the supper things, the wind started to blow hard. It seemed like a passing squall as the sky darkened and the swell grew steeper. As the evening drew on it blew harder and our course had us taking the sea on the beam, making it uncomfortable below as we lurched, slipped and dropped off waves, living inside this horizontal washing machine; outside our window was all froth, with loud bangs reverberating round the boat.

Day 8: *Sunday, 1 January 1978 (across the dateline)   Noon position ?*
Day's run 138 miles   Course E by S   Wind S Force 9
Barometer 992

John: Down to smallest sails, trysail and No. 2 staysail, we lurch on some 50 degrees off wind and sea as it booms up from the south. How lucky the water is still warm!

Alone at the helm at lunchtime with Peter, we had a long talk about how he feels he has failed and got the sack as mate. With Arun gone and the young, impressionable Dick taking his cue from Noel and Roger, Peter feels all alone. How cruel are humans one to another – long on mouth and so short on sympathy! I hope that after our chat Peter will

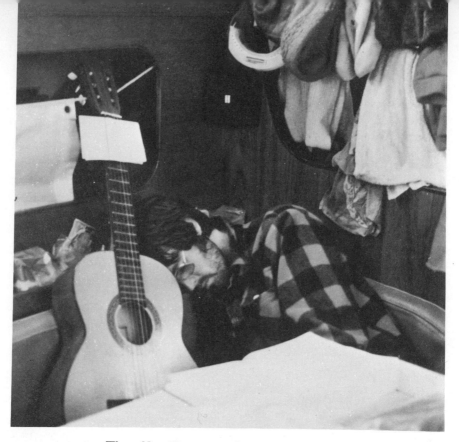

Three New Years were just too much for Pete

feel better, for in a tight situation the boat could wish for no stauncher ally than Peter Brand.

It was a rough day for sickness with the 'impossible' happening for Chris, Noel and J.C., and the routine debilitations hitting Roger, Steve, Alan and me. Only Tony, Dick, Colin and M.C. were left unscathed. Worst of all was the bowl of green bile beside Staff's lower bunk in the after-cabin. The plucky young Australian was knocked right out of action and I took to standing his watches until the return of calmer weather.

Marie Christine: A bad night for Johnny and me, with the boat heeled over. I alternated between lying on top and squashing him and trying to hang on to the upper side. At one stage we'd just dropped off to sleep when a bucketful of salt water shot through an open crack of our window, in spite of the storm boards being in position, wetting my face, hair, pillow, nightie, sheet and sleeping-bag. I wasted not a second in leaping up and shutting the window fast and with a towel tried to mop up some of the sea water.

All day long the gale kept on blowing a steady 45 knots, gusting over 55. We rode the waves like a bucking bronco with just two scraps of sail, the No. 2 staysail and trysail.

Alan went out with his crash helmet on before breakfast. Just as those on deck were asking what was the point of wearing it he was able to give them a demonstration. He lost his balance while making his way towards the wheel and hit his head with a crack on the mizzen mast. The crash helmet may have caused his unsteadiness but it also saved him a bump on the head! Anyway he claimed it to be highly satisfactory as he steered the boat with breaking waves all around. I just hoped he didn't suddenly want to be sick; he'd never get the helmet off in time and the alternative was too awful to contemplate.

Day 9: *Monday, 2 January   Noon position ?*
Day's run 158 miles   Course E by S   Wind S Force 6
Barometer 994

John: This was the roughest night we have had so far. At times the boat was left in the air by a wave with the resulting crash into the trough causing alarming flexing from the hull.

There seems to be a change in the actual physical appearance of Tony on this leg; he seems to glow with triumph and I can only put it down to a subconscious or even conscious belief that he has prevailed

Greenie in bone-dome

over his old rival Bob and the quiet cruising approach of Arun. With both adversaries gone, Tony at twenty-three, with his 'cold fish' approach to the rest of the crew, has many secretly praying he will succumb to the seasickness. Of all those on the boat I was least surprised to hear that it was blunt, intolerant Tony who had gashed his hand while opening a corned beef can in Auckland. The twelve stitches necessary to pull the gaping wound together were a measure of his explosive impatience.

The present thirty-six hours of bad weather is the worst we have had since leaving Scotland last August. The two watches keep the boat driving forward magnificently, blinded with spray even behind their misted-up goggles, mouths full of salt from spray and waves which beat the face. It is just such a challenge after five months on the boat together which lays each personality bare. The lack of sympathy for one another caused by the nagging aching drain on personal reserves shows clearly – a psychiatrist's dream! – but the boat keeps on going forward. At the end of it all each person will feel they have achieved something of major significance in their lives.

Towards late afternoon the wind abated and Stafford Morse showed his face on deck for the first time in a couple of days. Alan Green agreed to do his watch at night but I certainly hope he will be able to get over the sickness soon. Maybe when the wind goes aft of the beam he'll be okay. Surely after nine days we deserve a following wind.

At 1930 Peter and I set about trying to contact Portishead Radio at home in the UK. Debenhams are providing the fashion show at the London Boat Show which starts this week and they want us to pre-record a fresh tape each day for playing over the public address system at Earls Court. Communications can be difficult in the Southern Ocean:

1. We tried to contact Portishead direct – no reply.
2. No reply from Wellington Radio.
3. Auckland Radio came up to say Wellington had transmitter problems and advised us to try another frequency.
4. We got Wellington Radio.
5. They put us on to Red Phone Services.
6. Red Phone put us on to Traffic.
7. Traffic put us on to International.
8. International put us through to Portishead.
9. Portishead refused to accept the charge.
10. International put us on to Barwell Sports Management.
11. Barwell didn't answer their phone – 0930 was too early.
12. International said they'd try Portishead again.

13. Portishead agreed to speak with me but the interference was so great that the operator had to act as intermediary.
14. Portishead said they knew about the arrangement for the tapes but that they could only do them on a direct circuit, i.e. Radio conversation as in section 1 above!
15. International went to great lengths to arrange frequencies and told us Portishead would call us in fifteen minutes' time.
16. We were just going to go and sit down after two hours bumping up and down in the radio shack when Portishead came on the air to say the taping arrangements were taking a while to set up but that I could have the questions in advance.
17. Our power was running low but I answered the following questions for the tape:
   (a) *Debenhams'* position; (b) Weather conditions; (c) Distance sailed since previous day; (d) Current speed; (e) Whether under full sail or reefed; (f) Any sight of ships or competitors (nil); (g) Position reports on other competitors; (h) Any other news.
18. After this Portishead agreed to call us at 0900 GMT each day for a fresh tape.

The Southern Ocean is a vast grey empty place and we had felt far from the rest of the world. Now suddenly Peter and I felt very near to home. It was well worth the two hours of frustration.

Marie Christine: Very rough all night. The wind, still blowing from the same direction, causing us to jerk along heeled well over as we ride these steep grey waves broadside.

Alan, who has already recorded two hours of tape for himself, decided on a bit more at breakfast, his long white fingers clasping both microphone and cornflake bowl as he put into words the scene before him. Once more the saloon was festooned with dripping clothes hanging from the handrails above each seat. You had to put up with a wet dangling cuff or trouser leg brushing you in the face. The stove had been lit to dry the clothes around it, but after six large waves washing over the boat and fizzling down the chimney it was extinguished. There was a sudden lurch. 'There go my cornflakes,' Alan's phlegmatic voice spoke into the mike. Splattered on the wall opposite was a sticky mixture of cornflakes and sugary milk. He tied the mike to a dangling cuff and patiently set about mopping up his mess with paper tissues. I've learnt to laugh along with the others at these disasters. I think it is like a safety value. I'd be sick with disgust otherwise.

Day 10: *Tuesday, 3 January   Noon position ?*
Day's run 148 miles   Course E by S   Wind S by W Force 4
Barometer 996

John: *Great Britain II*, who have done so well since cutting inside to the west of the Chatham Islands, now report the sail track on their main-mast has broken free from the spar with the result that they can't hoist a mainsail until they have riveted the track back into place. It will be no easy job in the present sea conditions, even if they have a pop riveter.

This two-watch system is working really well and the crew are all in great spirits. Let's hope the trouble has come to a head and burst, and that from now on we will draw together as a team.

At supper time our tall, thin and lovable navigator appeared at the navigation table wearing a pair of silk gloves, the tornado whiteness of which was accentuated by the ultra-bright new nav. light which has been installed so he can see the chart at midday ('I'm a bit shortsighted you know'). Steve, the ship's mouthpiece, was quite unable to resist these gloves:

'Alan? We've seen the white gloves, the yellow bone dome, and the blowing down the sextant trick, now what is in the hat box?' This was followed by lots of giggles but in the end it seemed uncertain if Alan actually had a hat box. Instead a gleeful figure emerged from the swamp and threw me a soft parcel wrapped in a red poly-bag. 'Look at this, a waistcoat!' he cried, and sure enough big black letters in bold felt tip read WAISTCOAT. 'I bet he's got vast Elton John sunglasses for the tropics,' rumbled J.C., bouncing up and down on the seat.

Now Alan is secretary designate of the ancient RORC he has brought all sorts of gear with him as navigator: paper underwear, yellow nappy pins to secure thermal vest to trousers near his spine, JAVLIN polar jacket with the J and V inked out so his name appears on his chest (almost), two red helicopter suits borrowed from British Airways for storm conditions (one of which is used by a grateful Peter), Mary Blewitt's own sextant (she is the present secretary of RORC), which he uses across his face with his left eye because of an even weaker right eye, an excellent Wharton Chronometer borrowed from RORC, Tamaya Astro-nav. calculator borrowed from the makers, and a forest of charts, tables and instruments which are stuck all over the perspex spray screen by the nav. table, turning it from a window to a curtain. (That is why he needs the light on at midday.) All in all he is just the kind of person we need on the boat right now. He is well able to spend all day working on his navigation or reading a book; if drawn into conversation he gives his full attention but has no need to dominate the stage and needs no one to look after him.

Marie Christine: Perhaps one-quarter of this leg is over – as John and

I agreed, an encouraging thought to wake up on. We lay in our separate sleeping-bags discussing random thoughts till it was time to get dressed for breakfast at eight. Living in this six-foot by four-foot cell we had managed a fairly harmonious existence up to now, but I was beginning to feel irrational and set verbal traps for my poor seasick husband, who had no idea what I was angling at. It was like existing under a magnifying glass, having all this time to discuss the future, the past — our entire world. We were so different in outlook and temperament. John had always been totally insecure, an orphan then adopted but never knowing the love and comfort of a caring family. He worries about everything, always takes the pessimistic view that things will not turn out well, while I, blessed with a happy home and loving parents, have a built-in confidence and believe all will be well in the end, however bad the situation gets. I don't suppose either of us is right and perhaps the one view causes the other extreme. I knew what the boys meant when they said John depressed them. It's a form of brutal honesty. John will not accept any solace or crumbs of comfort. If he feels we are last, he will say so bluntly and not permit himself thoughts such as: 'We're last, but when the stormier weather comes we'll catch up.' I respect the courage of this honesty but there are times when I feel enraged by such an unmitigating view. My life bowls along with great gusts of enthusiasm. Only with hope in my heart can I get through the lean periods, but such hope to John is a foolish delusion. John is an achiever because he worries. Our views on Rio illustrate this. I am captivated by the thought of this exotic city and am ready to enjoy everything that comes my way. John is already dreading the heat and the parties and says he is going to spend his time there writing the book. I suppose we'll struggle on with our differences. This enforced idleness and proximity would be a strain on any relationship.

A merry lunch party. The two-watch system is a success at the moment and the crew seem cheery. Roger cooked lunch and was just about to come out of the galley when Staff vomited his lunch into a bucket blocking his way. Poor Staff. It goes on and on for him. At breakfast people enquire, 'How's Staff?' The answer comes back, 'Oh, I think he died in the night.' But they would do anything to get him back on his feet. John has been standing in for him on his watches when he can't make it.

Day 11: *Wednesday, 4 January   Noon position 53° 35' S, 156° 55' W Day's run 155 miles   Course E by S   Wind W Force 3 Barometer 994*

John: Young Dick is out airing the flaccid muscles of his shirtless, hairless chest at lunchtime, and the rigging is festooned with drying clothing and tea towels. The big-boy, red, white and blue, joins the similarly coloured radial-head spinnaker for the first time in many weeks. Whales lie brown and idle, gently blowing white fountains as we ghost by in water now deep blue, under bright sun and blue sky.

Everyone is relaxed and cheerful. Nobody is outside the circle. The navigator Green peers over the side and feeds the whales with his ancient paper underpants. No one dares tell him they're only blowing in disgust.

Marie Christine: The best day of this leg so far – warm sunshine and a clear, rain-washed sky, with a steady breeze from the north blowing us over a smooth, sapphire sea. We speed along with our gaudy spinnakers – starcut peeled to the radial-head with the big-boy as staysail.

We advanced the ship's time by two hours. It's like turning the corner for home; up to now we've been adding hours, the farther we go from Britain, until we'd added thirteen hours on to GMT. We are now down to a nine-hour difference, having put the clock back twenty-four hours at New Year.

There is a happy relaxed air amongst everybody on board and even I am coming out of my long black tunnel of misery and discontent. Lying in my bunk reading, my small cell changes from light to red to blue as a spinnaker is hauled into the cockpit and the gossamer gaudy silk filters sunlight through my leaky window. 'Come up here and have a look at this, M.C.,' Col, head of the sail-mending department, calls to me. Tucks taken by Bob when repairing the radial-head are now pulling the ripstop nylon. We discuss alterations and I'm pleased to find myself with a job for the evening.

Day 12: *Thursday, 5 January   Noon position 54° 20' S, 153° 10' W*
　　　　　Day's run 141 miles   Course ESE   Wind NW Force 3
　　　　　Barometer 997

Marie Christine: Tony lit the Tilley lamp for me and with the old familiar hiss as an accompaniment to the clicking of the sewing machine, I got the sail mended by midnight. It was back in use by 7.30 this morning. The sun shone again out of clear blue sky all day, flushing us out to enjoy the warmth like beetles from the woodwork. Damp clothes and smelly sleeping-bags were hung around to air and dry. The mizzen mast is always a favourite spot for dangling down bags, water-proofs, tatty jeans and so on. Our progress is moderate, but it appears that no one of the other boats are getting much more wind either, so we may as well sit back and enjoy it.

A good evening. Rog cooked a delicious supper of potatoes with cheese sauce and tomatoes, onions and corned beef, followed by pancakes which Alan had cooked during the afternoon and then reheated. I went over to help hand them out and was dismayed to see that our ingenious navigator in the absence of greaseproof paper had used single sheets of loo paper – the crêpes were getting the full treatment! We drank five bottles of port instead of our usual two and sang songs, watching a giant orange sun drop slowly into the sea. We scanned in vain for the green flash that comes a moment after the sun sinks below the horizon. Perhaps we are now too far south for this phenomenon at 56 degrees south. How different it is from leg 2! At 56 degrees south we were almost into the pack ice, muffled up in all our gear with the outside temperature below freezing. Two months on in the Southern Ocean's summer makes a great difference. Dick and Chris even had their shirts off today and were wearing shorts.

A new Barlow 32 winch drum has been cut through by the main halyard wire – surely it's a fault in the casting. John's never heard of it before.

Day 13: *Friday, 6 January   Noon position 56° 00' S, 149° 35' W*
Day's run 182 miles   Course ESE   Wind SSW Force 4
Barometer 998

John: It's sunshine and starcut spinnakers today. All is beautiful. But I'm sure we're slipping down the drain, so I had a chat with Tony and Colin, the watch-leaders.

'I'm not on this for a leadership kick,' said Tony, at twenty-three the most inexperienced watch-leader in the race, disagreeing as usual, on principle, with any suggestion.

The things that I think are wrong are that the decks are not getting

Crushed main halyard winch drum

washed, the watch hand-over is late, men are sleeping-in late; the saloon, the heads, the after-cabin, the swamp, the galley – none of those are being swept out; daily and weekly routines are not followed, not read and not reported; emergency drills are not being practised and we should be practising 'man overboard' and 'collision' drills; the day report book is not being filled in; stowage is haphazard – we have rusty tins all over the place; and the forward loo is very dirty. On deck the spinnaker sheet chafes on the red sheet; loose shackles; men walking on sails and ropes. When was the last mast-head inspection? Does J.C. trim as carefully as Chris? Chris is drawing on watch when he shouldn't be, and shouldn't be reading. We've bent the pulpit; the port lower spreader is chafed by the wire running backstay.

Act of leadership: Never get too tired, look ahead, don't drift.

Why was the pulpit bent? Helmsman is not alert. Watch-leaders need to be either at the helm or in the main cockpit for sail changes.

When were the torches last checked, emergency bags, life-jackets, knives, shackle-keys?

State of mental plonk, I think, exists. Something has got to be done about this anyway, and we'll have to meet at least every Saturday to discuss it.

The sun is warm because we are going at 8 knots in a 15-knot following breeze, so the wind only goes past us at 7 knots. It's funny to see people in shorts so far south.

Silver-grey petrels, which are known as ice-birds, flutter about the boat in great numbers. 'Did you know that when the fellow fell off *Condor* the birds all circled round him and then settled on the water by him?' Marie Christine asked, clearly thinking, what a nice thing for them to do.

'I suppose they were going to eat him,' I replied.

The sea is a milky-blue now as if it contained ice-melt, and we think we have crossed the Antarctic convergence.

The day ended on a poor note, with Tony's mismanagement of a change-down from a big-boy and radial-head spinnaker in the face of a steadily increasing wind from astern. Left too long, the big-boy dipped in the sea, tearing the sail and breaking the luff wire near the tack from the main body of the sail; then during the change down from the radial-head to the storm spinnaker, two poles were rigged and these crossed momentarily under the load, breaking the lazy pole end fitting at the mast. The pole fell to the deck, hitting the back of Dick's legs as he knelt at the mast handling the topping lift winch for the working pole. If it had hit him on the head it could have killed him; although, knowing Dick, it probably wouldn't have been able to.

Dick cutting the spi-strop so it can be lowered

After the radio contact with Portishead at midnight I couldn't sleep so I joined the watch on deck until 0400. Being the skipper is one thing, but being the owner as well makes the cash register ring even louder on a dark night. The serenity of a clear Southern Ocean dawn helps soothe the troubled brow.

Day 14: *Saturday, 7 January   Noon position 57° 43' S, 144° 42' W*
Day's run 207 miles   Course E by S   Wind WNW Force 6
Barometer 990

John: We're moving steadily forward under the radial-head spinnaker on our first two-hundred-mile run for this leg. What a change from the start from Cape Town!

I thought things were going rather smoothly until *Great Britain II* reported three bergs and *ADC* another two. We will take at least another fourteen days to reach Cape Horn and I'm haunted by the repetition of the fog and the worry of the ice watch in the dark in extreme weather. Once was quite enough for the moment.

'I'm just not getting enough time to make the film. I'm really worried about it,' Roger said, his unshaven face made haggard by days of refusing to eat his rations. I closed my diary slowly, unable to think of anything constructive to say. Maybe he felt this way because he'd just woken up.

'What do you suggest?'

'I dunno. It's a two-way thing. I do my bit to help the boat along, but I'm just here to make the film,' he retorted as he got to his feet to wash up the dishes of the lunch he hadn't eaten.

I was reminded of Tony saying that Noel and Roger were inclined to be unenthusiastic about sail changes, and I could foresee his getting 'a leadership kick' before we reach Portsmouth. No doubt it will come his way before long, as well.

Marie Christine: Late yesterday evening the big-boy was torn. It had dipped once too often in the water. The tack had torn away completely from the rest of the sail and the stainless steel wire in the luff had snapped. It had happened on Tony's watch. He had said to Colin that he would mend it, but matters didn't look too promising when he pushed off to bed after breakfast muttering that he *would* mend the sail some time. We might need it at *any* time so Col and I decided to get it done. He painstakingly spliced together the broken strands of wire while I zigzagged together the torn pieces of material with the faithful Reads machine. I was pleased when I finally finished. It had taken me all day. The saloon had been icy cold and the sailcoth was clammy and wet to handle. Comforting smells of supper came wafting in from the galley, J.C. cooking the last of the beans for eye-stinging hot 'chilli con coction', as he named it.

I felt a lot more cheerful as I drank my port in our 'happy hour' from 6.30 to 7. At least today I had done something useful. It's very hard being a passenger. I wish I could stop feeling guilty about doing nothing. 'Doing nothing's doing wrong,' chanted at me by an elderly aunt when I was a child, had left its indelible mark.

Day 15: *Sunday, 8 January (our hundredth day at sea on this Race)   Noon position 59° 24' S, 139° 33' W*
Day's run 163 miles   Course E   Wind NNW   Force 5–8 Barometer 984

Marie Christine: 'Wake up – breakfast,' a voice shouted from the other side of our closed door. John raised his sleepy head and looked at his watch. It was five minutes to eight. He has taken to not coming to bed till four in the morning, sitting up for the radio link with Portishead at midnight when he answers a few questions for relay at the Earls Court Boat Show in London and then going on watch from twelve to four. This enables one of the five to sleep in. But it usually means we wake up late for breakfast. I climb out of the bunk first, trying not to stand on the cold, wet floor but on John's deck shoes or my damp canvas gym shoes. (I keep my clothes wrapped in a bundle in a cupboard and try to get them out without everything falling out.) I swap my warm flannel boy's pyjamas for the cold jeans, T shirt and woollen jumper; on with the wellies and into the heads for a quick brush of the teeth, if the water left in the plastic mug from the night before hasn't been spilt; then out into the saloon and make the effort of going into the world. Half of the crew have been up since four and are usually pretty boisterous by breakfast time. The banter seems to reach fever pitch ... and how I long for a crisp copy of a daily newspaper to hide behind!

This morning Steve, who sets great store by being original, was cooking breakfast. To start with, an extravaganza of tinned peaches, apricots and pineapple. Clearly remembering food rationing after the war I can't help feeling slightly dismayed at what seems an extravagant use of the supplies. The syrupy fruit was delicious and I curbed my desire to ask how many tins had been opened. What did it matter? When all the goodies were eaten that would be that. Why should I care if we ate them now or later? Nevertheless, I thought this was typical of Steve, who to my mind was always on the make. He had the charm to get away with it; but then I thought back to other times: it was Steve who had ordered the huge three-pound steak in Cape Town at Rog and Noel's party; it was Steve who'd eaten the largest full breakfast, when Tom had treated us all to a farewell breakfast at an expensive hotel in Auckland. At any mention of a celebration, Steve would enquire, 'Can we have another bottle of port?' Not satisfied with the Long John whisky, on leg two he would ask when I was getting out the Glenfiddich malt? Perhaps my rather careful conserving attitude brought this out in him. I'd noticed the same in Col. Colin had been given six cardboard litre containers of apple, apricot and boysenberry juice to look after for his watch. I'd heard Tony and Steve wheedling Col to get out the juice but it was like trying to make a squirrel give away all his nuts before winter – Col was clearly going to hoard the juice for as long as he could. Colin and I probably got as much pleasure from knowing that the goodies were there as in the eating of them.

The next course was a masterpiece of originality: fried pumpernickel (which again we'd been saving – this was the first time it had been taken out) cheese sandwiches. It was quite nice and not unlike fried Christmas pud.

The sky and sea were a uniform grey as I looked out of the hatch on my way back to the cabin. How I longed to get home and be free to do what I wanted without any restraints! I lay in my bunk, immersed in self-pity, and wept.

John tried to comfort me. I was being pathetic and I knew it. We just had to see it through. We'd been at sea for a hundred days now, and two weeks on this leg.

I offered to cook supper – a lemon meringue pie took most of my time. We were well heeled over to port and the blind pastry cases came out of the gimballed oven burnt, so the lemon filling and meringue were poured in to take advantage of the uneven case. It was delicious apart from the lemon pips and chunks of lemon – I'd had no grater. Mince, dumplings and dehydrated runner beans had come before.

Day 16: *Monday, 9 January   Noon position 60° 10' S, 132° 40' W*
Day's run 195 miles   Course E   Wind SW by S Force 3–4
Barometer 990

John: The polar daylight and light winds make the night watches into quite an enjoyable experience. The cold is nothing like as severe as it was on the last lap, and everyone is secretly delighted. They don't brag about it, lest it should suddenly change and we find ourselves back in the long, dark tunnel again.

I've purposely shut my mind to thinking of home since leaving there on the second of August last year; but now I can see the tracks of the different yachts moving up in jerky black, red and blue lines towards Cape Horn, now only two thousand miles away – and I just can't help myself. I play 'Mull of Kintyre' as often as I dare on the cassette player, and tears prick my eyes. It'll be marvellous to get home and enjoy Ardmore again without the crushing worry of the past couple of years.

It's Noel's thirtieth GMT birthday today – he'll have another one tomorrow – so we took the chance of a party while it was calm. Excellent Fonseca Bin 27 port was the foundation, as ever, but Roger produced some rum and Chris a bottle of New Zealand white Montana wine. We all had a splendid time with Rocky, Richie Havens and 'Mull of Kintyre' being played in turns on the cassette machine.

Day 17: *Tuesday, 10 January   Noon position 61° 30' S, 128° 20' W*
Day's run 174 miles   Course E by N   Winds S by E Force 2–3
Barometer 989

Marie Christine: Our first iceberg of this leg was sighted early this morning. We passed her by to port in the early morning sunlight, a giant glistening white castle making its fatal journey north. At breakfast discussion turned to landing and planting the Debenhams' flag on the next one we saw. It just so happened there was one on our port bow. Staff and Steve were keen to make the assault and J.C. would paddle them to the berg.

As we drew closer we could see the heavy swell breaking on the berg. To land would be dangerous and difficult.

Plan B was put into action. The rubber dinghy was inflated and put over the side and Tony and I got in and were cast off. It was an uncanny sight to see the yacht disappearing behind the swell as she sailed away from us. The sky was overcast now, dark patches of snow cloud hung heavily on the horizon, the air was full of silver-grey petrels circling round us inquisitively. Close to the berg, a whale surfaced and blew. We could smell its fishy breath in the chill air. It would be feeding on the krill to be found there. I hoped it was fully absorbed in its search for food and wouldn't nose up under us, spilling us out into the icy water. My mind went back to a story Lance used to tell of the time a whale swallowed a fisherman. His mates caught the whale, opened him up, to find the man was still alive, his skin burnt from the acid in the whale's stomach and he was quite mad.

Our job was to take photos of the yacht as she sailed between us and the towering iceberg close by. 'What if they don't come back, Tony?' The boat was now out of sight. 'Well, we would just have to prepare for death,' he answered solemnly and then he wailed, half jokingly, 'My mother wouldn't like to see me sitting here.' I could just imagine the horror on my mother's face too. The rubber dinghy rose and fell on the huge oily grey swell. Then we saw her like a swan, the yacht dipped past

The day I put the wife in the longboat

us, her sails looking yellow and worn against the sharp, blue-white, castellated peaks of this ice mountain. She turned and came to pick us and our cameras out of the ocean. It had been a strange and rather refreshing interlude.

Day 18: *Wednesday, 11 January   Noon position 62° 30' S, 121° 10' W*
Day's run 214 miles   Course ENE   Wind SSW Force 4
Barometer 992

John: Colin sighted one of the most spectacular bergs we've ever seen dead ahead at 2.40 in the morning. I remained at the wheel when our watch ended at four in the morning to pass close to weather of the hazard at 4.30. All is beautiful. The majestic floating islands of ice vary in appearance with the quality of the light. On this particular morning it was overcast. A big snow shower lay to windward as we passed within a hundred yards upwind of the dazzling confection. It seemed to have the most delicious thick, white icing slurping over the edges of its sides while at the eastern end two slim pinnacles stood like toy soldiers dressed for ski warfare.

'I think it's toppling over,' Alan, the navigator, murmured through a narrow face-hole created by his red and black helicopter suit, a woollen balaclava, and a tightly drawn oilskin hood. It was pretty nippy.

I'd sacrifice the feeling in my toes to pass these ice towers. It would be

grand to see one collapse. The water at the foot of the bergs was a pale murky blue as the ice extended just below the surface to the pinnacles. Numerous silver-grey petrels, the ice-birds, were silhouetted against the surf which dashed relentlessly on the ice cliffs. What a strange, cold, grey, compelling place this is! Those birds have probably never seen human beings before; the whale grazing on the banks of krill pinned against the ice probably thought of the ice mountain as a temporary home. Nothing ever drifted by us in the Southern Ocean which could be associated with man whereas on other oceans we saw rubbish. Here the liquid ice appeared quite virgin.

As the day wore on the wind began to rise again from the south; thus the young New Zealander made several moves to get the course altered to the north. I felt we must stick with the Great Circle now if we're to see the advantage of the short-cut. Some of the need to go north stems from the head-winds we're having; but some of it comes from Chris, who's feeling the cold. Luckily, we have a pretty tough bunch on here now. It *is* cold. The water is 1½ degrees Centigrade, and the air fluctuates between 3 degrees C and close on freezing at night; and the wind-chill with 25 knots of wind combined with an air temperature of 3 degrees, gives minus 33 degrees on exposed flesh. I think we'll see no sudden jump north on this leg.

'Cold? It's not cold. It's warmer than the day we left Portsmouth. You should have been on the last leg,' Noel laughs at Chris, Staff and Alan. It's a well-known joke: anyone who complains is told, 'You should have been on the last leg!'

Day 19: *Thursday, 12 January   Noon position 62° 55' S, 115° 20' W*
Day's run 200 miles   Course NE by E   Wind S Force 4
Barometer 1004

John: It was 2.30 in the morning, the snow was stinging my face, the swell churned my stomach. Staff was already out of action. The bow dipped into the waves, nodding gouts of grey-green liquid ice into the headsails. The weight was dangerous for the big genoa. A tap on the perspex drop boards blocking the main hatch and Tony was away up on to the foredeck and down the forehatch to get the No. 1 yankee. Chris, Noel and Dick (responding to that tap with remarkable speed, bearing in mind the time and the temperature) were up, out of the main hatch and up on to the foredeck, while I ran the boat downwind. When the sail was changed, I suggested the four of them go below for a warm while I stayed on the wheel.

'The wheel is nothing to the foredeck,' they tell me — and they're right.

'No. We're fine. Quite warm, in fact,' says Noel, and Tony nods.

JC's streak in snow

In spite of all the irritation I feel at being locked up with them in this small tube, I have to admit they are just grand. I wouldn't change one of them if I had to do it all again. *Had* to, that is.

Chris stands at the weather-rail, slim and cold in white oilskins. I see him looking at Dick, hunched uncomplaining over the big silver Barlow 36 winch, snow crusting his red oilskin suit as he works the double-hander to bring in the yankee sheet.

'These Poms may not be the poufters I thought they were,' a glance said.

All day long there was one or more bergs in sight, and cape pigeons and storm petrels and ice-birds.

Marie Christine: Cold and bloody boring! – apart from magnificent icebergs all around us. I can't raise much enthusiasm for anything at present. Life on board for me is not unlike a prison sentence. Reading is my only solace. I have enjoyed enormously Somerset Maugham's *Of Human Bondage* and *The Painted Veil*, which I bought John for Christmas. But on reading it, don't think it was such a suitable gift as it tells the tale of an unfaithful wife, he hasn't read it yet but might think there was some hidden message! Saul Bellow's *Humboldt's Gift* was greatly enter-taining and thought-provoking. I just wished I hadn't read them so quickly. I'm left with a load of Nazi-type war stories which John bought in Auckland, and the odd pulpy saga. I've spent both afternoons with the machine out, mending sails and any of the crew's clothing.

We phoned Mum in Brighton on Thursday evening (eight our time and five a.m. in Britain). She took the early wakening well and sounded delighted to hear us. We hadn't spoken since October in Cape Town. We'd tried many times to get through but either couldn't raise Por-tishead or else the line wasn't clear enough. She and Becca were well; Becca had just gone back to school and was as happy as a lark. John gave her our position, 2,000 miles from Cape Horn, and mentioned that we had icebergs all around, to which Mummy replied, 'Good,' in a very steady voice, a very uncharacteristic reply. I can only think she hadn't heard. It was lovely to hear her voice and most of all that she and Becca were well. I could picture her so clearly in Brighton: after our having woken her she would switch on the electric blanket to warm the bed up just a shade, adjust the Teasmaid beside her bed and in a short while be sipping a cup of hot tea made with fresh milk out of a large floral bone china cup that I'd given her many Christmases ago, before I was married. She'd sit back and feel relieved that we were still alive and wonder what we were doing.

John went straight to bed, as he was getting called at midnight, but I stayed and talked to some of the boys. I was warmed by their interest in how Becca and Mummy were. It was such a contrast in this 57-foot fibreglass tube 63 degrees south, 115 degrees west, racing through the night down here in the loneliest part of the world, giant looming icebergs surrounding us – to Brighton. I couldn't really grasp that I'd been able to make contact. It was like not only phoning another planet but in a different era.

Day 20: *Friday, 13 January   Noon position 63° 08' S, 108° 55' W*
Day's run 198 miles   Course ENE   Wind W by N Force 4
Barometer 993

John: Friday the 13th – unlucky date for some.

At 3.30 in the morning, Steve blew out the saloon paraffin heater. There was a flash and a peculiarly tinny sounding crash – then we were in the cold again. 'Steve is not a practical man – more suited to the lectern,' I reflected on a chunk of fried Army hamburger kindly cast to us swine by the *Adventure* crew in Auckland.

'Good on the dialogue,' mused Roger, ATV cameraman.

'Better on the monologue,' someone muttered.

At the moment he's trying to disprove the design of the big-boy.

'It's only made to steady the rolling effect of the radial-head,' cracked J.C.

Steve, in the bile-green balaclava, was upstairs at the wheel, out in the blizzard, trimming the big sails like a good 'un. From our cabin, a drumming sound – Marie Christine running on the spot to get warm in our cabin. Alan, our tall, blind navigator, has turned out a new cold-defying suit of clothing: a white polo vest with 'E. A. Green' and two overlapping hearts pierced by an arrow inscribed in the area where there might have been a left breast pocket. 'This side up,' says a further felt pen directive, running up the vertical seam and pointing at his left arm-pit. Alan was quite fearless of the Velcro strip in place of vest buttons – there aren't too many hairs on his chest to get trapped in it anyway. 'Bought it in a mountain shop in Cowes,' he crows, fingering a colour o' death purple duvet waistcoat. The climbing instructors examined the material, declaring it synthetic: no eider ducks in that. But it doesn't worry Alan. The closest he's ever come to a moun*tain* – he emphasizes the 'ai' to tease me – is that wearisome drag up St James's Street to reach the Ritz, a rather down-market summit café.

We've eaten a great deal of fried food since everyone had to do their share of the cooking – except me, I hasten to admit, and two members of the crew who have trouble with spots around the eyes. This is most likely due to squinting into the snow for long periods at the wheel. But there is a popular belief that it's caused by the illustrated French magazine now residing in the forward heads which the Italian crew of *B & B Italia* gave us in appreciation of the Hobart connection we established on their behalf in the last leg.

Day 21: *Saturday, 14 January   Noon position 63° 00' S, 102° 40' W*
          Day's run 178 miles   Course NE Wind SW Force 6
          Barometer 986

Marie Christine: A night of strong winds and heavy swell. On the twelve-to-four watch the Arun storm spinnaker was torn apart. The head of the sail shot to the top of the mast and fluttered like a flag of truce. During this calamity the boat broached, dipping the lower part of the mainsail and boom into the water. The weight of water could have easily broken the boom. Later on during the four-to-eight watch, the boat seemed to be slewing crazily, led by the stronger Ratsey storm spinnaker which had been put up in place of the Arun one. This was more an illusion down below – so I was assured by the helmsman of the night. And who was I to argue, who never put my nose out except to throw the port bottles over the side?

John and I awoke from our uneasy sleep at 6.30 and lay clutching the sides of our bunk. The boat was close to broaching as she heeled over

Staff and Steve in stormy weather

into the icy Antarctic Ocean. After what seemed like a half hour of this, it finally happened – a severe broach that went on and on. The water was coming over the side, fast filling up the cockpit and pouring through our cabin windows. Those on deck were fighting hard to get the spinnaker, which now lay in the water, back on the boat. John flung his clothes on and rushed up. He was worried firstly that unless the boat got on to a more even keel another wave could capsize her, as happened to *Sayula*. Secondly, the boom was again in the water and could easily break with the weight of water pressing on it. Thirdly, it had been an expensive night up to now with one wrecked spinnaker. I lay below, cocooned in my warm sleeping-bag, straining to hear what was going on above. Our crew as usual saved the day. The spinnaker was hauled in all in one piece, an easier rig was hoisted and life returned to normal, that is, as normal as it can be after three weeks at sea in these wet and cold conditions.

Today was remarkable for the three outstanding meals. Staff, who hadn't been able to cook until now because of his seasickness, made a supreme effort at breakfast and cooked us eggs florentine (poached egg on spinach with cheese sauce). For lunch Chris, with a little help from me, gave us fried bubble and squeak with corned beef. Supper was voted top of the pole. Steve's creation was pizza on a pan-fried pastry base, baked potatoes, beans followed by the most delicious queen of puddings. We had all got pretty tired of eating the dehydrated food. It's excellent now and again but we had been eating it right up to the end of leg 2, about eighty days without much of a break. We've found that the three sacks of potatoes I got in Auckland have been enjoyed by all, also the eggs, cheese, onions, butter and flour have gone a long way to making better meals. After eating processed and canned foods for a time we were yearning for unadulterated tastes and textures.

During the afternoon Colin's watch steered downwind of a large iceberg a mile distant and were shocked to find themselves amongst a lot of bergy bits about the size of the boat, which would do serious harm to us if hit. The day was grey but fortunately the ice showed bright in the heaving, breaking sea and Colin steered the boat through the danger.

I'd not had a proper wash for days and my hair under my scarf was squashed flat. It felt extremely itchy. I decided to light my small gas stove and heat the tiny heads compartment; with the door shut it should soon warm up. I also mopped the ceiling and outside wall with a sponge to stop the cold drips. Armed with a pint of hot water in my blue bucket I managed a fairly warm wash of hair and self and felt terrific afterwards. For me it is a great boost to the flagging morale.

Day 23: *Monday, 16 January   Noon position 61° 05' S, 88° 10' W*
Day's run 203 miles   Course NE   Wind WSW Force 8
Barometer 986

John: Night-watch.

'Ten to twelve,' called Tony bluntly and briefly through the half-open door. Then he shut it again.

It's all but dark as one of the two windows is blocked by the life rafts kept in the cockpit for instant use. Anyway, it's so overcast tonight that dusk is really dark. I crawled gingerly over the bunk-rail which damaged my ribs on the previous leg, balancing on my not-too-wet deck shoes. I pull on my heavy tweed workman's trousers over the grey/white long johns. 'Come on, you silly twit,' I keep urging myself: step into yellow boots and pull up orange oilskin trousers; then on with the polar jacket and towel round the neck; wrestling into the huge oilskin jacket; check the safety harness, granny's golf hat on; and secure the oilskin hood; finally, snatch up the sopping mitts and red outers – each initialled 'J.R.' to stop the other bleeders from nicking them.

'Night-night. You cuddle down,' I croon spitefully at Marie Christine, just to make sure she's awake.

'Be sure and clip on,' she murmurs in reply.

Out through the cabin door and into the dark saloon. The off-going watch are quietly jubilant.

'Where's Tony?'

'Oh, he's up there already.' One of them nods at the hatch.

Up I go, harness-clip in hand, floundering over the perspex drop-boards. Top one in my hands. Clip on.

'Aye-aye.' Forced cheerful cry to help keep up the morale.

I don't hear the muttered encouragement from the other watch man as he dives below. Dropboards back in the slot; pull the main hatch over. Lurch fifteen feet along the weather safety line to Tony at the wheel. Sit down on the edge of the after-cockpit and concentrate on looking cheery. As he's on the wheel, he will be relieved in half an hour. That means I go on for a further half an hour after that. I'm trying to work out how the 240 minutes of the watch will be split between the five of us. I reckon that two of us will be doing two hours, two an hour and a half each; and the last one will get away with an hour.

'Wanna drive?' Tony shouts through a red balaclava.

'Okay.' I climb around behind the wheel.

'O-four-seven,' Tony shouts again, flipping his faded yellow safety tape over the compass and taking my place on the right edge of the cockpit. There is no joking – Tony doesn't go in for that. Any con-versation is stilted – but then we haven't time to consider one another really. It's hard work at the wheel. The quartering sea seeks to throw the stern to port, thus pointing the bow up into the wind. The helms-man must defeat every wave. Every once in a short while, the sea breaks white over the weather side. I turn my face away to stop the water from running down my chin and so inside the orange oilskins. My arms ache and I'm losing sequence with the waves. The speedometer reflects a loss of rhythm. The left wrist feels strained from a couple of nights back when the Arun storm spinnaker fell apart. Thirty-to-forty-knot winds eagerly strain for the advantage. A red figure appears in the hatch.

'Half an hour's up.' The blue mittens, a leaving present from Bob, mean it's Dick. Tony hesitates, turns to me:

'Do you want to do your hour and a half straight now?' Bloody hell, I think.

'No. Another half-hour will do for me just now,' I grin, and Tony's away along the combing sideways like a crab – and then straight down the hatch.

'Aye-aye,' cracks Dick in north-west Sutherlandese.

'Aye-aye, Dicker-boy. It's a wild night then.'

We swap yarns about old times at home, full of laughs, to mask the cold and wet. After a while, Dicker takes over and I sit on the edge of the cockpit. Dick's the leader of the 'it's nothing like as cold as the last leg; it's warmer every day' lobby – and he's right. I still find it bloody cold, wet and miserable. A small ice cube seems to have settled in my groin. It's spreading slowly. No, it's not the cold seat – it's a trickle of water.

And I thought I'd smoothed out my zips and Velcro strips. The spray is running along a trough in the oilskins and down through the fly. I shake myself in disgust and look at Dicker. Christ. What I'd give for some of that steam of twenty years ago, I think glumly, looking at him. Another figure in the hatch.

'Hurray! It's Noely. Boy, am I glad to see you.'

'I bet you are.'

And I'm off down into the saloon lit by the Tilley lamp because Noel and Roger are on watch. If it was Colin's watch we'd have to sit in darkness so Noel and Roger can sleep in their saloon bunks. I take off my oilskin jacket. Don McLean's 'American Pie' comes softly from the cassette player. It's warm and muggy with paraffin fumes. A wave breaks over the saloon top, comes down the chimney, and grey smoke belches out from the bottom of the stainless steel Taylor paraffin heater.

'There's water in the thermos,' Tony said, sitting on the starboard side of the white table, dark brows knitted over Somerset Maugham's *Painted Veil*, thick fingers interlocking, motionless. He looks a bit like his brother Nick – more like a cold Confucian monk. Roger's pale unshaven face is half-masked by the forward tilt of his woolly hat. Slumped on the forward end of the settee, yellow boots sticking out from under red oilskin trousers, he's sort of ready for an emergency, content he's fixed himself the only one-hour stint on the watch. Moving slowly and quietly, I make myself a cup of hot chocolate. I can't find the sugar. Never mind. With my feet on the stove, I nod off to sleep – half asleep really. I'll not need waking for my two-thirty watch.

The boat heaves and crashes, but it doesn't trespass on the peace in the cabin. Just occasionally the compressed squeal of air trapped under the hull when we're surfing breaks into my slumber. It sounds rather like a bicycle pump if you hold your finger over the end. People come and go and I realize my time is coming soon, too.

'It's nice, this sailing,' laughs Noely's mustachioed face from the other side of the table.

That's not exactly what I was thinking just now.

'Have a bit of chocolate.'

'Thanks very much.' There were only three of us in the saloon – Noel, Dick and me. Tony and Roger are on deck. Don McLean is still on. It reminds me of a bus trip Chay and I made from Montreal to Boston on our way to start rowing across the Atlantic: one of those unlooked-for experiences – beautiful spring woodland, mountains and small timber townships; ski-trails of Vermont – I always link it with a snatch from the song.

'D'you ever go to America, Noel?'

'Yes. For a day's filming in New York. I hated it. But I'd like to go back to the West Coast.'

'You have the three minutes to get the oilskins on,' Dick breaks in, grinning; and I lumber to my feet.

Outside it's broad daylight, and I'm buoyed by the thought I've only half an hour more. Then it dawns on me that it must be an hour – yes, I'm going to be a two-hour man. Must be me and Dick, who is next on after Tony.

Why do they come to the Southern Ocean at all? I look out over the sea and try to itemize things, to clarify exactly why people keep on coming here. Seems crazy to me.

My back is to the southerly gale which is striking the boat just aft to the starboard beam as we plough across the storm-driven swell. Occasionally I must look ahead for bergs and growlers; but looking out across the boat to port presents no difficulties. There are no demands on me in this role at the moment; and few bergs to watch. I just look at the sea and think about it.

On the horizon the snow hangs in ragged curtains like pale, grey woodsmoke. The clouds are simply large black areas of sky interspersed with lesser patches of grey. The sea is a cruel slate-grey to black marbled with streaks of spindrift. Patches of stark white foam are everywhere. They come from breaking seas and they must be checked to ensure they're not growlers, any one of which could sink us.

The weather astern is always catching us up. It looks fiercer somehow. The breakers seem more angrily white; waves explode at odd spiky angles for no apparent reason; our wake is a broad swathe of white scum stretching behind us. Kinks from our broaching don't appear in the end product, for the scar is too wide and the driving wind blurs the pattern. Close in under the lee, the wind shadow behind the mainsail looks like a fleeting patch of calm, almost an oil slick; as we surf Tony leans out to port, his arms half bent without changing his grip on the wheel. He can't bring the rudder round any more to port. Behind his muffled figure, dark spray-sodden red, the sea bursts into brilliant white foam above pale blue based on jet-black liquid ice.

The speedometer wavers on 12 knots. The boat roars; the leech of the mainsail thunders. The blue and white yankee sheet cracks bar-taut on the snatch-block which keeps it off the main boom; and the gold staysail sheet rattles in its roller on the deck. The wind howls in the rigging; the snow beats a tattoo on my hood. My toes are cold; my gloves are soaking; and tomorrow I promise I'll try and borrow Alan's rubber gloves.

Dick appears. Tony goes below. I take the wheel for my last half hour. Every wave tries to make me broach. Dick explains how we've been caught for this two hours each and how I must be fifth up if I want to do only one hour next time. I sing out loud. 'What a lovely day it is to be caught in the rain.'

I know why people keep coming down here to the Southern Ocean – they come for the comradeship and the struggle against something big. Boy, is it big!

Noel appears and suddenly I feel fresh and full of laughter. I don't want to go to bed. I warm my feet on the stove and see the other watch come on – then it's three hours' sleep until breakfast.

Marie Christine: 'It's so cold out there that even the dogs are frozen to the lampposts,' cracked J.C. as he squeezed his forty-eight-inch chest through the narrow hatch opening, coming in for his bowl of steaming porridge, brown sugar and milk, to be followed by a poached egg in the same bowl – no place for the squeamish here; if you don't like your poached egg flavoured with sweet porridge, too bad.

All day as the boat surfs and bounds along, morale is high. We are well ahead of *Adventure*, catching up *Treaty* and making better daily runs than some of the other boats. Down below the saloon is damp, water dripping from leaks in the ceiling. People are flopping down in their wet oilskins anywhere now, leaving wet seats when they get up to go out again. I don't blame them for relaxing anywhere below. It can't be a lot of fun out in the cold and wet. The stove needs almost constant attention, otherwise it goes out; a tricky operation involving lying on the wet floor with a box of dry matches in one hand, in the other a cloth to turn off the hot metal handle which automatically pricks the hole clear, then speedily relighting the burner before it cools down and needs more meths to vaporize the paraffin in the tubes.

John and I sat up for the prearranged radio schedule with Portishead at ten our time, 5 a.m. back in Britain. Hunched round the saloon table, the Tilley lamp creating a small circle of brightness, we talked away the hours between supper at seven and ten. Noel, ready for action in his red oilies, stretched into his bunk and brought out a pound of smoked cheese which he shared with Rog, John and me. It was delicious.

'I've got tons of the stuff,' Noel told me. 'I stocked up in Auckland. I couldn't face the thought of any more dehydrated food, but I didn't bargain for all this good grub we're having now.'

Rog chipped in: 'I'm sleeping on two huge salamis, they're pretty squashed now.' He too had quite a supply of biscuits, chocolate cakes and other goodies.

At five minutes to ten in the tiny aft cabin which was the radio shack I watched John remove the white plastic cover to the four-thousand-pound radio and switch on. The sleeping muffled shapes of Staff and J.C. shifted slightly when the loud crackling of static filled their cabin. 'Portishead, Portishead, this is 2 Oscar Victor Echo. 2 Oscar Victor Echo, do you read me, over.' Portishead came over loud and clear. We had arranged for a call at this time when we'd made contact a few days back, so they were listening out for us. But even so, I felt it was close to miraculous that we could be speaking across thousands of miles of ocean. We put a call through to Arun Bose in Durness and within seconds we could hear his reedy voice.

'This is John speaking, Arun, 450 miles from Cape Horn. All is going well here. How are you? Over.'

Arun answered clearly but briefly. He knew what it was costing and that at any minute the batteries might fail or we could be cut off.

'Can you get a quote for a dishwasher for thirty to forty persons to run off a 4-kw generator? It doesn't need to heat the water as this will come from the Wooden House supply.'

Arun took this query at five in the morning with no note of surprise in his voice as he repeated, in confirmation, John's rather unusual request.

'Do you ever think of us, Arun?'

'Oh, yes, all the time,' came back his anxious reply.

'Please ring Lance and Ada and Colin's parents and tell them we're fine.'

'Yes,' answered Arun, 'I'll do that right away.'

I hoped to goodness he didn't. I could just imagine Lance stumbling down the stairs to the phone in the dark, cursing us for putting 'that contraption' into his house and wondering what the emergency was that involved a 5 a.m. phone call.

We also managed to send a short telegram to Rebecca at her boarding school: 'Close to Cape Horn. Soon be home. Love Mumdad.' I could imagine Rebecca asking her geography mistress the whereabouts of Cape Horn and thinking she was glad to be where she was.

With regard to the dishwasher, John and I, as ever, had been talking of home. A trip of this nature is a perfect opportunity to stand back and view problems objectively. The School's courses went well: we were always full: but a penalty for being out in the wilds as we were at Ardmore was that you couldn't get domestic staff. This meant that I, with the help of Ada, did the cooking and the instructors took it in turns to do the washing up. It was not a popular job.

'Surely it would be possible to get a big enough dishwasher to do the job. If we've managed to get a boat built and raced half-way round the world already, I can't believe it's beyond us to get a commercial dishwasher or even five domestic ones, if a commercial one is out of the question,' John put to me.

Certainly we both felt it was time to make our lot a bit easier. It had been a long haul, since starting the School ten years ago, for both of us. On top of our six-month season, we had managed to make four major winter expeditions: from the farthest source to the mouth of the Amazon; crossing an ice-cap in Southern Chile, which we had reached by navigating the Magellan Straits in rubber dinghies; a sea trip to the Cape Verde Islands, stopping at the Spanish Sahara and the Azores; and finally our present 'jaunt', racing round the world. We are lucky enough to live in a beautiful part of Britain and yet the way we were managing our lives meant we hardly had a day off to enjoy the mountains, a fishing expedition or whatever the place had to offer. We both felt our life-style had to change. 'What is this life if full of care we have no time to stop and stare?' Hence the dishwasher idea.

Day 24: *Tuesday, 17 January   Noon position 59° 11' S, 80° 51' W Day's run 197 miles   Course NE   Wind SW Force 5 Barometer 994*

John: The same as yesterday except I borrowed Alan's rubber gloves; and Colin passed up cheese and biscuits with hot coffee through the after-hatch for J.C. and me.

Headsails were poled out during the day and the wind eased considerably.

At noon we are 480 miles from Cape Horn. *Pen Duick* went round at about 1800 local time on the 15th – that's two days ago! *Great Britain II* was 120 miles past on the noon chat show today, with *Condor* thirty miles short and *Flyer* sixty miles short. The rest of the boats are fairly bunched, and we are ahead of *Japy Hermès* and *Adventure*; about level with *B & B Italia* and *Treaty of Rome*. The rest are maybe a day ahead of us. We have, in fact, done well.

Marie Christine: We plod on, a bit nearer to Cape Horn, our present objective. We are curving north and the weather is kinder, not such steep seas and slightly warmer, but I'm still finding it freezing. I've had bad chilblains on my toes for about fourteen days, ever since my trip off the yacht in the rubber dinghy when my feet went quite numb (there was a good two inches of icy water swirling around in the bottom of the dinghy) and it was just too much for my poor circulation.

Day 25: *Wednesday, 18 January   Noon position 58° 27' S, 75° 18' W Day's run 173 miles   Course ENE   Wind SSW Force 5 Barometer 994*

John: It's Marie Christine's birthday today.

The midnight-to-four watch passed easily under a light wind with tri-radial and then radial-head spinnakers. It's much warmer now with the wind dead astern for Cape Horn.

I'm concerned at the damage which occurs through carelessness –

like Tony tearing the starcut while hoisting. That sail has been unmarked for two years. Ah, well!

It's a funny situation to be switching the saloon heater off as we approach Cape Horn. We've had it on for the past couple of weeks and now we find it's just too warm as we come north to the Horn.

We hit trouble in the early hours of the morning. First, we found the nylon sheave of the Lewmar port spinnaker halyard masthead block had disappeared – leaving the tri-radial spinnaker flying with only the stainless pin in the body of the block, preventing the whole shooting match from coming down, filling up with water, and tearing to ribbons with the speed of the boat through the water. The radial-head went up, and the other halyard; and as the genoa halyard had mysteriously gone up to the head of the mast during the night, someone had to go up to the mast to retrieve it.

At last we were able to use some of our other skills. Staff may suffer from seasickness, but he sure can climb rocks and masts. With no halyard to go up on, he used a single prussick loop attached to the standing part of the remaining spinnaker halyard which was carrying the radial-head spinnaker, and climbed the sixty feet up the mast steps in a very wobbly sea.

After this gallant deed the situation deteriorated rapidly. The radial-head was seen to be torn at the head, so it was brought down; but the clew got wrapped round the inner forestay, causing further damage; then the No. 1 yankee was put up and found damaged, so it came down. Then Colin decided to gybe the full mainsail, the only sail up at the time. He forgot to secure the main sheet track slider when he took in the sheet, so when the sail was gybed the slider slammed six feet across the boat and brought up with a crash. The Ratsey mainsail split from leech to luff, starting along the stitching of the leech reinforcing triangle just below the third row of reef holes. This is disaster. When I came out from my cabin for breakfast, the faces were glum. An extra week to Rio. No carnival for Roger.

'The sails are worn out,' wailed a few rather poor workmen describing their tools.

As soon as breakfast was over I scuttled back to my cabin to try to puzzle out what is going wrong. It was clear enough: we weren't doing any preventive work. We just waited for the sails to blow out and then complained they were worn out. The material is as good as ever – it's the stitching which is worn; this because with terylene cloth the stitching stands proud and wears first. In the days of canvas sails the stitching sank into the cloth, and so it was protected.

I called a meeting of the crew at one o'clock and Alan, the navigator, took the wheel.

I started a new routine. The watch on duty will divide into two parts:

two men on deck and the other three men working on maintenance, principally repairing the stitching on sails. This way we should be a step ahead of trouble – a stitch in time may save nine thousand.

Not much of a birthday for Marie Christine. She worked at the sewing machine with Colin from 8.30 in the morning right through until two o'clock on the following morning. By that time the mainsail was about half repaired, and they were exhausted. Peter repaired the No. 1 yankee in the cockpit, and the boat sailed along at 7½ knots under No. 2 yankee boomed out, working staysail, trysail out on the main boom and full mizzen.

We were not the only boat with problems. On the radio we heard that *Adventure*, 120 miles behind us, had broken her steering gear during the night when she broached under the storm spinnaker. Judith on *Treaty of Rome*, just ahead of us, told me they could not fly a spinnaker as their masthead spinnaker halyard block had failed. *Disque d'Or*, a Swan 65, was rounding the Horn without radio and taking water through a damaged rudder skeg. *King's Legend*, another Swan 65, has been out of contact by radio for a couple of weeks, and she had rudder skeg trouble on the last leg.

There was much excitement on the radio at noon. HMS *Endurance* was still 200 miles north-east of the Horn, but she was on the radio to all boats. The French were particularly excited. Two of their yachts in sight of each other gave widely differing positions, and shouted slanging matches at one another on the radio. *Tielsa* from Holland, *Neptune* from France, *Disque d'Or* from Switzerland were also in sight of one another as they rounded the Horn. *Adventure*, the joint Services yacht, came up with a signal for *Endurance* to send to Portsmouth, calling for further support from Her Britannic Majesty:

To Joint Services Sailing Centre from *Adventure*
Priority Unclassified.
Steering gear repaired but may well not last long.
Essential Leg 4 stores include three ball joints, one bottom steering box crank, one tie-rod.
Spare storm spinnaker on board. Blown out one; repairable, but not on board.

Peter and I crouched in the dripping radio shack at the back of the boat.

'Better ask Debenhams if they'll send us something,' the wiry Tasman grinned through his black stubble. 'Why not ask for new underpants?'

'Okay, I will,' I replied. 'Hello, *Adventure*. *Adventure*. This is *Debenhams*. Do you read me? Over.'

'Good morning, John. This is *Adventure*,' came the usual suave reply.

'In view of the massive aid you've just requested from Her Majesty's Government, I wonder if *Endurance* would send a signal for us?

'To Chairman Debenhams London
Mainsail, radial-head, No. 1 yankee, storm spinnaker all blown. Essential Leg 4 stores include new underpants for crew.'

'You could try them,' laughed *Adventure*. Some twenty minutes later, during a break in the inter-boat chatter, *Endurance* came on the air and said they'd heard we wanted them to make a signal for us, and was this true; and I replied 'Yes' and passed the signal. I wonder how Sir Anthony Burney, whom I've never met, will take our plea from Cape Horn.

Marie Christine: In spite of singing happy birthday to me when I appeared at breakfast, spirits were low. It had been a fairly disastrous night: the starcut was torn while being hoisted up. Later on with the radial-head up, a split was noticed, but in bringing down the sail, it got wrapped around the inner forestay causing further damage. The No. 1 yankee which was put up in its place also had a seam split, so that was brought down. Finally, at 6 a.m., with Colin at the wheel, the mainsail split from luff to leech, a distance of about fourteen feet from just below the third row of reef holes. The main had been the only sail up at the time. Unfortunately, he forgot to secure the main track slider and when he gybed the mainsail slammed over, causing the sail to split. Poor Col was filled with remorse.

'I'm afraid it's not going to be much of a birthday for you, M.C., we're going to have to get this patched as soon as possible.' Since the main had been taken down we had lost a good two knots in our speed.

The long task began. We started at 8.30 after breakfast with the leech tape which had torn apart. Carefully placing the two frayed edges together, we measured and cut out two strips of material to repair this edge of the sail. We were soon damp from sitting on the wet heavy terylene and hauling it about. It was depressing having to unpick stitches along the hem of the leech tape to accommodate the eventual patch. Here it was seven pieces of material thick and I knew what it would be like sewing it together again. We had the complete sail in the saloon and there wasn't much room for anything else other than ourselves, the Reads sewing machine and 'an inexhaustible supply of sewing needles'. People who needed to pass through had to crawl under the table, not an easy task when most of the space there was taken up with sailcloth. Most of the trips through were to the heads. 'Can't you go over the side?' Col and I would say to them impatiently, not wanting any interruptions. Wherever possible, we used the zigzag stitch on the sewing machine, but found we couldn't adjust it to take more than two thicknesses of the 12-ounce terylene. After securing the leech, we carefully matched up the split, making allowances for the material lost which showed as a frill along the entire edge of the tear, up to about two inches in the middle of the sail and slightly less either side. We still had the luff tape in one piece, which was a helpful guide.

Carefully we cut out a patch from a roll of the same material. We stuck one side of this to the tear with miracle sticking tape. This way we were able to machine half the patch in place; three outer rows of zigzag stitch and one zigzag row along the edge of the tear. We finally got this done by two in the morning. I was exhausted and kept saying to Colin, 'Let's leave it now, we'll do it much better in the morning when we've rested.' Seemingly tireless, he had kept going all day with hardly a break and now he was reluctant to turn in. What's more, he'd only had four hours' sleep the previous night. Sadly, I felt perhaps that my being thirty-four now, compared with his twenty-five, had a bit to do with it too.

We'd had a short break for a birthday supper at seven which we celebrated with a bottle of whisky and three of port in the half hour before J.C. presented me with an unusual gift, an Egyptian ten-pound note. I felt it was like being given an airline ticket to Cairo. Perhaps now that I had ten pounds to spend in Egypt, I might make it to the pyramids after all. A birthday cake completed the party. This hour break had been our only pause in the day.

Day 26: *Thursday, 19 January   Noon position 56° 25' S, 69° 16' W*
Day's run 201 miles   Course NNE by N   Wind SW Force 4–5
Barometer 1003

John: During the night-watch I considered our present plight, with the mainsail out of action. It should only take a couple of days to repair, and we were making 7½ to 8 knots without it.

Condor, Japy Hermès, 33 Export, Gauloises, B & B, Disque d'Or and now *Adventure* had all suffered major setbacks to one degree or another on this race. We must not be downhearted, but thankful that the mainsail business is the worst trouble we've had. We can guard against it by preventive maintenance of the gear.

All morning we kept a sharp eye out for land. It was cloudy as usual, but Alan snatched thirteen sights of the sun. He had his lines all over a sheet of paper; then he checked, re-checked, and treble checked. The Royal Ocean Racing calculator was nearly smoking with use. Steve was in the mizzen spreaders until he turned blue. Visibility was poor, with the low-lying Diego Ramirez Islands scattered, we hoped, somewhere

up in the murk on the starboard bow. Some fifty-five miles beyond them
to the east-north-east lay Cape Horn, the object of so many of my
dreams since boyhood.

A discussion broke out in the saloon about what it meant to each of us
to be rounding Cape Horn. Colin and Marie Christine are rather
short-tempered today — hardly surprising considering how they had
slaved on the mainsail repair; and the conversation became rather
heated as some of the younger fellows were typically supercilious. The
trip had been handed to them on a plate — free, gratis, and for nothing:
scarcely more than a break between dinghy circuits round a Rickmansworth gravel pit. And yet this was really the time of their lives.
How many people would they bore with tales of it in years to come? Just
over the horizon lay the 8.32 train and the mortgage. But I couldn't
have come without them either, could I? I'm a crabbed old git!

The Diego Ramirez were sighted at 4.40 p.m. in the afternoon, and
we will arrive at the Horn in the dark. The wind remained fair, but
visibility was poor with black clouds and rain squalls over the maze of
islands lying to the south of Tierra del Fuego. Darkness found us we
knew not where. With a chart full of Deceit islands and False Cape
Horns, we struggled with HMS *Endurance* on the radio, but apparently
she just could not read us, so we gave up. When we tried again, we
found the transmitter wouldn't work. Peter fixed it in twenty minutes.

It was a dark night. The cloud obscured the half moon above. Our
course started at east and gradually became more south-easterly as one
black headland after another swam up through the gloom ahead.
Squalls with heavy rain passed through, pushing the wind to 30 knots
on the dial before the helmsman, and the heavy genoa was heeling the
ketch harder over as each swell pumped its surplus into the body of the
sail.

'That's the one. It all fits into the pattern now,' muttered Alan, the
navigator, peering through thick glasses into a rain-sodden night.

'Remember Tom said he'd been here and found the light had fallen
over on its side. It's probably not working,' Steve opined.

Better men than me had lost their ships through making patterns of
land fit to justify their courses. The light must not be ignored.

At midnight I handed over the watch to Tony. A difficult time. We
saw we had just passed the Horn close to port, but already I could see
yet another grey mass ahead on the port bow. Still no light. Tony was as
worryingly unconcerned as ever. Alan was wisely insisting that we head
as close to windward as possible. We were making south-east or better.

Peter called me from the radio schedule to Portishead, and then
people began pushing scraps of paper at me as I sat on *Treaty of Rome*'s
old teak drawer — the only seat we had by the radio. 'Cape Horn 500
yards abeam,' read one for Tasmania. 'Send the same for me,' called

Steve from the galley, and I read out his Manchester address to the distant voice in England. 'To hell with it,' I thought. 'I'll send the same to Lance and Ada.' Then I returned to the chart table.

'I can see the light,' shouted Chris from the deck.

'Does it flash every ten seconds?' I called. There was a long pause.

'Yes. Flashing ten seconds,' came the longed-for reply.

We hadn't been five hundred yards off Cape Horn at all. It was Cape Spencer on Hermite Island. Cape Horn lay twelve miles to the southeast across San Francisco Bay. Anyway, we'd seen the light and we could lay it.

'Good thing we're not in a square rigger,' someone muttered.

I smiled to see the three circles drawn round the soundings on the chart: '(a) 52; (b) 44; (c) 61'. Ten years ago I'd drawn those as rendezvous points for a newspaperman, on the *Sunday Times* Golden Globe Race for the first non-stop single-handed circumnavigation. Knox-Johnson had won; I ended up in Brazil with a damaged boat – but I'd never have made it anyway.

Granny's green golf hat completed its circumnavigation tonight because the west coast of Chile is just north of here, where I'd worn the old friend to cross the grand Campa Nevada ice-cap back in 1972.

Marie Christine: Straight after breakfast Col and I continued our task. Today we had the job of hand-sewing the four lines of stitches, as it was not possible to get the sail through the arm of the machine. We worked away with our palms and double thread, Colin's ginger head bent over the heavy sail. We didn't say much apart from, 'Have you the thread and scissors?' Then the other would stop and search for them. Outside it was blowing hard and the boat was slewing along at its normal steep angle with the result that down below, items put aside would fall on the floor or get buried under the pile of sailcloth on the down side. Once the thread and scissors were found, we would continue to stitch together the gaping wound.

Those on watch and our navigator were keeping a sharp lookout for land. It was late afternoon and on Tony's watch that Hawk-eye Deakins spotted the vague grey outline that confirmed our position. I scrambled over the heap of sails, hanging on to the grab rail like a monkey, and peered out of the hatch in the direction the excited fellows on deck were pointing. It looked like a long, low dark cloud to me, jumping up and down, with white stitches on it.

'Come on, Marie Christine,' shouted Colin. 'We'll not get it finished by tonight if you keep rushing out.'

Reprimanded, I went back to my task. By now my fingers were feeling sore, but worse were my thumbs. The effort to push the angled needle through the sailcloth was considerable and although I had taped my gaping thumbnail up it was feeling pretty tender. My other thumb had been in the way when the needle I was pushing shot off the leather palm and scratched it deeply from the nail to the knuckle. This too was bound in plaster.

Having seen the islands, we expected to round Cape Horn during the night in darkness. While Col and I worked away in the saloon, John, Alan and those on watch kept a sharp lookout for the myriad of unlit islands close to the Tierra del Fuego. The night was dark and the little light shed from a slip of moon was hidden by frequent rain squalls. Wasn't this the graveyard of unlucky seafarers through the centuries? My unease mounted when John and Peter tried to contact HMS *Endurance*, which was in the area to escort the yachts round Cape Horn. They made contact but our signal was so weak they could not hear us; our transmitter was not operating. It began to dawn on me, watching John's and Alan's anxious faces as they came down to study the chart time and again, that they didn't really know where we were. 'Can you put out the Tilley lamp down there? It's ruining our vision,' an anxious voice called from above. Col and I continued by torchlight.

Land had been sighted on several occasions to either side of us but without confirmation of the light actually on Cape Horn, which should flash every ten seconds, we could not be certain where we were. Then suddenly, there was a shout of relief from on deck. 'I can see the light.' It was Chris. 'And it's flashing every ten seconds.' Col and I both scrambled up to see what we could of Cape Horn. Our heads over the hatch and squinting through spray and wind we could just make out the flash of light that was to many the dream of a lifetime, 'rounding Cape Horn'. As I stood there shivering in the raw damp air, I wondered what fairy godmother had been at my birth to decree that two days after my thirty-fourth birthday I would sail round Cape Horn. Clare Francis had been sailing since the age of five, the other four girls in the race had also spent much time cruising and racing – but not me. It's funny where Destiny leads one.

It was now past two in the morning. Alan set a course for the helmsman to steer in the certain knowledge of our position and John at the door to our cabin said, 'I'm turning in, M.C. – hope you won't be long.' His face wore a look of deep satisfaction. I knew what this night had meant to him after the titanic struggle of making this trip possible for all of us. 'Yes, I won't be long,' I answered.

Day 27: *Friday, 20 January   Noon position 55° 05' S, 65° 30' W*
Day's run 190 miles   Course NNE   Wind SW Force 4
Barometer 1008

John: Cape Horn. Cape Horn. I look back at it in the pearly light of an

early southern summer's day. It was four in the morning. All you sailors
that have rounded here and the struggles you've had. I'll never forget
you, I thought.

It was the first sunny day since I don't remember when. The land
looked just like the Scottish Highlands in winter – but it was summer
here.

We skirted along the southern shores of Tierra del Fuego until we
came into the narrow Le Maire Straits which separate it from the snowy
heights of Staten Island. Luckily the tide was with us, and we had 30
knots of wind from astern. As the line dropped from view once more, we
had seen no sign of human life except that small welcoming light
twenty-eight feet above the sea at the foot of Cape Horn. Only the great
wandering albatrosses wheeled about, the ghosts of men drowned at
sea.

'Here she comes,' someone shouted, and all heads scanned the
northern horizon. A growing red speck was making towards us from out
on the port bow.

'That's a funny looking ship for the Royal Navy,' said Steve.

'Oh, she was going to be a battleship,' quipped J.C., 'only they
couldn't afford the guns.'

We were suffering a bit from the after-effects of the champagne and
beer consumed at lunch to celebrate, but we made a brave sight with
full mizzen, newly repaired main and the patriotic colours of our
big-boy and spinnaker. As the red hull, with its boxlike white superstructure, came along with us, strains of 'A Hard Day's Night' drifted
across the breaking waves. The crew waved long and cheerfully. Steve
and J.C. sang our 'Southern Ocean Blues' into our Tannoy
loudspeaker, and a ragged cheer went up from the bows of the ice-
breaker, where bearded matelots in white pullovers lined the rail,
shouting encouragement – we thought it was encouragement, anyway.
Too soon they had to turn and head for *Adventure*, still 150 miles astern,
with her damaged steering. Sadly we took down our banner 'Closed on
Mondays for Staff Training', and *Debenhams* was left alone with the rafts
of drifting brown kelp once more.

'That was about the most exciting part of the whole trip,' was Marie
Christine's view, amazed that anything so important should come to
see us.

Marie Christine: As it turned out, I spent another hour in the saloon
with Col and the sail. He would have worked on until we had it finished,
but by now my hands were so sore I could hardly push the needle
through the material. Reluctantly he agreed to the halt when I said I
could go no further. We would continue in the morning.

Breakfast featured a most unusual recipe, but quite delicious;

Jacquet 'long-life' bread, crusts off, sandwiched together with cheese in the middle, dipped into pancake mix and fried, a cheese sandwich fritter, a Lenartowicz original.

My hands felt a lot better when we set to again on the sail. We had only half a seam out of the fifty-six feet of hand sewing left to do and by eleven we were ready for it to be taken out and put up. We heaved the sail out into the cockpit. I was shocked when I looked back into the saloon; the floor was littered with twirls of paper backing to the sticky tape we had used, shreds of material, cotton, forks, torches, books, bottles – it looked as if we had had a New Year's party down below instead of two days of serious sewing!

I held my breath as Tony, Dick and Colin hoisted the main; was the patch going to work? I couldn't bear the thought of getting it down and starting all over again, if it was wrong. It went up slowly and there was the tear. The untidy stitching looked marvellous from a distance and it seemed to set well. Colin reckoned the leech was too slack, but I missed the finer aspects of its set and felt pleased it was all in one piece again. 'We'll have a party,' John suggested. 'Some champagne to celebrate going round the Horn and mending the mainsail.'

J.C. had to open the bottles because of my fingers and with great merriment we toasted Alan the navigator for getting us there, John for making it all possible, the crew for keeping the boat going and Col and me for our stitching. By this time we had drunk two bottles of champagne and about two cans of beer each, quite heady when you're not used to much. Dickie's lunch of minestrone and baked potatoes brought us round a bit, but one by one those who weren't on watch crept away to sleep off the effects of the booze.

A sudden shout woke John and me from our doze – '*Endurance* is only five minutes away'. We both got dressed at the speed of lightning and rushed on deck to see the brave and welcome sight of HMS *Endurance*, scarlet-red flared hull with white painted deck and topsides making full speed towards us. It was a sunny day. *Debenhams* must have looked grand. We had up our red, white and blue tri-radial spinnaker as well as the matching big-boy, our newly mended main and mizzen and the large red ensign fluttered from its pole on the stern where John and I sat waving to the friendly crew of *Endurance*. We could hear her loudspeakers playing for our benefit 'It's been a Hard Day's Night'. Steve and J.C. bellowed in return through the loud hailer our own blues song, 'I Ain't Goin' Down to that Southern Ocean No More', to great cheers and applause from *Endurance*.

Meanwhile, Peter in the radio shack had been chatting with the radio operator.

'Peter,' I called, peering through the aft hatch, 'could I have a word with them?'

Colin and MC's hand repair of split mainsail
near Cape Horn

'Why, sure, M.C.,' he answered, rather surprised. To *Endurance* he said: 'Marie Christine Ridgway would like to speak to you,' and handed over the telephone to me.

'Could you tell your Captain I like the look of his boat more than ours. I have my bags packed. May I join you?'

A brief pause, then: 'The Captain would be delighted for you to join us.'

'How does the Captain suggest I get on to *Endurance*?' There was a distance of fifty yards of icy rough water between us.

'Well, you could swim or we could lift you by jack-stay.'

'Thanks a lot, but maybe I'll join you next time I'm rounding the Horn,' I answered, and then thanked them for making our day by visiting us.

They had been with us for two hours and then finally bid us farewell — we shouted three cheers for *Endurance* and as she passed close to our stern she blew her sirens in farewell.

'Well,' said Steve, having come down off the mizzen spreader. 'I think that has been about the most exciting part of the trip up to now,' and I could only agree as we watched the red ship disappear over the horizon.

Day 28: *Saturday, 21 January   Noon position 52° 40' S, 63° 10' W*
Day's run 115 miles   Course NNE by N   Wind NW by W Force 2
Barometer 1011

John: The wind died away during the early hours and there were mutters of 'South Atlantic High again. It'll take us a hundred days to Rio at this rate.' But everyone was in good heart.

J.C. and Steve cooked us a grand sausage and egg pie for supper last night, and the general improvement in the food has played a large part in keeping people cheery on this leg.

We only made 115 miles today as the wind failed on us, leaving warm sun and blue skies; ghosting along under the starcut on a flat sea. It was suddenly all so different from the cold grey days in the Southern Ocean. Clothing came out for airing; the main hatch dropboards were taken out; people blossomed into wide smiles, and all the talk was of Rio. Roger had his first shave since Auckland — but the others didn't bother.

Marie Christine: More sail-mending for Col and me. It's never ending — but I do quite enjoy it. Col's a cheery fellow to work with in spite of his doleful, limpid brown eyes which give him a sad expression, and it's good to be able to contribute something to the progress of the boat. This time it was the radial-head; a few minute tears where it had twisted round the forestay and part of the head of the sail had come unstitched. It's certainly a lot easier to handle this light nylon compared to the heavy terylene of the main. By lunchtime we'd fixed it.

Over the past three days I'd no chance to wash and I was feeling decidedly dirty. I set my stove going in the heads compartment, got two pints of hot water, and had a real good scrub, hair as well, and I even managed a face pack this time without interruption. I felt really terrific afterwards, with clean clothes the first time this trip (apart from socks and underwear) and I'd used dollops of Alliage body lotion and scent. After I had finished my toilet, it was so warm in the heads that I put the loo seat down and found myself a cushion and tried to catch up on my diary which I had also neglected over the past few days.

Day 29: *Sunday, 22 January   Noon position 50° 29' S, 60° 08' W*
Day's run 189 miles   Course NNE   Wind NW by W Force 5
Barometer 1010

John: When the wind returned it was strong enough from the north-north-west to force us into the No. 1 yankee, working staysail, drop the mizzen and put a reef gingerly into the just repaired main. We passed close under the eastern end of Grand Jason on a beautiful sunny morning. The Falkland Islands cover an area of some 4,700 square miles; of the 2,000 population, half live in Stanley. It's a rugged place of islands and inlets; treeless moorland rising to bare, craggy mountain; sheep farming, the way of life. So much like home is it that even the great skuas seem to circle us in recognition. Grand Jason is one of a line of islands and rocks trending out to the west from the north-western corner of the Falklands. It rises to 1,200 feet from a base of some five square miles. To our eyes, starved of land colours for a month, it seemed a balm of yellows, browns and greens, as it lay bathed in the pale morning sunlight.

'I think those white patches by the shore are a mass of penguins,' cried Alan excitedly, peering through his Russian binoculars. What appeared to be a half-moon shape area of white rock, where the top soil had been eroded away like giant bites out of the green and yellow flora, was indeed a football crowd of white-chested penguins, standing on terraces of black soil.

'Smells just like Handa Island at home,' laughed Staff as we came downwind of the birds. The water all around us was alive with the little fellows. They were only briefly visible as they shot up from below the surface, into the air, and down below again, 'like a dog running through wet grass', as Alan described them. Albatrosses and cormorants were everywhere too, and after we passed through a tide-rip near another low, rocky islet, we came upon a group of some thousands of albatrosses sitting together on the surface. They seemed to be fishing. When we drew near, the commotion from their tightly pressed bodies was so great, the water was lashed white as they all began their clumsy water-walking take-off. I found the passing of Grand Jason one of the most pleasant interludes of the entire voyage so far.

The wind held and we passed a school of whales, which brought cries of delight from the crew.

Day 30: *Monday, 23 January   Noon position 48° 26' S, 57° 18' W*
Day's run 182 miles   Course NNE   Wind SW by S Force 5
Barometer 1001

John: The middle watch of the night was miserable, with a near gale, wind and rain driving in our faces. By breakfast it was almost calm. Rain fell gently from a leaden sky, the horizon foreshortened by mist. Then the wind came again – from the south-west now – and up to 25 knots at that. The radial-head stayed up all day, giving way to the storm spinnaker at dusk. Only some 1,600 miles to Rio at midnight.

We know now that the last ten days of a leg are difficult. After thirty days there is a strong feeling of frustration which niggles at the back of the head. Sometimes a minor disagreement flares into a slanging match; like this evening, when Joan Baez was played full strength for

What's this?

the *n*th time since Marie Christine put our cassette out for general use –
and probable destruction. Alan is a quiet thirty-nine-year-old, fond of
ballet, opera, and classical music generally. He happened to remark
that he objected to political music. Steve, a flamboyant twenty-
five-year-old, verbose champion of minority causes in general, flew at
the retiring bachelor as if he'd tried to stop the last train out of Warsaw
before Hitler. Alan apologized.

Another discussion related to Marilyn Monroe's intelligence – a
subject which no one was really qualified to talk on with much sense. It
then swung to Raquel Welch, whom no one knew even distantly. Roger,
who usually ignores everyone, for artistic or personal reasons which are
never revealed, sets himself up as a sole arbiter of all matters: Cinema.
He gave a brief dissertation which effectively killed conversation. Any
further contribution could only be seen as a personal insult to the TV
man who was already morosely deep in his science-fiction paperback
once again.

It's all a reflection of the general air of tension which creeps in as we
get the scent of the fleshpots in our nostrils once again.

Day 31: *Tuesday, 24 January   Noon position 45° 40' S, 54° 40' W*
Day's run 171 miles   Course NE   Wind SW Force 4
Barometer 1008

John: The short steep seas we have found here in the lee of South

America produce the worst conditions for rolling we have had so far on the trip. 'Rolling down to Rio', as the song goes.

While Tony was at the wheel shortly after one in the morning, and I was lying in the saloon on the port settee, an awkward wave caught the stern and the full mizzen helped the broach along until the storm spinnaker pole on the starboard side was dumped deep in the sea. The top flew off the burning Tilley lamp. It arc'd across the saloon like a fiery comet and crashed into the starboard settee cushions, leaving behind a needle jet of nearly vaporized paraffin which spewed out over the table top. Just the right conditions for a fire in pitch darkness. It only needed the paraffin vapour to reach the still-glowing remains of the mantle and we'd have a blaze with everyone asleep in their bunks, and the boat rolling like a runaway cart-horse.

I flicked the lamp hard on to the floor and unscrewed the pressure pump on the lamp itself. All was well. A scorched cushion and a bit of a scorched floor – but what if there'd been no one in the saloon, I wondered. How many lives do you get on a trip like this?

Marie Christine: Reasonable progress, averaging just under 200 miles a day, winds variable, occasional calms. The slatting sails on the rigging sounding like wire coat hangers rattling in an empty wardrobe. Morale is up and down. We all seem ready to argue about anything. Is it because we are only about ten days away from Rio and we are all so impatient to be there? It was at this stage on the last leg that the trouble with Bob came to a head. John and I are spending more time in our cabin than before so as not to be drawn into disagreements.

Getting a lot warmer.

Day 33: *Thursday, 26 January   Noon position 42° 08' S, 47° 45' W*
Day's run 179 miles   Course NNE   Wind WNW Force 9
Barometer 1001

John: The day of the punch on the nose. All through this leg, indeed throughout the race, my plan has been to keep going at hull speed using the wind sail chart; by keeping a high steady average we have benefited from the over-pressing tactics of faster boats. In other words, we were on the unattractive but rewarding role of the fleet vulture, gaining only from the misfortunes of our competitors – ugly realism; but today the Young Turks, scenting *Treaty of Rome* only thirty miles ahead – and losing sight of the overall picture in the glare of the short-term gain – pushed the boat just too far, exacting a specified penalty: gear failure.

By 2.30 in the morning we were beam on to a severe gale, frequently gusting beyond the range of the 60-knot wind dial.

'At what speed do you reckon putting up the trysail, Tony?' I said from the wheel to the cowled figure in the after-cockpit with me.

'Forty-five knots,' came the short reply.

'It's gusting well over that now.'

'Only gusting.' Ten minutes of silence.

'Pretty long gusts of 70 or more,' I commented.

'All right, then.'

And the operation began; and they did it really well. Tony, Roger, Noel and Dick, four sodden red figures crouched against the main boom, shining dully in the moonlight between heavy showers. The trysail bag was found, at last, at the bottom of the after-sail locker; in half an hour the job was done. Tony and Noel came back to me at the wheel.

'D'you want to go below for a bit?' I asked them both.

'No. I feel much better now: a lot warmer,' Tony replied, his voice betraying the warmth of feeling he so seldom imparts.

'I'm fine,' Noel said in his most cheerful manner. Everyone was relieved the rotten job was done.

At breakfast the wind was the same, but the seas bigger and coated with spindrift. My message to watch-leaders was to get the No. 3 yankee up as soon as they thought the weather justified it. I should have been firmer, but it's got to be balanced with giving the watch-leaders room to lead.

Roaring along under trysail

Marie Christine and Steve crashed across the saloon and flung their combined breakfast into Noel's bunk, Marie Christine scalding her arm with coffee in the process.

By lunch the wind and seas were beyond anything anyone except me had ever seen. The No. 3 yankee was still up with a small staysail and a trysail.

'When are you planning to take the yankee off?'

'When we can get on the foredeck again.'

J.C. and Peter were thrown on to the table, smashing the folding leaf in three pieces. Marie Christine burnt her other arm passing out the soup; and in another crash the sharp French kitchen knife flew across the saloon narrowly missing her left eye as she sat on the leeward side.

Noel and Dick came down below, streaming spray and crowing with delight at an all-time speed record for the hour. 'The wind speed is right off the dial,' Noel chattered in his high-speed talk.

Tony crouched down at the wheel, with Roger, not the keenest sailor on the crew, at his aid. We broached. One huge wave burst on the foredeck, darkening the saloon in its passage aft. The boat shuddered, sails thundered; the second comber struck on the port quarter, piling grey water on top of the already overflowing main cockpit. J.C. let out a bellow of rage as high-pressure jets caught him in the crossfire from the sliding windows above his position at the cooker.

'Do you think people know what to do in this situation?' came Chris' worried voice. He was still a stranger aboard.

'Ease the mainsheet to come out of the broach, you mean,' I replied, watching the water level wavering at the second perspex dropboard up from the bottom of the companionway.

'Yes. The sheets have gotta be free to help the boat back.' Chris' voice held a note of alarm.

'Rudder's gone. Rudder's gone,' came the cry from above. The Young Turks chortled with excitement, stampeding up the companionway with a chant of: 'Let all the sails down. Let all the sails down.' I wondered idly what they'd break next. I didn't think it could be anything too serious.

Alan, at thirty-nine, was not overcome with the general feeling of glorious excitement.

'I thought you might like to know the rudder's broken,' I called through to his bunk in the swamp.

'I did hear something to that effect,' came a quiet English voice, 'but there's nothing for me to do. I thought I might as well just stay here.'

I smiled and wished there were a few more fellows aboard like him. There's nothing like experience for calming you down in this sort of situation.

Colin set about doing everything. I had difficulty in persuading him to see the situation objectively; get the others on the jury-rig steering system while he worked on repairing the main problem with the quadrant. There was no future in the jury tiller. In the long run the time of our arrival in Rio depended on how soon the main system was repaired. The job took four and a half hours. It could only be seventy-five per cent strength to Rio; four bolts had gone and two locating pins sheared. How lucky the weakest link had been something we could reach and fix.

Chris was concerned that we should radio our position to the fleet in case the sea should build further and overwhelm us. I didn't tell him that Peter had just discovered the aerial was broken – one of the Young Turks had trodden on it in his excitement. We never would discover who.

Marie Christine: A wild night – wind gusting well over 60 knots, boat lurching uncomfortably on steep waves. Several times I expected us to turn over and clung to the sides of the bunk, ready for the worst. Twice a stream of sea water shot down at my head from the ventilation hole just above my pillow. The first time I sat up, startled out of my sleep. This turned out to be the wrong thing to do as the stream of water continued and soaked the sleeping-bag on which I had been lying as well as my pyjamas. Switching on the light, I quickly found a towel and stemmed the flow. Poor John came in at four shivering wet and retired to a very damp bed.

Breakfast was a disaster. J.C. had just passed out the coffee when the boat did a massive broach. Steve and I, who were sitting side by side, ended up in a tangle the other side of the table. The contents of my plate of muesli and cup of coffee shot into Noel's bunk along with a whole heap of other stuff. Thinking we were capsizing, surprised by my rage, I uttered the worst swear word I knew three times and loudly. She didn't quite go over, but when we righted ourselves it certainly looked as if she had: Noel's ceiling had a mixture of tomato ketchup, coffee and muesli plastered on it. The varied contents of the table had shot all over the downside seat and floor – tapes, books and anything loose had catapulted into a heap with the rest. I scalded my wrist with the hot coffee but apart from that there were no injuries. 'Marie Christine – I didn't know you knew such words,' a delighted Dick said to me in mock reproach. Noel had the lousy job of cleaning his bunk while I mopped the floor and put things in a safer place. We were still lurching about in a very steep sea and the wind showed no signs of abating.

At lunchtime I was passing out the two mugs of soup from the galley into the saloon when a sudden lurch of the boat sent me spinning into the waterproofs. Now I could add leek soup to my fragrance of coffee and 'swoop' well impregnated into my jeans. The steep sea was traced with lines of spindrift and each wave was topped with a tumbling crest of foam. John felt it was time to take down the No. 3 yankee and said so.

Noel had just come down for his lunch. 'Absolutely fantastic up there,' he told us excitedly. 'We've easily broken the speed record, the wind's been off the clock for ten minutes at least. I'm sure it's gusting over 70 knots.'

I looked at John's anxious face. He wasn't sharing in Noel's exhilaration at all – he knew how much strain the boat could take without something breaking and was just waiting for it to happen.

Another lurch. A sharp-pointed knife took flight across the saloon and narrowly missed hitting my eye – I hadn't seen it but those seated on the other side looked shocked. It just wasn't my day.

Then it happened. A tremendous lurch. For the second time in the day everything shot off the table. 'Are we going over?' I wondered briefly. A strangled cry from above: 'Everyone on deck! Rudder's gone, rudder's gone!' There was a certain amount of panic and a lot of anxiety as the two watchers scrambled into their waterproofs to get on deck.

'Just take it calmly,' John barked. 'Get the sails down first.'

The boat was vibrating wildly with the flapping sails rising and falling heavily on the giant seas. We were now riding the breaking waves broadside; water was cascading over the deck as the boys battled at getting the sails down and secured. The wind shrieked remorselessly through the rigging. It was a queer sight to see no one at the helm as we rode the cresting mountains.

I couldn't help thinking that if this had to happen, how lucky it had occurred during daylight and nowhere near land. Our efforts were concentrated on keeping upright and fixing an emergency form of steering. The first fear that the rudder had gone was allayed when Colin found the fault – the quadrant had been subjected to such enormous strain that two of the four stainless steel bolts holding a vital plate had sheared off, leaving the other two bent and useless. Quickly he fixed up a temporary tiller, giving us more control over the boat; then painstakingly he removed the loosened plate and set about re-securing it. It took four and a half hours.

Colin warned that once back in use it would have to be handled with care. Rio seemed to be getting farther from us, not nearer. The wind gradually died and by evening we were becalmed for an hour or two, the heavy swell causing an uneasy motion down below.

John and I discussed the disastrous day in our cabin. We were both feeling fed up with life at sea. It was expensive, uncomfortable and most of the time unbelievably boring. How could anybody contemplate doing this a second time?

Close to the big ice on Leg 3

The most crowded start – Boxing Day, Auckland

Debenhams and an iceberg on Leg 3

Come the dawn Roger was still
filming the Carnival

Peter's playmate in Rio

John switching halyards on Leg 4

'Our leader' at sunset in granny's golfing hat

Day 34: *Friday, 27 January   Noon position 39° 50′ S, 45° 50′ W*
Day's run 131 miles   Course NE by N   Wind Variable Force 3
Barometer 1020

Marie Christine: Funny, how just when we feel we've had the sea, the wind lessens, the sun comes out and you feel prepared to give it another go. Today is like that – a cloudless blue sky, sparkling sea and warm, comforting sun. Can it really be the same world as yesterday, when we were all fearing for our lives? Damp gear was brought out to air. I climbed up the steps of the mizzen mast and tied up two excellent Point Five bags that zip into a double, hoping the sun and wind would banish the damp smell and stop the mould which I could see growing at the foot of each bag. They swung heavily in the wind like bodies on a gibbet. I hoped my granny knots were adequate and that they wouldn't fall into the sea. Time had come for a blitz on our cabin. I got the damp sheets and blanket out, pushed them through a grab rail and spread them on the hot deck. With dustpan and brush I swept up an unbelievable selection of rubbish from our empty bunk, bus tickets, hard old knobs of chewed gum, hairclips, coins from South Africa and New Zealand to mention just some of it – no wonder I'd had such vivid dreams.

With the calm, Alan had been able to get a good sight. Sadly this put

MC writing her thoughts and airing her socks

us way out to the east of our dead reckoning positions of the last two days. It seems that in the past twenty-four hours we have fallen 180 miles behind *Treaty of Rome*. We had managed before yesterday to narrow the gap to thirty miles. John is taking this news hard. However, it might mean that by being farther out to sea, we'll miss the notorious calm patches found up the coast towards Rio. Time will tell.

'How about another bottle of port?' suggested Col.

'A splendid idea,' intoned J.C. After the buffeting of the previous twenty-four hours we were all enjoying the calm of this evening and apart from our position, spirits were high. The orange sun was falling fast into a sea of grey and yellow scales. Eight o'clock came, the watches changed. Alan and Noel went on deck with sextants to take star sights. With each sextant altitude a ragged cheer went up from the cockpit, Steve's loud voice imitating a sports commentator: 'Oh yes, it's gonna be a good one – Will he make it? Yes he will – Hurrah!'

Alan paid no attention to the rabble as he shouted the readings of the heavenly bodies in an ultra-clear voice to Dickie, who was jotting down the figures with a non-too-patient expression on his face. I lobbed the three bottles of port over the side. 'He'd see stars all right if you hit him with one of those,' Steve quipped and I watched the corked bottles containing their messages bob out of sight in the bubbling wake.

Day 35: *Saturday, 28 January   Noon position 37° 30' S, 44° 35' W*
Day's run 162 miles   Course NE   Wind N by E Force 8
Barometer 1016

John: Pounding into heavy head seas, which forced us off our course for Rio.

The yacht *33 Export* is heading with an injured man for a rendezvous with a tug off the town of Rio Grande, quite a long way south of Rio.

Marie Christine: The wind is back again. Col, looking resigned and sweaty with his waterproof high trousers on and nothing else, was handing out from the galley plates of 'elephant's trunk' in batter – circular spam fritters. The night before I'd bartered a half Mars bar for Peter's gherkin. The deal had gone a further step this morning. Peter offered the half Mars bar to Alan for half his fritter. I will enjoy reminding Alan, when we meet in the future, of the time he almost sold his soul for half a Mars bar.

The sea was building up and as the morning wore on I retired to bed with a tummy ache, hoping it would pass. John handed me a plate with a potato and knob of butter which was all I felt I could eat of the lunch and the remains of a packet of dry pumpernickel. He forgot a spoon or fork but I managed eating it slowly and dipping it into the melted butter and thinking how I wouldn't mind eating just potatoes and butter for the rest of my days.

The afternoon bumped along. We were on the port tack and it was sticky lying head to toe with John forced into the angle of our bunk. Escape in the form of *Trinity*, a book written by an American about Ireland, took my mind off the discomfort. I poured us glasses of a dry red wine which we balanced carefully in between sips. I didn't want to spill it over our newly dried bedding. Ready for a change from sticky sweet port, I'd opened two bottles of wine which mostly I'd drunk in our cabin instead of beer at lunch or port before supper. I felt slightly sinful drinking this behind closed doors. Always before we'd been scrupulously fair in sharing everything with the rest of the crew, and, as a result, every sip was like nectar. My tummy still ached in spite of the wine, so John agreed to bring me some curry. I thought he had forgotten but eventually he brought it after I'd suffered a period of maudlin self-pity, lying in the darkened cabin.

The wind had been gusting 45 knots most of the day; by eight it was up to 50. The visibility was right down owing to driving rain. The poor boys, it couldn't be much fun for them.

We heard on the radio chat show that one of the boys on *33 Export* has broken his femur.

Day 36: *Sunday, 29 January   Noon position 34° 55' S, 43° 45' W*
Day's run 160 miles   Course N by E   Wind SW Force 4–5
Barometer 1015

John: Racing in moonlit seas, butting into steep waves breaking over decks, spitting salt out of the mouth, four hours of changing up from the No. 2 staysail and trysail to No. 3 yankee, No. 2 staysail and trysail; and then the No. 3 yankee and No. 2 staysail to the main, with three reefs. Then the wind goes on to the port beam (south-west); bilge pumped all over me at the helm while Steve was pumping the aft locker. Shortly after this Steve was sick.

Blue skies and 30 knots of wind for breakfast.

The first flying fish seen since Cape Town of one-inch in length, lying on the deck.

There was the usual dramatic weather change as the wind went round to the south. Blue skies and sun-bathing on gentle seas became the order of the day.

33 Export feel the life of their casualty is now in danger. It's the third day since he broke his femur and there's still no sign of a boat setting out to meet them from Rio Grande. They plan to rendezvous with *Japy Hermès* tonight and take on the doctor from that boat for the rest of the journey to the Rio Grande.

'Are you well today?' I asked Chris, up on deck.

'Yep,' he replied sourly, looking away.

I'm more than a little worried about his attitudes. First he threatened to stop trimming sails if we went through the Falkland Channel; then this afternoon as I was writing these notes he suddenly said, 'Can I read what you're writing there?' in a demanding voice.

For a young fellow, one of many in Auckland who wanted a passage, I'm afraid he's failed to impress. Marie Christine and I agree we'll put him off the boat at Rio. Sadly, I feel the same way about Tony. I didn't come on this trip for seven months of aggravation from him. It's only fair to tell them both as soon as we reach Rio.

Marie Christine: We plod on. The gale has blown out, but we're left with head-winds making progress slow. It's getting very warm. The swamp is particularly airless and smelly, but it is too wet to open the forward hatch. Our cabin is like a sauna. We've got another six weeks of this heat. I'd give anything now for the three-foot thick stone walls of our croft that keep the house as cool as a milking parlour even on the hottest day in summer. I've removed the storm boards covering our windows, which helps with the air.

Unable to sleep, I joined John on his twelve-to-four watch. The sky was studded with myriads of stars, the Southern Cross hung low in the sky, Jupiter and Mars were brilliant in the blanketing darkness. The boat, the sea, the sky had a timeless quality as we sailed through the night.

Day 38: *Tuesday, 31 January   Noon position 29° 50' S, 43° 20' W*
Day's run 151 miles   Course NE by N   Wind N by W Force 4
Barometer 1015

John: I am doing the night-watch in shirt-sleeves. What a change that is just from a few days back!

Dick saw three yellow-brown turtles during the forenoon and I spent the whole morning sorting out cupboards in our cabin; which is a very good job done because some of the water has been draining in through the windows and down into the cupboards with the result that much of the stuff is very mildewy now, as the heat increases.

The first adult flying fish were seen this afternoon. We were sailing along with a gentle north-by-west breeze. The heat was oppressive, so the crew took it in turns to surf along the wave tops in a bo's'n's chair which was attached to a spinnaker halyard on the leeward side. It looks exhilarating but there wasn't time for me to have a go before supper.

The stars were exceptionally bright in a black velvet sky, and for the first time I saw the two fluffy patches known as the Magellanic Clouds. They looked like miniature Milky Ways.

I'm really very disturbed by the thought of having to tell Tony and Chris to leave the boat at Rio. With Tony the problem is really rather complex; I've not been able to bridge the age gap between us, twenty-two and forty, with any degree of mutual sympathy; and over the months it's become clear that our objectives are widely divergent. Tony, fresh out of college, I think only endures his job as chief instructor at the John Ridgway School of Adventure as a means of achieving personal advancement from an executive position aboard a yacht in this race at such an early age. His carelessness with the equipment and apparent disregard for the future life of the boat, his frequently uncooperative attitudes at meetings and his reluctance to carry out any maintenance tasks except those that appeal to him are not the attitudes I require in a watch-leader. In spite of all this he is a hard worker, driving the boat forward, and regardless of cost I would keep him on, but for one factor which isn't applicable to the other yachts in this race: we have to start work together immediately on returning to Scotland, on a long and arduous new season, whereas on the other boats the crews split up and can achieve release in that way. Tony would be a destructive and negative force in his present state of mind, and I just can't afford his influence to infect the others; and so he must be gone, really, before everybody turns their minds to Ardmore and the new season.

With Chris the situation is simpler. He's had a free trip, seven and a half thousand miles from Auckland to Rio round Cape Horn; I've spent ten years assessing people as possible instructors at the John Ridgway School of Adventure, and after forty days with Chris I know his attitude is unsuitable.

Day 39: *Wednesday, 1 February   Noon position 28° 10′ S, 44° 00′ W*
Day's run 152 miles   Course WNW   Wind NE Force 7
Barometer 1015

John: Pitiless head-winds, from the north-east and a metallic blue sea to match. Everyone struggles with the frustration of little or no progress towards Rio which is only three hundred miles away, and most of the boats are now in. With favourable winds we'd do well on handicap; but as it goes now, our chances are ebbing away.

Day 40: *Thursday, 2 February   Noon position 26° 05′ S, 44° 30′ W*
Day's run 154 miles   Course N by E   Wind NE Force 7
Barometer 1014

John: Gale force winds now slow us down to 5 knots – and that to the west of Rio!

The Barlow 32 main halyard winch drum crumpled during the night, and so we had to rig the halyard down to the cockpit – which is rather a complication if we have to do any tacking.

The heat is taking its toll, and people are sleeping all over the place on deck during the day.

I've been reading a book called *The Katyn Massacre*, which is about the Russian massacre of the Polish officer and intellectual class during the last war; and we got into a discussion about this in the evening. Predictably, Steve was absolutely for one-sided disarmament, whereas I was in favour of disarmament in stages by both sides equally. John Covington had no real view about it, and Peter didn't want to say anything in case there was a row; Colin had little to say, and Stafford Morse was weakly with Steve Lenartowicz.

Day 41: *Friday, 3 February   Noon position 24° 05' S, 45° 00' W*
Day's run 124 miles   Course NNE   Wind ENE Force 3
Barometer 1014

John: The heat bores on. We made a landfall on Brazil some hundred miles south-west of Rio.

My main concern is with the crew. I feel we need a fresh start at Ardmore this summer. The 1977 instructors have taken my delegation of responsibility for weakness; and so they have become stale and uninterested in returning there. There are a thousand young loud-mouths who'll tell you how to sail a boat, and be delighted in smashing it for you. But very few who can tell you how to get a boat in the first place for them to crew on.

This morning we were making five knots to windward – straight at the land. Steve and then Colin had a go at the bo's'n's chair from the spinnaker halyard, and we had to run 20 degrees off our course to stop them from bumping the side. In fact, Colin did bash his eyebrow against the toe-rail.

I asked the crew if they wanted to go on swimming or stop using the bo's'n's chair and make the course for Rio.

'It doesn't matter. We'll get there some time,' Tony said dully.

'Well, it's no more important than stopping for an iceberg,' I agreed. 'It's some trip when you can do both things, if you think about it.'

'If we'd set out to race in the first place, it would matter. It's too late to bother now,' Dick said.

I was livid at this attitude and so retreated up to the bow with Marie Christine.

'That Dick McCann is going to get a piece of my mind in a minute,' she said. Marie Christine is much more frightening than me, so I felt rather sorry for Dick if she let fly.

'Okay, we'll get shot of all three – Tony, Dick and Chris,' I snarled,

Steve swinging from the spinnaker halyard

once we were out of earshot. 'Those buggers think they've got me cornered. Well, they're wrong. I'll run the School without them – no bother. Breath of fresh air is what we want.'

'Give them an inch and they'll take a mile,' Marie Christine agreed, lips tight across her teeth with fury.

'Bloody ridiculous. If they say they've got no money for the fares, you know what I'll tell them?'

'What?'

'You'll have to do what I had to do for this boat you've been on. Borrow. Borrow from your proud parents!' I stamped off to our cabin and got out the staff file from my briefcase. I read every letter from people who wanted jobs in 1978. I had the applications which had arrived before October 1977, and there'd be more recent ones waiting in Rio which would have been sent out by Ada. I went back to Marie Christine in the bow with my lists.

'We can make it easily without them – and we will.'

And so the day wore on, stifling hot, and nearly calm. *Japy Hermès* seemed really choked off on the radio, for they were only five miles from the finish and absolutely becalmed.

After an excellent supper followed by Steve's Atholl brose, I sat and chatted with Colin's watch by the wheel. Then Tony asked to have a talk with me up on the bow. It was dark and nearly calm.

'I wondered if you were going to do anything about the crew after this leg?' Tony asked, hesitantly, when I was comfortably sat on the buckled remains of the stainless steel pulpit.

'Yes. Matter of fact I am. But we don't want another Auckland. I'm waiting until we're ashore in Rio, and then I'll call a meeting,' I replied guardedly.

'Yes. I can see it coming and I don't want it to happen. I want to do something about it.' Tony stumbled on the words, his arms flailing the night in an effort to make his point.

'Okay then. There are two things I'm not satisfied with – loyalty and manners. They matter a lot to me. I was going to tell the whole crew that you, Dick and Chris were being put off at Rio. I was prepared for the rest of them to leave in sympathy. The entire crew could leave within twenty-four hours if they wish. I would accept that. The rules require a crew of five only. Marie Christine and I would need three others and we could pick those up in Rio – no bother.'

'But I don't want to leave. I've had a difficult time with my watch on this leg. You wouldn't have much trouble with me on the next leg.'

'I realize it was asking a lot for you to deal with all four of them,' I said. 'It's a good thing you spoke with me tonight. If you hadn't, all three of you would have gone tomorrow.' I wondered if he could see the tears of tension on my cheeks.

Our conversation moved on over a wide range of subjects. I felt he was my man. I would keep the other two on as well; talk to them individually in Rio.

It's a game all right! Tempers get short when you are becalmed after forty days and the other boats are whooping it up in port.

Day 42: *Saturday, 4 February   Noon position 30 miles WSW of Rio de Janeiro Day's run 67 miles Course E Wind W by S Force 0–2 Barometer 1014*

John: On deck with Tony, Dick and Chris just before dawn in very light airs some dozen miles south of Punta de Castelhanos on Isla Grande, fifty miles west-south-west of Rio de Janeiro, high up in the night sky I saw a golden satellite-sized object moving rapidly at a shallow angle towards the earth. I took it to be a comet, trailing a symmetrical fantail cloud of white. Suddenly, it disappeared as if it had disintegrated, and the white cloud gradually dispersed, changing its shape as it faded to nothing.

The sun was well up by breakfast, already heating the day. A pale breeze nudged us very gently towards Rio – it was going to be hard on the nerves after six long weeks. Only *Adventure*, *33 Export* and ourselves were still at sea. Today saw the start of the Carnival in Rio, and Roger sometimes says the Carnival is the only reason he came on the trip.

After breakfast I said I would like to see the whole boat cleaned up before we arrived in port, and to encourage the limp enthusiasm of some, I said I'd clean up the crew's heads, because anyone sitting in the saloon would see its filthy condition if the door was open.

While in my cabin I heard Alan telling a story about his National Service days as an Able Seaman in the Royal Navy. Shortly after joining a ship at the age of eighteen Alan had been told by a crusty old chief petty officer to clean some brasswork just aft of the funnel.

'But, Chief, the smoke'll tarnish it again straight away.'

'Are you going to argue with me, Green?'

'No, sir, I'm just going to clean the brasswork,' said Alan.

'Just about as bloody stupid as us cleaning up this boat now. Who cares if it's dirty when people come aboard? It's a bloody waste o' time,' I heard young Dick moaning to anyone who'd listen.

If you imagine each leg of the Race to be about forty days, you could say that at the end of leg 3 we were coming to the end of the third period of Lent – that's how it seemed to me as I knelt before the crew's lavatory and began the hour-long task of cleaning the heads properly in a calm sea.

Behind me Colin and Peter were scrabbling about beneath the floorboards in the swamp in search of a putrid smell which seemed to be coming from somewhere just aft of the mainmast step. I doubted whether Dick was doing anything. As I had cleared the air with Tony the previous night I might as well deal with Dick while I had time on my hands ... I could almost hear Lance's North Eastern voice back at Ardmore saying in my ear: "The trouble with you is you're too bluddy impetuous!'

'Who's bluddy boat is it anyway?' I thought, swelling with foolish self-righteousness.

'I wonder if you two fellows could leave that for a moment – I'd like to have a word with Dick. Could you ask him to come down?' I called to Colin and Peter, and in a couple of minutes they'd extricated themselves and left.

'You wanted to see me,' said Dick in his stubbornest tone.

'Yes. I'm afraid I think it's about time we had a little talk.' I looked down at the bowl, suddenly wondering where to begin.

'Come on ... Don't make a big thing of it, just say what you want to say and get it over.'

Running my hand round the rim of the bowl where the Harpic had begun to bite, I collected some of the thick yellow urine scale across four fingers.

'This is what you could see no sense in cleaning up before we reach Rio. As well as looking awful, there are going to be flies in Rio. They are going to settle on this and on the food in the galley. Some people will call the result Rio Runs. Maybe someone will get so ill he won't be able to finish the trip.'

He said nothing, looked sullen.

'We had an agreement at the start of this leg, didn't we?'

'Yes.'

'Well, I'm afraid I'm not satisfied you're carrying out your side well enough. I think you're ill-mannered and disloyal. If you wish to continue on this boat I want you to write me a thousand-word essay on your understanding of good manners and loyalty. If not, I would like you off this boat within twenty-four hours of our arrival in Rio.'

'What? Me write you an essay? ... Never!'

'In that case please be clear of the boat the day after we arrive. I think that's all we have to say to one another, thank you.' I got on with the bowl and Dick left.

I remembered having to write a thousand words on 'Manners maketh Man' for my housemaster in my last year at school after sending a junior with my cricket bat to the French master; the accompanying note read: 'Could you please get this bat repaired in the village when you go down, the blade is split at the bottom.' I never forgot writing that essay.

When eventually I came on deck, Noel, Roger and Dick were huddled up in the bows. 'It's going to be just like entering Auckland,' I thought ... Six weeks is a long time and it was a hot day.

In the dark we crossed the finishing line. There was no moon. On our way to the Rio Yacht Club we rounded the Sugarloaf and saw the illuminated statue of Jesus Christ. It was isolated from other lights and so high up in the mountains that it appeared to be in the sky – another priceless memory after 7,500 miles at sea.

The Iate Clube de Rio de Janeiro – to use its proper name – was sumptuous; but with a £7,000 entry fee it's not surprising. Cape Horn and the bergs seemed far away already.

Early next morning I told Dick he could stay on with the crew. Did *I* know much about manners and loyalty at twenty years of age? Had I forgotten what it was like to be unable to express my thoughts? Wasn't I being rather petty? I wouldn't leave him stranded. There was plenty of crew trouble on the other boats. Seven of the nine Italians had walked off; two had left *King's Legend* and one from *Flyer*. Some would have to go from *Treaty of Rome*. I felt Corado de Majo, the Italian skipper, was not alone when he told me: 'I thought the sea would be the chief problem on this voyage. It is not. It is the people.'

Marie Christine: Calm all night. We can see land and are nearly there but any wind there is is coming from the wrong direction. Johnny is itching badly with prickly heat.

'Got any books, M.C.?' – How could Col feel like reading when we are so close?

'No, but I'll play Scrabble.'

We sat in the burning sun for what I hoped would be my last victory of this leg. By mid-afternoon it had dropped dead calm. Some even thought we were going backwards! A school of dolphins were playing gently a little distance from the boat. 'Let's go and swim with them,' shouted John. We jumped into the cool water and swam towards them. Sadly, they didn't want to be near us and swam away – maybe it was our unwashed bodies. I looked back at the boat rising and falling on the swell and thought of the other time I'd 'got off'. It couldn't have been more than three weeks ago. Here was I basking in the blue, calm water, thinking of that ice.

By evening the breeze freshened. We might actually arrive in Rio tonight. As the sun set we passed along a spectacular mountainous coastline girdled with silver beaches.

At 10.30 we crossed the finishing line, having passed close to the fabled Ipanema and Copacabana beaches. Gentle surf rolled on to the now empty sand but we could see the brilliant lights of the multi-storey flats and hotels, stretching along this mecca for the world's richest and most beautiful sun-seekers. Rio and the Carnival were ours.

9

Rio

Marie Christine: After six weeks at sea we were now on dry land again ready to enjoy whatever Rio had to offer. I had fished out a rather crumpled cotton skirt and top, dusted the mould from my high-heeled sandals and made my way along a wobbly plank stretching from the neighbouring boat to an arc of light on the pontoon. Glancing down into the inky water I saw a bloated dead rat floating belly up. This is no place to fall in, I thought to myself.

Waiting under the lamplight was Susan, Alan Green's fiancée. As they made their way arm in arm towards the yacht club, our ex-navigator had much to tell his girlfriend. It was late in the evening but the waiters were still busy taking orders from the tables placed outside the opulent, Portuguese-style club house. We greeted friends off other boats as we sat down and ordered exotic drinks under a starry sky and giant coconut palms.

Later, although we hadn't been officially cleared by Customs, John and I decided to get away for a steak. We hurried out of the club past the gate guards and found a near-by restaurant. It was now about midnight. We did not realize that in Rio most eating places stay open until three or four in the morning. We thought we were lucky to have found a place that was open and would serve us, ignoring its dingy decor and empty tables.

Having been warned by Alan to watch out we weren't 'rooked', we cautiously and with great language difficulties found out how much it would cost – or so we thought. We opened our long-awaited letters from home to a deafening background of monotonous samba tunes while we sipped our cool lagers.

'Don't turn round, John, but an amazing sight is going to walk past our table in a second or two.'

I watched John's eyes open wide as a young mulatto girl swung her naked hips inches past him. She was stunning – velvet dark skin sprinkled lightly with sparkle. She wore the briefest of lamé bras and a tiny triangle, held in place by a string, exposing rounded buttocks. Unselfconsciously she ambled towards the cashier, snapping her fingers in time to the samba's insistent rhythm.

'I hope that won't put you off your steak,' I muttered darkly as I watched John's eyes fixed on the lady in gold. When eventually the steaks came they weren't the best we had ever tasted but we ate the fresh food with relish. The next shock came with the bill: it was twice what the man had quoted, which we had thought pricy anyway. We paid and left, learning our first and most important lesson of how to survive in Rio.

Wandering back to the yacht club by a different route we passed crowds of excited Brazilians in exotic gear dancing to the hypnotic samba tunes blaring out of loudspeakers. This was the start of Carnival. I felt the boys were in for some surprises.

Over the next five days everything stopped. Rio was completely taken over by Carnival, a kaleidoscope of dazzling pinks, greens, blues, yellows, lamés silver and gold, glittering sequins, giant tinted ostrich feathers, satins, silks and dark wobbling flesh of every imaginable shape and size. Day and night the samba contests went on. The boys had their cameras and Rog and Noel went out to film on the second night. The luscious ladies, determined to be in the limelight, would provocatively advance towards the camera and commence a special erotic belly dance, part shake, part samba. They just loved to be photographed and the fellows enjoyed taking the photos; it certainly made a change from shots of sails going up and down.

The days – or should I say nights? – took on a pattern: a few drinks at the club and then out into the streets to see and join in the spectacle; back at six in the morning with glazed eyes; flop out exhausted on deck under the awning we'd made from one of the sails (it was too hot to sleep down below); and then off again in the evening. Not much got done but that didn't matter – it was Carnival.

The day after we arrived Pam and Ron Lynskey came down to the boat and introduced themselves. Ron was the B.P. manager in Brazil. After a tour of the boat, when they'd seen our cramped cabin, they very kindly offered to put John and me up at their apartment for the duration of our stay in Rio. It was heaven to sleep again between sheets on a still, soft bed and we even had the luxury of our own marble bathroom. The vast apartment overlooked the South Atlantic where it met the shore, giant rollers of surf endlessly breaking on the crowded, silver-sanded beach. Rio was hot beyond words but in this air-conditioned apartment we were able to feel human again. Each day I would come back from the yacht with the boys' and my dirty laundry, which was now covered in

Rio

mould and smelling. Into the washing machine and tumble drier it would go, and soon we were respectable again, no longer the tramps that we had been when we first arrived.

Pam and Ron couldn't have been kinder. They anticipated and understood our every need. They took all of us out to dinner; up to see the figure of Christ high up on the mountain top with a breathtaking view of Rio; introduced the boys to other friends who took them into their homes and with their kindness really made our stay in Rio happy.

Once Carnival was over we started work on the boat. Apart from the repair to the steering, which Colin was supervising, there were no major repairs to be done. However, there was the usual cleaning, sail-mending, checking, and re-stocking of supplies for the final leg. It was just as well, as the heat was sweltering and any physical effort made us run with sweat. The days passed by all too quickly. A lunch break would end up as a three-hour session sitting under the coconut palms in front of the club house, drinking Caiperinis and sipping the strong Rio coffee while swopping yarns with friends, followed by a swim in the pool and back to the boat just to tidy up the job of the morning.

The boys' lives were brightened even more by meeting an international group of girls who were on a bus tour of South America. They were mostly young teachers and nurses who had saved up for this trip of a lifetime. Instant friendships and romances started; they found they had much in common. Close to the end of our stay we took a boatload of friends for a sail to Itaipu, a beach a short distance from Rio, most of our passengers being the girls off the bus. It was strange to have a nearly all-female crew for a change. We feasted on exotic fruits, chickens and salad, chilled beer and Caiperinis and swam and snorkelled in the milk-warm water. It was a memorable day.

A few days after our arrival when John went back aboard the boat one morning he was surprised to find the entire crew assembled in the aft cockpit being interviewed by Rog and Noel. Chris, our young extra hand from New Zealand, was in the process of criticizing John for not going on deck when the steering broke. Naturally enough, at the sight of John they fell silent. John went below to sort out a few items he needed in our cabin, feeling pretty annoyed. After a while Rog came down and asked him if he could hurry up and leave so that they could get on with the interview. John was deeply hurt at this criticism behind his back and for a few days avoided meeting certain crew members.

John and I had joined a gymnastics group on the sandy beach below the apartment. From 6.30 to 7.30 each morning we stretched, gyrated and pulled every muscle in our bodies. Needless to say, after the first

Brazilian picnic

session we felt half crippled. John was the more enthusiastic of the two of us and I'm afraid my attendance record was not as good as his. We had both felt terribly unfit after six weeks at sea, and the lithe Brazilians put our bulges to shame.

During the rest of the day John was grateful to have some privacy and quiet. He spent most of his time sorting out accounts and problems and writing in the cool of the apartment.

During the last week John asked me to collect some money from the bank. Before going I decided to check on the name of the man I was to see. I had heard that currency transactions could be difficult and I didn't want a wasted trip. While I was struggling with one of the yacht club phones, trying to contact John back at the apartment, a large, well-dressed Brazilian offered to help. We couldn't get through so I told him my problem.

'There should be no trouble with your currency. I am going that way – perhaps I can give you a lift,' he suggested in halting English.

I gratefully accepted. I would have taken a taxi but the drivers were like kamikazi pilots. We left the club and purred along the highway in his Mercedes towards the commercial and banking area of the city. Our conversation was limited somewhat by my speaking very little Portuguese and my companion even less English except for uttering 'Oh-my-God' when another car came too close. (Driving in Rio needs nerves of steel; it seemed as though each person behind the wheel of his car imagined himself a Fittipaldi, accelerating and braking violently.)

We appeared to be taking a rather long route, but not knowing the area I didn't feel I should comment. Suddenly my companion looked at his watch. 'Oh-my-God – we will not get to your bank in time. They close at three.' It was now five minutes to three. I was disappointed but said it didn't matter, I would try the next day – cursing myself for wasting time with the phone.

'Would you like a drink somewhere?' he kindly suggested. I was feeling thirsty and replied that a glass of orange would be most welcome and could we stop near Copacabana as I would do some shopping there afterwards.

We drove on and on and this time I was getting suspicious.

'We're well past Copacabana, aren't we?' I queried sharply.

'Oh, just a bit, but I wish to take you to a quiet place for a drink. The cafés here are noisy and dirty.'

'Well, please not too far, I have a lot to do and I can't spend all afternoon out.' I was beginning to feel a trifle alarmed.

My fears were confirmed when we drew up at a motel and my chauffeur picked up a key from a pay barrier. Naïvely I'd walked into a trap: it was more than a drink this gentleman was offering me. I learned later that this particular motel was notorious for just this sort of assignment, letting out rooms for fifteen minutes.

Then followed some rather unpleasant dialogue and a struggle during which I managed to persuade my companion that this particular round-the-world yachtswoman had no intention of complying with his wishes. He drove me back to Copacabana warning me that other Brazilians might act more violently than he had. I was fuming with rage at his arrogance. I didn't tell John for two days.

The Prize Giving for leg three was to be held beside the giant swimming pool at the yacht club a few days before the start of leg four. It was a grand affair and we had dressed up for the occasion. Waiters swirled around the many tables offering glasses of coconut milk and rum or passion fruit laced with some mysterious liquor. I went to the ladies before the actual prize-giving and was amazed to see four semi-naked women, screaming at the top of their voices, sticking sequins on to various parts of each other's anatomy. Feeling somewhat overdressed in my bare-back lowcut long dress I smiled politely at them and returned to our table to tell the boys to expect some entertainment later.

Prizes were handed out from the raised stage and the victors of leg three had a long walk up under the spotlights to receive their awards. Finally all the girls taking part were called up in turn to receive giant bunches of roses. The drinks had taken effect and there was rowdy cheering and stamping from the other crews as each of us went forward to accept the flowers. This glamorous occasion seemed a far cry from the often frightening and squalid times we had endured at sea.

Then the stage was cleared, the band struck up and the dancing girls came on. It wasn't long before some of the bolder crew members were up gyrating with the ladies. John and I danced for a while and decided to leave just as people were being thrown into the pool.

Later the situation turned ugly. The catering manager called the riot police, who arrived waving truncheons and throwing tear gas (as one yachting journal put it: 'at least it was a change from salt spray in the eyes'). We were lucky to have missed the baton charge and tear gas but there were quite a few fellows wandering around the next day with very red eyes.

10

Leg Four – Rio to Portsmouth

Day 1: *Wednesday, 22 February 1978*

John: A sultry morning, overcast, with mist obscuring the Cagarras Islands only two and a half miles offshore from the Lynskeys' apartment window in Leblon.

I gave the PT a miss and instead had an early breakfast. Packing was a rush but eventually we were in Pam Lynskey's dark blue Chevette threading through the usual Grand Prix traffic along the Copacabana. We arrived at the yacht club in sweltering heat, clutching huge brown paper bags full of fresh rolls and sticks of salami.

'The Fonseca Port's come,' beamed Tony. 'It's been driven all night from São Paulo.'

Sure enough, the diminutive Senhor Rodriguez was as good as his word. Looking distinctly anxious while clutching a slim plastic briefcase with one hand and mopping his damp brow with a big handkerchief in the other, he directed the stacking of five black cases of the precious liquid on the dockside. The hundred or so crew members in the Race looked really cheerful as they gulped down last drinks and club sandwiches at the trim white tables beneath tall palms. This was the start of the last leg. We were heading for home. At the end of this trip we would have sailed right round the world. Red launches took us out to those yachts safely anchored in the bay away from the treacherous pier where so many boats had been damaged by the swell.

On *Debenhams* the decks were being scrubbed down, sheets and sails got ready, and the anchor weighed. We waved goodbye to Pam returning in the launch, remembering how kind the Lynskeys had been to us all. Then the trusty little Lister diesel pushed us out to the start line at five knots, creating a welcome breeze out of a stifling calm.

There was plenty of time so we practised starts, then ate a pleasant lunch of chicken and salad. I was at the wheel when Tony smiled shyly and said, 'Well, if I don't speak to you again, have a good trip.'

As if on cue, the grey mists dispelled for the start. Blue skies and a

Rio yacht club

blazing sun saw sixteen boats on their way to Portsmouth. We crossed the line, which ran off-shore in front of the imposing Escola Navale, on the starboard tack in a gentle south-easterly breeze. Luffing up *Tielsa*, the big red Dutch ketch, we quickly dropped her astern before tacking off into Botafogo Bay. I could see Dirk Nauta, *Tielsa*'s skipper, cursing my luck; but it must have been outside his power because we struck it lucky. By keeping well tucked in to the western side of the two-mile-wide entrance to the vast Guanabara Bay we avoided the worst of the tide which was still coming in after forecast high water.

I heard a great clapping sound behind me while I was at the wheel. It was the yellow-shirted horde on *Condor* applauding us for being in front of their seventy-seven-foot monster. We were all delighted.

The most noticeable thing about *Debenhams* was the space. With only ten instead of thirteen the atmosphere of crowding was gone for the first time since leaving Ardmore, 23,000 miles behind.

When darkness came we had only covered twenty miles in five hours, but we were well pleased.

The new watches were:

    Watch 1: Tony, Dick, J.C., Peter

    Watch 2: Colin, Steve, Roger, Noel

I split Dick from the influence of the TV crew to ease the load on Colin, and put in the ebullient Steve, who was also showing great enthusiasm as navigator. His rendition of 'Show Me the Way to Go Home' at the start line had heartened us all. If Dick didn't like Peter, well, he'd just have to lump it. I really thought he must get to like him. Tony, Colin, Steve and Peter I would take anywhere; Dick too if after a year or two's experience he could see the wood for the trees.

Day 2: *Thursday, 23 February   Noon position 23° 06' S, 41° 45' W*
        Day's run 124 miles   Course E by N   Wind W Force 4
        Barometer 1015

Marie Christine: I awoke to the gentle swaying of the boat. We had a following wind and were carrying the radial-head spinnaker; as I lay there trying to summon the energy to get up the thought kept running through my head 'We're going home, we're going home.' The boat was making a steady 5 knots – not fast but reasonable for this area where we expected head-winds or worse, still calm. 'Five hundred miles to go before we get the S.E. trade winds,' Steve, now in the role of navigator, had told us yesterday. The motion was like being gently rocked in a hot air balloon. Melon, black grapes, fried eggs, bacon and fresh rolls washed down with tea and lime for breakfast and life seemed surprisingly good. The sun was shining, but it was not the unbearable heat of Rio. We sat in the spacious saloon munching our breakfast and marvelling at the new living space. From thirteen on the last leg we were down to ten, Alan Green, Chris and Stafford Morse having joined us only for the previous leg.

Day 3: *Friday, 24 February   Noon position 21° 50' S, 40° 25' W*
        Day's run 130 miles   Course ENE   Wind SW Force 2
        Barometer 1020

John: We made a hundred and thirty miles in the day, rolling along pleasantly under the radial-head and big-boy for most of the time. The tall sails of *Tielsa* lay astern and the red and yellow spread of *B & B* was up on our starboard bow.

I had a wobbly time at the mast-head changing the big-boy and radial-head halyards to their correct sides; then we gybed soon after and Colin had to change them again. Not many volunteers for that job.

The radio chat show positions put us nicely in the middle of the field. The boat is strangely quiet with just the two watches of four plus Marie Christine and me. Let's hope it makes for less friction too; it's rather nice being just the ten of the original 'dirty dozen' on this leg.

Day 4: *Saturday, 25 February   Noon position 19° 51' S, 38° 07' W
Day's run 189 miles   Course ENE   Wind SE by E Force 4
Barometer 1022*

John: The Rio coughs and colds persist. Few people have washed, and the floors have not been swept nor the heads cleaned since we left port. Very soon I shall have to start nagging again. I hope I can find the will. I shall have to ration the drink, too, which is another tedious duty. J.C. is the only person drinking port at the moment, the rest preferring Caiperini, the Brazilian drink, with limes, for a change while our small stock holds out. Left alone with a port bottle J.C. will consume three-quarters of it during happy-hour. His favourite topic of conversation at the moment is how his friend contracted VD in Rio.

Marie Christine: Squalls with heavy rain showers have replaced our balmy airs of yesterday. The boat is heeled over and a few of us felt sick. Today we can see *Great Britain II*, *B & B* and *Tielsa* ahead of us. It's very hot. After breakfast John and I went up on deck, hoping for a shower of rain to cool us. Tempers had flared as the new watch took over and failed to listen to the advice of the off-going team: 'The squalls only last a few minutes; don't bother to alter the sails – just ease them off.' But the mizzen was lowered and a reef put in the main during a particularly black cloud-burst; it passed and the boat speed dropped away with the vanishing wind. 'Why can't you listen?' came an irate voice from below.

'We'll manage for a while,' shouted John, urging the on-party to go down and finish their breakfast. After a spell of calm I put up the mizzen sail again and with help from Peter took the reef out of the main. In a short while the rain came down like stair-rods and I managed very successfully to shampoo my hair and wash myself, hanging on to the backstays as the shampoo stung my eyes blind. I wiped them dry with my towel and opened them just as a mighty lightning flash struck the sea close by to the instant giant accompaniment of rumbling, roaring thunder. The lightning and rain moved away as quickly as it had come; in the squall we had overtaken *B & B* and she now lay about two miles astern of us. I went below feeling great – cool and clean for a change.

The vegetables were not lasting well at all. I chucked out a load of almost liquid courgettes and cucumbers. We'll just have to eat up everything perishable. Noel is showing enormous will power and eating only one meal a day. At this rate he will certainly lose some of the weight he gained in Rio.

Day 5: *Sunday, 26 February   Noon position 17° 44' S, 36° 53' W*
Day's run 154 miles   Course NE by E   Wind SE by E Force 4
Barometer ?

John: Up at three o'clock to plan a meeting to clear the air. This was held up in the cockpit with all ten of us present. I read a written statement because I wanted to be clear about what I'd said in case I needed to refer to it again. There was plenty of tension as I read:

> This is a clearing of the air meeting, and I'll start first of all with the Rio television interview which we'll remember; certain people gibbering away behind my back about how they would run the boat *if* ... a rather large *if* ... they were the owner and skipper. My arrival seemed to halt that vainglorious interview. I can only think it was because things were being said behind my back which those concerned couldn't say to my face. I was sufficiently hurt by that to be unable to face some of you for several days. During that time I'm pleased to be able to say that a number of people – Colin, Tony, Steve and Peter – rallied round and got the boat ready for sea. We are now into day five. Some people haven't had a wash. There are putrid smells coming from various parts of the boat because some lockers and cupboards haven't been cleaned. The floors have not been swept once since we left, neither have the heads been cleaned. Certain people are getting set to scuttle off the boat when we arrive at Portsmouth, leaving it in a rather worse condition than they found it. Well, I'm the skipper and the owner of this fine yacht, which has brought you all safely this far round the world. It's my food you have eaten; my drink you have drunk; my clothing you have worn these past six months. Not one of you has contributed a penny towards the voyage. It is in the shadow of my reputation that some of your heads have now grown to the point where you wonder which poor sucker of an owner to freeload off next on the Atlantic Triangle or Parmelia Race. A bold cry for people who had hardly been to sea, much less crewed in an ocean race before this voyage. One or two of you, having only just resisted the temptation to break your agreement to work for me this summer when you realized you had got yourselves a free passage to New Zealand, became apprehensive lest you were left stranded in Rio, a rather less than hospitable place. Well, we've come to the sticking post, gentlemen. At the end of this talk I shall ask each one of you – Tony, Steve, Peter, Dick and J.C. – if you intend to honour your agreement with me to sail from Portsmouth to Ardmore and work through to mid-October. As you know, my objective was to sail round the world from Ardmore to Ardmore on the occasion of the tenth anniversary of the John Ridgway School of Adventure. I chose to have a crew of instructors from the school – rather than older,

experienced racing men – to give instructors the value of the experience, as I have done on my previous expeditions. The purpose of entering the race was to give impetus to the voyage to ensure the boat got back to Ardmore in time. This it has almost achieved. My interest in the race now roughly parallels that of Tabarly. If it suits me I shall continue; if not, then I shall make for Ardmore. If some of you gentlemen seek to break your agreement with me and get off the boat at Portsmouth, then quite clearly my interest is to shape a course directly for Ardmore to undo the damage you have done me, as soon as possible. My intention – if I go to Portsmouth – is to sail from there to Ardmore probably early on 9 April. I intend to try for a berth in Camper's Marina, while people are away and the boat is unattended. My intention is to make the best possible time from here to Portsmouth within the confines of the wind sail chart above the chart table. To improve the condition of the boat, I would like the following steps to be taken:

One: watch-leaders continue with their present duties, and to detail people to carry out the tasks which follow.

Two: Steve continue as navigator.

Three: Dick to draw up rotas and stick them over the chart table of
  (a) daily head-cleaners
  (b) daily floor-cleaners (by floors I mean forepeak, forward heads, swamp, saloon, chart table and wet area, galley and after-cabin)
  (c) a progressive check of all lockers by one of those on watch in stable conditions by day when only a helmsman and one other are required to attend the boat. This is to eliminate the rotting stores and the putrid smells. Dick to be responsible that all floors are kept screwed down.

Four: Peter to draw up a list of maintenance work to be done and improvements to be made so that the boat arrives in UK in a better condition than when she left. These tasks are to be carried out whenever stable day conditions permit, by two people on watch not concerned with the wheel or trimming sails. That includes the television crew (who make up twenty per cent of the crew) unless they are otherwise engaged in planning their film or cleaning their equipment.

Five: J.C. to be responsible for bringing the galley up to the standard of cleanliness which was agreed when I took him on as cook for the voyage.

Six: Marie Christine to be responsible for the issue of drinks on the scale of one beer per day, one drink at 'happy-hour', i.e. three fingers of port or equivalent other drink. In the saloon I expect the seats to be

kept clear of clothing. On leaving your seat please ensure the cushions are straight.

'Well, that's all, but I'm just going to ask each of you whether you do
intend to honour your agreement to sail with me from Portsmouth to
Ardmore and work through the coming season.

'Tony?'

'Yes.'

'Steve?'

'Yes, but can I say something? I hope we can be friendly about this?'

'Yes, I'm sure we can. Just need to clear the air ... Peter?'

'Yes. I'll be going to Ardmore.'

'Dick?'

'You said in Rio I could make up my mind in Portsmouth.'

'All right, Dick ... J.C.?'

He came round to saying yes, he would sail up to Ardmore, and leave
as soon as we got the place going again; and this suited my idea, too.

After this talk I asked Roger if he'd like to film a meeting of people
saying whatever they felt like to my face. One of the first questions was
from Roger behind the camera:

'Do you think the film has been the main problem on the voyage?'

Again, I read the answer because I had prepared one in case someone
asked:

> The film has proved to be a disappointingly divisive element in the
> voyage. My original agreement with Denton and Creasey of ATV
> was for a live *cinéma vérité* film, using real situations and recording
> sounds from the saloon and chart-table microphones. Too often it
> has degenerated into a dockside armchair skipper-knocking session.
> For me the visits to Auckland and Rio were marred by this rather
> dreary side of things. When you get home, back in the office, the
> classroom, on the truck or on the muck-spreader or even in the dole
> queue, no one will be able to take away from you that you once
> crewed a boat that sailed right round the world. It's a pity the
> memory should be scarred with pettiness.

Dick and Tony asked no questions and left the interview as soon as
possible. J.C., as usual, commanded most of the camera time. He said
that the crew felt I should have spent more time on deck and less time
writing the book. What had I to say on this?

Marie Christine burst in, saying, 'What a bloody cheek!'

My answer was: 'On the first two legs I'd been at the wheel for every
crisis, night or day. I believe the leader must never be too tired to
act correctly in a crisis. On the third leg I did the midnight to zero

four hundred hour watch each night. Regarding the book, my sixth: everybody who came on the crew knew that the book, the television film and Debenhams were realities without which there could be no voyage.'

J.C. then said that Dirk Nauta of *Tielsa* does everything, is always there overseeing every action, and that this sort of leader is much easier to follow.

'I've found that instructors need responsibility,' I replied. They don't like to be cogs in a machine as they were at school or university, so I have always tried to give them that responsibility. I have done the same on this voyage – maybe too much so in the case of having three watches and a mate. I have twenty years of leadership experience, and much of the criticism I have heard over those years has been aimed at leaders unable to delegate responsibility, so that the subordinates are stifled. If I'd wanted to be running a single watch myself, then some of the crew would not have been on the voyage, and the crew would have been smaller.

Roger then asked a question. He said he felt that I was blaming the film for the trouble – using it as an excuse to cover up the trouble there would have been in any case; and I was frightened lest my image was damaged.

My answer? I felt sure there would have been trouble anyway. There had been trouble on every boat, but I doubted if any other skipper would have allowed this type of critical film to be made. I had nothing to prove – that had all been done long ago. My concern was that the film had made the expected troubles that much more difficult.

In reply to a question from Roger, Peter said that he didn't think the film was the main cause of division, but that he was concerned what might be written about him in the book.

I replied that of course the film was no aggravation to an ordinary crew member, but that if he, Peter, had remained on as mate, then he would have found the film at least as aggravating as I had.

Steve made the point that he felt the film was the bit of power the crew had over me in reply to my writing about them in the book.

I replied that my books were all fairly self-critical; I couldn't set myself up as a psychoanalyst, and that in any case they all had recourse to the libel laws. Once again I said that I didn't think I could have got eight better fellows of a similar age and background, and that I also thought the same about the TV men, Roger and Noel. Nobody had said it was going to be easy.

Steve said that not all the dockside, behind-the-back interviews were critical. It had even been said that some people wouldn't wish to sail on any other boat.

I said that I wish that they'd told me that in Auckland when I had severe doubts about many people's loyalty to the project. Why had they not tried to persuade Bob to carry on?

Marie Christine had to be calmed down at some points as she felt no one had any right to criticize me at all as they were all on a free trip of a lifetime. I wished I shared her conviction, but I was nevertheless rather pleased when I heard Colin say the same.

After this, J.C. took the conversation round in circles a bit and so we left it.

The boat got a thoroughly good clean-up, and people looked quite cheerful, with the exception of the film crew who looked glum. I wasn't sure why. With any luck this would clear the air for a few days.

Day 6: *Monday, 27 February   Noon position 15° 18' S, 35° 13' W*
Day's run 195 miles   Course NE by E   Wind E by S Force 3
Barometer 1020

John: The weather stays hot, and we're moving steadily up the east coast of South America. The rain squalls are still sporadic. With an easterly air stream the sailing is easy, and neither watch needs me at night, as usually only two of the four are on deck at a time. I sleep poorly. Marie Christine went to sleep in the more comfortable leeward berth in the saloon.

As usual, I worried about the confrontation of yesterday; and Marie Christine also had a headache all day. The struggle is between Roger and me: it's one of personal ideology. I see him as a lone crusader, hunting to destroy politicians and management as a race apart from the good honest worker – and I think he includes me in the number for destruction. With Tony, Steve, Colin and Peter – even J.C. – there is no fundamental problem. But Bob, and his disciple, Dick, are the tools of Roger's trade.

What a lot of twaddle, I thought. Why worry about it? Just look forward to seeing Rebecca again soon.

Marie Christine: After two sweaty hours in our bunk, I moved out and slept in the saloon, on the portside seat. The soft cushions were luxurious after our hard bunk and the boat was at just the right tilt to force me into the angle of the seat. I just hoped nobody would sit on me in the darkness.

After breakfast I collapsed on my bed. We were going into the wind and I felt sick. After a while John poked his head through the window and called: 'Come on up, you'll feel better up here.' The engine was on for its regulation four-hour daily battery charging and the noise filled our tiny cabin, so I made the effort and hoisted myself out of our high bunk and went up.

I took the wheel over from Dickie and felt instantly better – which made me think seasickness with me, which is rare anyway, must be psychological. The wind was blowing 20–25 knots and I found the wheel heavy to turn as the boat was knocked off course by waves and wind. The sun shone faintly through a thin layer of cloud and I could feel my skin burning as we sped along the surface of the ocean at 8 knots. We'd touched briefly on the subject of the book yesterday during John's 'air clearer' but I knew Peter was still worried. It seemed easier for him to talk about his personal worries while I was at the wheel, my mind half on keeping us on course. A very sensitive person, he seemed concerned that I in particular was writing rotten things about him in my diaries. I suppose they all feared that and in a way felt that for them the film offered a come-back. I tried to explain that most of the time I was obsessed with my own pathetic efforts of trying to keep going. 'In any case,' said I, 'no film, no book, no *Debenhams*, no trip for Peter or any of us come to that; it boils down to hard cash. You should be thankful I'm writing it!' Righteous indignation was rising in me ... Dear Peter, he's too sensitive for his own peace of mind. I'd not damned him in any of my scribblings; he'd be more likely to take offence that he's mentioned so seldom.

Determined to get a good suntan, I lay out in the centre cockpit after lunch, reading a book. I'd undone the strap of my bikini top so that I shouldn't end up with a line of a different colour across my back. I'd heard mutterings and laughs from the watch who were in the aft cockpit but thought nothing of it. They were always larking about. Suddenly I felt an icy cold splash across my back, accompanied by screams of laughter from the fellows – 'Oh, M.C., you're no fun, you were meant to sit up.' Peter, the culprit of the rotten deed, laughed down at me.

'In this state? I'd only sit up if the boat was going over. I don't think you'd be looking at me then.' I glowered back. 'There'll be reprisals. Just you wait,' I muttered ominously.

Day 8: *Wednesday, 1 March   Noon position 10° 25' S, 31° 59' W*
Day's run 161 miles   Course NE by E   Wind SE by E Force 4
Barometer 1018

John: As the log puts it, after eleven hours of blank entries in the remarks column, 'Not much happens these days, or nights.' We are still well placed, ahead of *B & B*, *Treaty of Rome* and *Japy Hermès*. Also *Adventure* – they have trouble with their forestay *King's Legend* and *ADC* are stuck sixty miles off the coast near Recife, while we keep on with a fair wind 240 miles out.

'Smell that oily smell. It means there's a whale about,' said Marie Christine at the wheel.

'Probably me,' grunted J.C., his huge bulk spread across the teak after-hatch cover.

Sure enough, a great school of leaping dolphins appeared. We had heard that in the old days at Ardmore the crofters located the shoals of herring by the oily smell in the loch. Marie Christine was delighted, therefore, when the dolphins appeared to back this theory.

In the late afternoon while I was on the radio to the fleet 'Jaws' bit the Walker log spinner from the end of the sixty-foot log line, and the idea of swimming lost its appeal.

It was a grubby night of squalls and heavy rain. Near midnight Tony, Dick and Peter crouched around the wheel, hypnotized once more by J.C.'s resonant tones. This time it was a lengthy monologue concerning the master marketeer's experiences with the occult. J.C. was being serious, the preamble extensive. Dick was beginning to take the mick with explicit gestures, but the orator plodded on. Unknown to the weary audience, Concorde was approaching at something around twice the speed of sound. A great crack rent the heavens, and the marine Moses was silenced, refusing to say any more about the occult. Some fellows felt the expense of developing Concorde was money well spent.

Marie Christine: Last night I lent Peter a book I'd been given in Auckland. Erica Jong's *How to Save Your Own Life*. Both John and I had read it while out at Taupo. He had reacted violently against it, while I (maybe not agreeing with all she had to say) found in it a certain ring of truth. Peter had found it riveting and had spent half the night reading. He had read half the book and at breakfast was keen to discuss what he'd read. His views at this stage were similar to but not quite so reactionary as John's. I felt outnumbered as I held high the banner for downtrodden women. There was so much hypocrisy in both Peter's and John's arguments, although perhaps of all those on the boat these two treated me most as an individual with a right to voice an opinion. I occasionally got the feeling that whatever I said on certain subjects would be dismissed out of hand by the others because of my sex. I was living in a man's world and I felt unless I could equal them in strength and toughness I would never be totally accepted.

We are moving along well. The S.E. trade winds are blowing constantly and we are beating at 60 degrees off the wind. The boat is heeled over slightly. The heat bothers us all in varying degrees. John's prickly heat is a constant source of irritation to him and, combined with his seasickness, makes it all a helluva struggle. The saving grace for him is that we're homeward bound. Noel is also bothered by a skin irritation.

He never complains. But again the heat doesn't help. Thank God for the breeze. If it dropped calm it would be close to intolerable. One thing we've noticed which I never realized before is that drinking a can of beer at lunchtimes brings out beads of sweat all over our faces and bodies. We're having to eat up the fresh stuff fast now. It's going rotten very quickly. Poor Dickie has had a few nasty things fall on him. We've had some delicious salads using everything we've got. Noel still remains unmoved, having his one and only meal at breakfast. I've never come across such will power.

I made lunch today for Colin, whose turn it was, in return for his watch sorting out the three sacks of potatoes which were rotting fast in the aft cabin. We sorted the putrid, slimy mess out into the aft cockpit. It was lucky for J.C., who shared this cabin with the tatties, that his sense of smell was far from acute. I felt sick but relieved to be preparing lunch instead. Thank goodness we've got the Batchelors dried food to fall back on. I wonder how the other boats are doing. We are all able to talk more to each other on this leg which leads to a much happier atmosphere. Is it because of the smaller number around or because it's almost over? Perhaps a bit of both.

Dickie was airing his views on some obscure subject this afternoon – 'You do talk rot,' piped in Tony. 'Yes, but he's fluent at it,' came in J.C., quick as a flash. J.C. is now the only port-drinker of an evening, the rest of us are enjoying the Caiperinis while the limes and cachaça last. I suppose it reminds us of Rio, which most of the crew enjoyed best of all the stops.

Day 9: *Thursday, 2 March   Noon position 8° 00′ S, 30° 46′ W*
Day's run 177 miles   Course NE   Wind SE Force 3
Barometer 1017

Marie Christine: Not much wind this morning. We easily get irritated with each other still out here not moving very fast.

Usage of fresh water has become quite a controversial topic. In past legs J.C. has wisely rationed the water: for washing one mug daily per person, trying to keep the overall use each day to five gallons. Our full capacity is 375 gallons, which at that rate should be enough for seventy-five days, leaving a surplus for emergencies such as one of the tanks puncturing or the water going bad. However, there is a move afoot advanced by Tony and J.C. in particular to use a great deal more of the fresh water. The rest of us (especially me) are happy enough to increase our consumption, but when it comes to doing the washing up in fresh water, the rest are in uproar. One would never get so steamed up about such minor points on land but out here everything becomes a giant clash of will. 'If we run out of water I suppose we could call in to the Azores. The crew wouldn't like that,' John said to me later. He wasn't happy at the thought of so much being used but hadn't the energy or interest to enter into the arena. Later in the morning I went up and enjoyed a good scrub hidden behind the genoa on the foredeck in a downpour. In spite of our debate, I couldn't alter the habits of seven months and just use tap water.

The wind increased by midmorning and in no time we were shooting along at 9–10 knots, our fastest speed. I took the helm for a sail change during the afternoon. My course wasn't altogether constant and, regrettably, a few waves splashed over the foredeck, wetting the watch. With shaking fists, screams of abuse and a bucket of sea water, they returned to the aft cockpit, to have their revenge on me. I got wet but not as wet as them!

Day 10: *Friday, 3 March   Noon position 5° 00' S, 29° 34' W*
Day's run 233 miles   Course NE by E   Wind SE by E Force 6
Barometer 1016

John: Our best run ever – 218 miles over the ground with a 25-knot south-easterly wind just forward of the beam, and a small sea. The boat moved sweetly under a new rig: No. 1 yankee, genoa staysail, double-reefed main and full mizzen.

I'm pleased to see that Dick and Peter are getting on well. It shows that Dick has grown up a lot on the voyage. It would be difficult to dislike Peter, who worked away for most of the day with needle and palm to repair J.C.'s sailing shoes.

I noticed him writing with a Bic transparent biro the other day.

'I'm just catching up on my diary,' he grinned. 'Then, when the biro runs out I'm going to kip.'

I looked at the biro and, sure enough, the column of ink was gone.

'Have you ever run a biro dry before?'

'Oh, yes. I usually do,' he replied seriously.

'Well, you're the first person I've ever met. I thought I was the only person on this boat who did miserly things like that.'   Peter has a small black leather zip-up bag about the size of a handbag with a string handle. He is the neatest and most self-reliant person on the boat. I'm always surprised at the number of jobs that can be done using the contents of that bag: pliers, knives, sharpening stones, needles, threads, bits of leather. We've never seen all the contents laid out. At the moment he's making a macramé net for a green leather bag to hold a miniature brandy bottle full of Cape Horn water. How refreshing after 180 days to talk with someone who has done something besides the conventional State education and plate-glass university, all gummed up with predictable left-wing ideology.

Day 11: *Saturday, 4 March   Noon position 2° 17' S, 28° 23' W*
Day's run 204 miles   Course NE by E   Wind ESE Force 3
Barometer 1016

Marie Christine: Many of the eggs are rotten. The cook punctuates his efforts with groans and sounds of disgust as he cracks another baddy into a glass before committing it to the hissing pan. It's too hot to keep anything fresh – even ourselves, as we lounge in slumped attitudes round the saloon, feet stuck up on the table to allow the slight draught to circulate and cool sweating limbs.

Midmorning, on our port beam, the sea became alive with dolphins squeaking as they rushed towards us in what seemed a frenzy of excitement. There must have been at least a hundred, their sleek, tight, silver bodies leaping from the water in graceful curves. They stayed with us for half an hour, racing beside our smooth white hull, filling me with their *joie de vivre* as I steered our boat towards the Equator. I glanced down at my brown hand holding the wheel. I had worn a simple twist of gold, shaped as a dolphin, above my wedding ring from the beginning of our voyage, given to me by my brother's wife, Carole. If I was allowed just one memory to treasure from this journey, it would be of these joyous creatures.

I had taken to sitting on the pulpit on the bow. It was a peaceful and quiet spot up here, looking forward at the great swoop of the empty horizon. At times it was like riding a horse as the boat dipped and rose on the sea as we sped along at 8 knots or more. Other times it was a place to sit and think away from the others on the boat. But with only ten on board now, there are plenty of places one can sit on one's own. This evening I feel quite sunburnt, particularly my tummy and lower lip. Maybe they're the two areas that stick out most!

Day 12: *Sunday, 5 March   Noon position 00° 18' S, 27° 36' W*
Day's run 126 miles   Course NNE   Wind SE Force 2
Barometer 1018

Marie Christine: By breakfast, the wind had almost died and we weren't moving very fast. It's oppressive below, so after sorting things out I went on deck and found a slab of shade to shelter from the fierce sun. Dickie, Col, and I think Peter, are all suffering from 'gunnel bum', a particularly nasty affliction caused by too much salt and wear on the arse resulting in prickly spots which itch like mad. Dickie had been dabbing his for days with diluted Dettol but it wasn't getting any better.

'I reckon it's like nappy rash and you should expose it to the sun', I suggested to the slightly shocked sufferers.

'Wouldn't you mind, M.C.?'

A hot day for the helmsman

'No,' I answered, 'as long as I don't have to take mine off!'

Dickie now wanders round with his swimming trunks up at the front and down at the back.

In the afternoon I offered to shave Steve's bushy beard off. He had been complaining of the heat and thought it would help to be rid of it. I was rather sorry to do it, particularly after combing it before the cutting; it was a very fine bushy beard. I couldn't decide which he most resembled, Shadrach, Meshach or Abed-nego. Anyway he could always grow it again. We set up the barber's bench on the aft hatch and with none too sharp scissors with rounded ends, in case the boat lurched, I snipped it off. 'Are you going to keep any for Rebecca?' Col asked from the wheel with a smile on his ginger face. He'd heard the story of how seven years ago Steve had had his long flowing locks cut by me at John's insistence if he wished to be an instructor at the John Ridgway School of Adventure, and Becca had gathered up the hair and carried it around for days in a paper bag. To finish off the job well, I shaved off the stubble, much to the amusement of the others. The job was done. Steve's chin was pale compared to the rest of his face, in fact he looked entirely different.

'M.C. looks different too – she's got a hairy chest.'

I looked down and saw I was covered in Steve's beard.

'Jump off the bow with a rope and we'll pull you in from the stern,' John suggested, coming up from below. Fortunately I was able to offer my sunburn as an excuse. I had no intention of taking a dip.

At 4.30 we crossed from the southern hemisphere into the northern, celebrating crossing the line with a can of Whitbread's pale ale. Later we had a double dose of Caiperini, watching the sun go down over the Equator, glancing back and remembering some of the times we had enjoyed and endured south of the line.

Day 13: *Monday, 6 March   Noon position 1° 36' N, 27° 17' W*
Day's run 108 miles   Course NE   Wind SE Force 2
Barometer 1018

Marie Christine: We appear to be well and truly in the doldrums. It's oppressively hot and we're hardly moving. I went on deck before breakfast to try and dry off the sweat before getting hot again, eating breakfast. *B & B Italia* was out on the horizon on our port beam. 'She's going faster than us,' muttered Tony at the helm. 'She'll probably have a floater up.' I looked at our radial-head spinnaker, our lightest and most suitable sail for these conditions, but sadly the wind was insufficient and the great gaudy balloon kept collapsing.

Below, plates of bacon and egg and fried bread were being passed round. I took mine but couldn't stomach the musty-flavoured egg which I quietly flipped into the black rubbish bucket.

Out on deck the sun seems to drill into the skin. I feel tender from too much sun and try and find shade. The bright blue deck paint absorbs and holds the heat. It's not possible to walk barefoot over it. Bodies of those not on watch are lying limply out of the piercing sun, if they're lucky on sails on the foredeck. There are two really good places up there in the shade.

I spend most of my time talking to Peter about anything and everything and nothing. He's currently trying his hand writing poetry, inspired by reading some Scott Fitzgerald, and is amazed at how long it's taken him to write just four lines. I try to reassure him by saying that in this heat, doing anything would take twice as long.

During the morning, we were depressed to see *B & B* gradually overtake us and disappear over the horizon. There was nothing more we could do but it's bad for morale. She is closest to us on handicap and allows us 1 hour 14 minutes over the distance between Rio and Portsmouth. Sadly in a race with bigger boats like *Pen Duick*, *Condor* and *Great Britain II* the smaller ones at the back of the field tend to feel rather left out and unimportant, but seeing *B & B* on day 13 so close should be very exciting. I'm sure that if we were the two largest boats in the fleet we'd feel much more of a sense of drama in this situation. By supper time the great heat was slightly less. I'm thankful I suggested that John and I would wash up each evening after supper. The galley is a hell hole during daytime.

Day 14: *Tuesday, 7 March   Noon position 2° 46' N, 26° 53' W*
Day's run 143 miles   Course NE   Wind NW Force 3
Barometer 1017

Marie Christine: An oppressive night. I lay bathed in sweat in the saloon trying hard to slow my pulse rate. Between the hour from four to five we covered one-tenth of a mile. 'Will we ever get out of these doldrums?' I heard muttered in the thick darkness.

By eight in the morning an unexpected breeze had sprung up from the north-west. We were hoping for the north-east trade winds. 'Don't get excited,' John said to me as we sat up on the bow after breakfast. 'It's probably just wind from these rain clouds.' To either side and ahead of us were giant black thunder clouds, typical of the doldrums. As one moved along ahead of us we could see, from on top of the swell, the faint outline of another yacht. We were to discover later on the chat show that this wasn't *B & B* as we'd thought, but we never found out who it was.

Happily, the wind increased slowly in strength from the north-west

JC and JR stretched out in the shade

and we rode up and down on the growing swell. John was feeling queasy and I was trying hard not to think of my breakfast.

Round about lunchtime we saw a rickety old fishing vessel, very similar to a fleet of Chinese boats we had seen in Cape Town. It altered course and headed towards us. We'd now got our wind and were determined to make the most of it while it lasted. The doldrums were very fresh in our minds.

'We can't stop,' John said. 'But perhaps you'd better call them on the radio, Peter, and explain that we're in a race.'

I was rather sorry – a lunch party with some Chinese fishermen would have provided a welcome diversion from the present company. But instead, Peter made contact with a French drilling boat called *Astragal*. Suddenly I heard my name mentioned over the static:

'Do you have Mrs Ridgway on board?'

'Go on, M.C.,' shouted John. 'Go and speak to him.'

In amazement I rushed in to speak to the captain, who turned out to be charming.

'You must be very brave, Mrs Ridgway' . . . he paused . . . 'to be alone with nine other men.'

And so our daft conversation continued. I just hoped there weren't too many other boats listening in. They'd certainly have a good laugh.

Day 16: *Thursday, 9 March   Noon position 6° 46' N, 24° 39' W*
Day's run 154 miles   Course N by W   Wind NE Force 3
Barometer 1019

John: The talk is all of home, disregarding the weather that might lie to the north of the Azores. Roger has put felt-tip pen lines for each day until Easter Sunday on the polystyrene tiles which line his bunk on the port side of the saloon. I think he'll be lucky to make that target. *B & B*, *Japy*, *Debenhams*, *Adventure* and *Gauloises II* are all close together and only crawling north. Everyone is cheerful but struggling to contain frustration caused by the slow progress. We're all making great efforts to avoid upsetting each other. After the three previous legs we all know the signs, I reckon.

I'm trying to get things done on the boat. Colin and Peter are helpful, but I don't raise much enthusiasm from the rest. I've cleaned up most of the deck with Vim, but it takes a long, long time in the sun. Colin got the gelcoat repairs done today and Marie Christine smoothed them down with emery paper.

I discovered that we had lost the Hella port and starboard electric navigation light from the pulpit; the retaining lock had failed. We'll have trouble with paraffin oil lamps in the Channel, but Peter has a plan to convert them to electricity.

Little things like chafing spinnaker halyards and the topping lift round the main halyard indicate that people's minds are not on the job.

Day 17: *Friday, 10 March   Noon position 8° 56' N, 25° 37' W*
Day's run 160 miles   Course NNE   Wind NE by E Force 3
Barometer 1020

Marie Christine: The wind blew a constant force three all day from the north-east, pushing us along at a steady 6 knots, not brilliant progress but beautiful sailing. The sky and sea are bright blue. John and I, sitting up on the pulpit, watch the flying fish take hurriedly to the air, the wet blue sheen of their tight bodies glistening in the brilliant light as we plough through the gentle swell.

Life continues at a fairly easy pace. The two watches take care of the running of the boat and now we're not conserving water the kettle and saucepan really are constantly on the go. 'Anyone for tea?' the cry goes up from a head poking out of the galley window. The offer of tea covers a multitude of beverages. Tea with milk or lime, cocoa, coffee, real or instant and malted milk, the latter being the most popular; it seems a bit incongruous drinking this delicious bedtime drink in the middle of the day under the scorching equatorial sun on a racing yacht – not quite what the manufacturers had in mind for it.

I've taken on the appearance of a palomino, with my clothes off, the more tender parts of my tummy and front have peeled. 'You'll never learn,' John sharply reprimands me. But the more leathery areas of my back, legs and arms are a good rich brown. I can't think why I should bother trying to get a tan except that I always do. 'Pure vanity – and you'll shrivel up like an old nut,' threw in John for good measure. I thought of England in March, those cold, windy, wet days.... How I'd love to be home to see Bec and Mummy! But this was perfection out here today.

Day 18: *Saturday, 11 March   Noon position 10° 33' N, 26° 19' W*
Day's run 117 miles   Course NW by N   Wind NE by N Force 1
Barometer 1022

John: We were becalmed until lunchtime in the north-east trade winds, which is pretty peculiar – and it's rather hard on people's nerves. We lost another seventy miles to *Gauloises II* on the day's run, and they were only thirty miles ahead of us last night at the radio chat show.

Steve's navigation is going really well. The smooth seas mean he is not hampered by seasickness, so he spends a lot of time innovating with the £35 Silver Reed 104 calculator. There is no doubt in my mind that it's a good idea to have a full-time navigator on a race of this kind. He's able to immerse himself in the detail of the present and future situations dictated by pilots, weather charts and radio weather data.

On the first leg the critical feature turned out to be the location of the South Atlantic High, a large high pressure system which remains reasonably static and which has no wind at the centre. On this, the fourth leg, it is the Azores High which may prove to be the key to the jigsaw. The winning boat will be one which skirts the centre of the High, either going to the east or west of it, and clearing it by a sufficient distance to keep the wind in the sails.

Having said all the above, I have noticed that in the Southern Ocean on legs 2 and 3 there was little or no weather information available, and that the various weather systems which came through were really unavoidable as we were moving comparatively slowly. Certainly the satellite ice report from Washington would have been useful, but we couldn't afford the kind of radio equipment necessary to receive that. Then on legs 1 and 4 we didn't have a specialist navigator, but most of the crew spent time thinking about what the High might or might not do; and few of the boats on leg 1 could say they read the weather absolutely right.

The actual process of astro navigation necessary for the maintenance of a steady course across the world's oceans is simple. If you have all day to fiddle at it you can make it quite complex, and maybe at the nth degree of precision this will pay off in a race. I have a feeling that all fifteen boats in this race had chosen their course for legs 2 and 3 before they left Cape Town and Auckland and that mostly alterations were minor and brought about by force of local weather.

By contrast, coastal navigation, particularly round Britain, I have found infinitely more hazardous. Our strategy for this leg from Rio to Portsmouth appears to match that of all the other boats. Broadly, it seems that we're all following the tracks of the most successful navigators on this leg of the 1974 race. Rather unimaginative, you might think, but on the evidence of that race there looks to be little choice at the moment. We set off from Rio with the intention of getting as far to the east as possible by the time we crossed the Equator, bearing in mind the direction of Portsmouth and the fact that the doldrums are supposed to be a narrower band on the western side of the Atlantic. Once through the doldrums lying just to the north of the Equator, we expected to pick up the north-east trade winds blowing down from the Iberian Peninsula. The brief period of north-westerly wind was an unexpected bonus which gave us even more easting, and there was a good deal of east-north-east in the trades when they arrived, albeit in a weak strength; so we are able to proceed pretty much due north, clipping the westernmost of the Cape Verde Islands by about 120 miles.

At the moment the centre of the Azores High is over the Iberian

Peninsula, and if it stays there – which is unlikely – we should be able to pass inside to the east of the Azores, and then make directly north-east for the Channel on the expected westerly air stream. If this plan comes off we will have sailed a shorter distance than many boats presently to the west of us.

Marie Christine: The wind dropped away in the night and in the hours between midnight and eight we covered about fourteen miles. The sun rose quickly into the immense sky and out on deck it was blisteringly hot as the sails slatted back and forth, empty of wind. Rog and I both put out washing. It hung limply in the still air and dried within an hour. The sea, a luminous blue, heaved gently like undulating silk, while a sinister black fin, lazily circling the boat, finished any ideas we had of a dip over the side. Peter in underpants, dark glasses and floppy denim cap, sitting sideways on to the wheel, which he balanced idly with a brown foot, told me gory yarns of sharks in Australia – how one man had survived a massive bite as a brute seized him by the abdomen and then for some reason spat him out, inflicting a ring of numerous deep teeth marks.

'I'm bored with the radio,' John announced later as he sat in the shack balancing himself on a big oblong buoy which we'd found in Rio and was now his seat.

Becalmed Peter and Dick

'I'll do it,' I jokingly replied.

'Okay, you're on, but don't make a muddle of my book and be sure to get all the positions and the weather.'

I wonder whether I hadn't bitten off more than I could chew. The radio wasn't all that difficult to operate but one had to remember to turn on to high power before speaking, to press a switch in the handle of the receiver when talking and come up with the necessary radio jargon such as 'over' after talking and 'over and out' at the end of a conversation. I tried to sound confident and it passed relatively smoothly. I spoke to *Adventure* and *33 Export* and told them I was standing in for John who was exhausted after spending the morning in the water towing the boat along!

Days 19 & 20: *Sunday and Monday, 12 & 13 March   Monday: Noon position 15° 58' N, 27° 33' W*
Day's run 216 miles   Course N   Wind ENE Force 6
Barometer 1020

Marie Christine: The wind has increased from the north-east to about 25–30 knots. It's an uncomfortable motion banging into the seas. Every so often we fall into a trough. On hitting the water the noise and shock is so great, you wonder how long the boat can take this pounding. John and Steve are feeling sick. It's miserable for them. I can't say I feel terrific.

I spent most of Sunday reading a disturbing book about cruelty and murder against a tribe of Paraguayan Indians and Monday reading *The Katyn Massacre*, the appalling killing by the Russians in 1940 of most of Poland's intellectuals, officers and leading class. Both stories of genocide read in the vacuum out here have shocked John and me deeply. Whatever else a long journey at sea permits, it is a good place to stand back and think long and hard about problems. I felt in great sympathy with the people held in captivity, particularly when it's uncomfortable out here as I feel I'm serving a prison sentence too. Each morning when I creep back into our cabin, John greets me with 'Day 19' or 'Day 20'. The time passes so slowly. Steve reckons we should arrive in Portsmouth on 30 March, so we're over half-way in time and distance. This going to windward is very wearing on everyone and the boat, John likened it to being put in a box and shaken about for days without stopping. Quite a good method of torture. The saving grace is that we are making good headway; our heavy boat ploughs through the seas and we are clocking up 200 miles each day.

John: Full tick in the north-east trades with a big swell hitting us in the starboard bow. It's as if Someone up there says: 'Well, we've got them this far. Now, while they're still penned up in the tube, we'll shake 'em about for a week or so – and while that's keeping them occupied, we can go off for a cup of coffee and think up something else.'

This state of torment through the fleet is reflected in the terse radio messages on the chat show in the evenings.

While at the wheel in the morning I was chatting with J.C. and happened to glance out to starboard. We'd seen a lot of flotsam in the past few days, and I was not terribly surprised to see a shiny black buoy about fifty yards out on the beam – and carried on talking. But my mind was saying, 'It can't be a brand new black conical buoy right out here.' Suddenly I realized. It wasn't a buoy, but the great glistening black head of a whale, lying in the water like an exclamation mark; just sort of treading water on its tail, and coming up to get a breath of air every so often. At 8½ knots we soon left it astern, and I saw its mate blowing out to port.

In the afternoon Dick was sent to Coventry by the rest of his watch for being objectionable. It made a pleasant change to see him suddenly become polite.

Day 21: *Tuesday, 14 March   Noon position 19° 03' N, 28° 15' W*
Day's run 215 miles   Course NNE   Wind E by N Force 6
Barometer 1022

John: The boat is getting a hammering in this bumping and there will be plenty of maintenance work to be done to piston hanks and sails when we come out of the trades in about four days' time.

I spoke to Richard Morris-Adams in the evening. A few days ago we were first British boat, but that has faded with the light airs around the doldrums. Richard was as cheery as usual, thank goodness.

We've been puzzled by the increase in the bilge water since entering the trades; 30 to 60 pump strokes an hour means about ten to fifteen gallons coming in somewhere. After supper, Tony, Colin and I got the boards up over the engine and tried to trace the leak. I hoped it wasn't the fresh water tanks, but it tasted salt okay when I dipped a finger in it.

'I can hear a hiss coming from the next compartment forward,' Tony muttered, head down into the engine compartment, probing the area with the beam from his torch.

So the boards went back over the engine, and came off the forward half of the saloon floor. Out came Arun's heavy grey toolbox, the remaining cases of Fonseca Bin 27 Port, the Honda generator, the sewing machine, etc., etc. Then down under the next set of floorboards, while Marie Christine pumped the bilge dry at the main companionway.

'There it is, third keel bolt from forward,' Tony pointed.

'That'll be the bumping on the ground in Rio.' It was my fault for not being on the boat, I thought. It wouldn't have happened if I'd been there. Let's hope it doesn't get worse.

Days 22, 23 & 24: *Wednesday, Thursday & Friday, 15, 16 & 17 March*

Marie Christine: Beating to windward still. It's a strain on the boat and on all of us. I've taken the easy way out and have kept low, finding escape in the books I'm reading: *Escape or Die* (RAF escape stories of the Second World War) and Robert Graves' autobiography *Goodbye To All That*, mainly describing his time in the trenches during the 1914–18 war. At one particularly tense passage of the book, John burst into the cabin. I was so keyed up that I let out a shriek. Poor John, he was more shocked than I.

However great the discomfort is, we are consoled by good distances covered each day – we're eating up the miles between us and Portsmouth at the rate of over 3 degrees latitude a day. Our expected time of arrival has now been brought forward a day to 29 March. So long as we don't go straight into the Azores High! John has resumed his position as The Chatterer on the chat show but I come in at the end to take down the meteo or weather forecast, which the French boats kindly relay to the rest of the fleet. Occasionally it's in halting English but usually in French – great concentration is needed to copy down the columns of figures positioning isobars and millibars – it's important for us now to get the correct daily pattern of the High. The boats ahead are not so free with weather and wind conditions any more. The competition is getting tighter.

Day 25: *Saturday, 18 March   Noon position 31° 50′ N, 27° 36′ W*
Day's run 183 miles   Course NE by N   Wind E Force 5
Barometer 1035

John: Our crisis with the Azores High is nearly at hand. We're coming to the end of the north-east trades, but we are still holding an easterly wind and making north at a fair speed. If only we can cut the corner a bit and pick up a westerly air stream for the English Channel – but I fear it will not be that easy.

At last the flying fish are gone. It is the end of cryptic notes in the log such as, '0120 Mizzen down; R P McCann attacked by giant flying fish; no mercy', and '0400 Almost saw a giant squid'.

This morning I found all the rubber strips which pad the main mast where it passes through the deck in the swamp had come out and the mast was flexing against the edge of the hole, and so down to the shoe on the keel. Colin braced the mast above the deck with a handy billy and lazy sheets to genoa winches to ease my refitting of the rubber pads.

'fraid I'm going to leave it. I've found something much more serious,' the bearded ginger face called anxiously through the main hatch. 'The pin on the forestay bottle screw is almost completely out. Call Tony.'

Tony clambered reluctantly from his bunk and so began a two-hour delay with all the sails down to try and rescue the forestay. The toggle and pin at the deck were bent, and these were replaced, but the stripped threads on the body of the bottle screw were more of a problem. Without Arun we didn't know the whereabouts of a replacement, or even if we had one at all. Still, the repair looks good. Let's hope it'll hold.

Day 26: *Sunday, 19 March   Noon position 34° 12' N, 26° 15' W*
Day's run 122 miles   Course ENE   Wind ESE Force 3
Barometer 1039

John: The bottle screw holding the forestay tight to the deck up in the bows is a most pressing worry. On the radio I managed to speak with Arun at home in Scotland. He confirmed there is no spare bottle screw on board, but the plan had always been to use half-inch galvanized shackles in its place if it got damaged. There were plenty of these available, and Colin and Tony got the job done within the hour – very strong and efficient it is, too. The hand of Arun is ever present, and it is in this sort of situation when attention to detail and a lengthy pre-planning stage pays off.

Marie Christine: At least the calm will give the seasick sufferers some respite. For the first night in a long time I was back in my own bunk. It was now cool enough and certainly last night the boat was hardly heeled over. I think the boys thought John and I had fallen out with each other, we'd been sleeping apart for so long.

'Could we do an interview with you, M.C., after breakfast?' Rog asked as he munched on an Army hard tack biscuit. (It was just about all he and Noel were eating these days. They were trying hard to slim by missing out the meals but kept their energy up by a constant stream of cups of sweet cocoa and high-carbohydrate Army hard tack. I suppose I've heard of less likely diets.)

I'd guessed that this was coming up. I'd seen Rog concentrating over the last few days on compiling what looked like a list of questions. He and Noel were ending their journey at Portsmouth and wanted to get everything recorded by then. As I expected, these were the final questions like, 'What was the worst moment?' 'Has it been worth it?' etc. Having two people on board making a film of our ups and downs has not always contributed to the harmony of the crew but it has underlined

*Emergency repairs on
last leg*
1. $\frac{1}{2}''$ *shackles in place
   of stripped Gibb
   rigging screw*
2. *Pete's electrified
   paraffin lamps*

the whole transitory experience, and with luck the film that will come out of it will be there to remind us of the awe-inspiring ice, the magic of seabirds, dolphins, whales, the laughs, the rows.

'Yes,' I could say. 'It has been worth all the discomfort, tedium, separation from my family, the winter of '77–78 when we raced around the world.'

Everyone is cheerful. The sun is shining, but where is the wind? By the afternoon it had dropped away completely.

I sewed a zip into Dickie's jeans and watched countless purple-veined Portuguese Men o' War drift past, their curious bubble sails catching the slightest puff of a breeze. Although they haven't spoken directly about it since the air-clearing chat John had shortly after departing from Rio, it seems that Dick doesn't want to return to Ardmore and will be leaving the boat at Portsmouth. John feels it's better he should leave then than come on up to Scotland if his heart's not really in it. I get the feeling now that old Dick is perhaps a bit sad that we'll all be parting soon. I wonder what he'll do. He's been with us for nearly two years.

Day 27: *Monday, 20 March   Noon position 35° 31' N, 25° 17' W*
Day's run 124 miles   Course NE by N   Wind Variable, calm
Barometer 1041

Marie Christine: Not much wind about, but a breeze from the N.W. picked up in the afternoon. Could we be through the High?

John phoned Arun during the afternoon to discuss items such as canoes and sailing dinghies which Arun was repairing or taking delivery of. Within five weeks the courses at Ardmore would be starting up. There was not much time to spare and John had been happily busy with his favourite hobby – accounts – ever since the wind had dropped away; his pocket calculator had been brought out of retirement and the bed was scattered with files. After the chat show, when we were able to get the positions of all the other boats and a not very detailed weather report, we sat down to discuss our tactics. The wind had picked up a bit and we thought we were through the High until we heard that *Treaty of Rome* and *B & B*, both directly north of us, were becalmed but it looked as though the High was moving east. It was a toss up. We put it to the vote. To go north and not to the east was the outcome by overwhelming majority.

Day 28: *Tuesday, 21 March   Noon position 37° 08' N, 24° 12' W*
Day's run 83 miles   Course NE by E   Wind SE Force 2
Barometer 1040

Marie Christine: It was the wrong decision. We are B . . . calmed, not a breath of wind, smack in the middle of the High, blue sky and warm sun again.

I unscrewed the floorboards in our cabin for an inspection of the bilges. It was pretty nasty – no water but all the jars and bottles are covered with a grey slime. I think it's where a bottle of cooking oil must have leaked and emulsified with the salt water, probably with some paraffin added from the galley for good measure. I also took out a jagged, broken Glenfiddich bottle – funny that we never smelt the whisky fumes when it broke.

Back in shorts and suntop, I joined John at the wheel. Santa Maria, the most easterly of the Azores, was thirty-five miles astern on the port side and remained there all day. The gay radial-head spinnaker hung limply, empty of air. There was nothing we could do to get the boat moving.

Peering over the side we could see many different kinds of pulsing jellyfish. The most plentiful variety had four orange blobs in the middle of a glob of opaque jelly, not unlike a raw quadruple yolk egg. There were strings of pale jelly with specks of black spaced like a string of beads – fish eggs perhaps? The Portuguese Men o' War were still around, but less brightly coloured. I saw one large mass of clear jelly with three silver sardines trapped in its centre. Later in the morning we saw dolphins jumping far out on our port bow. It seemed they were catching fish. They came nearer and one big fellow leaped high, his blue, beige and white body sending a shower of silver fish scattering in terror. A good day to have had a marine biologist on board.

We heard on the radio tonight that *Adventure* and *Japy Hermès* to the east of us have been becalmed all day too – *B & B*, sixty miles ahead, has only just got a light westerly breeze. It helps to know we are not alone in this predicament. Even if we had made for the east yesterday, it wouldn't have helped. The front boats have strong winds now from the south-west. *Great Britain II* and *Pen Duick* managed runs of 260 miles. They'll be home in time for Easter!

Col made a delicious supper of chilli con carne and nutty brown bread. We drank an extra bottle of port to celebrate our fourteenth wedding anniversary. John told Eric Loizeau on *Gauloises* during the chat hour, adding: 'and it's the calmest one yet!'

I was putting some water on for a hot drink after supper but there was very little water coming out of the pump. J.C. bustled down, whipped up the floorboards and to our horror discovered that the good tank was quite empty. This left us with about fifty gallons of very musty water in the other tank. I felt awfully like saying, I told you so. It seemed to me all this leg we were far too casual and extravagant with the water and now we were down to iron rations. 'It tastes like earth worms,' John muttered, wrinkling up his nose in disgust as he sipped at a glass of murky water.

Day 29: *Wednesday, 22 March   Noon position 38° 28' N, 23° 27' W
        Day's run 162 miles   Course NE   Wind NW Force 3
        Barometer 1036*

John: The wind returned at noon and we're away again at last. I made radio phone calls to Arun, and we also spoke with Rebecca and Gran who are in the best of spirits because Rebecca's school holidays start today. We can't wait to see her. Waiting for our turn to come up on the radio, Marie Christine was upset by the usual series of husband to wife calls from distant ships to the United Kingdom. I'm sure the radio interference makes the bad marriage situations a lot worse.

The evening radio chat show puts *B & B*, *Japy Hermès*, *Adventure* and *Debenhams* on the same latitude and close together. *Condor* broke her long radio silence and revealed she was ahead of *Pen Duick*, now only forty miles south of Looe in Cornwall. She's two hundred miles from the finish and will be in tomorrow morning. She went north round the High – I wish we had. It's easy to say that in hindsight. I rang Robin Knox-Johnston to congratulate *Condor*; after all their troubles they deserved this victory. They went round the west and north of the Azores High, while *Great Britain* and *Pen Duick* went south and east. How easy it is to see that we should have followed *Gauloises* on the same route now.

Day 30: *Thursday, 23 March   Noon position 40° 13' N, 20° 35' W*
Day's run 176 miles   Course E   Wind NNE Force 4
Barometer 1040

John: In the afternoon I saw a kittiwake. These delicate seagulls, with wing-tips black as if dipped in ink, breed on Handa Island at home, and I'll probably sail round Handa about thirty times this summer.

We are now comprehensively last. *Adventure, B & B* and *Japy Hermès* were farther to the east of us passing through the High, and this has paid off for them. Suddenly, they are all three about a full day ahead of us, having got the wind that much earlier.

I find it hard to disguise my relief at not being a navigator on this leg; even Steve has quietened down a bit. Being last boat into Portsmouth will at least be 'unforgettable'. Nothing wishy-washy like middle-of-the-field – a real feast for the masochist.

Day 31: *Good Friday, 24 March   Noon position 40° 43' N, 18° 42' W*
Day's run 60 miles   Course E by N   Wind N Force 1
Barometer 1040

John: Moving steadily in the direction of Portsmouth. *Condor, Pen Duick* and *Great Britain II* finished in that order. *Condor* blew a spinnaker at the Needles and split her main in two on a gybe at the finishing line; but she beat *Pen Duick* by five hours. We are feeling the knife as *Japy Hermès, B & B* and *Adventure* pull away from us.

Marie Christine: The barometer is still high. It seems we can't move away from the high pressure area – it follows us. There is a gentle breeze and the sun is shining. It's really a lovely day but marred by our all-consuming passion to get moving fast.

We spent most of the morning trying to phone Ardmore. When John got through to Lance there was such interference that Lance could barely hear what John was saying and understood John to say that we would be back at Ardmore on 30 April. 'But the first course starts on the 29th,' came Lance's frantic reply. Just him and Ada and twenty-two business men – no wonder he was flapped! John made certain he understood we'd be back by the 15th and then we gave up. There was too much interference.

In the evening we phoned Mum again to say we expected to be in on Thursday.

'What time do you think?' she asked and I jokingly replied,

'Three in the morning and if you're not there I'll be raging.'

'We'll be there; don't worry,' came the staunch answer. Nothing was too much bother for her. Noel's turn was next. He spoke to his girlfriend who said when she heard it was Thursday, 'Oh, but we were expecting you on Tuesday. Can't you make it for then?' Would that we could, I thought, but there didn't seem much hope, trapped in these light airs.

Day 32: *Saturday, 25 March   Noon position 41° 25' N, 16° 55' W*
         Day's run 168 miles   Course NE   Wind NW Force 3
         Barometer 1036

John: There is so little maintenance to do on this GRP boat that the least task becomes a huge effort for anyone to accomplish. Peter cleans the cockpit, cooker and floor so thoroughly that those who follow him are just inclined to give things a quick rub over. The problem is made worse by the TV crew, who do nothing beyond the minimum routine housework. As they make up one-half of one watch – the one including the navigator – this throws all boat repair work on the other watch or Colin. The result is that this work, which should be a joy in itself, becomes something to be avoided, if at all possible, by Tony, Dick and J.C. – except that Tony will always repair sails if necessary. So again Colin and Peter end up doing the lot. Some people look for jobs and others resent doing anything at all. These can be identified by the state of their oilskins, the tatters of which reflect their general attitude to care and maintenance. If oilskins are ever mentioned, their ruined oilskins are pointed out as evidence of their hard work on deck and the poor quality of the suits. On the other hand, Peter's oilskins are so well looked after they still look nearly new – and he works as hard as anyone. The difference lies in his experience: years of travelling the world with little money in his pocket. Others from another school of life could best be described as consumers.

We've passed through an area of sea which looked as if unmelted snowflakes were sticking up from the surface. On closer inspection these turned out to be thousands of sails belonging to baby Portuguese Man-o'-War jellyfish.

Marie Christine: Not the best Easter Saturday I've spent. I had taken to my bed with a tummy ache and a riveting book about American politics when there was a knock at the cabin door half-way through the morning. A small deputation stood huddled round the door. Peter, the spokesman, confronted me with their plea: 'M.C., we've found the three survival containers full of tins of sardines, Mars bars and other goodies. Can we use them?'

'Why come to me?' I asked. 'Is it because I'm a soft touch?' He grinned. 'I think you really should ask John. I hope he agrees. Sardines would be delicious.'

We were now down to very basic food, mainly the dehydrated which we'd grown tired of. I was losing weight fast. John, who was cleaning out the galley and feeling cross that it wasn't cleaner, mumbled: 'I'll think about it.' Thoughts of the sardines obviously swayed his feeling and for lunch Peter cooked us a tasty dish of macaroni, sardines and black beans. If we had to take to the life rafts out here, there was a good chance of being picked up fairly soon. There didn't seem to be any shortage of ships around.

Day 33: *Sunday, 26 March   Noon position 43° 52' N, 14° 40' W*
Day's run 213 miles   Course NE   Wind SW Force 4
Barometer 1032

John: Many of the big boats are finished now; even *Gauloises*, who took the bold route round to the north-west of the Azores. She will almost certainly have won this fourth leg of the race on handicap. It seems only a few days since I laughed with Eric on the radio, saying 'One of us will be wrong' as we approached the Azores.

'See you in Portsmouth,' he replied.

I was wrong.

Four pilot whales surfaced just ahead of us, coming in the other direction at full speed. Luckily they dived just in time.

Tonight it was J.C.'s turn for the scourge of the radio telephone. He called his girlfriend to tell her our expected time of arrival in Portsmouth.

'I'm getting married and going to live in Nigeria,' she told him.

At least it was a reverse-charge call.

Marie Christine: Peter, dressed from top to toe in his scarlet polar suit, fluffy side out, with two mitts sticking out of his hood for ears, hopped into the saloon during breakfast. 'Happy Easter, folks – I'm the Easter Bunny.' He clasped in his paw a box of Quality Street chocs which he passed round to us all. It was a grand idea and made us all feel a bit more festive. I'd got no Easter eggs hidden away in my cupboards so I decided a cake would go down well.

The wind was blowing us along at a good speed and the boat was steady with spinnaker and big-boy. Unfortunately shortly after breakfast the big-boy dipped once too often into the heavy swell and tore badly. Without its steadying influence the spinnaker caused the boat to roll unpredictably, making life and jobs below difficult. In the galley my cake-making session was one setback after another. The first blow was finding the sponge mix quite sodden along with all the other contents in the cupboard; salt water had leaked in and was swilling up and down ruining everything it touched. My first half hour was spent cleaning and drying it out. Finding we'd more margarine that I'd thought, I beat in sugar, the last two eggs and flour and put the two baking trays in the oven. I'd found some reconstituted apple flakes left over from breakfast; the boys would love apple crumble, I thought to myself. In no time it was ready for the oven. I searched high and low for the second metal shelf, finally locating it behind a wooden board which was tied up, Houdini style, by J.C.'s bunk. I couldn't give up now, so breaking a nail or two I untied the knots, put the shelf into the oven and then found this particular dish wouldn't fit. Just as I was shutting the oven door one of the cake tins lurched forward, spilling half its contents on to the floor. I shoved the lighter tin back in, muttering oaths – my patience was running out. Deciding to make some icing, I found everything and set to, tasting the icing sugar after I'd been creaming it for a bit with the Army margarine, which was all we had left. It tasted musty – I should have known. Scuttling into our cabin I located the Long John whisky, a good drop of which would disguise any mustiness; but try as I might I couldn't open any of the metal lids. They had seized solid with the salt. In desperation I attacked a new bottle of open Glenfiddich malt, which opened straight away. Regretting the waste, I sloshed a good dollop into the chocolate icing. Eventually the cake was done, the crumble cooked, also some pies . . . It had taken at least three hours – at home a job of thirty minutes!

We managed to get a clear line through to Lance at Ardmore in the afternoon. He sounded pleased to hear us. It was cold up there with snow showers, but the house was warm and home-brewed beer was going down well. It was grand to hear his familiar voice, which made John and me feel a lot closer to home. Next we rang Richard Morris-Adams. 'Don't worry about coming in last,' he reassured us. 'We'll have a great reception for you when you arrive – I've got two magnums of champagne all ready for you.'

After these two good calls I felt really buoyed up and excited. I sorted out presents I'd bought in Rio for friends and family, wrapping up Becca's and my mother's, an assortment of treasures. Giant blue butterflies framed, semi-precious stones set as bunches of grapes or polished into eggs, a tiny blue, heart-shaped Brazilian stone hung on a silver chain, a carnival doll. There would be great excitement from Bec as she opened her share.

We are really moving now, we must take great care not to damage the boat. There is a heavy sea and the wind is strong.

Day 34: *Easter Monday, 27 March   Noon position 46° 29' N, 11° 30' W*
Day's run 225 miles   Course NE by E   Wind SW Force 6
Barometer 1021

John: Crossing the Bay of Biscay and heading for the western entrance to the English Channel. We planned to press up the middle of the Channel, giving Ushant a wide berth because of the giant oilslick on the French coast caused by the wreck of the supertanker, *Amoco Cadiz*.

The wind increased during the day and I took a turn on the midnight watch. Ships are like fast-moving icebergs in heavy weather. Thank goodness, Peter's job on converting the oil lamps to electricity has been such a success.

Day 35: *Tuesday, 28 March   Noon position 48° 00' N, 6° 00' W*
Day's run 230 miles   Course E by N   Wind SW Force 8–10
Barometer 1005

Marie Christine: These last two days have passed slowly, the hours punctuated by the hoarse cry of 'Log' from one of the watch sitting out his spell below and the man at the helm yelling back the reading off the trailing Walker log, also giving wind speed and direction. It's been blowing up to 50 knots from the south-west and we've been able to clock up 200 miles for both days – our wind has come at last.

Channel fever, as Bob used to call it, has brought on a certain amount of recklessness (or maybe it's just carelessness owing to our being so close to the finish), resulting in the following damage: a tear and broken batten in the mainsail, spinnaker guy chafed through unnecessarily, two broken spinnakers, bent stanchions and severely bent pulpit. It's hit John hard; being exceptionally careful himself, he can't understand why others let the damage occur. To be fair to them, they do make great efforts to repair whatever is broken. John sees it in terms of cost and a spinnaker guy costing £50 to replace, that was chafed through in a morning owing to no one noticing it happen, has sent him into a state of gloom. Once again I'm in the dilemma of feeling annoyed for John and yet understanding how easily it happens. I suppose it would help if those who let it happen were to apologize but that never occurs to them; and then John feels they just don't give a damn, which I don't think is the case. I keep telling him: 'Hold out for another thirty-six hours and it will all be over' – except for the trip to Scotland, which I fear may be worse than anything we've seen so far, and with a weaker crew. Rog and Noel are leaving the boat at Portsmouth and possibly Dick and J.C.

On deck it's magnificent: the grey seas are huge, breaking all around, the wind blowing gale force 8 for the last two days. Visibility is not good and a constant watch is kept for shipping. We've seen a few large ships not more than a mile distant. It's possible they might miss seeing us and if they hit us I don't suppose they'd know and we would sink rapidly. The last two nights just before dropping off to sleep John has asked me where the life-jackets are. He is now doing the twelve-to-four watch again during the night for extra vigilance.

Roll on Portsmouth! Life will seem so easy after this struggle. I keep thinking of Bec running into my arms and hugging her tight – not so long now. We expect to get in to *Vernon* between Wednesday midnight and 6 a.m. on Thursday morning, so my joke to Mum about arriving at 3 a.m. may not be so far from the truth!

I had a short spell on the wheel but found it just too heavy for me in these big seas and strong winds.

Day 36: *Wednesday, 29 March*

John: A beautiful moonlit run across the Channel took us to a position where we could see Start Point some fifteen miles to port at breakfast time. With the storm spinnaker, full main and mizzen, Steve laid us on a course to Portsmouth. Morale was high in the sun of a beautiful early spring day.

Marie Christine: The sea this morning is a completely different colour: it is Channel green, I suppose owing to the shallower water we are now in. We have our radial-head spinnaker up and are making good speed for Portsmouth, I can't really believe this trip is almost over; it seems as though there was never any other way of life and it's hard to imagine Rebecca, my mother and all our friends just waiting to see us in a few hours' time.

Roger and Noel spent the morning packing up their kit. Roger washed and shaved but Noel just washed.

'Why don't you take those whiskers off?' I asked jokingly.

'Never. I'll get much more love and sympathy if I look as though I've had a hard time.'

I had to agree he looked a real old weather-beaten salt with his rough chin and long hair tied in a pigtail.

The day passed more slowly than any I'd ever known. The wind was dying on us all the time. I sorted out a few things in our cabin and put them into a bag for going ashore. I felt a wave of affection for this tiny cabin that had been my home for the past eight months. How I had cursed it in the heat and the cold and when the condensation had run in rivulets down the walls and dripped off the ceiling! We had been through so much and now I felt fickle as I packed my bag to leave it for a more well-appointed, comfortable room away from the heaving, rushing water that was inches from where I stood.

With the wind and tide as it was we decided we would pass round the south of the Isle of Wight and by seven in the evening we were off St Catherine's Point. Steve, who had been rushing up all day long to take sights, in an idle moment turned on the radio and twisted the knobs to hear what was on the air. By sheer coincidence he happened to tune into Radio Niton, who were at that moment putting out a traffic list. We were amongst the ships being called. Peter straight away contacted Niton and we phoned through to Race Control giving them our position. There was practically no wind now and John, never very optimistic, thought we would not be in before morning. After supper I decided to turn in. If I could sleep it would for me bring our arrival closer.

I awoke at eleven, when we were just rounding Bembridge Ledge. The wind was picking up again and it looked as though we might make it in tonight after all. There was a further message from Race Control to say that a boat was coming out to meet us. The excitement welled up inside me ... at last it seemed real, we would soon be there. I dressed hurriedly and got out on deck just as the lights of a Trinity House Pilot boat shone on *Debenhams*. It was after midnight and freezing cold, when out of the blackness came our two navigators of legs 2 and 3, Tom Woodfield and Alan Green, shouting congratulations at us. They passed our mail over and a bottle of milk to Dickie, who had requested this back in Rio. His face was a picture of satisfaction as he gulped it down in preference to the champagne I had opened as we approached the finishing line. Also out of the darkness loomed another boat; on board were our old pal Richard Morris-Adams and friends and family of some of the boys.

We sailed on and over the finishing line. My mind went back to the start last August, of our hopes and fears then. It was a mammoth task to have undertaken but we had made it by the grace of God.

The rest was a blur ... docking in *Vernon* amid thunder flashes, sirens, fog horns, hooters, in fact anything that would make a loud enough noise. We were the last boat of the fleet to arrive and those on the quay were determined to cheer us in. The illuminated quayside showed crowds of well-wishers, who must have had a long wait, it was now the early hours of Thursday morning. As we slowly motored in I searched the crowds for two special figures that had been so much in my thoughts during the last 30,000 miles. One small girl with a brightly coloured bobble hat was jumping up and down and waving excitedly, holding on to her granny. We tied up and somebody lifted Becca up into my arms. It had seemed an awfully long time. Soon Mummy was up too. Hugging her tightly, I was speechless with happiness to see them both again.

What was left of the night was spent eating steaks very kindly laid on by Captain O'Kelly and HMS *Vernon*, drinking champagne and talking to friends. There was so much to say. People had come from all over to welcome us. Ron and Val Lincoln, who had been to Ardmore for several years were there. There were Jim Wheeler and Jim Archer-Burton, both in their sixties, who had come to Portsmouth to see us and, thinking we wouldn't be in till morning, had gone to bed at their hotel a little distance from *Vernon*; they had been awakened by bangs, explosions and sirens and, realizing it was us arriving, quickly dressed and hurried to see us.

We left the following afternoon for Brighton. Mum spoiled us rotten for the next week while we enjoyed to the full everything being on dry land

*Arrival at Portsmouth — a grand turn-out
in the early hours*

had to offer. But the greatest treat of all was being reunited with her and Becca again.

We decided that ten days would give the boys enough time to see their families and friends before heading north for the summer in Scotland. John and I also had a fair bit to do, and travelled up to London from Brighton now and again. ATV and the publishers wanted to see us and we still hadn't completely organized the dishwasher project which we'd put into motion over the radio back in the Southern Ocean, far from the hurly burly we were now sucked into.

After one day in London of achieving very little, we decided to work through the night – this way there should be no interruptions. William Heinemann, the ultra-correct publishers in Queen Street, Mayfair, were slightly taken aback when John and I asked for a couple of blankets and permission to stay through the night so we could get on with typing out logs. I don't think the late Somerset Maugham or any other of their illustrious authors had ever made such a request. It was five in the evening and the night watchman could not be found, the blankets had gone missing, it was obviously not going to be easy. Richard Creasey, who was with us, piped up: 'Come to ATV. We're much more flexible,' winking at Roger Smith our obliging editor; 'there's no problem there with blankets or night watchmen and there are plenty of typewriters. You'll have the whole place to yourselves.'

It seemed a good idea as we looked round the spacious offices three floors up in the heart of London. Richard's office had a brown sofa and a cocktail cabinet; there was a vast ladies' loo outside in the hall with unlimited hot and cold water. I was still marvelling at the luxury of being able to turn a tap and use as much water as I wanted.

After the cleaners had left at about eight, John and I were alone and we worked hard without interruption. By about 1.30 I felt all in. We pulled the brown cushions on to the floor, laid out the two first-aid blankets. I had a wash, changed into my nightie and flitted back into Richard's office. John was already in our makeshift bed and we were soon both fast asleep.

About an hour later the door was thrown open and torches flashed in our faces.

'I think we've got them,' shouted one of the burly figures framed in the doorway. What was this? Could the boat be sinking? I asked myself and then realized we weren't at sea as I looked up from the floor. Silhouetted in the doorway were four policemen and three security guards staring down at John and me in our shaky-down on the floor.

'Will the gentleman come outside,' a stern voice ordered. They turned their backs as John struggled into his trousers and he then joined them in the outside office. I strained to hear what was being said in the brightly lit next-door room. A man wearing white overalls had been seen climbing into this multi-storey office block; the police had arrived and had been searching the building with the security officers. Out of the window I could see a black maria and two police cars with flashing lights.

After some gruff enquiries the police decided John was not the intruder in white overalls but instead a trendy ATV executive getting in a bit of overtime with his secretary. There was no point in trying to tell them the truth, they would never have believed we were man and wife and had just come back from sailing round the world so we left it like that. The police and guards left, apologizing for interrupting us, and John reckoned he heard the odd snigger as they made their way out of the offices.

Poor Richard, his reputation would be blackened now.

II

From High Seas to Highlands

John: We left Portsmouth early on a grey April Sunday morning. It was nearly flat calm so we used the motor to help us against the unfavourable tide in the Solent. It seemed strange to be under way again after a week of London life and oddly disappointing that there was none of the drama of a 'start' for us this time. We passed through a great fleet of half-tonners down by Lymington; racing in the Spring series they made a brave sight under clouds of bright spinnakers. Once past the Needles, heading west for Land's End, *Debenhams* was on her own. No radio chat show this time.

The wind held between N.E. and N.W. for the next several days, exactly unfavourable for my fourth wintry passage north up the west coast of Britain. Snow squalls up to 50 knots alternated with periods of calm, but morale was high, we were homeward bound. In place of Dick, J.C. and the TV crew we had two old friends, Richard Morris-Adams and Bruce Reynolds. Also Simon Godden and Will Michelmore joined us as part of a trial period prior to becoming instructors at Ardmore for the season.

The fresh faces, combined with the nearness of home, made this passage the most enjoyable leg of all for me. I was able to be a watch-leader and spend half the time on watch, safe in the knowledge that Tony and Steve could look after the boat while I slept. We passed within a few hundred yards of the Mull of Kintyre, the first part of Scotland to greet us, and our cranky salt-stained cassette player coughed out Paul McCartney's song until it was fit to bust. Peter had brought us the tape from Tasmania, and we'd played it all over Christmas in Auckland far away.

Following the route of the original delivery trip in January 1976, we basked in pleasure among the red and brown hills of the Inner Hebrides. The mantle of snow on the high tops gave me a spiritual warmth better than any tropic sun. Islay, Jura, Corrievrechan, Mull, Muck, Eigg, Skye – we reeled them off. We called in at Mallaig to pick up

Roger Smith and his son Giles for the last twenty-four hours, and Richard very kindly bought a huge joint of beef to celebrate our last night at sea.

Six days out from Portsmouth we arrived at Ardmore flying every flag in the locker. It was a warm sunny morning in the shelter of the hills. A great shout went up as we saw Heckie Ross on the cliff top of Ardbeg. Waving his stick in welcome he suddenly lifted Mona his sheepdog in his arms to see us better. We picked up the mooring under the wood at 10.30 a.m., Saturday, 15 April 1978. In 255 days (174 at sea) we had sailed right round the world from Ardmore to Ardmore. It had been my dream for fourteen years.

Granny Ross, near on ninety, was sitting in her rocking chair just the same as ever, when we came in to her house next to ours on the hill.

'Well, Ridgway – so you're back. "A good neighbour close at hand is better than a brother far away." I came outside to the fence last August to wave you off and I came out again today to wave you back. I don't suppose I'll go out again.'

We were back.

Some Thoughts in Retrospect

John: I have purposely let a little time pass before trying to get the voyage into perspective. Now I feel twenty years younger, the burden of the monthly boatbuilders' bill is no more. Rebecca seems unchanged. I love to hear the birds singing over the wood in the spring sunshine; there was none of that at sea. The lambs are being born and winter is past. When I look at the boat from the garden gate, as she lies serenely below the wood, I heave a sigh of contentment. I'm awfully proud of what she's done.

Marie Christine and I have written this book as we went along, neither reading the other's material. I hope we have captured the passions of the moment; it seemed more honest than writing with hindsight. The reader will be able to see the mistakes I made. There were plenty of them:

The crew was too big. Thirteen people was intolerable. Two watches of four would have been sufficient. I didn't realize how easy it was going to be to pick up replacements along the way. I spent too much nervous energy worrying about the feelings of the crew; if the extras had not been present the business of running the boat while on watch would have occupied my thoughts and expended my energy in a more healthy way, as on the trip from Portsmouth to Ardmore.

The TV film was as much a part of the voyage as the Southern Ocean. We tried to achieve something new in television and it was difficult. Roger and Noel were two fellows trying to do a job. Their outlook on life was entirely different from mine, so squeezed into a tube together as we were for long periods, conflict was as certain as bad weather. Both of them did a good job in keeping the boat going and I wish them well. While it is easy to jib at the pricks caused by the film-making, it should not be forgotten that without the communications media there would probably be no John Ridgway School of Adventure.

As Corado di Majo, skipper of *B & B Italia*, said in Rio: 'I thought the sea would be the biggest problem. It was not; it was the people.'

I would like to thank Richard Morris-Adams and Richard Creasey for their help when it was most needed – in the thin times.

My selection of a crew was made with a view to having a team of instructors for the school on our return. This meant choosing from a tiny group of people, some of whom were maybe not quite mature enough to cope with the rough and tumble of such a large-scale project, and their process of testing themselves and the boat was an added strain for me. Now I can see that three good men to help get things going on our return to Ardmore would have been sufficient because as it turned out there were plenty of people keen to be instructors when we got back, and there was time to run a course for them. But all those who sailed with us tried their very best and I thank them sincerely for it. All my carping should never hide those long hours they spent on watch in *all* weathers.

The boat was first class. Arun Bose fitted out a powerful cruising hull which acquitted itself very well against the racers. Her time would have won her third place in the 1974 race! I hope she will have many years of hard work ahead of her at Ardmore, for which she is now ideally suited.

I look back on the voyage as the realization of a lifetime's dreaming. To have the dream come true right in the mainstream of my life and of the school's existence was wonderful. Of course it was a struggle but that is what made it all worth while.

Marie Christine: Here at Ardmore very little has changed, now a month after our return and back into the swing of things. It almost seems as though we were never away, except for a few small reminders: the kitten, so small when we left, is now bigger than its mother; the salmon in their four cages have grown – and so has Rebecca. Beside the kitchen door is a yearly record of her height. On 15 April, eight months after we all went away, Becca has marked her extra two inches and written in her childish hand: 'The day Mummy and Daddy came back to Ardmore from sailing round the World.'

John has turned his hand to gardening. He has dug a square of rich earth in front of the ruined croft next door, overlooking the boat lying peacefully at anchor in the sheltered bay.

Home is every bit as good as I'd remembered it at sea. It would be nice to think we'll stay at home for a bit – after all it's the place we both always long to be when we are away! Living in our stone croft-house high on a green hill, running courses here at the adventure school and growing tatties for the winter: it's a recipe for contentment.

But a leopard doesn't change his spots overnight and John, no doubt, some time in the future will get itchy feet and we'll be off again. I say *we*, for I can't think I'll have the sense to say no the next time John gets the atlas down and enthusiastically tells me what he's planning for us.

The winter of 1977–78 when we sailed round the world has for me been a memorable one. Memories of the struggle: overcoming fear and putting up with squalor and discomfort, but these are nothing when compared with the excitement of the four starts, the exhilaration as *Debenhams* surfed along at 12 knots, the wildlife that we saw, the comradeship felt towards each other as well as towards our fellow competitors, and the knowledge that we achieved what we set out to do and sailed right round the world.

None of this, however, would have been possible for me had it not been for those at home, and to them I am forever grateful: Lance and Ada Bell, who stayed at Ardmore and held the fort during the worst winter for thirty years; my mother, Lady D'Albiac, for looking after Rebecca and being such a staunch supporter of the project, even though I know she would have been happier if we had not gone at all; wise little ten-year-old Rebecca, who never once said: 'Don't go, Mum.' As well I must thank the boys for keeping the boat going and our spirits up; *Debenhams*, our boat who never failed our trust and brought us safely home; and most of all John, for dreaming up the idea and making it happen.

Appendices

APPENDIX I

Suppliers of Goods

We would like to thank the following for supporting the venture with supplies

FOOD   Batchelors Foods Ltd, Sheffield
    Dehydrated foodstuffs at each port for entire voyage
Carnation, London
    Evaporated milk and dried milk
Caters Bros. (Provisions) Ltd, Dagenham
    Tinned and fresh groceries for entire voyage
House of Clarks, Dagenham
    Popcorn
Jacquet, Paris, France
    Long life bread at each port for entire voyage
Kraft Foods Ltd, Cheltenham
    Cheese slices
Mars Ltd, Slough
    Mars Bars, Galaxy, and Twix
Quaker Oats Ltd, Southall
    Cereals and pancake mix
Standard Brands, Liverpool
    Royal Food products and Planters Dry Roasted Peanuts
Tate & Lyle Refineries, Croydon
    Sugar and tea
Whitworths Holdings Ltd
    Raisins

DRINK   Grants of St James's, London
    3 Dozen bottles Glenfiddich Malt Whisky
Mentzendorff & Co. Ltd, London S.W.1 (Guimaraens-Vinhos S.A.R.L, Portugal)
    10 Cases of Fonseca Bin 27 Port at each port for entire voyage
Whitbreads
    Beer and Long John Whisky at each port for entire voyage
    (I would like to add that my husband is a teetotaler – or *was* at the start
of the voyage – M.C.R.)

CLOTHING   Clarks Footwear, Street
    Deck shoes
  Debenhams, London W.1.
    Blazer, slacks and tie for entire crew
  Jaeger Holdings Ltd, London W.1.
    Sweaters
  H.R. Marrum (Sports) Ltd, Northampton
    Romika boots
  North Cape, Aberdeen
    Polar suits, sweaters, socks and gloves
  Pringle of Scotland Ltd, Hawick
    Sweaters
  Slazengers Ltd, Croydon
    Shorts and shirts
  Vango (Scotland) Ltd, Glasgow
    Jiffy Tops

EQUIPMENT   Altro Ltd, Hertford
AND FUEL   Flooring
  Boots the Chemists, Nottingham
    Pharmaceutical items
  BUPA, London W.1.
    Medical check-ups to each crew member at start of voyage and medical
  insurance for entire voyage
  Century Oils Ltd, Stoke
    150 gallons of Paraffin which lasted right round the world
  Honda U.K. Ltd, London W.4
    Loan of a portable petrol-driven generator
  International Paints, Plymouth
    Anti-fouling paint and advice
  Kean Leisure Ltd, London W.5
    Thermos flasks
  R. A. Lister & Co. Ltd
    Servicing our Lister 15 h.p. Diesel around the world
  Lucas Electrical, Birmingham
    Electrical service around the world
  National Coal Board Co., London
    Two Freshness water filters
  Rigel Instruments Ltd, Sutton, Surrey
    Clock, Chronometer and Barometer
  Supreme Plastics Ltd, London N.4.
    Plastic bags
  Swifts of Exmouth
    Tableware
  Trendella Ltd, Bolton
    Clear Seal for charts

APPENDIX II

Power

We decided to use only one fuel – paraffin. After careful consultation with R.A. Lister & Co. Ltd we used their 15 h.p. SW2 MGR2 Marine diesel engine as the main power unit on the boat. This engine was run as much as 6 hours per day right round the world using top quality paraffin plus four per cent 20W lubricating oil provided by Century Oils in place of diesel. The engine powered the 12 v Lucas AC5 alternator which charged two 6 v lead acid batteries used for interior lighting and the navigation and deck lights. There were two more of the same batteries for engine starting. Also it charged two more for TV film equipment and four more for the Pentland Bravo radio set used for communications between the boats and also to shore stations. This makes a total of ten batteries on charge.

The central 150-gallon tank of paraffin beneath the main cockpit floor also supplied fuel to the Shipmate cooking stove and the reserve oil navigation lamps and Tilley lamp as well as the Taylor paraffin cabin heater. One hundred and fifty gallons lasted us right round the world.

APPENDIX III

Medical

We had little or no sickness and injury besides a few cases of 'gunnel bum' and the twelve stitches Tony needed in his gashed hand in Auckland.

Seasickness was the most general hindrance and the crew included several who suffered to a greater or lesser extent. Apart from our visit to Dr McCallum, the Cape Town chiropractor, which cured Marie Christine, no pills or measures were taken as the victims all agreed that on a six-week voyage endurance was the only cure – the sea always calmed down after each storm. There were no trees to go and sit under.

Sufferers	*Non-sufferers*
Arun Bose	Bob Burns
Steve Lenartowicz	Peter Brand
John Ridgway	Noel Smart
Marie Christine Ridgway	Dick McCann
Roger Deakins	Tony Dallimore
	Colin Ladd
	John Covington

Steve Lenartowicz was our medic. When he joined the crew in the spring of 1977 he was still teaching in Manchester and asked what he could do to help with preparations until he joined us at Ardmore in June. As he had no skills or experience relevant to the voyage I suggested he train himself as medic and set about making up a medical kit, which he did at a cost of about £150.

Steve's efforts were boosted when BUPA agreed to sponsor the British crews in the Whitbread Race by providing an extensive pre-race medical in Portsmouth, a comprehensive medical kit and handbook, insurance cover during the Race, and medical facilities in the three ports of call. I am most grateful for this excellent support.

The inter-yacht radio chat show was also a comfort. There were several doctors and surgeons in the fleet, as well as Dr David Dixon aboard *Condor* who was always most helpful.

APPENDIX IV

Damage Report

Introduction

At first sight the list of damage may appear long, but in fact I consider its content remarkably small. Bearing in mind the pressures of racing, heavy weather, and the sheer distance involved I thought the boat and gear stood up extremely well. A good deal of the success is owing to Arun Bose of Cape Wrath Boatyard for his part in the overall planning and assembly of the components, the rest is due to the careful way the crew looked after the boat.

Manufacturers might look with dismay upon the frequent mention of their products. I was dubious about our chances with simple standard Proctor spars; before the start in Portsmouth I noticed other boats appeared to have so much more robust specially strengthened gear, but I have to admit that I was pleasantly surprised and all my fears proved groundless. The Brookes and Gatehouse electrical gear endured massive changes of temperature from tropical calm to frozen interior condensation in the Southern Ocean, storm-driven spray inside and outside. Could I really have expected a better performance?

The Barlow winches performed well; the breakage of the two No. 32 drums was probably due to a fault in the casting, as both came from the same batch and were new in Auckland where we changed the self-tailers to new conventional drums.

Damage Report

Taken from Day Report Book kept throughout the voyage

Ardmore–Portsmouth

3 Aug. 77
Brand new Marina blue genoa sheet badly chafed through use in Barlow 36 self-tailing winch.

4 Aug. 77
Snatch block lost off boom owing to lack of a 'safety' line. (Gibb)
Forward end of foot rope groove on main boom chafing foot of mainsail. (Proctor)
Main boom vang snapshackle broken in accidental gybe. Some other arrangement is necessary. (Lewmar)

6 Aug. 77
One of two shackles linking spi-pole goosenecks lost a pin, resulting in a temporary loss of pole heel control. These shackle pins should be included in normal 'round the boat' shackle checks. (Proctor)

Portsmouth–Cape Town   Leg 1

28 Aug. 77
Chart table light switch broken (they always do!).
Spi-guy chafed through at pole end. Replaced by sacrificial loop. (Proctor Pole)

29 Aug. 77
Genoa halyard parted at rope/wire splice (two years old).

5 Oct. 77
Wire spi-guy parted at back of eye splice.

Two alloy guard rail stanchions broken on starboard side amidships by flogging sheets. (S. S. Spars Ltd)

12 Oct. 77
Refill needed in Cape Town for Chubb fire extinguisher used in saloon battery fire. successfully extinguished.

Cape Town

Genoa halyard sheave replaced and new shims and plates fitted.
Replaced some stanchions with local stainless steel type.

Cape Town to Auckland   Leg 2

31 Oct. 77
Mizzen halyard shackle lost.

1 Nov. 77
Yacht speed (amplified) dial stopped. (Brookes & Gatehouse)
Main gybed and vang snatch block broken. (Lewmar)

5 Nov. 77
Winch handle locking device broken. (Barlow)

11 Nov. 77
Wire tack strop for yankee broken.

13 Nov. 77
Main boom kicking-strap tang broken (just fell apart). (Proctor)
($\frac{3}{8}''$ stainless steel rod; see Leg 3 on 21 March 78 for recurrence.)

14 Nov. 77
Barlow 24 winch used for port main mast running backstay jammed. Pawls jammed – maybe due to use of this winch as boom preventer when on starboard tack. (Barlow) Mended same day.
Port side log impellor under hull broken off while passing through loose ice. (Brookes & Gatehouse)
Alloy guard rail stanchion broken on port side amidships by flogging sheets. (S.S. Spars) Stainless steel stanchions (4 fitted in Cape Town) superior for this heavy work.

15 Nov. 77
Steering quadrant coming loose from stock. (Canpa)

22 Nov. 77
Steering quadrant looser. No further spinnakers until Auckland. (Canpa)
Main sheet track stops jammed – pins bent under weight of slider – no longer used, use control lines to winch and cleats instead. (Proctor)

23 Nov. 77
Boom eye for main sheet suddenly broke. $\frac{3}{8}''$ stainless steel! (Proctor)
(Note similar failure on boom vang fitting 13 Nov. 77 and 21 March 78)
Spi-pole track lifting off mast. Probably due to overloading with No. 1 yankee (poled out). (Proctor)

25 Nov 77
Main halyard sheave quite worn. (Proctor)

Auckland, Dec. 77

Quadrant repair. New quadrant casting retaining plate manufactured.
A much thicker and stiffer plate which we hoped would not bend but hold the
quadrant clamped tight to the stock and key.
4×No. 36 and 2×No. 32 new Barlow winch drums fitted by Barlow in place of
self-tailers F.O.C.

Auckland–Rio   Leg 3

6 Jan. 78
One Barlow 32 winch drum cracks when used for wire mainsail halyard. This
drum then swapped for the other 32 which was serving the genoa halyard.

5 Jan. 78
Port side of pulpit bent by spi-hole guy because watch-leader was not looking at
the job in hand.

6 Jan. 78
Starboard Proctor spinnaker pole had been left in position after a gybe. As the port
pole was brought forward to lower the radial-head spi the two poles touched – this
sheared off the male end fitting on the starboard pole at the mast.
This was repaired by Colin Ladd, who drilled and tapped the piece that came off,
drilled the piece which stayed on, and then bolted the two together. Finally he
glued the joint.
The repair lasted all the way to UK – but the glue didn't hold, which is not
surprising considering the great load at this point.

13 Jan. 78
Winch handle lost over the side. (The only one in the boat's life so far.)

15 Jan. 78
Problem with teak seating pad on port running backstay winch. Probably through
overloading in use as main boom vang anchorage.

18 Jan. 78
Sheave gone from port masthead spi-halyard block. (Lewmar)

19–25 Jan. 78
Last snatch block lost overboard. (Lewmar)
3rd (aluminium) stanchion forward from aft on port side broken. (S. S. Spars)

26 Jan. 78
Main bilge pump sprang a leak (Whale). Repaired.

27 Jan. 78
Steering quadrant fails in heavy seas. Four bolts broken, two locating pins
sheared. Keyway should be on front of stock not on the side. Four-and-a-half hour
repair job by Colin Ladd.

28 Jan. 78
Becket gone from topping lift handy billy on main boom. (Lewmar)

30 Jan. 78
6" crack found in Barlow 32 winch drum in use for main halyard.

1 Feb. 78
Barlow 32 winch drum collapsed under main halyard when taking in 2nd reef (see
30 Jan. above).

Rio de Janeiro

Echo sounder cockpit repeater disconnected (flooded), but sounder still working at chart table. (Brookes & Gatehouse)

Log repeater at cockpit disconnected (never worked since Portsmouth). (Brookes & Gatehouse)

Starboard lower spreader mounting plate on mainmast found to have been pulled down about 2 mm. This due to the hole in the mast for the through bolt (to which shroud tangs are attached) being slightly oversize. The plate was removed and re-riveted using long monel rivets. (Proctor)

Steering quadrant repaired by Brazilian Navy dockyard by filling stripped holes with bronze and re-tapping. (Canpa Quadrant).

Rio–Portsmouth   Leg 4

24 Feb. 78
Harrier log fails at chart table. (Brookes & Gatehouse)
Walker log streamed.

1 Mar. 78
Walker log spinner bitten off.

9 Mar. 78
Red/Green electric navigation light on pulpit lost, wires pulled out from lamp as it dangled over bow. (Hella)

12 Mar. 78
Starboard hinge on Canpa forehatch broken by wave slamming it shut on an 18 mm sheet.

14 Mar. 78
Third from forward keel bolt leaking. Mastic between keel and hull may have been loosened by bumping on the bottom at mooring at Rio de Janeiro or general wear and tear.

18 Mar. 78
Forestay toggle and pin bent at deck when pin slipped three-quarters out. Threads found to be stripped on bottle screw body. Half-inch galvanized shackles used as a replacement.

21 Mar. 78
Stainless steel tang on main boom, which anchors the wheel type boom vang, broke for the second time on the voyage. On both occasions the failure has occurred after 12–14,000 miles and the $\frac{3}{8}''$ stainless steel rod has sheared at the weld on to the plate which is riveted to the boom.

The problem of holding the boom down when running was never finally solved, eventually we broke everything we used.

Sail Damage

We suffered probably the least sail damage in the fleet. The Ratsey sails were outstanding. They did ninety-eight per cent of the work and the small amount of damage is a remarkable tribute to them and to the care of the crew.

The colours ran badly in the Arun storm spinnaker and tri-radial.

Sails carried

Ratsey & Lapthorn Ltd	USA Ozs	in 36″ Vectis material	Arun Sails Ltd* Arundel, Sussex (Reserve)	USA Ozs
Mainsail	9.5	P = 56.00′	No. 3 Yankee	9.5
		E = 17.00′	No. 2 Staysail	9.5
		slab reefing (3 rows)	Tri-radial spinnaker	2.2
Mizzen	7.8	Pz = 29.50′	Storm spinnaker	4.0
		Pz = 9.50′	Big-boy	2.0
		slab reefing (2 rows)		
Trysail	9.5	Luff = 30.50′		
		LP = 10.50′		
Heavy genoa	6.8	Luff = 64.00′		
		LP = 32.25′		
Light genoa	4.3	Luff = 64.00′		
		LP = 32.35′		
No. 1 yankee	6.5	Luff = 62.00′		
		LP = 22.00′		
		Head pennant		
No. 2 yankee	7.8	Luff = 56.00′		
		LP = 19.00′		
		Head pennant		
No. 3 yankee	9.5	Luff = 47.50′		
		LP = 14.25′		
		Head pennant		
Genoa staysail	6.5	Luff = 35.50′		
		LP = 21.00′		
		Head pennant		
No. 1 working staysail	9.5	Luff = 35.50′		
		LP = 12.00′		
		Head pennant		
No. 2 staysail	9.5	Luff = 26.66′		
		LP = 10.00′		
		Head pennant		
Radial-head spinnaker	1.5	I = 63.00′		
		J = 21.50′		
Starcut spinnaker	1.5	I = 63.00′		
		J = 21.50′		
Storm spinnaker	4.0	I = 63.00′		
		J = 21.60′		
Mizzen staysail	2.2	Luff = 37.25′		
		LP = 22.75′		

* No connection with our companion Arun Bose

Ardmore–Portsmouth

4 August 1977
Ratsey No. 1 working staysail head burst from luff wire.

Portsmouth–Cape Town

3 Sept. 77
Two fairly small holes in clew of Arun big-boy sail. Trapped between radial-head spinnaker sheet and capshroud.

3 Sept. 77
Ratsey radial-head spinnaker blown right out of its 'frame'. Broach in too high a wind in the dark.

5 Oct. 77
Ratsey radial-head spinnaker, man-sized hole torn while being pulled inboard after squall broke wire guy at night.

Cape Town–Bob Burns made a check and service of all stitching.

Cape Town–Auckland

4 Nov. 77
Arun big-boy torn in two, one panel up from the foot. Caused by dipping the sail in the sea.

11 Nov. 77
Small hole in Ratsey No. 1 yankee two feet in from luff in hanks up from the tack. Caused by flogging when poled out. Hanks wearing through luff of sail.

15 Nov. 77
Piston hanks came off Ratsey No. 3 yankee and sail torn near luff when flogging. Hank off Ratsey No. 1 working staysail.

17 Nov. 77
Small hole in Arun storm spinnaker.

19 Nov. 77
Small hole in Ratsey No. 1 yankee, six panels down from head and 2" below seam, three feet in from luff. Probable cause piston hanks during flogging when poled out. Some piston hanks jamming at this time and stitching on foot and leech deteriorating.

23 Nov. 77
In a broach Ratsey No. 1 yankee blew out. Torn from mitre seam half-way up luff down to a point half-way along foot and across to a point half-way up leech.
    This was a major repair and took many days for Bob to repair alone. The lack of this sail off N.Z. coast slowed our progress enough to alter our final handicap position on this leg. After this incident sail repairs were carried out by more than one person whenever possible.

24 Nov. 77
1. Damaged piston hanks on Ratsey No. 3 yankee.
2. Arun No. 3 yankee damaged stitching and cloth around tack thimble and talurit damaged. Perhaps material was pulled too tight along luff when sail was made.

26 Nov. 77
Two small slits in Ratsey mainsail caused by remains (now removed) of broken kicking strap tang fitting on main boom.

27 Nov. 77
Very small hole in body of Ratsey mizzen staysail.

Auckland Sail Repairs (Shore Sail Company)

1. Anti-chafe patch on Ratsey mainsail in way of lower spreaders.
2. Ratsey radial-head – new luff tapes and reinforced head.
3. Ratsey No. 1 yankee – new joining strip on both horizontal and vertical tears.

Auckland–Rio de Janeiro

6 Jan. 78
Arun big-boy luff wire parted three feet up from tack. Sail tore horizontally then vertically to a point four feet along foot from tack. (15 knots of wind across the deck.) Wire spliced and cloth repaired.

13 Jan. 78
Arun storm spinnaker head torn off two feet down.

17 Jan. 78
Ratsey starcut spinnaker small hole due to wrap round forestay when hoisting.

18 Jan. 78
1. Two small holes in Ratsey radial-head spinnaker caused by wrap round inner forestay when lowering.
2. Ratsey mainsail (unreefed) blown out from leech to luff in gybe when main track slider ran free across the boat. Tear from bottom of third reefing cringle reinforcing patch across panel to luff.
     This was a major repair job carried out in two days and nights by Colin and Marie Christine. Some forty hours work for both people.
3. Ratsey No. 1 yankee damaged, hanks and also leech tabling coming adrift.

19–25 Jan. 78
Piston hanks coming off the Ratsey yankee sails. General stitching of sails carried out.

1 Feb. 78
Three Ratsey mizzen luff track slider tapes broken. General wear and tear.

Rio de Janeiro–General check and servicing of stitching.

18 March 78
Stitching chafed at Ratsey mainsail clew where No. 1 reef point passes over clew/foot tabling.

26 March 78
Arun big-boy luff wire parts for second time. One panel badly torn. Caused by dipping in the water and shock load caused luff wire to part, and then sail material followed suit.

I still can't believe we sailed so far, so fast, with so little damage.

APPENDIX V

Expenses

There have been two Whitbread Round the World Races. Each has been won by a multi-millionaire. To make a race you need competitors, and for the average owner a great financial race has to be won before reaching the start line at Portsmouth.

Sponsorship is hard to come by and I am most grateful to Debenhams for the £25,000 they put into the project.

I regret having been the only person on board with financial responsibility for the boat. The (at times almost unendurable) burden would have been better shared with the crew. The two main worries were:

1. That some uninsured damage would leave us stranded in a far distant port. The £2,500 insurance premium left plenty of scope for disaster.
2. That we might be delayed and so fail to return to Ardmore in time for the 1978 season starting 29 April.

I doubt if the costs listed below could be reduced. Given a free hand I believe I could have spent £1 million on an eighty-foot boat, crew and expenses. Other competitors are believed to have come pretty close to this huge sum.

There were some pitfalls. Something more than a normal boat is needed to enter the Whitbread Race and the entry fee of £150 soon becomes several thousand pounds. For example, the rules sensibly require inflatable life rafts sufficient for the whole crew to be fitted with double bottoms as protection in the freezing waters of the Southern Ocean. We had two eight-man Avon life rafts for use at the John Ridgway School of Adventure but we were dismayed to find that, like most rafts on the market, they were only single-bottomed as needed for the normal temperatures of cruising waters. I am most grateful to Kenneth Catt of Avon Inflatables Ltd, who not only fitted the life rafts with double bottoms but repacked them in rectangular containers and supplied us with twelve life-jackets free of charge. This saved us well over £1,000.

Income

	£	
Highlands & Islands Development Board	11,300	(Adventure School development loan, boat used for voyage during closed season. Repayable over 10 years at 8% interest)
Debenhams	25,000	(£10,000 paid before the event, £15,000 on 1 February 1978)
ATV	3,500	(Includes feeding two-man TV crew for 8 months)
Wm. Heinemann	5,000	(£2,500 in September 1977, balance on receipt of manuscript in '78 after voyage over. Also possible foreign rights sales arranged by Wm. Heinemann)
Fonseca Port	1,500	(Paid in advance of the voyage plus 10 cases of port for each of the four legs of the race)
Sunday Telegraph	500	(approx. – 5 articles)
	£46,800	

Outgoings – from July 1975 (*no* account taken of inflation or VAT)

The building of Debenhams

Hull and deck	⎫	
Timber	⎪	
Sails and rigging	⎪	
Transport and cranage	⎪	
Engine and fuels	⎬ Total, excluding VAT	
Fittings	⎪ £73,269.18	
Labour	⎪	
Sundries (race insurance £2,500, accommodation, etc. etc.)	⎭	

Ports and expenditure on food and spares
Cape Town	£250	
Auckland	£1,250	
Rio de Janeiro	£500	£2,000

Total   £75,269.18

The above costs are specific to the boat alone. The numerous hidden costs involved in the three-year project are not covered. Things like the value of my own time spent in creating and managing the project, special moorings which had to be laid and the use of my diving equipment, boats and compressor for their frequent inspection; insurance for the period up to the Race when the boat was used in a sail-training role, the use of equipment and vehicles already owned by the School which was transferred to help the boat building for the Race; some rations, some clothing: all this cannot be valued but I doubt if it would exceed £5,000, so £80,000 would seem to me to be a fair figure in total. The £46,800 in loans and sponsorship left me with some £33,000 to find privately. Fortunately this expenditure can be regarded as an investment in extending the facilities of the School of Adventure.

Index

About the Authors

John Ridgway is an ex-Paratroop captain who, with his wife Marie Christine, runs the John Ridgway School for Adventure in northwest Scotland, where each season scores of business men and women, children and young people learn leadership and outdoor skills such as sailing, canoeing, climbing, mountain walking, and personal survival in one of the most remote and ruggedly beautiful parts of Britain.

John Ridgway is the author of several successful books. His first, *A Fighting Chance* (Lippincott), the account of his rowing across the Atlantic Ocean with Chay Blyth, was a world bestseller. Another, *Amazon Journey: From the Source to the Sea* (Doubleday), has become a classic among "achievement" books. In *Round the World with Ridgway* Marie Christine Ridgway has for the first time collaborated in the writing of one of his books.